Carl Crow

Handbook
for
China

WITH AN INTRODUCTION BY
H.J. LETHBRIDGE

HONG KONG
OXFORD UNIVERSITY PRESS
OXFORD NEW YORK MELBOURNE
1984

Oxford University Press

Oxford London New York Toronto
Kuala Lumpur Singapore Hong Kong Tokyo
Delhi Bombay Calcutta Madras Karachi
Nairobi Dar es Salaam Cape Town
Melbourne Auckland

and associated companies in
Beirut Berlin Ibadan Mexico City Nicosia

First published by Kelly and Walsh, Limited, Shanghai, 1933
This edition reprinted, with permission and with the addition of
an Introduction, by Oxford University Press, 1984

ISBN 0 19 583788 6

OXFORD is a trade mark of Oxford University Press

Printed in Hong Kong by Liang Yu Printing Factory Ltd.
Published by Oxford University Press, Warwick House, Hong Kong

INTRODUCTION

BETWEEN the wars Carl Crow's *Handbook for China* was a standard reference book for the foreign visitor to that country. It was first published in Shanghai in 1913 as *The Travelers' Handbook for China*, and four further editions appeared, a fact which testifies to its quality, popularity, and durability.

The author, Herbert Carl Crow (always known as Carl), was born in Missouri in 1883 and attended the state university there. His career followed a familiar American path, that of the newspaperman who becomes an author, like Bret Harte, Mark Twain, Stephen Crane, Dreiser, Dos Passos, or Hemingway. Carl Crow first started out as a printer's apprentice and graduated into journalism, to become in 1906 a member of the editorial staff of the *Fort Worth Star-Telegram*. Then, in 1911, he moved across the Pacific to Shanghai as associate city editor of the *China Press*, one of the leading Shanghai newspapers, and only rivalled by the *North-China Daily News & Herald*. In his day, Carl Crow was a respected and well-known newspaperman and writer, author of *Four Hundred Million Customers* (1937), a genial work on China and the Chinese, which was translated into French, German, Swedish, Danish, Spanish, Dutch, and Polish, a remarkable tribute to its appeal. Crow, although comparatively unknown today, was once regarded as a leading authority on China and the East and his reputation as an observer of the Oriental scene was high, especially in his native land, the United States.

The Travelers' Handbook for China was first published by the Hwa-Mei Book Concern, but later editions, those of 1915, 1921, 1925, and 1933 (the

fifth and last), were issued by Kelly and Walsh
Limited, Shanghai, the celebrated China Coast
publishers, with branches in Hong Kong, Singapore,
and Yokohama. This firm had been established in
Shanghai by J.M. and J.F. Kelly sometime in the
1860s; later the brothers were joined by Arthur
Walsh, a printer, also an Irishman, and the firm was
henceforth known as Kelly and Walsh, and survives
as the name of a bookshop in Ice House Street,
Hong Kong. By the 1880s the original partners had
either died or retired, but the firm continued to
flourish under new management. By the First World
War it had become the largest and most reputable
printing and publishing establishment of English-
language material in the Far East. It declined as
a result of the Japanese take-over of Shanghai's
International Settlement in 1941, and of course was
eclipsed by the coming to power of the Chinese Communists in 1949. The Hong Kong branch of the firm
never achieved the eminence of the parent Shanghai
company and was later bought out by a Hong Kong
bookseller.

Carl Crow, journalist, writer, and proprietor of a
successful advertising agency, founded in 1914, left
Shanghai for the United States in late 1937. His
retirement from the Orient, after a sojourn of
twenty-six years, was influenced, one imagines, by
the region's politics: for in his last year in Shanghai
the Japanese had devastated the Chinese districts
of Chapei and Hongkew and had even menaced the
International Settlement. Strongly pro-Chinese,
Crow was *persona non grata* with the Japanese
authorities. Like so many Americans at that time,
he deplored Japanese imperialism and adventurism.
During the war years, after 1941, he worked for the

American Office of Information, and died in New York, where he had settled with his wife, in 1945. In his own country, he was regarded as a journalist of some distinction; and the prestigious *New York Times* honoured him with an obituary that set out his career in some detail. Nowadays, the name of Carl Crow is hardly remembered, except by a few Old China Hands, a fast vanishing breed, and by collectors of what booksellers like to call 'Orientalia'.

Five editions of the *Handbook for China* appeared in Crow's lifetime, each updated and slightly expanded; and the demand for this useful compilation steadily rose as China was opened up to the traveller, globe-trotter, and tourist, the vast majority of whom arrived by sea, using the great ports of Hong Kong or Shanghai (both administered by foreigners) as entry points to the country. The volume of visitors was governed, obviously, by the growing accessibility of China, due to improvements in communications and transportation, above all railways, and by the provision of Western-style hotels and hostelries, including YMCAs for the teetotal, the pious, the prim, and the less affluent. The construction of hotels (mostly Western-owned) in Hong Kong, Shanghai, Peking (Beijing), Tientsin (Tianjin), and other large cities, was a key factor in the opening of China to the tourist trade (the nineteenth-century traveller was not a tourist in our modern sense of the word). In them the foreigner felt safe; food, sanitation, and service were of an acceptable or familiar standard; and the Chinese staff normally spoke some English. As a consequence, visitors did not feel utterly disoriented in a foreign place. Americans started to arrive in droves from across the Pacific, by cruiseship and liner, people who deified the bathroom and modern plumbing, as Sinclair Lewis suggests in his novels *Main Street* and *Babbitt*. Now they were no longer terrified of travel in the East. When they saw the welcoming portals of, say, the Peninsula or Peak hotels in Hong Kong or the Cathay and Astor in Shanghai, they could relax. Such places provided a little Western oasis or enclave, from which sorties could be made into the native quarters of the city; or, one could simply stare at Chinese life through the hotel's plate-glass windows. The many Hilton and Sheraton hotels in the Asia of today are just as comforting, one concludes.

However, in the inter-war period parts of China were not within easy reach of the average traveller; only the intrepid or venturesome foot-slogger could traverse certain regions, and then he would be forced at times to use age-old forms of Chinese transport: the wheelbarrow, the donkey, sedan chairs, sampans, and junks. He would need to rest in Chinese inns (not to everyone's taste), as Crow warns in his chapter on general information. Tibet was closed to foreigners: lamaseries did not welcome outsiders or intruders. Outer Mongolia (under Soviet influence), Inner Mongolia, and Kansu (Gansu) were forbidding places to visit; and once Manchuria (renamed 'Manchukuo' by the Japanese in 1931) fell under Japanese domination, a traveller experienced added difficulties there: he could be mistaken for a secret agent by the spy-obsessed Japanese military. South-west China — the provinces of Kwangsi (Guangxi), Kweichou (Guizhou), and Yunnan — also provided difficult terrain. But it was possible to navigate the Yangtze (Chang Jiang), to pass through the river's tremendous gorges, and reach Szechuan (Sichuan) and arrive at last at its main city, Chungking

(Chongqing), which from 1938 to 1946 became the Nationalist capital after the fall of Nanking (Nanjing) to the Japanese.

The pattern of travel was very much dictated in the Twenties by the railway. Railroad building had been neglected by China but promoted, after 1895, by the imperialist powers (notably Russia, Britain, and France) in their respective spheres of influence, so that China's railway system remained, until the Communists reorganized it after 1949, patchy and largely disconnected. It was possible, before hostilities broke out between China and Japan in 1937, to go by train from Shanghai to Tientsin and Peking via Nanking. The traveller took the so-called Shanghai Express, a train as famous in its day, as celebrated or notorious, as Europe's Orient Express (immortalized by Agatha Christie and Graham Greene). A journey by the Shanghai Express also conjured up visions of intrigue, conspiracy, and adultery. This famous train had sleeping-car and dining-car accommodation. It attracted those who had money and liked comfort and European amenities. One should also mention the Kowloon–Canton railway: the Hong Kong passenger embarked at the spot, adjacent to the Star Ferry's Kowloon terminal, now marked by the former railway station's clock-tower. From Canton it was possible to entrain for the north and other parts. The French Yunnan line, terminating at Haiphong in French Indo-China, provided the foreign traveller with an entry into southern China. Haiphong was connected with Europe by the Messageries Maritimes shipping line, whose boats plied between Marseilles and China and Japan.

In the Thirties the motor car became a popular mode of transport in China. The Nationalist Government built over 60,000 miles of good roads and introduced cross-country bus services. The Nationalists also promoted air transport. But these developments came to an end, necessarily in most parts, with the outbreak of the Sino-Japanese war (1937–45) and the Japanese seizure of Nanking, the Nationalist capital, in December 1937. It was still possible for the enterprising to travel in China after 1937, but it became riskier. Auden and Isherwood's book on China was aptly titled *Journey to a War* when it appeared in 1939. The golden age of travel in China thus spanned the years 1918 to early 1937: things were never to be the same until the winding up of the Cultural Revolution in the late 1970s, when China once again cultivated the tourist.

The Twenties and Thirties were not the age of cheap travel; that was to come later, after the end of the Second World War, with the invention of the jumbo jet. Only the rich, members of the upper and middle classes, could afford to travel to faraway or out-of-the-way places. Students did not go on a 'grand tour' of the Orient; and far fewer went in search of a nirvana induced by drugs (that, too, was also to come later). European dope-fiends, to use a pre-war locution, such as Alesteir Crowley, Jean Cocteau, and Nancy Cunard, obtained their supplies, and opium dreams, at home.

Apart from journalists, diplomats, consular officials, businessmen, writers and scholars, the great majority of travellers in this period were simply sightseers, a class of persons who, guidebook in hand, gazed expectantly or rapturously at churches, palaces, tombs, and other generally admired, or admirable, monuments; or who went shopping for exotic gewgaws, bric-à-brac, and eastern antiques.

Others simply enjoyed the excitements or pleasures of a sea voyage, for most came to China by ship. There were many lines to choose from: the celebrated P. & O. (London to China), the Canadian Pacific Railway (Vancouver to Hong Kong), the Pacific Mail Steamship Co. (San Francisco to Japan and China), and the Nord-Deutscher Lloyd (Bremen to China and Japan). There were also many steamships that operated mainly or exclusively in Far Eastern waters: Chinese, British, American, French, Dutch, and, of course, Japanese companies.

Needless to say, China could also be reached from the North, by the Trans-Siberian Railway, whose southern branch ran down to Mukden (Shenyang), and from that city to Peking and Tientsin. Not everyone enjoyed staring hour after hour, day after day, at the endless and melancholy Russian steppes or relished glacial stops at lonely Siberian railway stations, where coal or wood was taken aboard as fuel. The journey from Russia to Manchuria (Dongbei) was an adventure in itself and appealed, naturally, to railway maniacs and to masochistic travellers, of whom there are more than one would suppose. This great railway, the longest in the world, is celebrated in William Gerhardi's classic novel *Futility*.

The cruise-ships and liners that called at either Hong Kong or Shanghai — American vessels mostly went to the latter — did not stay long in port (wharfage or anchorage fees were high) and passengers could, therefore, not stray too far afield; shopping sprees, a measure of sightseeing, and the sampling of night-life (more exotic and *louche* in Shanghai — 'The Paris of the East' — than in decorous, colonial Hong Kong) were favoured pastimes. Travellers who had more time at their disposal always headed for

Peking, China's ancient capital, which lost that status in 1928 when the Nationalist Government removed the capital to Nanking. Nevertheless, Peking was a 'must', the traveller's bourne. Peking offered so many marvels, the Forbidden City above all. For there its last imperial occupant, the Emperor P'u-Yi, still held 'shadow' court. He had been forced to abdicate in 1924 and remained in the Imperial Palace until enthroned by the Japanese as the puppet emperor of Manchukuo in 1934. (P'u-Yi's odyssey is related in Reginald Johnston's *Twilight in the Forbidden City*.) Other places of note to look at or visit were the Altar or Temple of Heaven, where the emperors of China once made their annual sacrifices, built in white marble in three circular terraces, the Confucian Temple, the Lama Temple, the Observatory (dating from Kublai Khan), and the famous Summer Palace outside the capital, partially destroyed and vandalized by the Allied Army in 1860. The Bell Tower and Drum Towers also had their admirers. There was much else to view of course; and a visit to Tientsin was obligatory.

The sights of Peking were, one imagines, the main attraction for the ordinary traveller or tourist in China; but there were other itineraries that catered to more specialized or adventurous tastes, such as the ascent of the Yangtze, which has been referred to, a journey undertaken by the writer Somerset Maugham in 1920. Kwangsi, noted for its extraordinary landscape and sharp mountain peaks, much celebrated in Chinese painting, tempted the Hong Kong resident. But the big game hunter — once a famed European species — did not regard China as suitable terrain to show off his skills. There was tiger in South China, but the killers of the larger beasts infinitely preferred India or Africa, the land of Trader Horn, the home of the great white hunter. Who would go to China simply to blaze away at snipe in the environs of Shanghai? There were more peasants than pheasants to shoot. Only naval or army officers, bored with camp life and with time on their hands, showed superlative enthusiasm for such sport, as one infers from Christopher Cradock's *Sporting Notes in the Far East*. On the other hand, houseboating in the waterways of Shanghai did have a large following, as Crow himself tells us.

Pre-war, Hong Kong was not the tourist centre it has since become; but many ships entered the sheltered waters of its harbour and docked or anchored there. The colony thus received a constant stream of visitors and sightseers, on whom many Chinese shopkeepers came to depend. P. & O. liners always visited the colony en route to Shanghai and Yokohama; so too did the Messageries Maritimes and other lines, whose ships sailed from the British Isles or the Continent. One should mention that Hong Kong was popular as a rest station with China missionaries. Protestant missions had built numerous bungalows and homes on Cheung Chau Island for their pastors. Catholics had a hospice for their priests at Bethanie, opposite University Hall in Pok Fu Lam Road. To this somewhat stark edifice came many priests from China to rest or recuperate. The little cemetery attached to Bethanie testifies that it was the final resting place for some, worn out with toil among the Chinese. The Peak Hotel (destroyed by the Japanese), reached by cable car, was also popular with convalescents, as well as tourists, and with those who simply wished to escape from China's enervating summer heat.

Macau, like Hong Kong, had not developed a tourist industry at this time, although it was well visited, especially by Hong Kong residents. Macau was then notorious for its gambling casinos, brothels, and opium dens, and for its corruption. It was a sleepy Portuguese-style town, with grinning, ebony-hued Mozambican soldiers guarding the Governor's palace. Macau was a place to which one took one's girl-friend or mistress for surreptitious love-making. There were many things to see, mostly ruins: the façade of the old church attached to the Jesuit College, the Grotto of Camoens, the Moro fort, and the Protestant cemetery, in which Robert Morrison, the pioneer of Protestant missionary work in China, was interred in 1834. Samuel Couling commented laconically in 1917: 'It [Macau] lives chiefly on its *fan t'an* gambling houses'.

In the aftermath of the Revolution of 1911 China was destabilized. Even the Nationalists, under the energetic, and apparently reforming Generalissimo Chiang Kai-shek, were not able to impose order or to suppress the Communists, who retreated in 1934–5 — in the famous Long March — to remote Yenan (Yan'an, in Shaanxi Province) and there set up their own Soviet government (1936–45). Nor could the Generalissimo restrain the Japanese from seizing Chinese territory, notably Manchuria and parts of North China. Banditry was also a curse in this period, prevalent in marginal areas (some examples are given in H.G.W. Woodhead's autobiography), and kidnapping was rife: it was not uncommon, at times, for Europeans to be held to ransom, even slain. Another peril was rioting. After 1911, and the fall of the Ch'ing (Qing) dynasty, anti-foreignism did not decline. Rather it was further exacerbated by political events, such as the clash in Nanking Road, Shanghai, between British-controlled police and Chinese demonstrators in 1925, a clash that gave rise to the China-wide May Thirtieth Movement, which was to paralyse the economy of Hong Kong. At times, then, the traveller or tourist could not venture far from secure areas, such as Hong Kong or Shanghai, although Peking was normally a haven for the foreigner, the population less truculent or intransigent than Cantonese or Shanghainese. It is necessary to make this obvious point because Carl Crow's handbook tends, perhaps, to underestimate the potential dangers of travelling in a bandit-ridden and war-torn China. From 1911 to 1949 there was always conflict somewhere in China.

Raymond Dawson, in *The Chinese Chameleon: An Analysis of European Conceptions of Chinese Civilization*, did not discuss the effects that the cinema, and Hollywood in particular, has had upon perceptions of China and the Chinese. In Hitchcock's film, *Rich and Strange* (1932), a young couple on a voyage round the world are shipwrecked in the East and are picked up by a Chinese junk. The woman makes friends with the ship's cat. The cat disappears one day. She is later startled when she discovers it has gone into the cooking pot and that its pelt has been nailed to the deck to dry. In Josef von Sternberg's *Shanghai Express* (1932), the lives of a Chinese warlord (Warner Oland), a *demi-mondaine* (Marlene Dietrich), an upper-class stiff-lipped British officer (Clive Brook), and an Eastern seductress (Anna May Wong), are woven together in a story of intrigue and adventure. The war-lord and his minions take over the Shanghai Express. Concupiscently eyeing Dietrich, and licking his lips, Oland tells the passengers: 'The white woman goes with me'. The great Sternberg had never been to China, but he had images of that country: it was a world of excitement, conspiracy, lechery, decadence, and depravity. And the traveller in China, one infers, expected to discover some of these elements: the caress of silken fingers, the languors of exotic love. Such clichés appear in Maurice Dekobra's *Lune de miel à Shanghai* (1943) and in Vicki Baum's *Hotel Shanghai* (1937). These novelists were extremely popular before the last war, indeed best-sellers. The point is that not all tourists went to China in pursuit of aesthetic thrills: the *moyen sensuel* outnumbered the former.

Whoever goes to China, for whatever reason, will find Carl Crow's book excellent reading. It contains a great deal of information and pinpoints what the tourist should see and delight in. The enthusiasts of the Cultural Revolution smashed much but not everything; a lot survived. Pre-war, the *Handbook for China* was reputed to be the best guide there was. It is still worth slipping into one's pocket as one sets out to explore China, that vast country.

H.J. LETHBRIDGE

BIBLIOGRAPHY

Arlington, L.C., *Through the Dragon's Eyes* (London, Constable & Co., 1931).

____ *In Search of Old Peking* (Peking, Henri Vetch, 1935).

Auden, W.H., and Isherwood, Christopher, *Journey to a War* (London, Faber & Faber, 1939).

Blofield, John, *City of Lingering Splendour* (London, Hutchinson, 1961).

Cable, Boyd, *A Hundred Years of the P. & O.* (London, Nicholson & Watson, 1937).

Caldwell, Harry R., *Blue Tiger* (London, Duckworth, 1925).

Christie, Agatha, *Murder on the Orient Express* (London, W. Collins, 1934).

The Chinese Year Book (Shanghai, North-China Daily News & Herald, 1912–39).

The China's Who's Who (Shanghai, Kelly & Walsh, 1922–7).

Cradock, Lieutenant Christopher, *Sporting Notes in the Far East* (London, Griffith, Farran, Okeden, & Welsh, 1889).

Crow, Carl, *Four Hundred Million Customers* (London, H. Hamilton, 1937).

____ *Foreign Devils in the Flowery Kingdom* (New York, Harper, 1940).

'Carl Crow: an obituary', *The New York Times*, 10 June 1945.

Gerhardi, William, *Futility: A Novel on Russian Themes* (London, Richard Cobden-Sanderson, 1922).

Greene, Graham, *Stamboul Train* (London, William Heinemann, 1932).

Jernigan, T.R., *Shooting in China* (Shanghai, Methodist Publishing House, 1908).

Johnston, Reginald F., *Twilight in the Forbidden City* (London, Victor Gollancz, 1934).

Tyler, William, *Pulling Strings in China* (London, Constable, 1929).

Woodhead, H.G.W., *Adventures in Far Eastern Journalism* (Tokyo, The Hokuseido Press, 1935).

Handbook for China

(INCLUDING HONGKONG)

by

CARL CROW

With Six Maps and Plans

FIFTH EDITION
Revised Throughout

百 聞 不 如 一 見

"One seeing is worth a hundred tellings"

KELLY & WALSH, LIMITED

HONG KONG . SHANGHAI . SINGAPORE

1933

To
Mother and Helen

As was the case in former editions of this book, the author is indebted to a great many people for valuable and indispensable aid in the work of revision. Mr. Arthur de C. Sowerby who contributed the section on Flora and Fauna to the fourth edition has revised that section and added new material. Mrs. Victor Keene was of great assistance in bringing the Shanghai section up to date and Mr. Seth W. Clarke supplied the information regarding routes and fares. Mr. Reginald Sweetland and Mr. T. O. Thackrey have read most of the proofs. Among the others to whom the author is indebted are: Messrs. Hallet Abend, R. N. Swann, George F. Shecklen, Julean Arnold, Percy Finch, W. J. Kelly, J. B. Loucks, E. C. Stocker, W. J. Meade, Hin Wong, K. C. Chow, Y. Obie, Rev. F. A. Brown, Mrs. A. Bland Calder, and Miss Grace Mertsky. This list of acknowledgments is closed with the guilty and uneasy feeling that others who have helped have not received here the thanks and acknowledgment that is due them.

CONTENTS

GENERAL INFORMATION

 HEN the first edition of this book was published about twenty years ago, the author went to quite a little trouble to explain that although China was a strange and remote country, it was really possible for travellers to visit the country at a minimum of discomfort and inconvenience. In detail it was explained that even in China there were hotels which served foreign food, steamship lines which connected the principal ports, railways, and in the larger coast cities English speaking guides. It was noted that "as it is becoming more generally known that it is possible to visit the very interesting country of China without foregoing the usual comforts of life or facing extraordinary dangers, travellers are turning to it each year in greater numbers." At that rather recent period, China was off the beaten track of tourists and those who came to China except on business deserved the more dignified title of travellers. The short period of twenty years has made great changes, not only in China itself but in the knowledge of the world regarding the country. It is now on the main travelled road, with thousands of visitors each year who find that instead of "foregoing the usual comforts of life," they find in China comforts and entertainment which cannot be duplicated elsewhere.

China is becoming modernized with amazing rapidity. Journeys which a few years ago required days of travel by small boats or sedan chairs may now be made in hours by airplane or motor car. In its principal city will be found the highest buildings outside the United States and

1

hotels and cabarets which are world famous. But in spite of these changes which mark the progress of modern China the country remains as interesting and strange as it was to Europeans who more than five hundred years ago read Marco Polo's amazing, interesting but unbelievable account of the land of the "Great Khan."

A comparatively small part of China is open to travellers, but this part, is the most interesting, and most important. It includes the great semi-foreign port of Shanghai, the mysterious former capital, Peking, now known as Peiping, the southern metropolis, Canton, the heart of southern China, the beautiful city of Hangchow, the tomb of Confucius and many other places of less political, historical or commercial importance, such as Soochow, Chefoo, Mukden (the ancient capital of the Manchus), the Yangtsze River for six hundred miles from its mouth, and the old Portuguese colony of Macao. Hongkong, as a British Crown colony, is not politically a part of China, but its population and atmosphere is predominantly Chinese and no one has seen China without having seen Hongkong. Any one, no matter what particular personal interest has brought him to China, may profitably spend several months visiting these readily accessible places.

Of course, some of the very interesting spots cannot be included in any ordinary itinerary. Chengtu, the great metropolis and capital of Szechuen Province, Sianfu, old capital of the country, as well as many other places intimately connected with Chinese history, are so far from the ordinary and modern routes of travel that they can be visited only by those who are willing to spend some months in the country and make special and often tedious arrangements for these interior journeys. Equally inaccessible to the ordinary traveller are many of the rivers and a wealth of mountain scenery surpassed by few countries. But each year new routes of travel are opened, new hotels established and the inaccessible spot of to-day may be on a main travelled road to-morrow.

The interest of a visit to China is not confined to any one class. The size, population and undeveloped wealth of the country give it an absorbing interest to statesmen, religionists, merchants, bankers, and all who have to do with the affairs of the world. It has in the past few years more or less monopolized the spotlight on the stage of international politics and apparently will continue to occupy this position for a good many years to come. But China is not interesting only to the serious minded. The artist finds new and rich treasures in the comparatively unknown Chinese art. For the curio collector there are the great stocks of rare brocades, bronzes, pictures and porcelains, while the casual visitor who does not care to do more than see China in a hurried trip will find every moment crowded with strange sights and will carry away never-to-be-forgotten impressions. And those who find fascination in night clubs and night life will discover in Shanghai, perhaps, a few new thrills, certainly a few new colour combinations in the tapestry.

It is a trite expression that Chinese civilization has little in common with that of the West. Until a comparatively recent period, China was isolated from all other countries and developed a culture unaffected by the forces and influences which moulded Europe and were transplanted to America. The result is interesting to the casual traveller as well as to the serious student. One cannot be in China many hours before noticing customs which strike him as being directly contrary to what he has always thought to be the established order of things. So long as he remains in the country evidences of this contrariness continue to accumulate, a never failing source of interest, amusement, entertainment and possibly knowledge. If he remains long enough to become a student of Chinese customs, art and literature, he will find his interest does not flag with more intimate knowledge, but rather that China—any one of the many aspects of China—affords a study at once fascinating and inexhaustible.

The present Republic of China extends over an area of about five million square miles; more than twice that of the United States. This area includes Mongolia, Manchuria (Manchukuo), Tibet and Eastern Turkestan, in addition to the eighteen provinces, special administrative districts, concessions and settlements, which make up China proper. However, the average traveller need concern himself only with Manchuria (Manchukuo) and half of the eighteen provinces. Thibet is one of the very few places in the world which remains practically forbidden to the alien, not only because of its remoteness but also because of the suspicions and hostility of the Thibetans. Mongolia is more accessible and better known but there is little in its vast desert plains to compensate for the difficulties, hardships and expense of the journey. Eastern Turkestan is even less attractive and more remote.

The eighteen provinces which have furnished the stage for the long and absorbingly interesting drama of Chinese history occupy about two-fifths of the entire area of the country. It is within this area that a great part of the large population of the country is found, Tibet, Mongolia, Manchuria and Eastern Turkestan being very sparsely populated. For many years the population of China was placed at 400 millions, a figure which could only be called an intelligent guess, for there has never been a complete census of the country and few local censuses which were accurate. Within the past few years, there have been quite a number of years where an accurate count of the population has been made and although in most cases these counts have been shown that many of the more important cities have a much smaller population than they were supposed to have, the total population of the country is nearer 500 million than 400 million. This tremendous population gives statisticians an opportunity to make some very interesting speculations. If the populations of Austria-Hungary, Belgium, France, Germany, Italy, England, Scotland, Ireland, Wales, Japan,

Serbia and Roumania had been wiped out by the Great War, or some other catastrophe, these countries could have been entirely repeopled by Chinese and leave enough residents of China to give it a population as dense as that of the United States.

The area and population of each province, according to official figures published in 1932 by the Nationalist Government are as follows:

Province	Area sq. mile	Population	Persons per sq. mile
Anhwei	54,826	19,832,665	362
Chekiang	36,680	22,043,300	601
Chihli (Hopei)	115,830	34,186,711	295
Fukien	46,332	13,157,791	284
Honan	67,954	30,831,909	454
Hunan	83,398	28,443,279	341
Hupeh	71,428	27,167,244	380
Kansu	125,483	5,927,997	47
Kiangsi	69,498	24,466,800	352
Kiangsu	38,610	33,786,064	875
Kwangsi	77,220	12,258,335	159
Kwangtung	100,000	37,167,701	372
Kweichow	67,182	11,114,951	167
Shansi	81,853	11,080,827	134
Shantung	55,984	30,803,245	552
Shensi	75,290	9,465,558	125
Szechuen	218,533	49,782,810	228
Yunnan	146,714	9,839,180	67

Figures pertaining to the area of China are as impressive as those relating to the population. 'For a traveller to encircle China he would need to journey a distance considerably greater than half the circumference of the world. Of this distance, some 4000 miles would be coast line, some 6000 miles would be bordering on Soviet Russia, another 4800 miles would touch British possessions, while of the remainder, some 400 miles would be contiguous to country under French rule and about 800 miles be described as of doubtful sovereignty.'

The visitor to China will not find it necessary to leave the railway, airplane or steamship lines in order to make an extensive visit to the country. There are more than 5,000 miles of railways, the Yangtsze River is navigable by ocean steamers for a distance of 600 miles from its mouth, and several hundred miles farther by river steamer and house boat, and many lines of coast and river steamers connect the most important cities. Motor roads are building so rapidly that any list of them published to-day would be incomplete next month. At all principal points hotel accommodations will be found, many of them under European control and management, and the others by Chinese who through experience have learned how to cater to the whimsical demands of the foreigner. A great many new hotels of a foreign or semi-foreign style are established every year, and there is a constant improvement in all of them.

Along the beaten path the stranger will find the way made easy for him. Hotel servants, railway and steamship attendants speak English and are familiar with his needs. The more venturesome who are willing to leave the railways, steamship lines and hotels, travel on wheelbarrows, donkeys, or in sedan chairs and junks, and live in native inns, can visit any part of the country at small cost, and enjoy rare experiences. But no trip of this sort should be lightly undertaken. Indeed, the inexperienced traveller who leaves the beaten track in China is only tempting trouble and danger and making discomfort certain. Provisions must be carried and servants and interpreters engaged. The needs of the traveller will depend so much on the object of his trip, the season and the territory to be traversed that no guide book formulae would be of much value. The advice of experienced travellers must be sought, and followed.

Climate and Clothing.

If the territory of China were superimposed on that of North America, it would reach, east to west, from

Seattle to Halifax and north to south from Winnipeg, in Canada, to the interesting Isthmus of Tehuantepec, in Mexico. Climatic conditions might well be expected to show great differences in such a vast area, but the great plateau of Mongolia and other factors of lesser importance tend to establish rather uniform temperatures over a great part of the country. The ascending air from the heated sandy deserts of Mongolia creates in summer a current of air from the Pacific ocean, while in winter because of the great cold on the Mongolian plateau the current takes an opposite direction when the prevailing winds are from the west.

Although there are no very definite physical marks by which the country is divided, China is generally considered, geographically, as separated into three sections, North, Central and South. The former may be said to consist of the basin of the Yellow River (Hoang-ho), Central China the basin of the Yangtsze and Southern China that of the West River. The winter months of North China extend from November to March, during which time the rivers are frozen and the weather is very cold. The port of Tientsin is kept open in winter by the use of an icebreaker. In a very severe winter only navigation may be temporarily interrupted. In the spring and autumn there are frequent dust storms. In the summer the temperature in Northern China is nearly as high as in other parts of the country and there is a heavy rainfall with frequent floods in many sections. The spring and autumn, as in most other parts of the world, afford the best seasons for a visit as the temperature is then equable and there is little rainfall. In Central China the range of temperature is not so great as in the North and the rainy season comes earlier in the year. However, there is freezing weather in winter and a temperature of 100 degrees in summer, which is several degrees hotter than the highest recorded temperature in Hongkong. In fact the interior of Central China is a place to be avoided during the heated season. During

April and May the rivers are usually swollen. Theoretically, February and March are dry, but as a matter
of common experience they are often cold and wet. In
South China the winter months are usually dry and the
summer season rainy. In Hongkong and Canton tropical
conditions prevail, the average mean temperature for
Hongkong being 76 degrees with that of Canton 100 miles
distant several degrees higher. The coldest month in
Hongkong is February with an average mean temperature
of 58 degrees. The traveller who desires comfort will go
to South China in the winter and visit the Yangtsze Valley
and the north in the spring or autumn.

No section of China can be called particularly comfortable in summer, the heat being about the same as in
similarly located parts of the United States. The rainfall
increases as one journeys southward, the annual average
being 20 inches in Peking, 44 in Shanghai and 84 in
Hongkong. The summers on the sea coast are very moist,
the great humidity adding to the discomforts of the heated
season. The mean humidity at Shanghai is 80 and at
Hongkong 77. Mould will form on shoes, clothing and
leather bags unless aired in the sun at every opportunity.

An interesting and dangerous feature of the
metereology of the China Coast is the typhoon. "These
cyclonic storms are formed over the Pacific in a region
not far removed from the islands of Yap and Guam
(telegraph stations), and moving north-west strike the
coast of Indo-China, or veering northeast reach the coast
of China or Japan. The storm center is marked by very
low barometric pressure, and the wind blows round this,
inward toward the centre, from right to left (against the
hands of the clock), at a speed that may reach from 50
to 110 miles an hour, the usual rate in the north part of
the China Sea being 90 miles. Typhoons rarely reach
Shanghai, being more often diverted inland south of that
port or recurring toward Japan. They average on the
coast sixteen a year."* In former years these atmospheric

* The China Year Book.

disturbances caused great loss of life, and damage to shipping but with improvements in weather reporting by the Siccawei (Jesuit) observatory in Shanghai and other agencies ample warning of the approach of typhoons is now given and ships bound for threatened areas remain in port or if at sea seek the nearest shelter. Even with these warnings there are many annual shipwrecks and fatalities.

Clothing that is easily washed is essential for the summer months, when everyone is clad in white. The traveller need not equip himself with a wardrobe before leaving home, for on his arrival in China he will find numberless tailors ready to make up any garments he wants at a fraction of the price he would pay elsewhere. Although the charges for laundry work are increasing, they are still ridiculously cheap as compared with charges in other parts of the world.

Many large shops and department stores will be found in Shanghai, Hongkong, Hankow, Peiping and Tientsin, where the traveller will be able to purchase almost any article he may require, while there are few places which do not offer a small assortment of foreign clothing, toilet articles, etc. Foreign (European) tailors and dressmakers are located in Shanghai, Peiping, Tientsin and Hongkong for the service of those who want clothing more stylish than that supplied by Chinese talent.

CUSTOMS HOUSES.

There are three kinds of customs houses in China—the Maritime Customs, which collects a duty on maritime exports and imports; the "Old Customs Houses," which date from many centuries B.C. and levy certain duty and fees on inland traffic; and the *Likin*, a system of transit duties levied at various points in a rather irregular manner. In addition there is a duty levied at some city gates, corresponding to the old *octroi* duty of France. The only customs houses the traveller comes in contact with are those of the Chinese Maritime Customs at his port of entry or of departure. Until recent years the customs officials paid slight attention to the baggage of travellers. But with the imposition of high import duties on perfumes, liquor and other articles which are classed as luxuries and therefore offer a temptation to amateur as well as professional smugglers, the baggage of all incoming passengers is more or less carefully examined and import duty is collected on all except purely personal effects. Travellers should note that the customs duty of China is levied on exports as well as imports, and that if goods other than personal effects are taken out of the country it is necessary to pass them through the customs before they can be accepted by the shipping companies.

SHOPPING.

Few people who have never visited China realize what fine modern shops are to be found in the principal cities, Shanghai, Hongkong, Hankow and Tientsin. In all of these places there are large department stores with well selected stocks of European and American merchandise, book stores, chemist shops, specialty shops, tailors, etc. Here the traveller will be able to purchase anything he may need and at reasonable prices. The many who before setting out on a trip to China provide themselves as for a long journey into a wilderness simply encumber themselves with a lot of useless and unnecessary baggage. The shops of Shanghai are famous and can compare favourably with the shops of large continental cities.

Silks, porcelains, brasses, bronzes, cloisonné, embroideries, carved jade and ivory comprise only a few of the many beautiful and distinctive things that can be purchased in China, and for the wise shopper the prices will be satisfactorily cheap. It must be remembered that the small curio dealer seldom has a fixed price for anything in stock. He expects to sell for the highest price he is able to get, while the wise shopper will adopt the Chinese custom and use his wits to make the purchase as cheaply as possible. Bargaining is considered by the Chinese as indispensable in most retail transactions.

To this there are many notable exceptions in the principal cities where enterprising Chinese have established stores catering especially to the foreign trade. At these places there is a fixed price and the goods are of dependable quality. This applies especially to silver, silk, and fur shops. In all cases, careful inquiry should be made of local residents before making purchases of any great value.

Peiping (Peking) is the great storehouse of fine Chinese curios and the finest curio shops are to be found there. Shanghai perhaps ranks second, with some shops which rival those of Peiping in the richness and variety of their stocks. A rather different class of goods will be found in Hongkong, Canton and other southern ports where the offerings of old porcelain and other valuable art objects are not so numerous, but there are more interesting articles of modern manufacture than can be found in the northern ports. Some mention of the articles procurable in the various cities will be found in the following pages.

Money and Exchange.

Several volumes might be written and in fact have been written on the subject of Chinese currency, without exhausting the subject. Although in foreign trade the unit of currency is the *tael*, the unit in purely native transactions is the *cash*, the small brass or copper coin with a hole in the middle. According to theory, which in no place squares with practice, the coinage is as follows:

10 Hao..	1 Cash or Li
10 Cash	1 Candareen or Fen
10 Candareen	1 Mace or Tsien
10 Mace	1 Tael or Liang

It is first necessary to explain that the system of coinage indicated by the above table does not exist except in this and in other books whose authors attempt an explanation of China's currency. Of the five coins mentioned only one, the cash, exists and it is so rapidly passing out of existence that it is rarely seen. A number of *tael* coins have been minted but they are so rare that few old residents of China have ever seen one. The Chinese *tael* is really nothing more than a weight of silver (about one ounce) of a certain degree of fineness the weight and the degree of fineness being different in almost every locality where the *tael* is used as a unit of value. The Shanghai *tael* which is fairly well known in all parts of the country is worth at the time this is written about $—.30 (U. S. currency), or 1/4. The gold value, of course, fluctuates daily with the value of silver since the *tael* is only an ounce of silver. A few years ago the tael was worth about four times its present gold value. While the gold value of this unit fluctuates dizzily there is often an equal fluctuation between the *tael* and the copper cash, the copper penny and the ten cent piece, the twenty-cent piece and the dollar. In commenting on this variability in Chinese currency the well informed author of *Chinese Characteristics* said:

"The system is everywhere a decimal one, which is the easiest of all systems to be reckoned, but no one is ever sure until he has made particular inquiries, what number of pieces of brass cash are expected in any particular place to pass for a hundred. He will not need to extend his travels over a very large part of the eighteen provinces to find that this number varies, and varies with a lawlessness that nothing can explain, from the full hundred which is the theoretical string, to 99, 98, 96, 83 down to 33, and possibly to a still lower number. The same is true, but in a more aggravated degree, of the weight by which silver is sold. No two places have the same ounce, unless by accident, and each place has a great variety of different ounces, to the extreme bewilderment of the stranger, the certain loss of all except those who deal in silver, and the endless vexation of all honest persons, of whom there are many, even in China."

The common medium of exchange in the interior was until a few years ago the string of copper cash and lump of silver. The latter are known to the Chinese as *sycee*, a term which is applied to all uncoined silver used as money. The word *sycee* means "fine silk" as the silver when heated can be drawn out in silk-like threads. The Dutch who came first to China called these lumps of silver *schuyt* or *boat* because of the resemblance to a common Chinese boat. Other Europeans who came later changed the Dutch word to "shoe" because of a similar fancied resemblance to the Chinese shoe. Every native bank is equipped with scales on which the shoe of silver is weighed to determine its value in *taels*. It may then be exchanged for copper cash or other coinage with which the business transactions of the country are carried out.

Happily for the traveller, he need not concern himself with this currency unless he intends going far into the interior. When the foreigners began to settle in the treaty ports, they objected to a currency system which required them to carry about five or ten pound lumps of silver as spending money. To avoid this, they introduced the Mexican,* and other silver dollars and its successor the Chinese dollar or "yuan" which contains the same amount of silver as the old Mexican dollar is now the standard currency of most ports. Its value, like that of the tael, is determined by the market price of silver. Before the Great War it was usually exchangeable at two Mexican for one American dollar or ten for one pound sterling. For a few months after the war the Mexican or local dollar came to be worth more than the American dollar, owing to the increased value of silver, then slumped in value until it was worth less than a shilling. Many foreign and Chinese banks issue paper notes payable in local dollars. Prices at hotels and stores are quoted in dollars, while all large business transactions, professional

---

* Wherever the dollar mark is used in this book it refers to the Chinese or Mexican dollar.

fees, etc., are in taels. Usually the two are exchangeable at a rate of about four dollars for three taels.

In addition to this dollar currency, smaller silver coins of a nominal value of ten and twenty cents and copper coins representing ten cash are in circulation. But it must always be remembered that a coin in China represents nothing more than the actual market value of the metal it contains and as these coins are minted by provincial mints there are many coins of the same face value which have very different market values. A few years ago a Mexican dollar would be exchanged for less than 100 of the large Chinese coppers. At the time this is written, with the price of copper lower, the dollar is exchangeable for about 200 coppers, and you will receive 14 coppers for each silver ten cent piece. At the money changer's you will receive for a dollar five 20-cent pieces, one 10-cent piece and two to four coppers. The rates of exchange between all coins fluctuate daily.

These small coins are accepted, usually, on all purchases of less than fifty cents, but many shopkeepers, take advantage of exchange. For instance, if you make a ten cent purchase in Shanghai and tender a Mexican dollar in payment, you will receive only 90 cents in change. But if you first have your dollar changed into small money, you will be able to make the purchase and have more than 100 cents remaining. In Peiping and Tientsin will be found ten and twenty cent pieces which are of full value while in Shanghai there are 10, 20 and 50 cent paper notes redeemable at par.

This disparity between the dollar value and cent value in China helps to perpetuate the *chit* system. At all hotels, the traveller will be asked to sign *chits* for drinks, cigars, etc. If he paid cash for these articles as he purchased them, he would pay for them in "small money" that is, small silver coins and coppers. But when he settles his bill at the end of his stay, the amount is reckoned in "large money," and he pays 10 to 20 per cent more than if he had made cash purchases.

When you offer your dollar to the money changer or the shopkeeper, he will often bang it violently on the counter, and, if not satisfied with the result, subject it to further tests because there is a great amount of counterfeit money in circulation. In the banks expert Chinese clerks juggle silver dollars so rapidly that the eye can scarcely follow their movements, and they throw out a spurious coin each time there is a discord in the silver harmony. One of the most famous of these spurious coins was not a counterfeit but a dollar from which part of the silver had been extracted. The deception was discovered by subjecting the dollar to heat which would melt solder, when it would be found that the dollar was in three pieces. The face of the coin had been removed and a hollow scooped out of the center and filled with brass to give it the proper weight. Then the face was soldered back, the coin presenting a surface of pure silver and the correct weight. This is the famous "three piece dollar," and its existence offers a striking commentary on the cheapness of the labour of the skilled Chinese artisan who finds it worth while to undertake such tedious work for the sake of the few cents' worth of silver he is able to filch from the bowels of the coin. Of recent years, with the increase in the earning power of Chinese workmen, the manufacture of the "three piece dollar" has become unprofitable and the few which are found in circulation are valuable as curios.

When the money-changer gives you silver dollars in exchange for bank-notes, he will often stamp each dollar with his own *chop* or trade-mark. If in Shanghai, the chop will be applied with a rubber stamp. In some places it will be put on with a steel die, which eventually defaces the original marks of the coin and gives it a cup-like shape. This *chop* is the money-changer's guarantee that the coin is genuine. If it proves otherwise, return it to him and he will make good the guarantee his *chop* implies.

Travellers are advised to carry with them, even if they have the usual bankers' letter of credit, a certain amount of funds in travellers' checks or circular notes issued by

well-known banks. These checks can always be cashed
at hotels or on board a steamer and will often be found
convenient. The banks in the Far East observe many
holidays and often the traveller is subject to vexatious
delays while waiting for the banks to resume business
before being able to replenish funds.

HUNTING AND FISHING.

Wild game abounds in all parts of China, and this,
the most populous of countries, offers many opportunities
for the sportsman. Doubtless this is due to the fact that
the private ownership of firearms by Chinese has been
severely restricted and the only game they secure is by
means of primitive traps or firearms which are owned
clandestinely. A shooting expedition can best be arranged
in connection with a houseboat trip. The section reached
by houseboat or by the Shanghai-Nanking railway from
Shanghai is a favourite one for hunters and also the section
between Shanghai and Hangchow. The pheasant is the
most common game bird in China and is to be found in
nearly all parts of the country, particularly along the
Yangtsze river. Pheasant, snipe and duck are to be found
in the vicinity of Shanghai. Bamboo partridge, sand
grouse, duck and snipe are to be found in large numbers
and add variety to the day's game bag. Writing of a trip
through Shensi in the winter months, a correspondent of
the London *Times* says: "Nine deer, two wolves and
scores of pheasants were shot from the road-side.
Pheasants were so plentiful that the muleteers were often
seen flicking them off the road with their whips. Ninety
were once counted on a small patch of ground a stone's
throw distant." Tigers and panthers have been killed
within ten miles of Foochow and many wild pigs are to
be found in Chekiang. Strict regulations forbid the
importation of firearms into China, but do not apply to
sporting guns, although all owners of firearms must
register at their Consulates. It is also necessary to secure

from the Chinese authorities permits to carry guns and ammunition into the interior and permits to hunt game.

SERVANTS.

Chinese servants are justly famous and nearly every traveller who visits China adds to the praise which is accorded them. With some exceptions the servant is patient and industrious and loyal to his employer. He will work long hours without complaining, seems never to require any time to sleep, eat or rest, and is usually cheerful and smiling. Without being told he learns all the requirements of the household and the likes and dislikes of the master and mistress. The servant usually tries to make himself indispensable to his employer and often succeeds. No matter how much one may determine not to be he rarely avoids being spoiled by the Chinese "boy," and when he returns to lands less well supplied with servants, will often long for the long-gowned boy of the China Coast.

The Chinese servant seldom asks for a day off, but on rare occasions finds it necessary to go to some distant place to worship at the ancestral shrine. In this event the master will find his regular attendant replaced by another who apparently knows the needs of the household as well as if he had been in it a year instead of a day. If the servant is treated kindly, he usually responds with unswerving loyalty and it is the rule rather than the exception that a bond of real affection forms between master and servant.

As a final good quality of Chinese servants, it may be mentioned that they are very cheap. A good house boy may be employed at a maximum wage of $35 monthly, and an excellent cook for $30. Coolies are content with $18, and amahs, who do the work of maids or nurses at $25 to $35. Out of these wages they will furnish their own food, clothing and quarters, though it is customary for them to live on the premises. There is a very sharp line dividing the duties of different employees and though the foreigner

2

will often find this annoying, he will do well to accept it rather than to try to break down customs which had crystallized for centuries before he was born.　The house-boy who so willingly works all day and half the night will not carry a parcel, for that is the business of the coolie and the boy or cook cannot perform the task without losing face.　As master of that most important part of the household, the kitchen, the cook insists on and is usually granted certain privileges, among them being the domination of the other servants.　The coolie expects as a matter of right to have all the old bottles around the place and would probably not stay long with a master thrifty enough to dispose of them himself.

Admirable as the Chinese servant is in every other way, he has one fault.　He holds by ancient right and custom the privilege to "squeeze" his master on all pur-chases made.　He will collect commissions from the tailor, the laundryman, and all others with whom his employer has any dealings.　This system of commissions and petty grafting is so ingrained in custom, that no one need attempt to combat it.　A little checking up now and then will keep it within bounds.

Hotels furnish servants for their guests, but when a prolonged stay is intended, visitors often employ additional servants.　Steamship and railway lines offer special cheap rates for servants, who may accompany the traveller at slight additional cost.　However, few Chinese servants are of any great value in travelling, most of them being helpless when taken away from home into a strange part of the country.

TRANSPORTATION.

Considering its vast area, China's 5,000 miles of railway cannot be considered to cover the country very thoroughly, but as the railways connect the principal points the mileage is ample to meet the requirements of the average traveller.　All the lines are included in the system known as the Chinese Government Railways, except a few which are provincial enterprises. With the usual exceptions, travel on the express trains in China will be found comfortable and satisfactory. Sleeping car and dining car accommodations are to be had on all long journeys, as between Shanghai and Peiping, but the traveller should always make sure that he is taking the right train as neither meals nor beds are to be had on some of the ordinary mail trains. On some of the most important lines the check system of handling baggage is in vogue and trunks may be checked through to destination. On other lines the passenger must look after his own baggage. Plenty of porters will always be found to carry baggage to and from trains but he is wise who leaves this business to the management of the hotel runner.

China developed a large and thriving domestic commerce centuries before railways were dreamed of and this was accomplished by means of water transportation. To this circumstance is due the fact that nearly every important city of China is so located that it may be reached by one of the many coast or river steamship lines. The sailings are frequent and though the boats are small, most of them are comfortable and set a satisfactory table. One of the most comfortable, cheapest and generally most enjoyable trips the traveller can make is by one of the good Yangtsze River steamers plying between Shanghai and Hankow. On the smaller streams steam launch lines have been established connecting the larger ports with hundreds of smaller towns and these in turn are connected with villages by small boats.

In the treaty ports the ricsha is the most popular means of getting about. Its invention is credited to Rev. Mr. Globe, an American missionary, who, while living near Yokohama in 1869, converted a baby carriage into a vehicle in which his invalid wife could travel about. From this modest beginning the ricsha has spread to all parts of the Far East, except Manila, and may be found as far distant as South Africa. Its full name is *jin-riki-sha* and its Japanese etymology is given as *jin*, man; *riki*, power; *sha*, vehicle, or, literally, man-power-vehicle. Foreigners on the China coast have robbed the name of its first syllable and call it *rikisha* while some who live in Japan rob it of its last and call it *jinriki*. Only newcomers dignify it with its full name.

The first class ricshas in the principal cities are equipped with rubber tires, and are very comfortable. Just why the ricshas of conservative Peiping should be so much cleaner and more comfortable than those of progressive Shanghai no one has ever been able to explain satisfactorily. The charges vary in each place, but average about 60 cents an hour, $1.00 a half day, or $1.50 for a whole day. Treaty port residents use them for short trips about town, paying about 15 cents a mile, and usually ten cents for shorter trips. Never make the mistake of asking the coolie what the fare should be. He will immediately know that you are a stranger and demand many times the legal fare. Very frequently the coolie will demand from the newcomer a dollar for a trip from the steamer landing to the hotel when the correct charge is 10 or 20 cents. If you over-pay him your reputation for prodigality will soon spread, and you will be bothered by excessive demands. If you argue with him, he will enjoy nothing better, as it gives him an opportunity to show off his gift of repartee to the crowd which always assembles, and you are at a disadvantage in not knowing Chinese billingsgate. The only safe rule is to pay what you think is right and then walk away.

As in other parts of the world motor cars have practically driven public carriages from the streets of the larger cities. In all important ports motor cars can be hired at rates ranging from three or four dollars an hour for the ubiquitous Ford to higher prices for cars of greater aristocracy. Almost every city the tourist will visit possesses motor roads, private cars and garages. In many places it is possible to make excursions into the country and quite a number of cities are connected by motor roads and motor bus lines.

In the interior Chinese cities, the streets are often too narrow even for ricshas and sedan chairs are generally used. Travel in them is not very comfortable, but offers a novel experience. The tariff varies, but a rate based on $2 a day for each coolie employed will be especially liberal. Donkeys will be found useful in Soochow and many other cities. The rate should be settled with the donkey driver before starting out. It may prevent a stormy scene at the end of the journey but probably will not as the donkey driver will always ask for more than the agreed-on price.

Houseboats, wheelbarrows, mountain chairs, palanquins and several styles of mule carts are among the many means of transportation which one may find and use in China, when one leaves the railways. It would be impossible to give any general rates which would apply in all parts of the country, or at any one place during all seasons, for the tariff usually follows the ancient rule of being as much as the traffic will bear. The ever valuable old resident or the travel agency must be called upon to supply the information. In any event it will be well, in all transactions of this sort, especially in case of journeys of any length, to bear in mind the following excellent advice given by the late Dr. Arthur H. Smith in his *Chinese Characteristics:*

"Of all subjects of human interest in China, the one which most needs to be guarded against misunderstanding is money. If the foreigner is paying out this commodity (which often appears to be the principal function of the foreigner as seen from the Chinese standpoint) a future-perfect tense is 'a military necessity.' 'When you shall have done your work, you will receive your money.' But there is no future-perfect tense in Chinese, or tense of any description. A Chinese simply says, 'Do work, get money,' the last being the principal idea which dwells in his mind, the 'time relation' being absent. Hence when he is to do anything for a foreigner he wishes his money at once, in order that he may 'eat,' the presumption being that if he had not stumbled on the job of this foreigner he would never have eaten any more! Eternal vigilance, we must repeat, is the price at which immunity from misunderstandings about money is to be purchased in China. Who is and 'who is not to receive it, at what times, in what amounts, whether in silver ingots or brass cash, what quality and weight of the former, what number of the latter shall pass as a 'string'—these and other like points are those in regard to which it is morally impossible to have a too definite and fixed understanding. If the matter be a contract in which a builder, a compradore, or a boatman is to do on his part certain things and furnish certain articles, no amount of preliminary precision and exactness in explanations will come amiss."

In the past few years, two new methods of transportation have become important in China, with the development of airways and motor roads. This development is so rapid that it would be futile to get out here a list of the airways and motor roads which are available as it would be out of date by the time the book is published. But the more important developments are found in the fact that it is now possible to travel from Shanghai to Nanking (via Hangchow) by motor car and that by means of a regular and successful aeroplane service, it is possible to leave Shanghai after breakfast and have dinner in Hankow.

CALENDAR.

Officially, China has adopted the western or Gregorian calendar. A resolution putting the western calendar into effect was adopted in November 1911 and when Dr. Sun Yat Sen took his oath of office as President of China on January 1, 1912, it was officially recorded as "the first day of the first year of the Chinese Republic." Since that time all official documents have been marked with European dates, but in private life and in native business contracts the old customs prevail although the publication of old style calendars is now prohibited by law. Under the old calendar, time is reckoned by lunar months consisting of

29 or 30 days each, so that twelve lunar months make either 354 or 355 days. The beginning of the year, however, is determined by the sun, for New Year's day must fall on the "first new moon after the sun enters Aquarius, which makes it come not before January 21 nor after February 19." When the sequence of twelve lunar months does not meet this requirement for the beginning of the year, the discrepancy is remedied by the insertion of an extra or intercalary month, making 13 in the year, an occasion for joy on the part of landlords and grief on the part of those who pay rents. The calendar was almost identical with the Babylonian, Chaldean and Julian calendars and doubtless came from the same source. Each Chinese month begins with the new moon, which enables the most ignorant and illiterate to follow the passage of time, so that the Chinese calendar, strange and crude as it might appear to Western experience, was really an ideal calendar for the masses of China.

FESTIVALS AND HOLIDAYS.

There are twenty-four annual festivals provided for in the Chinese almanac, that is, two festivals for each moon. Most of these have no historical or other significance but mark changes in the seasons or supposed changes in the weather, such as spring, summer, autumn and winter and the days of moderate and intense heat or cold while others have to do with seasons supposed to be propitious for the planting or harvesting of certain crops. The occurrence of these festivals is fixed in that there are only two of them in each moon but no fixed rule determines the incidence of the days except that the day known as Chin Ming, Brightness and Purity, comes just 108 days after the Winter Solstice.

There follows a list of the festivals in the order of their sequence. Since the calendar is lunar, these festivals have no fixed position in the Western calendar but for sake of illustration we give the dates on which festivals occur in a typical year.

1st moon—
| *Lee Chun* | "Beginning of Spring" | Feb. 4. |
| *Yu Shui* | "Rain Water" | Feb. 19. |

2nd moon—
| *Chin Tse* | "Awakening of Torpid Insects" | Mar. 6. |
| *Chun Fen* | "Spring Solstice" | Mar. 21. |

3rd moon—
| *Chin Ming* | "Brightness and Purity" | April 5. |
| *Kuo Yu* | "Sowing Rain" | April 20. |

4th moon—
| *Lee Shia* | "Beginning of Summer" | May 6. |
| *Siao Man* | "Moderate Rain" | May 21. |

5th moon—
| *Moun Chun* | "Planting of Rice Sprouts" | June 6. |
| *Shia Tse* | "Summer Solstice" | June 22. |

6th moon—
| *Siao Shu* | "Moderate Hot Weather" | July 8. |
| *Da Shu* | "Intense Hot Weather" | July 23. |

7th moon—
| *Lee Chiu* | "Beginning of Autumn" | Aug. 8. |
| *Chu Shu* | "End of Hot Weather" | Aug. 24. |

8th moon—
| *Pei Lu* | "White Dew" | Sept. 8. |
| *Chiu Fen* | "Autumn Solstice" | Sept. 23. |

9th moon—
| *Han Lu* | "Cold Dew" | Oct. 9. |
| *Shuan Kiang* | "Frost Coming" | Oct. 24. |

10th moon—
| *Lee Tung* | "Beginning of Winter" | Nov. 8. |
| *Siao Hsueh* | "Moderate Snow" | Nov. 23. |

11th moon—
| *Da Hsueh* | "Intense Snow" | Dec. 7. |
| *Tung Tse* | "Winter Solstice" | Dec. 22. |

12th moon—
| *Siao Han* | "Moderate Cold" | Jan. 6. |
| *Da Han* | "Intense Cold" | Jan. 20. |

In addition to the above there are some other special days connected with the weather. In the latter part of the fourth moon there is a day called *Feng Loong* or "The separation of the plant beds." In the latter part of the fifth moon there is a day called *Chu Mei*, the beginning of damp weather, a period which lasts for 30 days, coming to an end the latter part of the sixth moon with *Mou Mei* or "end of damp weather." During the fifth and sixth moons there are three special periods of ten days each known as *Chu Fu, Chun Fu* and *Mou Fu* or beginning, middle, and end of hot weather. The three periods, 30 days in all, comprise presumably and usually the hottest weather of the year.

Some religious festivals are also included in the Chinese almanac. There are two days appointed for the worship of Confucius, also two days for the worship of the war lord, Kwan Kung. These semi-annual ceremonies occur in the spring and autumn. With the change to a Republican form of government Chinese officials have abandoned the gorgeous mandarin robes of their predecessors for frock coats and silk hats, and there have been changes in the old ceremonials of worship. It is curious that there is no special ceremony in connection with the birthday of Confucius, since Chinese are so punctilious about the observance of the birthdays of their famous men. It is merely noted on the calendar as the 27th day of the eighth moon.

Some of the festival days are observed by ancestral worship in the homes, probably the principal of these days being the one known as "Brightness and Purity," which falls in the third moon. In addition to the usual ancestral worship in the home it is also customary at this time to visit the ancestral tombs. There is also home worship on the Winter Solstice and the first day of the tenth moon as well as on new year eve and during the new year holidays.

There are three big festivals which play the greatest part in the lives of the Chinese. These are: New Year, the Fifth day of the Fifth moon and the Harvest Moon, which is always the fifteenth day of the eighth moon. All business accounts are supposed to be settled on these days, although the rule is more rigorously observed on New Year than at any other period.

The latter is really the one big holiday of the year, the holiday lasting, in theory at least, from new year's eve up to (and including) the 17th day of the first moon. New Year day itself is the most important day of the period, for the enthusiasm with which the holiday is celebrated diminishes daily, and long before the seventeen days are over, most Chinese families have settled back into the industrious routine which makes up their lives. But the holiday is a complete one while it lasts. On New Year day every shop is tightly closed, the wheelbarrow coolies and all but the most humble workers, take a day of rest, for some of them the only day of rest in the entire year. Those who have worn cotton for twelve months appear in silk and there are feasts ranging in magnificence from an extra portion of pork for the poor to tremendous banquets for the rich. The day is made joyous by the shooting of fire crackers. Ancestral scrolls bearing the names of all ancestors for many previous generations are displayed and offered the reverence which has come to be known as ancestor worship. In every household there are feasts and games and lavish hospitality. On the second day some of the smaller shops remove one shutter, so that they may transact business while giving the appearance of being closed and each day one or more additional shutters are removed while the big and prosperous shops keep tightly closed for the entire period prescribed by custom, that is, until the fifth day and some for a much longer period.

On the eve of the formal opening of the shops, the evening of the fourth day of the new year, all shops and families welcome the God of Wealth with ceremonies which are supposed to gain his good favour and secure financial success for the remainder of the year. On the morning of the fifth all except the most aristocratic shops are opened with a great banging of fire crackers and the current of trade resumes its usual flow.

But this does not end the New Year festivals, for from the fifth day until the thirteenth family feasts continue and this is an especially happy time for the children. The thirteenth is the beginning of the lantern festival which lasts to the seventeenth, this being the period of the appearance of the first full moon of the year. Groups of youths from the same neighbourhood, students, or members of guilds form processions carrying lanterns often of grotesque and fantastic design and these processions are to be seen in the streets every night while all the houses are also well lighted. The most ambitious lantern display is on the 15th, a night which is known as *Yuan Siao*, literally meaning the first full moon of the year. As is the case with many other festivals there is a special food for this occasion, corresponding to hot cross buns on Good Friday or roast turkey on the American Thanksgiving day. On this festival everyone eats a rice dumpling, shaped like a ball in semblance of the full moon. It is made of kneaded rice and flour, stuffed with sweets and boiled. The seventeenth is the last of the festival period and on the eighteenth everyone no matter how aristocratic goes back to his usual routine.

Like other people, the Chinese hold a great many superstitious beliefs in connection with the New Year festival and believe that the state of the weather on different days indicates the success of the year. Nothing could, in their minds offer a more happy augury for the year than for the entire new year period to be bright and fair. As the period is usually marked by foul days as well as fair, the prophecy of events works out in the usual human way of mixed good and evil. Each of the first ten days of the new year has a special significance as follows:

1st	day	Chicken
2nd	„	Pig
3rd	„	Dog
4th	„	Sheep
5th	„	Cow

6th	„	Horse
7th	„	Man
8th	„	Corn
9th	„	Heaven
10th	„	Earth

It is generally believed that the six principal domestic animals were created in the first six days, in the order named above, man on the seventh day, corn on the eighth, and the heaven and earth on the last two days.

Chin Ming, the day of brightness and purity, corresponds to All Souls Day in the Christian faith. On this day the spirits of all the dead come to earth for something to eat. The first duty of every one is to visit the ancestral tombs and provide the spirits of the ancestors with food and spirit money. Ancestral worship is universal and the sacrifices and devotions to the ancestral spirits are on this occasion more liberal and devout than on other times of the year. Since the spirits of the wicked as well as those of the good come to earth, the season is one when there are many spirits of predatory and criminal habits about. For that reason the entrance to every household is decorated with tender branches of the willow, a device, which, it is believed, will drive away all evil spirits. The special food for this day is a ball of boiled rice, coloured green with the juice of cabbage leaves and stuffed with sweetened bean flour.

Lee Hsia marks the first day of summer, and is the day on which all, adults and children alike, are supposed to be weighed. Duck eggs boiled in salt water and unripened ears of wheat form the special food of the day while there is an almost universal belief that a dish of sweet fermented rice, if eaten on this day, will have a powerful effect in warding off the usual summer ills.

Tuan Wu, the fifth day of the fifth moon, is the famous dragon boat festival. It is supposed to be the anniversary of the death of Chio Yuan, loyal and righteous official of the ancient feudal state of Chu, located in what is now Hunan Province. Chio Yuan was made the victim of an intrigue by traitors and in despair drowned himself in Mih Lu Lake. The people of the state of Chu, in appreciation of the unselfish public service of this official threw shoes of rice into the lake so that the fish might eat the rice instead of the body of their respected official and at the same time and for the same purpose men rowed boats up and down on the water, beating drums and tom toms to frighten away the evil spirits. That was the origin of the festival but to-day the rice shoe, instead of being used to feed the fishes, is a delicacy which is the feature of the Chinese feast of the day while the sailing of the boats has become a racing event in which rival crews compete. The work of devil dispelling is taken care of by a famous devil-dispelling spirit, Chun Kwei. His likeness, as well as his name, is displayed on a scroll hung up in the hall of every better class Chinese house.

This is the day on which there is a general clean up of the house, and walls, floors and furniture are given a more thorough cleaning than on any other day of the year. As a part of this general cleansing attempts are made to rid the premises of the five traditionally most poisonous insects, that is, centipedes, snakes, toads, spiders, and scorpions. The house is disinfected, the most popular disinfectant being wine mixed with sulphur, and this is sprayed into every nook and corner. At noon everyone takes a sip of this mixture. In addition sawdust mixed with strong medicinal roots is burned in every room, the pungent fumes presumably driving away all insects. Children have a lucky character painted on their foreheads and many of them wear coats made of black and yellow striped cotton, in imitation of tiger skins. At every household door a cluster of sword shaped rushes is displayed.

Chi Chiao, the seventh day of the seventh moon, is a festival of the greatest importance to the Chinese maids, for it is on this night that those heavenly lovers, the Herdsman and the Weaver Girl, are supposed to meet. The festival is described by E. T. Chalmers Werner in his *Myths and Legends of China:*

"In the myths and legends which have clustered about the observations of the stars by the Chinese there are subjects for pictorial illustration without number. One of these stories is the fable of Aquila and Vega, known in Chinese mythology as the Herdsman and Weaver-girl. The latter, the daughter of the Sun-god, was so constantly busied with her loom that her father became worried at her close habits and thought that by marrying her to a neighbour, who herded cattle on the banks of the Silver Stream of Heaven (the Milky Way), she might awake to a brighter manner of living.

"No sooner did the maiden become wife than her habits and character utterly changed for the worse. She became not only very merry and lively, but quite forsook loom and needle, giving up her nights and days to play and idleness; no silly lover could have been more foolish than she. The Sun-king, in great wrath at all this, concluded that the husband was the cause of it, and determined to separate the couple. So he ordered him to remove to the other side of the river of stars, and told him that hereafter they should meet only once a year, on the seventh night of the seventh month. To make a bridge over the flood of stars, the Sun-king called myriads of magpies, who thereupon flew together, and, making a bridge, supported the poor lover on their wings and backs as if on a roadway of solid land. So, bidding his weeping wife farewell, the lover-husband sorrowfully crossed the River of Heaven, and all the magpies instantly flew away. But the two were separated, the one to lead his ox, the other to ply her shuttle during the long hours of the day with diligent toil, and the Sun-king again rejoiced in his daughter's industry.

"At last the time for their reunion drew near, and only one fear possessed the loving wife. What if it should rain? For the River of Heaven is always full to the brim, and one extra drop causes a flood which sweeps away even the birdbridge. But not a drop fell; all the heavens were clear. The magpies flew joyfully in myriads, making a way for the tiny feet of the little lady.

"Trembling with joy, and with heart fluttering more than the bridge of wings, she crossed the River of Heaven and was in the arms of her husband. This she did every year. The husband stayed on his side of the river, and the wife came to him on the magpie bridge, save on the sad occasions when it rained. So every year the people hope for clear weather, and the happy festival is celebrated alike by old and young."

Chun Chiu is the middle of autumn, the fifteenth day of the eighth moon, when the full moon is usually seen in its greatest glory. In well-do-do families a feast is spread on a table in the open court yard, the feature of the feast being a round moon cake.

On *Chun Yang*, the ninth day of the ninth moon, is the day of "going on high." If there are any hills in the neighbourhood of a city all those who can tear themselves away from their daily duties climb to the hill tops. If, as in Shanghai, there are no nearby hills, the amusement places which boast roof gardens are very popular. While the festival may have had some religious or other significance in the past, it is now little more than an outing enjoyed by the younger generation.

In addition to the above festivals and anniversaries which have been observed for centuries, the Republican form of government has brought with it new days to be observed, as follows:

January 1st	Anniversary of establishment of first Republican government in Nanking.
February 12th	Declaration of Unification of South and North.
March 4th	Chinese Arbor Day.
May 1st	Labour Day.
October 10th	Republican Anniversary.
November 12th	Dr. Sun Yat-sen's Birthday.

Rapidly changing political conditions are already rendering some of these anniversaries obsolete and the only day which is generally recognized by Chinese and foreign firms and the consulates is October 10, anniversary of the establishment of the Chinese Republic.

HOTELS AND INNS.

European or American style hotels will be found in all the cities usually visited by foreign travellers; these hotels range in size from the large and luxurious foreign establishments of Hongkong, Peiping or Shanghai to more modest places under Chinese management in the cities less visited by foreigners. All foreign hotels in China except in Manchuria, are conducted on the American plan, providing an inclusive charge for rooms, meals and the usual service. This charge will be found to range from M.$10 per day upward, though M.$15 is the more customary minimum charge. The daily tariff includes the usual three meals a day, and, in addition, afternoon tea and an early breakfast consisting of tea, toast and fruit, served in the bed room. With an increasing number of travellers to China each year, the hotels of the principal ports are often crowded to capacity and it is advisable to make arrangements in advance as far as possible.

In addition to the hotels which cater to foreign tastes alone, there is an increasing number of Chinese inns which are becoming Europeanized, serving an approximation of foreign style meals. Some of these are quite satisfactory. The food served at others is a more or less edible travesty on the five course *table d'hôte* which all Chinese cooks believe to be necessary to the sustenance of the foreign life.

All these hotels carry stocks of tinned provisions and the traveller who cares to take the trouble to plan and supervise the preparation of his meals can get along quite comfortably. Fresh eggs, chickens and good tea are to be had in any part of the country. Chinese food is quite wholesome and many old residents eat it regularly, but it contains too many strange dishes to be palatable to the inexperienced. Those to whom a cup of coffee is indispensible are advised to accustom themselves to one of the

brands of coffee that can be "made in the cup" and carry
a supply with them. Most Chinese cooks have strange
ideas as to the preparation of coffee and in fact a good
cup of coffee is a rarity even at the best hotels.

At most steamer landings and railway stations, hotel
runners will be found to take charge of baggage. A small
charge is made for this service. Unless one makes special
demands on the servants, tips at all hotels in China may
be confined to the dining room boy, room boy and coolie.
If much entertaining is done and special dinners ordered,
the head waiter will expect a tip. Each one must decide
the amount of these tips for himself, but as a basis for
the calculation it should be remembered that a Mexican
dollar represents a maximum two days wage for the
average hotel servant.

If one leaves the regularly travelled routes of China,
marked by railway and steamship lines and foreign hotels,
he should be equipped either with letters of introduction
to local residents or with an interpreter and a competent
staff of servants. With a few letters of introduction, the
stranger may travel to nearly every part of China and
find a hospitable welcome at mission stations and the
messes maintained for the employees of foreign firms.
Where these messes are not available, the Chinese inn
will always be found. It will at least afford shelter and
an opportunity to prepare the food which the prudent
traveller will carry with him. However, it should be
thoroughly understood that no trip away from the main
travelled routes should be lightly undertaken. The traveller
who makes a journey of this kind without adequate reason
and complete preparation deserves the trouble and discomfort he will undoubtedly meet.

BRIGANDS, PIRATES AND REBELLIONS.

For the benefit of timid persons who may forego the
pleasure of a visit to China because of alarming stories it
may be well to point out that these dangers are very
small. It should be remembered that China covers a very

3

large territory, and brigands may ravage some parts of it without in any way disturbing the sections ordinarily visited by foreigners. All in all, travel on the regular routes is ordinarily as safe in China as in any other part of the world.

GUIDES.

In places where a guide is necessary, it is always advisable to secure one from the hotel or through one of the offices of a travel agency. The plausible gentry who hang about hotel entrances and gates of native cities should be avoided. Most of them are not guides, but runners from curio stores sent to lure the unwary traveller to a reckless purchase. The letters of recommendation they frequently carry have been forged, loaned, or rented for the occasion. The advice of any guide as to purchases should be accepted with a great deal of caution, for according to universal custom he is entitled to a commission on sales and it is to his interest to lead the traveller to shops where the commission and the price is the highest. It is not an unknown occurrence for the guide and the shopkeeper to take advantage of the tourist's ignorance of the language and arrange the terms of the commission in his presence while pretending to be haggling over the price.

The payment for guides employed from travel agencies ranges from $1.50 to $3.00 per day, to which must be added transportation and other travelling expenses. If the guide is discharged away from his place of employment the expenses of his homeward journey must be paid.

Some try the experiment of taking a servant with them throughout a trip, to act as interpreter, guide and general handy man. Though the venture is sometimes successful, it is more often a failure, for the average Chinese servant, capable as he may be at home, is usually quite useless on a journey, and, instead of caring for his master, needs quite a little looking after himself. To this general statement it must be added that there are quite a

number of experienced servants some of whom have
accompanied travellers on the usual railway and steamship
lines while others have done duty on the less travelled
routes in the interior. In every case, letters of recommendation should be demanded and verified.

FOOD AND DRINK.

The foreigner in China will miss few of the luxuries
of food to which he is accustomed at home and will find
many new delicacies he cannot procure in any other
country. Nearly every variety of vegetable known in
Europe or America is cultivated in China and in addition
there are many native foods which it is a delight to know.
During the season, persimmons as large as tomatoes may
be had by all who care for them. Delicious mangoes,
reminding many of the Missouri pawpaw, are served ice
cold for breakfast. The lychee, which is exported in
large quantities, is equally delicious whether eaten fresh,
or dried. All the year round the fruit stands of China
will be found fully stocked in appetising variety and in
the larger ports there are regular shipments of American
fruit. Indeed while other countries can offer superior
quality, few have the variety of fruit that can be secured
in China.

China is especially rich in poultry and game. Pheasant,
duck, quail, rice birds, snipe, wood cock and venison appear
almost daily on the bills of fare during the season. Many
of these articles of food, which might be accounted luxuries
in other places, are very cheap in China.

One bit of advice which the traveller will hear over and
over again is that he should not eat any food which has not
been thoroughly cooked and should especially avoid green
salads. This is good advice though one will often see it
ignored by old residents with no apparent ill effects. It
appears that the old resident may, without harm to himself, do many things which would send the newcomer to
the doctor, thence to the hospital and possibly to the under-
taker. Even the old resident is careful about the water

he drinks and will have none which he is not certain has been both filtered and boiled. As the traveller cannot always be certain that this has been done, he will be wise to drink none but bottled waters, of which he will find a variety on sale everywhere. The Chinese themselves seldom drink water, but consume huge quantities of weak tea which has been made with boiling water. As regards alcoholic drinks, no country offers a wider variety or cheaper prices.

PIDGIN ENGLISH.

When the first British and American traders visited the coast of China they found the great barrier to intercourse existed in the ignorance of each other's language. A long period of study is required of a foreigner to gain even a working knowledge of one Chinese dialect and the English language offers to the Chinese student difficulties almost equally as great. Trade could not wait for these academic accomplishments and the situation was met through the use of *pidgin* or *business* English. *Pidgin* represents the Chinese attempt to pronounce the word *business*, and *Pidgin English* actually means *business English.* This language consists of several hundred English words, adapted to Chinese pronunciation and used without regard to English grammar, but as they would be used in a Chinese phrase. In fact the language originated through attempts of the Chinese to make word-for-word translations from Chinese into English, expressing the sounds of English words by means of Chinese characters. Early trading at Canton was carried on largely by representatives of the East India Company, who, coming to China from India, brought with them a few Hindustani words which came into general use on the China Coast, and which add picturesqueness to the pidgin English glossary.

Many attacks have been made on this jargon, especially by cultured Chinese. and it is rapidly disappearing, just as a similar pidgin English has practically disappeared in

Japan. But for the present, except for the small number of foreigners who speak Chinese and Chinese who have a foreign education, pidgin English is a useful if inelegant means of communication. It is often used between Chinese themselves, for when two from different Southern provinces meet, each finds difficulty in understanding the local dialect spoken by the other. It was spoken to a great extent in the revolution of 1911 by officers of the Republican army, who, brought together from all parts of the South, communicated with each other through pidgin.

There are many parts of China where pidgin English is unknown, but the traveller will find that a knowledge of the jargon, which is picked up in a few days, will suffice for all his needs so long as he remains in the treaty ports or on the usual travelled routes. Interpreters will be needed on any trip into the interior.

In *pidgin* English, one word usually does the work of several, the jargon, like the Chinese language, being uninflected. For instance *my* is used for I, me, my, mine, our, ours, and we. *He* expresses he, she, it or they. *Catchee* is a modification of the English word catch, signifying ownership or acquisition. *"He have catchee one piecee wife"* means "He has married." *Belongee* is the English word belong, as pronounced in *pidgin* and has a variety of meanings. *"What side you belongee?"* means "Where do you live?" *"He belongee too muchee boilum tea"* means "He has boiled the tea too long." *Can do* is used for yes, or with the rising inflection as a form of interrogation. The Chinese servant will seldom use the word yes, and when he does use it, he often means no. There are no words for *yes* or *no* in the Chinese language as the question is answered by a careful affirmation or denial of the original statement. *Maskee* is a very useful word which means all right, correct, never mind, however, but, anyhow, and nevertheless. It is the Chinese equivalent of the Russian *Nichevo*, the Spanish *quien sabe* or the Japanese *eskataganai*. *Chop chop* is equivalent to hurry—seldom done in China. *Chop,* when used alone, means trademark, brand, or name. *Number one chop* means "first-class quality." *Walkee* is used for all forms of travel, motion or progress. Not only men and horses, but boats, birds and wagons, motor cars and machines *walkee.* *Chit* is sometimes a letter, but more often it is the memorandum of indebtedness which you sign at the hotel or club. *Cumshaw* is a tip or present. It need not be large, but is always expected. If you eat a meal in a Chinese restaurant, ten per cent will be added to your bill as a *cumshaw* for the servants. *Face:* character, self-esteem. To *lose face* is the worst punishment a Chinese can endure. This is a *pidgin* phrase which appears to have come into use the world over. *Finish* is complete, or exhausted. When your boy tells you *"Ice have finish,"* he means there is no more ice. *How fashion?* is a familiar form of interrogation meaning Why? or What is the matter? When the boy tells you *"Ice have finish,"* you should ask *"How fashion?"* to which he will almost invariably reply *"My no savvey,"* meaning that he knows nothing of the reason for its finishing and disclaims all responsibility therefor. *Joss* is from the Portuguese word *dios* and means idol, god, or luck. A *joss-pidgin-man* is literally, a God-business-man, or a clergyman, and there is no disrespect or irreverence implied. *Larn-pidgin* is the apprentice, who without pay will do most of the work around your house and be blamed by the regular servants for everything that goes wrong.. *Look-see-pidgin* is the general term applied to everything done for show or effect and is used for all forms of hypocrisy. *Plopa* is the Chinese pronunciation of the English word "proper" and is used for right, correct, or nice.

Prof. E. H. Parker in his delightful book *John Chinaman* gives the following example of a typical pidgin conversation between himself, when British Consul at Canton, and a Canton barber:

" Mornin,' barber-man."

" Mornin,' Missi Consun; wanchee my cuttee heh."

" Yes; no wanchee cuttee too muchee; can cuttee littee."

" Oll ligh! My savee. My cuttee any man heh: plento man catchee my shabe he, ebbily mornin.' Beforetime Hongkong gobbunor ollo time my shabe he."

" What ting have got to-day, barber-man?"

" New piecy wice-loy hab go *ngamún* (*yamén*) to-day."

" That Chinaman talkee he belong good man?"

" No man savey: moos wait littee time, can see. Some man talkee he moos wanchee stop lat gambaloo."

" Have got too muchee gamble housee that creek side!"

" Yih! Beforetime Sir Blook Lobisson no pay he stop lat side."

" What for that viceroy he soldier-man no look out?"

" He no likee. S'pose Missi Hance no bobbery [bother] he, he no likee too hat [hard]. Missi Hance no savey China talkee: moos wanchee new piecy largee Consun talkee he."

" Mr. Hance knew all about it: he told the flower-boats to clear out long ago, and the *wai-yün* [the viceroy's deputy] have got order."

" Missi Hance numba one good man: he lat hat [that heart] too muchee soft. My tinky Missi Consun too muchy soft hat, too."

" Any man talkee my so fashion? What ting that Chinaman talkee my?"

" Lat Chinaman talkee consun-side too muchy bijinis; Missi Consun any ting can makee. Maskee what ting, ollo belong ploppa."

" Chinaman talky my so fashion?"

" Yih! Any man talky; suppose no got Missi Consun, no can!"

" What for no can? What thing my got number one?"

" Ollo man takee, fullin man come Canton side before-time Missi Mayers numba one: Missi Mayers hab go way; olo Chinaman talky Missi Consun numba one onsz-tan [understand]."

The most complete pidgin English vocabulary contains but a few hundred words, and one who is used to a larger vocabulary will be surprised what a wide range of conversational and controversial subjects these few hundred words will cover. He should be careful, however, about the indiscriminate use of pidgin English, for cultured Chinese naturally dislike being addressed in that jargon. An old story is told on the China Coast of the recently arrived missionary lady who sought the aid of the local mandarin in replacing the mission organ which had been damaged by rain leaking through a hole in the roof. "Have got before time one piecee organ, belong makee sing song," she explained. "Have puttee organ house inside. Roof topside have makee break. Lain come chop chop makee spoilum organ. Just now must catchee one more piecee." The mandarin listened attentively but did not appear to understand, so she repeated the story several times. Finally the light of understanding broke over his face, and he replied, "Ah, I understand. A rift in the lute, *n'est-ce pas?*" He was a graduate of an American university and had lived long in Paris.

Those who wish to pursue the study of pidgin English are advised to purchase those amusing little volumes *Pidgin English Sing Song* by Charles G. Leland and *Broken China* by A. P. Hill.

ROUTES AND FARES.

China, with its extensive seaboard, numerous harbours and busy ports, is at cnce a terminus and a point of transit for steamer lines from all parts of the world. At almost any time will be seen side by side in her extensive waterways all manner of craft, from the luxurious passenger vessel to the veriest tramp, that somehow coughs its way across the seas. Nearby lie the trim coasters, that maintain a railroad like schedule, and native junks of myriad shapes and sizes, all of them part of the many-linked chain that connects China and her products with the outside world.

Routes to China can be broadly divided into groups: from America; from Europe by Suez; from Europe by air; from Europe by rail; from Australasia; from Africa; from the Middle East; and from neighboring countries, roughly bounded by Japan in the North, the Philippines in the South and Siam in the West.

FROM UNITED STATES AND CANADA.

Four steamship lines connect North America with China, American Mail Line, Canadian Pacific, Dollar Steamship Company and Nippon Yusen Kaisha. The Dollar Steamship Company operates a weekly service from New York via the Panama Canal, California, Honolulu and Japan to Shanghai and Hongkong. American Mail Line steamers leave Seattle and Victoria every fortnight, sailing direct by the Northern Route to Japan and China. Canadian Pacific steamers sail every two weeks from Vancouver and Victoria for Japan and China with calls once a month at Honolulu on the westward trip. For Los Angeles from Seattle connection is made with Canadian Pacific steamers at Victoria by the "Princess" boats, the fare for which is included in the trans-Pacific fare.

The Nippon Yusen Kaisha maintain a fortnightly service with their California-Orient steamers between Los Angeles and China via San Francisco, Honolulu and Japan. Among these ships are the three new motor vessels of the "Asama Maru" type. A Northern service is operated every two weeks between Seattle and China via Victoria and Japan. A further service is maintained between China and South America as far as Valparaiso by the Nippon Yusen Kaisha West-coast service, which sails monthly via coastal ports of South America, Balboa, Mexico, California, Hawaii and Japan. Steamers proceed direct from Kobe to Hongkong, but connection can be made with Shanghai by other Nippon Yusen Kaisha steamers.

Apart from the passenger lines there are numerous cargo vessels plying between China and America, several of which have limited passenger accommodation.

First class fares from the West Coast of North America to China range from G.$150 to $400 depending

on the route and the accommodation desired. Length of
voyage from North America to China varies according to
line between fourteen and twenty days.

Recently the tendency has grown for travel from
Europe to China via America, and to encourage traffic
over this route favorable sterling rates have been applied.
Holders of first class steamship tickets on a Pacific line
may secure a free baggage allowance of 350 lbs. on the
American railroads provided they can produce their
steamship tickets prior to checking their baggage.

From Europe via Suez, passenger services are
maintained as follows:

FROM ENGLAND:

Peninsular & Oriental Steam Navigation Co,—
fortnightly, Blue Funnel—monthly, Nippon Yusen Kaisha
and Glen Line—fortnightly.

FROM NORTHERN EUROPE:

Norddeutscher Lloyd—monthly, Hamburg Amerika
Line—twice a month, Nederland Royal Mail and Rotterdam
Lloyd—combined weekly service, connecting with steamers
of the Java-China-Japan Line at Batavia.

FROM THE MEDITERRANEAN:

Lloyd-Triestino, monthly service from the Adriatic,
Messageries Maritimes from Marseilles and all lines from
Northern Europe.

A feature of the Suez route is the number of cargo
vessels carrying passengers, some as few as two, others
as màny as thirty. Generally these steamers are longer
on the voyage, forty to sixty days to Northern Europe as
against twenty-five to thirty-five by the faster passenger
vessels. Fares tend to an accepted level and no great
disparity is noticeable among the rates offered by the
larger passenger lines. First class to England is about
£100 and second class £70, while to the Mediterranean,
fares are about £9 cheaper in first class and £2 in second.

FROM EUROPE BY AIR:

No less than four air lines can be said to link China to the West. Of these only one will maintain direct flights between Europe and China, the Eurasia Corporation. At the present time flights by this route are not extending beyond Lanchow, but it is expected very soon that a regular trans-continental service will be inaugurated.

The other three lines are the Imperial Airways, whose planes fly from London via Paris, the Mediterranean, Egypt and Persia to India, where scheduled connection is made for China; the Royal Netherlands India Airway (K.L.M.), whose service extends from Holland via Europe, the Mediterranean, India, Burma and Siam to the Netherlands East Indies; the Air Orient, which operates between Paris via Europe, Mediterranean and Indo-China. All these air lines maintain a weekly service and it is highly probable that this will soon be extended to China.

FROM EUROPE BY RAIL:

There is at the moment one method of approach to China by rail, via Siberia. From Berlin the shortest route lies through Warsaw, Moscow, Omsk, Irkutsk, Manchuli, Harbin and south through Mukden to Tientsin or Dairen, whence a Dairen Kisen Kaisha steamer is taken for Shanghai. The journey from Berlin to Shanghai occupies about fifteen days, but with improved conditions can undoubtedly be reduced by a third of this time. Fares from Shanghai to Berlin approximate G.$350.00 in first class and G.$250.00 in second class.

Intending passengers should pay particular attention to the question of visaes and before arranging their journey and should consult their consulate as to existing formalities. In general four visas are necessary, Chinese, Japanese, Russian and Polish and in the case of citizens of the United States, German. No free baggage allowance is given on this route, save such hand luggage as is permitted in the compartment. Travellers are recommended to use first class in Soviet Russia. Heavy baggage may be bonded through Russia to avoid the rigorous customs examinations.

FROM AUSTRALASIA:

Travellers from Australia and New Zealand may reach China by the direct route or via the East Indies. Three lines operate a direct service, the Eastern and Australasian Steamship Company, the Australian Oriental Line and the Nippon Yusen Kaisha. Each of these sails from Melbourne via Sydney, Brisbane and intermediate ports to Manila and Hongkong. In every case a monthly service is maintained from Melbourne to Hongkong, all fares are about £48 first class and £21 second class.

Via the East Indies steamers of the Burns Philp and Koninklyke Paketcaarp Maapschacppy sail monthly from Adelaide via ports of East Australia, the Celebes to Java, where by trans-shipment passengers proceed to China ports by the Java-China-Japan Lyn via Manila or direct from Batavia. First class fares by this route are £75 from Adelaide to Hongkong and about £80 to Shanghai.

FROM AFRICA:

There is no direct passenger service from Africa. The Osaka Shosen Kaisha steamers leave Cape Town every month via the East Coast of Africa for Singapore, where travellers may trans-ship to any of the numerous lines serving the China Coast. The journey can also be made by Koninklyke Paketcaarp Maapschacppy steamers which leave Cape Town each month via the East Coast ports and Mauritius for Java with trans-shipment to a steamer of the Java-China-Japan Lyn or Koninklyke Paketcaarp Maapschacppy direct services from Batavia.

FROM THE MIDDLE EAST:

All European liners call at Indian or Ceylon or Straits ports before reaching China. There are, however, several lines, such as the Nippon Yusen Kaisha Bombay service, the British-India Steam Navigation Apcar Line from Calcutta, which sail monthly and fortnightly respectively.

From the East Indies the Java-China-Japan Lijn and the Koninklyke Paketcaarp Maapschacppy maintain fortnightly services, the former both from Sourabaya to Shanghai via the Celebes and Manila and from Batavia direct, and the latter from Batavia by trans-shipment at Singapore.

From Neighboring Countries:

Services from Japan are provided by all passenger lines from America, by most of the European and African lines on their homeward voyage and by the Nippon Yusen Kaisha express steamers from Kobe and Nagasaki to Shanghai. Northern China is served by many local lines of small steamers, calling at ports of Chosen (Korea) and South Manchuria prior to arrival at Tientsin.

From the Philippines, there are regular sailings of steamers of the Australian lines, of the Java-China-Japan Lyn, the lines from America on their homeward voyage, Hamburg Amerika Line and the Norddeutscher Lloyd.

Through Bangkok, Siam is connected by local steamers of the China Navigation Company, who operate a network of local services in the China Seas, and by occasional passenger-carrying freighters. Indo-China is served by the large steamers of the Messageries Maritimes from Saigon and local steamers.

Along the China Coast itself and up the rivers inland run a waterways clockwork system of local services, of which the chief are the China Navigation Company, Indo-China Steam Navigation Company, Nisshin Kisen Kaisha, Dairen Kisen Kaisha, the Yangtsze Rapid Steamship Company, Douglas Steamship Company, Osaka Shosen Kaisha and the China Merchants' Steam Navigation Company.

Many interchange arrangements exist between lines in the Far East and the traveller will find this a matter for consideration in long voyages. Round trip fares are quoted by practically all lines at generally two single fares less 10% to 12½%. Stopover privileges are generally granted, save in the busy season (February-March-April-May-September-October-November).

For anyone travelling to China from America or Europe it will generally be found to be advantageous to purchase a Round-the-World ticket with stopover privileges. On the other hand, if the traveller intends to spend some considerable time in Far Eastern waters, he will find travel by most lines reasonable in price and, judged by accepted standards, comfortable in accommodations.

TELEGRAPHS AND RADIO.

China has an inland wire (or landline) telegraph system extending to most cities. In addition to this it has a network of radio-telegraph stations covering seventy-nine of the most important cities. Both the radio and wire systems are under the Director General of Telegraphs and Telephones, Ministry of Communications. Supplementing the above are the railway telegraph stations which are under railway management.

There are:—1,079 Telegraph Administration offices, 79 Radio Administration offices, 650 Railway Telegraph offices.

The rate for service between points in China is 10 cents per word Chinese Currency (at present equivalent to a little more than 2 cents gold) for Chinese plain language (non-secret transmission of Chinese characters by a four-figure-group system). 20 cents per word for Chinese language (secret code) and for foreign language or commercial code. The rates for the telegraph and radio systems are the same.

China now has both radiogram and cablegram services to all parts of the world. Chinese Government Radio Administration circuits connect Shanghai directly with the United States (at San Francisco), Germany (at Berlin), France (at Paris), Netherlands East Indies (at Batavia), Philippine Islands (at Manila), French Indo-China (at Saigon), Switzerland (at Geneva) and

Hongkong. Amoy has a circuit direct to Manila. Future plans provide for the operation of a direct circuit from Shanghai to Great Britain (London) and from Shanghai to Japan (Tokyo).

Cable services go from Shanghai to Europe via Japan and Siberia over the Great Northern route. From Shanghai to Europe, via Hongkong, India and Mediterranean points over the Eastern Extension route. From Shanghai to the United States via Manila, Guam and Hawaii over the Commercial Pacific Cable route. In addition to these cables there is the Japanese Shanghai-Nagasaki Cable, Chinese Chefoo-Dairen Cable, the Foochow-Taiwan (Formosa) Cable and several coastwise cables.

The rates to foreign countries are, in almost all cases, the equivalent to the rates from the several countries to China, converted into Chinese currency. Due to fluctuations of international exchange the rates vary from time to time and if a list were given herein it would remain effective for only a short period. Rates for the international radio and cable services are in nearly all cases the same and may be obtained without difficulty at any radio, telegraph or cable office in China.

The Chinese post office has developed into a very efficient organization, reaching almost every corner of the country, and affording an excellent service at very reasonable rates. The Chinese post office handles correspondence addressed in the Romanized version of Chinese names and shows remarkable ability in deciphering the many spellings which are used. Formerly there were sixty agencies of foreign post offices maintained at the various treaty ports but all these were closed on January 1, 1924, according to agreements reached at the Washington Conference.

CHINESE NAMES.

The lack of uniformity in the Romanized spelling of Chinese names is often a source of confusion. When foreigners first came to China they either expressed

Chinese sounds with their own alphabets or gave their own names to places. Arbitrary systems of spelling sprang up, and though the Chinese post office has adopted an official Romanization for all place names, there remain in common usage many methods of spelling the same names. For instance, Soochow is variously spelled, Suchow, Suchau, and Soutcheou, while Shanghai will often be spelled Changhai, Schanghae, etc. Further confusion arises from the fact that many cities are known to foreigners by names which the Chinese do not use. Canton is known to Chinese as Kwangchaufu. Chinese also experience difficulty in finding the phonetic equivalent of foreign names. The Eames family (the late opera star Emma Eames was born in Shanghai) is known as Aemih; Jardine is expressed by Cha-teen; and Lane, Crawford, & Co. by Lane, Ka-la-fat. In Chinese usage the family name is first, thus Li Hung Chang was a member of the Li family and not a "Mr. Chang" as he was frequently called by editors in foreign countries.

Place names in this book follow the spelling adopted by the Chinese Post office. If the traveller will learn the meaning of the few common suffixes it will help toward an understanding of the place names. *Chen* means town; *chow*, prefecture or department; *chun*, village; *fu*, department; *hsien*, district or county; *shen*, province. Following are the names of some of the principal cities and towns in China with their meaning:

Anching—" Safe and happy."
Chaiyu—" Good fish."
Changsha—" A long strip of sand along the river."
Changsueh—" Always giving good crops."
Chinhai—" To pacify the sea."
Chinkiang—" To pacify the river."
Chungking—" Happy again."
Foochow—" Blissful city."
Haichow—" Sea city."
Haiyin (Chekiang)—" Sea salt."
Hankow—" At the mouth of the Han River."

Hongkong—" Fragrant port."
Ichang—" Can be prosperous."
Jihchao—" Sun shining."
Kaishing—" Good and prosperous."
Kiangwan—" Bend of the river."
Kiangyin—" Back of the river."
Kiaochow—" Gun city."
Kirin—" Good forest."
Kiukiang—" Nine rivers meeting at one place."
Kweilin—" Cinnamon forest."
Liangshang—" Good village."
Linghai—" Near the sea."
Machen—" Flax city."
Nanchang—" Southern prosperity."
Nanking—" Southern capital."
Ningpo—" Smooth wave."
Panpu—" Oyster port."
Paoshan—" Mineral hill."
Paoting—" Guarantee to pacify."
Peking—" Northern capital."
Samshui—" Three rivers."
Shanghai—" Above the sea."
Shangshan (Kwangtung)—" Fragrant hill."
Shasi—" The market on the sand (sea shore)."
Sian—" Western safety."
Soochow—" A city of awakening."
Taichong—" Big granary."
Taiping (Anhwei)—" Peace."
Taiyuan—" Big. plain."
Tientsin—" Heavenly ford."
Tinghai—" To control the sea."
Tsinan—" South of the Tsi river."
Tsingtao—" Green island."
Tungkwan—" East light."
Wusih—" No tin." The original name was Yu Sih,
        "have tin," but when the tin in Sih Shan
        (Tin Hill) was exhausted the name was
        changed to its present form.

Wuwei (Anhwei)—" Nothing to do " (A lonely place).
Yunnan—" South of the cloud."

TREATY PORTS.

This is the term applied to the 48 ports of entry
wherein foreigners are allowed to reside and carry on
business by reason of agreements to that effect in various
treaties or voluntary concessions on the part of the
government of China. Foreigners are not allowed by
treaty to own land, reside, or carry on business in any
other place, though this restriction does not apply to
missionaries and in practice many foreign firms hold
property and carry on business in places where they have
no technically legal rights.

The treaty ports are as follows:

Port	Province	Date of Customs Opening		Estimated Population
Aigun	(Heilungkiang)	July	1909	5,800
Amoy	Fukien	April	1862	470,000
Antung	(Shengking)	March	1907	268,198
Canton	Kwangtung	Oct.	1859	3,000,000
Changsha	Hunan	July	1904	1,243,044
Chefoo	Shantung	March	1862	592,800
Chinkiang	Kiangsu	April	1861	503,325
Chinwangtao	Chihli	Dec.	1901	5,000
Chungking	Szechuan	March	1891	974,365
Dairen	(Shengking)	July	1907	262,237
Foochow	Fukien	July	1861	1,508,630
Hangchow	Chekiang	Oct.	1896	1,136,060
Hankow	Hupeh	Jan.	1862	1,466,860
Harbin	(Kirin)	July	1909	220,000
Hunchun	(Kirin)	Jan.	1910	3,700
Ichang	Hupeh	April	1877	55,000
Kiaochou (Tsingtao)	Shantung	July	1899	200,000
Kiukiang	Kiangsi	Jan.	1862	238,207
Kiungchow (Hoihow)	Hainan	April	1876	43,000
Kongmoon	Kwangtung	March	1904	70,000

Kowloon	Kwangtung	April	1897	—
Lappa	Kwangtung	June	1871	—
Lungchingtsun	(Kirin)	Jan.	1910	500
Lungchow	Kuangsi	June	1889	13,000
Manchouli	(Heilungkiang)	Feb.	1907	5,000
Mengtze	Yunnan	Aug.	1889	10,900
Nanking	Kiangsu	May	1899	902,941
Nanning	Kiangsi	Jan.	1907	300,000
Newchwang	Shengking	May	1864	61,000
Ningpo	Chekiang	May	1861	1,041,455
Pakhoi	Kwangtung	April	1877	20,000
Samshui	Kwangtung	June	1897	6,000
Sansing	(Kirin)	July	1909	22,500
Santuao	Fukien	May	1899	8,000
Shanghai	Kiangsu	June	1854	3,144,868
Shasi	Hupeh	Oct.	1896	95,900
Soochow	Kiangsu	Sept.	1896	350,900
Suifenho	Kirin	Feb.	1908	1,500
Swatow	Kwangtung	Jan.	1860	75,000
Szemao	Yunnan	Jan.	1897	15,000
Tatungkow	(Shengking)	March	1907	4,300
Tengyueh	Yunnan	May	1902	260,000
Tientsin	Chihli	May	1861	1,250,000
Wenchow	Chekiang	April	1877	90,000
Wuchow	Kuangsi	June	1897	100,000
Wuhu	Anhui	April	1877	240,000
Yatung	(Tibet)	May	1894	—
Yochow	Hunan	Nov.	1899	20,000

Names of territories enclosed in brackets do not belong to the eighteen provinces of China proper. Some being in Manchuria (Manchukuo).

WEIGHTS AND MEASURES.

It is only fair to the reader to state at once that there are no weights and measures in China as they are known in other countries. In theory the system is a very good one, being based on the decimal notation, but in practice every dealer or every guild fixes an individual

standard which may or not be like that of any other
dealer or guild.   Thus while the *picul* is in name a
standard of weight in all parts of the country, it is always
necessary to determine how heavy the *picul* is.   As the
picul is composed of a variable number of *catties* which
may also vary in weight and as each one of the smaller
divisions of weight is subject to variations it is quite
impossible for any foreigner ever to tell just what is
meant by a *picul*.   Says Dr. Arthur H. Smith in his
Chinese Characteristics: "So far is it from being true
that 'a pint is a pound the world around,' in China a pint
is not a pint, nor is a pound a pound.   Not only does the
theoretical basis of each vary, but it is a very common
practice to fix some purely arbitrary standard, such as
twelve ounces, and call that a pound.   The purchaser
pays for sixteen ounces and receives but twelve, but then
it is openly done by all dealers within the same range, so
that there is no fraud, and if the people think of it at
all, it is only as an old time custom of the salt trade.   A
similar uncertainty prevails in the measurement of land.
In some districts the acre is half as large again as in
others, and those who happen to live on the boundary are
obliged to keep a double set of measuring apparatus, one
for each kind of acre."   The same author continues, in
discussing what he calls the Chinese disregard for
accuracy—"Under these circumstances, it cannot be a
matter of surprise to find that the regulation of standards
is a thing which each individual undertakes for himself.
The steelyard maker perambulates the street, and puts
in the little dots (called 'stars') according to the
preferences of each customer, who will have not less than
two sets of balances, one for buying and one for selling.
A ready-made balance, unless it might be an old one, is
not to be had, for the whole scale of standards is in a
fluid condition, to be solidified only by each successive
purchaser."

With the foregoing explanations the following tables
of weights and measures are appended:

MEASURES OF WEIGHT

```
 10 Li..................1 Fen (Candareen)
 10 Fen................1 Ch'ien (Mace)
 16 Liang ..............1 Chin (Kin) or Catty
100 Chin ...............1 Tan or Picul
 10 Ch'ien..............1 Liang (Tael)
```

For purposes of foreign trade these weights are fixed as follows:—

```
1 Liang......583.3 grs.—1-1/3 oz.—37.783 grammes
1 Catty......1-1/3 lb. or 604.53 grammes
1 Picul......133-1/3 lbs. or 60.453 kilogrammes
```

According to the *China Year Book*, from which this information is taken, the *catty* ranges in native trade from 12 to 43 1/2 ounces, and the number of *catties* to the *picul* will vary from 90 to 280.

MEASURES OF LENGTH

```
 10 Fen ................1 Ts'un (inch)
 10 Ts'un...............1 Ch'ih (foot)
 10 Ch'ih...............1 Chang (Pu or Kung)
108 Chang..............1 Li
```

For purposes of the foreign customs trade the length of the *ch'ih* is fixed at 14.1 inches or 0.358 metres, this arrangement being reached in the Anglo-Chinese agreement of 1858.

A *li*, theoretically 2,115 feet or two-fifths of a mile, is usually regarded as a third of a mile. One will often find that the distance from A to B is reckoned at 20 *li* while from B to A is 25 *li*. This discrepancy is explained by the fact that the road one way is uphill. In rainy weather when roads become difficult the "distance" between points will increase 50 to 100 per cent.

Some of the "standard" lengths (in English inches) in various trades, etc., are as follow:—

```
Carpenter's    ch'ih............11.14
Mason's        „  ............11.08
Artisan's      „  ............12.569
```

Board of Revenue's „ 13.181
Tailor's „ 13.85
Customs House „ 14.098
Junk Builder's „ 15.769

MEASURES OF AREA

In measures of area the following tables are used:—

10 *Ssŭ*..............................1 *Hao*
10 *Hao* ....1 *Li*
10 *Li*...............................1 *Fen*
10 *Fen* ....1 *Mow*
100 *Mow* ....1 *Ch'ing*

———

25 Square *Ch'ih*.................1 *Pu* or *Kung*
240 *Pu*...........................1 *Mow*
100 *Mow*........................1 *Ch'ing*

The *mow* is known to most foreigners as consisting of one-sixth of an English acre, that being the standard fixed by treaty in Shanghai. In other parts of China the *mow* means whatever local custom may have established as its meaning and nothing more. It is known to vary in different parts of the country from one-fifteenth to one-third of an acre.

MEASURES OF CAPACITY

Measures of capacity are probably used less in China than in any other country, for most fluids and grains are sold by weight. Wooden measures are used for retail transactions in rice and grain but in the wholesale trade these commodities are weighed rather than measured. Most of the measures of capacity which one sees in the rice dealers' shops are really measures of weight, local custom decreeing that a certain measure full of rice be equal to one, five or ten *catties*. Though the Chinese merchant always makes a concession to the customs of foreigners and sells his silk by the yard, the Chinese customer when buying some qualities will pay for it by the ounce. Eggs, too, are sold by weight rather than by the dozen as in our own enlightened lands where we pay as much for a dozen small eggs as for a dozen large ones. However, on the rare occasions when the Chinese do use measures of capacity, their theoretical table is as follows:—

10 *Ko*..................................1 *Sheng*
10 *Sheng*..............................1 *Tow*
10 *Tow* ....1 *Shih*

These terms may mean much or little for the *tow* according to one authority ranges from 176 to 1800 cubic inches.

At the time this is written the Nationalist Government of China is making a determined effort to regulate and standardize the whole system of weights and measures of the country and doubtless in a short time the inconsistencies mentioned above will disappear. Formerly the Chinese people travelled about very little and they were not greatly inconvenienced by the different standards which existed in other parts of the country. Now with the building of railways, there is a great deal of travelling and the old standards will not do.

STAMP COLLECTING.

Shanghai and other cities in China are perhaps the most interesting in the world to a philatelist, or stamp collector. Although postage stamps did not come into use in Shanghai until 1862, when the British post office began to use the stamps of Hongkong that were introduced in that year, the stamps of other countries, arriving on mails, provided material for the early collectors; and the modern collectors dream of the chances the old-timers must have had to find rarities on the incoming mails of those days. Fifty years from now, collectors will doubtless think we of to-day were the lucky ones, for stamps of every country come to Shanghai on letters, not to mention the stamps of China itself.

The French post office soon established an agency here, which used the ordinary French stamps, until in

1894, they were overprinted with the name "China." The American postal agency was established in the late seventies or early eighties, but used ordinary American stamps until a few years ago when they were surcharged. The Germans had their post office also, using ordinary German stamps, from during the eighties, but in 1898 began overprinting the stamps with the name "China" to head off speculators from buying the stamps here and sending them to Germany in order to make a profit on the difference in exchange. The Russian and the Japanese post offices later joined, so that until the World War, there were no less than seven different countries having post offices here, all issuing stamps, and each office carrying letters to its home country at the domestic rate, which was a distinct gain to its patrons but a serious loss to the Chinese post office.

During the world war the German office was closed, and the Russian office stopped when the Trans-Siberian railroad was closed. Then at the end of 1922 all the other foreign offices were closed, leaving the field to the Chinese post office.

In 1865 the Shanghai local post office first issued stamps, and continued doing so until about 1896. From the early nineties and for about six years there were also local post offices with their own stamps operating in Amoy, Chefoo, Chinkiang, Chungking, Foochow, Hankow, Ichang, Kiukiang, Nanking, Weihaiwei and Wuhu, and perhaps sold as many stamps to tourists and collectors as were used postally. The Chinese post office did not issue its own stamps until 1878, and from then until 1897 the post office was managed by the Maritime Customs. Later China joined the Postal Union, and has now a postal service that is second to none in efficiency and low charges for the service it renders.

There are several causes that make Chinese stamps harder to find here in China than they might be. One is, that foreigners generally spend only a few years here, and, if collectors, take their stamps home with them as a souvenir of their stay in the East. Then, also, a very large proportion of the Chinese issues and practically all of the stamps issued by the foreign offices in China were used on letters leaving the country, and, finally, the Chinese themselves have begun to collect stamps, and naturally they prefer the stamps of their own country.

Forty years ago the 1878 set of Chinese stamps were sold for 10 cents for the three stamps. The set of three stamps is now listed at G.$4.25, and they are getting to be harder to find each year. It is impossible to tell how much a complete collection of Chinese stamps would be worth. In the first place, there is no complete collection in existence. An Austrian multi-millionaire who devoted himself to collecting, and who paid thousands of dollars for single specimens, if he lacked them, was not able to show a complete collection of Chinese stamps. The famous "Post Office" Mauritius stamp, of which about twenty are known, and which sells for $20,000 is a common stamp when compared to any one of half a dozen of the stamps of China and the foreign offices. But no Chinese stamp has yet brought as much as a thousand dollars. Leaving out a few rarities, which the ordinary collector would never obtain, a Chinese collection may be made as cheaply as that of most of the other countries.

There are about 350 main varieties of Chinese Empire and Republic stamps, and all but about fifty can be bought for less than a dollar each—most of them for a few cents, and about twenty for a cent or two each. Minor varieties are plentiful and some very rare and expensive. When the collector goes in for the stamps of foreign offices in China, especially the numerous French issues, the number runs up above a thousand, but a fair proportion are low in price. As they are obsolete, owing to the closing of the foreign offices, they will probably become dearer.

Auction sales of stamps are held nearly every Saturday afternoon in Shanghai during the stamp season; they are advertised in the daily papers. It is absolutely necessary, however, to examine the lots before the sale, as no dependence can be placed on the descriptions given in the catalogues. Auctions are only for local buyers, as the catalogues are not available until a few days before the sales. In spite of all drawbacks, those who know a bargain when they see it can often do well at the auctions.

There are plenty of forged surcharges in the market, and many of them will deceive any but an expert. There is not much danger of being taken in by forgeries, if the collector lets the surcharges alone.

HISTORICAL SKETCH

CCORDING to legends which have very little historical support, Chinese history begins about 2500 B.C. with the reign of the three emperors, who in a remarkably short space of time brought a barbarous people to a comparatively high stage of civilization. The first of these semi-mythical rulers was Fu Hsi (or Fuhi), who instituted marriage, taught his subjects to fish with nets, domesticated wild animals for their use, invented the flute and lyre and replaced former methods of communication (by means of knots tied in strings) with a kind of picture language which has been developed into the present Chinese ideographs. His grave is now pointed out in Chechow, Honan, where thousands assemble annually to do reverence to his memory. The following emperor, Shen Nung, carried the cultural advance of the people still further. He taught agriculture and the use of herbs as medicine, and is now known as "The Imperial Husbandman." The third emperor, Hwang-ti, extended the boundaries of the empire, reformed the calendar, established cities, and introduced the use of carts and boats, while his consort taught the rearing of silkworms which remained a Chinese monopoly for many centuries. Foreign historians regard these three emperors as merely representative of different stages of early civilization, while the old Chinese historians ascribe to them supernatural qualities.

After the death of Hwang-ti several unimportant rulers succeeded and a little later (2357 B.C.) the famous ruler *Yao* was placed on the throne. He and his successor,

Shun, are doubtless the most popular figures in Chinese history. During the reign of *Yao*, the country was harassed by a great flood, which from the Chinese descriptions bear a resemblance to the deluge of the Bible. The minister of public works having failed to control and subdue the flood, the task was undertaken by Yu, his son. He built great canals, dug tunnels through mountains, and at length the flood subsided, after having devastated the country for nine years. He is credited with the accomplishment of engineering feats which would compare creditably with the building of the Panama Canal.

Yao finally handed over the government to his colleague, Shun, and he in turn gave it to Yu. Yao and Shun are two of the greatest figures in Chinese history and historians have vied with each other in ascribing to them every possible virtue and holding them up as examples to be followed by all other rulers. In the revolution of 1911 when the monarchy was exhorted to hand over the government to the Republicans, the examples of Yao and Shun in voluntarily surrendering the throne were cited.

Yu, the canal builder, founded the first of China's long succession of dynasties, which lasted from 2205 B.C. to 1766 B.C. This was the beginning of China's more or less authentic history. There were frequent revolutions during his reign, as was true of all succeeding dynasties, but the Chinese people continued to advance in the arts of civilization. The dynasty, starting with the able and resourceful Yu, fell, during the centuries, on evil days and the eighteenth emperor, Kie, was a cruel tyrant, whose name is synonymous with all that is infamous and vicious.

Tang, the Prince of Shang, led a revolt, overthrew Kie, and established the Shang or Yin dynasty, which stood from 1766 to 1122 B.C. Tang is accounted one of the great emperors of China and many writers have united in their praise of him. After a successful revolt against

Chou-sin, the last ruler of the Shang dynasty, Wu Wang set up the Chow dynasty and rewarded those who had helped him and his father, the Duke of Chow, by granting them titles and certain portions of the kingdom, establishing a feudal system, not unlike that of mediaeval Europe of a rather later date. He also fortified his position as emperor by the introduction of elaborate court ceremonials, and introduced distinctive court and ceremonial dress. The dynasty was the longest in the history of China, extending from 1122 B.C. to 249 B.C., a period of almost 900 years, probably the longest dynasty in the history of the world. The undisputed portion of Chinese history begins with this period, for the stories of the earlier period are mainly based on records which the two great sages Confucius and Mencius showed to be unreliable, and the present accepted chronology was not known until after the time of Confucius. Indeed no dates in Chinese history earlier than 722 B.C. are authentic, but records existing at that time show such a high state of civilization as to corroborate the Chinese claims for the great antiquity of their race. The Chow dynasty is notable for the fact that during its rule the three great philosophers, Confucius, Mencius and Laotze were born.

The feudal system which had been established by the founder of the dynasty at length resulted in great growth for the various feudal states at the expense of the central government. As the centuries passed, the fiction of allegiance to the central power was abandoned, and the rival states engaged in petty warfare among themselves, stronger states gobbling up the weaker ones, until finally there arose an historical predecessor of Napoleon, a man strong enough to conquer all others and unite the country under one rule. This was Shih Hwang-ti, the Duke of Tsin, who overthrew the thirty-fifth and last emperor of the ruling dynasty and in 221 B.C. established the Tsin or Chin dynasty. From that date China remained an empire for more than two thousand years, although the throne passed to many houses. It was divided several times

between rival thrones, but these short periods but briefly
interrupted the unity of the country.

Shih Hwang-ti, who assumed the title of emperor,
realized the weaknesses of the former administration and
in order to form a strong central government abolished
the feudal system. In its place he divided the country
into a number of provinces, over each of which he
appointed a governor-general. He removed his capital to
the city which is now known as Sianfu, and there built
magnificent palaces which far surpassed any previous
architectural attempts in China. His reign was one of
great internal development, for he constructed many roads
and canals and was responsible for other public improvements. But a portion of the people refused to accept his
sovereignty without protest and the scholars continued to
tell of the glories of the old feudal system which he had
abolished and to plan its restoration. As a reprimand to
them and as an indication that his dynasty had begun
anew and would not be bound by traditions or precedents
he ordered all the books of the empire burned, including
the vast libraries which previous monarchs had collected.
The only exceptions to this order were what were considered practical books on astrology, divination, medicine
and husbandry. As a further means of silencing the scholars
and writers of books he ordered several hundred of them
to be buried alive. It is not surprising that his name
has been execrated by all Chinese scholars since that time.

The empire of China had by the advent of his reign
extended from the original seat near Sianfu until it
comprised what is now that part of China proper north
of the Yangtsze river. The extension of the northern
boundaries had brought the Chinese into contact with the
Tartar tribes of the north, and Shih Hwang-ti built the
great wall around the confines of his kingdom to protect
it from Tartar attacks. Work on this ambitious under-
taking was begun in 214 B.C. What is now Chinese
Turkestan was conquered and became a Chinese colony
and caravans passed through establishing trade with

Persia and Rome. Shih Hwang-ti died six years after work on the Great Wall was begun and the throne passed to his youngest son, with the title of Second Emperor. Defeated rulers of the old feudal states were naturally jealous of the success of the Duke of Tsin and one of them, the Prince of Han, led a successful revolt against the Second Emperor, who was put to death after a short and inglorious reign. This dynasty lasted but fifteen years, the shortest of all in the history of China. It receives little praise from the Chinese historians but it at least gave to China the name by which the country has since been known to foreigners. The word *Tsin* or *Chin* became corrupted into China.

The Han dynasty which followed marked the establishment of the unity of the Chinese people, and the Chinese, with the exception of the independent and truculent Cantonese, still call themselves "The Sons of Han." The Prince of Han began his reign by repealing the decree regarding the destruction of books, and aided in the restoration of the libraries. He set the example for future rulers by offering sacrifice at the tomb of Confucius, and the dynasty originated the literary examinations on which China's great civil-service system was formed. The struggles with the northern tribes began during this reign, the most serious being with the tribes of Mongolia, ancestors of the Huns with whom Attila, 600 years later, scourged Europe. Chinese arms were successful and the territory of the country was enlarged, taking in a large section south of the Yangtsze and the present province of Kansu.

The power of the Han dynasty declined after nearly two centuries of rule, one of the causes being a nation-wide outbreak of pestilence which started in A.D. 173 and continued for eleven years. A Taoist priest claimed to have discovered a magical cure for the pestilence and on the strength of this claim secured enough followers to take possession of some of the northern provinces and seriously threaten the throne. Wang Mang, Tung Cho-

and Tsao Tsao, who have since been known to history as the "Three Traitors," took advantage of this period of disorder to seize the throne and separate the empire into three parts, each of them appropriating one of the kingdoms.

Although they had divided the country amicably, the three kingdoms did not remain at peace and the half century which the period of the Three Kingdoms endured was marked by continual warfare between the rival rulers. This was China's period of chivalry and a great many of the most popular poems and dramas are founded on the stirring events and deeds of daring which occurred during this time. In the end the Kingdom of Wei triumphed and assumed rule over the others. The occupants of the throne were descendants of the founder of the Han dynasty, so Chinese history regards the period of the Three Kingdoms as merely a brief interruption of the Han reign.

After the final downfall of the Han dynasty in the fifth century there was constant warfare for the mastery of the country and several short-lived dynasties succeeded, these being Tsi (479 to 502), Liang (502 to 557), Chen (557 to 589), and Siu (589 to 619).

Tai-tsung at length conquered the country, establishing the Tang dynasty, which existed from 619 to 902, during which time the frontier of China was extended to eastern Persia and the Caspian Sea. During this dynasty lived Empress Wu Hou, one of the consorts of Kao-tsong, who seized supreme power and ruled the country for some time. Her accession to authority established the precedent which enabled the Manchu Empress Dowager, Yehonola, to rule China during the latter part of the last and the beginning of the present century. The peace of the country was disturbed several times by Tartar attacks and by internal rebellions, all of which were successfully put down. Korea was conquered and made a vassal State in the hope that it would serve as a buffer against the Tartar attacks.

The Emperor Wu-tsung who began a rule of six years in 841 abolished all nunneries and monasteries and ordered all missionaries out of the country. Buddhism, however, soon revived and was given a semblance of state sanction a few years later when a succeeding emperor claimed to possess one of the bones of Buddha. The history of the latter part of the dynasty records the acts of a feeble government which was finally overthrown. There followed five brief dynasties under which the country was ruled from 907 to 960. These dynasties were little more than military despotisms, set up by successive victorious generals, in many respects similar to the government under which China has since existed.

The next substantial dynasty was the Sung (960 to 1280), and though it was allowed a long rule it was not undisturbed. The Tartars continued to grow in strength and in 1125 successfully renewed their attacks, taking possession of the capital at Kaifeng, and forcing the government of China to pay tribute. The Emperor removed his capital, first to Nanking, and then farther south, to Hangchow.

A few years later, the Mongol chieftain, Ghengis Khan, began the conquest of the country, having previously formed a confederacy of the Mongol states. The Mongol rulers found their hardest foes would be the Tartar occupants of the north, so a treaty was entered into with the Sung Emperor, wherein it was agreed that he should join forces with the Mongols to drive out the Tartars, and should occupy Honan undisturbed. The Tartar tribes having been defeated, the Sung rulers moved into Honan, in accordance with the terms of the treaty, but were ordered to leave.

The work of conquest so ably begun by Ghengis Khan was carried on by his son Ogotai, who conducted expeditions overrunning Poland, Hungary and Russia. Kublai Khan, grandson of Ghengis, followed as the Mongol leader and completed the work of conquest. His armies were sent against the Chinese and the Sung dynasty was wiped

5

out, the last emperor of the dynasty being drowned near Canton.

The conquest of China, which had occupied the attention of the Mongols for more than a century was completed in 1260, when they set up the Yuan dynasty which was destined to remain in power a shorter period than that occupied by the conquest which made the establishment of the dynasty possible.

Kublai Khan made partially successful attempts to reconcile the Chinese people to his alien rule, and then began fresh attempts at conquest. An attack on Japan failed, but Annam was added to the list of tributary states and remained so until it became a dependency of France in 1864. The Burmese were forced to pay tribute. The emperor was as energetic in public works at home as he was in conquests abroad and is credited with adding many improvements to the Grand Canal, which was widened and lengthened. It was during his reign that Marco Polo, the Venetian adventurer, visited the country and gave to Europe its first authentic and detailed knowledge of the Great Khan and of China.

The idea of foreign rule was hateful to the Chinese and many secret societies sprang into existence having for their purpose the overthrow of the Mongol dynasty. In the early part of the fourteenth century the long-threatened revolt broke out, led by an obscure servant in a Buddhist temple near Nanking. Through the years of easy living as rulers the Mongols had lost their prowess as fighting men and the rebels met with little resistance. As the leader captured one section of the country he established law and order and left the people of that district to live in peace while he went on with his victorious army. In 1355 he captured Nanking and thirteen years later, when master of the entire empire, he proclaimed himself emperor with the reign title of Hung Wu, establishing the Ming dynasty.

In was during this dynasty that China began to come more in contact with European nations. In 1511 Portuguese traders arrived at Canton and received a friendly reception. Six years later Fernando Peres de Andrade entered Canton and was allowed to proceed to Peking, the capital of the Mings. A short time later, his brother arrived on the Southern coast, and not being satisfied with the reception he received, committed depredations on the coast, from Foochow to Ningpo. The Chinese retaliated by killing many of the Portuguese who were then living in the country and Andrade was put to death. Friendly relations between the Chinese and Portuguese were later established and in 1557 Macao was leased to Portugal. In 1622 the Dutch appeared, were driven off by the Chinese, and retired to Formosa, where they established posts and protected them with forts.

The Ming dynasty, after ruling nearly three hundred years, fell before the Manchus, a tribe of Tartars living near the present city of Moukden. One of the last Ming emperors neglected the administration of the country to meddle in the affairs of the tribes and in doing this aroused the resentment of the small but strong and truculent tribe of Manchus. Nurhachu, the Manchu chieftain, led an attack against the Chinese and in 1618 invaded the Liaotung Peninsula. The invaders put to rout the Chinese who opposed them and on capturing a city compelled the Chinese to shave the front part of their heads and braid their hair into queues, as a sign of their subjection to the invaders. This was the origin of the queue which became such a distinguishing characteristic of the Chinese during the rule of the Manchus and has, since their overthrow, been gradually disappearing.

The Chinese brought cannon to the northern provinces from Macao with which to defend themselves against the invaders and succeeded in holding them in check. In the meantime two rebels, starting from Shansi and Shensi, met with great success and overran a large part of the Empire. One of the rebels assumed the title of emperor and advanced on Peking which he entered to find the last Ming emperor a suicide.

General Wu, who was holding back the Manchu invaders at the border, determined to avenge the death of his emperor, and like the Sungs several hundred years before, entered into an agreement with the Manchus who were to aid him in driving out the rebels. The allies marched on Peking, routed the rebels, and General Wu pursued them to the south. Returning to Peking he found that the Manchu Regent had placed his own nephew on the throne with the title of emperor and inaugurated the Ts'ing or Manchu dynasty. The Chinese in the South struggled for fifteen years against this usurpation of power, but in the end were compelled to acquiesce to the Manchu rule.

Exclusiveness and intolerance of any intercourse with foreigners distinguished the foreign relations of the country during almost the whole of the Manchu reign and it was only by show of force that they were compelled to allow trade to be carried on. As early as 1635 England had granted a charter to English merchants authorising them to trade in China and as a result Captain Weddell sailed for the East with a small fleet of vessels. His fleet was fired on by forts near Canton. He retaliated and silenced the forts. The Chinese authorities then granted the right to trade at Canton, subject to severe restrictions.

The value and importance of Chinese trade became better known and in 1793 England sent Lord MacCartney to negotiate a treaty with China providing for more satisfactory relations between the two countries, but little was accomplished by the mission. About twenty years later Lord Amherst headed another embassy from England but was not received by the Emperor of China and returned home without having accomplished anything. For more than forty years after the embassy of Lord MacCartney, England continued her unsuccessful efforts to secure from China some satisfactory agreement providing for trade relations between the two countries.

During this period all English trade with China was

in the hands of the East India Company, but the monopoly came to an end in 1834. On the Chinese side, all foreign trade had been in the hands of a monopoly similar to that of the East India Company, the famous "Co-hong" of Canton. In fact all foreign commercial relations had been delegated to this guild of Canton merchants, with which the foreigners could deal and which had the authority to place many restrictions on foreign trade. Although England ended the monopoly held by the East India Company the Chinese saw no reason for similar action. The Co-hong was unwilling to relinquish its rights and the foreigners had no means of dealing directly with the government. At that time the residence of foreign traders in China was limited to a small area of Canton. They could sell their goods only to members of the Co-hong and make purchases from them alone. No one was allowed to teach them the language and they could not leave the confines of their restricted residential area without a Chinese guard, nor were they allowed to go into the city of Canton. Strained relations between foreigners and Chinese resulted. The Manchu government at Peking, always assumed the attitude that commerce was beneath the dignity of the Court and did not deign to notice it.

About 1836 the Chinese government did unbend to notice foreign trade, for it became alarmed over the outflow of silver, a great part of this being due to the sale of imported opium smuggled in by foreigners, usually with the connivance of Chinese officials. In 1839 it was decided by the Chinese government to make a determined effort to abolish the opium traffic. A commissioner appointed to carry out the plans of the government arrived in Canton, and seized and destroyed the opium in the foreign warehouses.

Further demands were made on the foreign merchants and a year later war broke out between Great Britain and China, the fighting being concentrated around Canton. China, with antiquated equipment, was worsted on every side, but the conflict dragged on until the arrival of Sir

Henry Pottinger, in 1841. The war was then carried to the north, Sir Henry being instructed to make terms of peace with no authority less than that of the Imperial government. The fleet sailed up the coast, taking, in rapid succession, Amoy, Ningpo, Woosung and Shanghai, then proceeded up the Yangtsze and captured Chinkiang. By the time Nanking was reached, two imperial commissioners representing the Chinese government were there waiting to arrange for peace.

The treaty of Nanking was concluded on August 29, 1842. It provided that Canton, Shanghai, Amoy, Foochow, and Ningpo be opened as treaty ports where foreigners could reside and carry on trade. The island of Hongkong was ceded to Great Britain and an indemnity of 21 million silver dollars was to be paid, six million of which was compensation for the opium destroyed. Fair tariff rates were to be maintained and communication between the two nations was to be on terms of equality. Similar treaties were later concluded with the United States and with France. Under the provisions of these treaties, foreign firms were established at the five ports. A few Christian missionaries from America and Europe had arrived in the country before this time, and had remained under a rather doubtful legal status but with the opening up of the ports, more active missionary work was possible.

In 1851 Emperor Hien Feng ascended the throne and about the same time the Taiping Rebellion broke out under the leadership of Hung Hsio-chuen. The teaching of a Protestant missionary in Canton was the indirect and innocent cause of the rebellion, for Hung, with half-formed ideas of Christianity, became a fanatic. For a time he organized religious societies in the neighborhood of Canton, for the purpose of destroying idols. As the society grew in membership it became political and anti-dynastic. Hung announced himself as the "Heavenly King" and led his forces against government troops with the openly announced purpose of overthrowing the Manchu dynasty. The rebels marched northward from Canton to the Yangtsze Valley sacking cities and devastating the country through which they passed. There is scarcely a city on this route which does not show to-day some evidence of their visit. They seized Hanyang, Wuchang, Hankow, Anking, Kiukiang and Nanking, the latter city being selected as their capital. In 1853 a military expedition was sent from there against the capital of Peking, but was repulsed at Tientsin. The great Chinese statesman, Li Hung Chang, who was then a young officer in Anhui, first came into prominence as a result of this rebellion. He employed two Americans, Ward and Burgevine, to command an army which had greater success against the rebels than that which attended the efforts of the regular Imperial forces.

While this rebellion was progressing northward, the friendly relations which had been established between Great Britain and China again became strained. The Chinese complained that opium was being smuggled into the mainland of China from Hongkong by means of vessels flying the British flag. The British asserted that they were still harassed by useless and malicious trade restrictions. The Chinese authorities seized and threw into jail the native crew of the Arrow, a small vessel flying the British flag, and the negotiations which followed led to serious differences of opinion, both sides preparing for war.

The first contingent of British troops was sent out in 1857 under Lord Elgin, who had been appointed Lord High Commissioner for Great Britain, but the force of 5,000 men with which he started was diverted to India to help put down the Sepoy mutiny. Meanwhile a French missionary had been murdered by the Chinese and the French government found in this a reason for joining with the British.

The French and British forces sailed up the coast and easily took the Taku forts (Tientsin), when peace terms were discussed. It was agreed that Newchwang, Formosa, Swatow, and Kiungchow be opened as additional treaty ports and the British be given the privilege of trading in the Yangtsze Valley. An indemnity of two million taels was to be paid to Great Britain and to France and the tariff revised to provide more favourable terms for the importation of French and British goods.

The following year had been set for ratification of the treaties, but the Chinese government refused to agree on any place for exchange of ratifications. The French and British fleets again proceeded to Tientsin and found the harbor blocked with piling and heavy chains, while they were fired on by the Taku forts. Another force of 20,000 men which followed the initial expedition captured the forts. The Chinese sued for peace, but British emissaries sent to meet the officials coming from Peking were captured and thrown into prison. The allied forces advanced on the capital and a new treaty was signed October 22, 1860, the original indemnity being increased to eight million taels. Kowloon, on the mainland near the island of Hongkong, was ceded to Great Britain and Tientsin was opened as an additional treaty port.

While the Imperial forces were engaged with their foreign adversaries, the Taipings had taken advantage of the opportunity to extend their operations and resumed possession of a section south of the Yangtsze river. When the rebellion started it was believed to be inspired by purely Christian motives and foreigners who had long since grown tired of the evasions and deceptions of the Chinese government readily gave their sympathy to the Taipings, while misinformed missionary societies in England and America held prayer-meetings for their success. But the quasi-religious motives in which the rebellion originated were soon forgotten and when missionaries called on the "Heavenly King" at Nanking they found in him an arrogant fanatic living a dissolute life which gave the lie to his christian pretensions.

Foreign sympathy finally veered to the side of the Imperialists and foreigners took an active part in the fighting against the Taipings. General Ward, the

American employed by Li Hung Chang, was killed while leading an attack against the rebels and to succeed him in command of the troops he had trained and organised Great Britain loaned to the Chinese government the services of Captain C. E. Gordon of the British army. Captain Gordon reorganized and augmented the Imperial forces, placed them under foreign officers and continued the successes of his predecessor. His final triumph was the surrender of the Taiping stronghold of Soochow. Li Hung Chang violated the agreement of surrender which provided that the lives of the Taiping leaders should be spared, whereupon Captain Gordon refused to remain with the army.

However, his work was completed, for soon thereafter the Taiping capital of Nanking fell before the Imperial army, which had kept it in a state of siege for eleven years, and the rebellion ended in 1864. Some of the leaders committed suicide and the few who escaped execution quickly dispersed. The rebellion ceased to be, and the rebels returned to their farms and shops as quickly as they had taken up arms. But the country had suffered devastation which is still attested to by the ruins of cities. It is said that over 20 million lives had been lost and half the country devastated.

Emperor Hien Feng died in 1861, leaving as the heir to the throne his son, T'ung-chi, a child of five years. What proved more important in the future history of China was the fact that he was survived by Tsze Hsi, the little emperor's mother, who, owing to the birth of the child, had been raised from the position of favorite concubine to that of imperial consort. With the legitimate empress, who was childless, Tsze Hsi became joint regent. For fourteen years, the two empress dowagers ruled, the mother of the emperor by virtue of her superior abilities slowly gaining the ascendancy. But in his nineteenth year the young emperor died, an event probably not unwelcome to the plotters around the throne, who hoped thereby to be able to seize power for themselves.

In this conflict the former concubine Tsze Hsi, out-
witted them all, and secured the selection of the infant
son of her sister who had married a brother of the late
emperor.   This coup gave her renewed power and
prolonged the regency in which she had, by this time,
become dominant.   The infant emperor, Kwang Hsu,
ascended the throne in 1875 while the Empress Dowager
continued the dominating figure in all governmental
affairs. His selection had been prompted by her boundless
ambition and in it she had violated one of the most
sacred traditions of the Chinese. The conditions of
ancestor worship demanded that each successor to the
throne be of a generation just succeeding that of his
predecessor. Kwang Hsu did not fulfil that condition,
for he was a first cousin of the unfortunate emperor
whom he succeeded. There were many criticisms of this
act and the prestige of the Manchu court was weakened
in the eyes of the Chinese.

Korea had long been a vassal state and foreigners
naturally looked to China to redress any wrongs they
might suffer there. In 1866 some French missionaries
were murdered in Korea, and soon thereafter an American
vessel which made a peacefull call at a Korean port was
burned and members of the crew brutally murdered. Both
France and the United States demanded satisfaction but
China replied that she was not accustomed to interfere in
the affairs of her vassal states and paid no attention to
the reprisals made by both France and America. Shortly
after this Japan found it necessary to retaliate for Korean
attacks on a Japanese gunboat. The Korean government
was compelled to pay an indemnity and to give the
Japanese the privilege of trade and travel. In order to
neutralize the predominant Japanese influence established
by this arrangement, the Chinese government then threw
Korea open to the trade of the world.

France, in 1864 had annexed Cochin-China. Twenty
years later France manifested desires for Tonkin, north
of Annam, as a country through which it would be possible

to tap the trade of the rich Chinese province of Yunnan. Tonkin appealed to China for protection. Negotiations followed and China agreed to cede certain territory to France. When French troops came to take possession, they were fired on by the local garrison, owing to the fact that no date had been set for the actual transfer and the Chinese garrison was not advised of the arrangement.

Although following this occurrence, the two countries were actually at war the fiction was kept up that each was engaging in reprisals. The French fleet entered the harbor at Foochow and after lying at anchor there for several weeks opened fire on the Chinese fleet, gaining an easy victory. Chinese strongholds in Formosa and the Pescadores were taken as easily. In the meantime the Chinese troops gained such successes over the French on land that the latter were content to forget their early demands for a heavy indemnity, and the final terms of peace, concluded June 9, 1885, cast no discredit on China. She gave up her claims to sovereignty over Tonkin while France agreed to respect China's southern frontier. The conflict ended with a gain in prestige to China for she had been able to hold her own in a war with a first-class power.

Another break with Japan came in 1894. Each country had agreed not to land troops in Korea without giving formal notice to the other but China ignored or forgot this agreement when serious disturbances broke out in Korea. Japan protested and China agreed to withdraw the forces but while this arrangement was being perfected a steamer arrived with more Chinese troops. A mutiny on board made it impossible for the Chinese commander to comply with the Japanese demands for a surrender. The fire of Japanese cruisers sank the transport and as a logical sequence war was declared at once.

If the war with France had given the Chinese an exaggerated idea of their fighting abilities, the conflict with Japan soon created a different impression for it was immediately apparent that China was no match for her small but recently modernized neighbor. The cause which probably contributed most to the defeat of the Chinese was found in their own official corruption. The funds which had been raised several years before for the building of a modern navy had been diverted by the Empress Dowager and used for the construction of a summer palace. The navy consisted of old vessels, inadequately supplied with ammunition. The units of the Chinese navy were either sunk or put to flight and the Japanese then made a successful attack on Port Arthur, a fortified position which the Chinese deemed impregnable.

The treaty of Shimonoseki was signed as a result of this war and China suffered heavily. The independence of Korea was recognized; Formosa and the Pescadores were ceded to Japan; an indemnity to Japan of 200 million taels was agreed to; Shasi, Chungking, Soochow, and Hangchow were to be opened as further treaty ports. The war had conclusively proven the weakness of China and as a result she suffered many acts of foreign aggression.

During the drawing up of the Shimonoseki treaty, Russia interfered, apparently on behalf of China, to prevent the lease of Port Arthur to Japan. Shortly after the treaty was signed, however, Russia forced China to lease this important fortress to her, thereby giving her one of the strongest naval bases in the world. The murder of two German missionaries was the pretext by which Germany in 1898 seized Kiaochow (Tsingtao), an important port on the coast of the province of Shantung. It was here that they built up the important commercial centre of Tsingtao which in the great war fell into the hands of the Japanese and has since been returned to China. Great Britain leased Weihaiwei, in return for assistance in paying the indemnity to Japan. France secured Kwan-chowman, in Kwangtung, declaring this was necessary in order "to restore the balance of power in the Far East." China was being dismembered by the powers.

In the early Summer of 1898, Emperor Kwang Hsu, who had previously left all governmental affairs to his aunt, the Empress Dowager, and former concubine, unexpectedly took over affairs of government himself. To the surprise of everyone he entered on a series of reforms as ambitious as they were visionary. He gathered about him some of the most progressive and radical reformers in the country and for 100 days issued edict after edict which threw down established institutions and set up new ones. The Manchu nobles were to be sent abroad that travel might broaden their minds. Temples were to be replaced by schools in which western learning would be taught, and the publication of newspapers, which hitherto had been carefully suppressed, was to be encouraged and promoted. Every new idea which appealed to him was made the subject of an edict.

The reactionary forces of the Manchu court set in before any of these proposed reforms as changes were effective. The Manchu nobles appealed to the old Empress Dowager to assert her rights as an "ancestor" and again take over the control of the government. In September 1898 the visionary period of reform came to an inglorious end. The Emperor was seized by a band of palace guards and for the remainder of his life remained a prisoner completely under the domination of his aunt. In a very short time all the reform edicts had been nullified and the government of China was again in the hands of the reactionaries, who marked their triumph by executing some of the hopeful reformers.

A similar reaction took place in the provinces. The chagrin at the defeat of China by Japan had led to an increased appreciation of the advantages of western learning, and many societies had been formed to promote the translation of European books. The change came with the acts of aggression by the foreign powers and the granting of concessions for the building of railways. This anti-foreign feeling was most intense in the province of Shantung, where it resulted in the organization of the

Boxers, a fanatical secret society having for its purpose the driving out of all foreigners from China and the complete elimination of foreign influence. The leaders declared themselves immune from harm by foreign bullets and gave each member a talisman which would insure similar protection for him. Under the encouragement of provincial officials the movement rapidly grew in strength.

In the spring of 1900, the long-threatened trouble broke out and not until then did foreigners appreciate the gravity of the situation. A number of Shantung villages populated by Christian converts were destroyed, the converts and missionaries killed. The whole of North China was soon overrun by Boxers who tore up railway tracks, robbed, looted, and massacred. In a short time they had reached the capital itself. A small mixed body of marines was hurriedly brought to guard the foreign legations. Foreign residents gathered in the legation compounds and a state of siege began in the early part of June. The Chancellor of the Japanese Legation and the German minister, were murdered. On June 14, Peking was entirely cut off from communication with the rest of the world and little was known of the fate of the foreign diplomats, missionaries and other foreign residents until almost two months later.

A mixed force of about 2,000 men consisting of British, French, German, Russian, Austrian, American, Japanese and Italian troops left Tientsin for Peking early in June. It was set upon by large bands of Boxers and retreated with serious losses. The foreign settlements in Tientsin were attacked and, fearing that an attempt would be made to cut off communication with the sea, the allied foreign fleets captured the Taku forts. Reinforcements of foreign troops arrived and Tientsin was cleared of Boxers, but with a heavy loss to the foreign allies.

After the taking of the Taku forts, China rashly declared war on all foreign countries, the final gesture of a dying civilization and there was no longer any doubt as to the issue. Forces of the regular Chinese army joined the Boxers and all of the resources of the Chinese government were pitted against the foreign troops.

Many additional forces were sent to Tientsin to join in the relief of the legations, but international jealousies and misunderstandings caused inexcusable delays. On July 6, the Japanese government decided to embark two divisions which had been mobilized. British troops from India began to arrive in the early part of August and at the same time American troops from Manila. A relief column of 20,000 men set out for Peking on August 4 and after meeting with many difficulties and some loss of life arrived on August 13 and on the following day entered the city and raised the siege. The Boxers during all this time had kept the legations under fire and there had been heavy loss of life. The band of marines, sailors, soldiers and civilians who made up the guard for the legations had never numbered more than 500 and at the time the siege was raised, 90 had been killed and 131 wounded. When the foreign troops entered, the Empress Dowager and the Emperor fled to Sianfu.

Peking had suffered terribly from the Boxer activities. In their efforts to destroy all foreign property, fires had been set which spread over a large part of the city. Foreign and Chinese houses alike had been looted, and a great part of the city was in ruins. The arrival of the allied forces added to the devastation for the foreign soldiers looted uninterruptedly for several days. Order was finally restored, and then began a long series of negotiations, hampered, as the relief had been, by the jealousies of the foreign nations.

Each had a long list of indemnities justified because of property and lives lost and as a punishment to China. At length it was decided that China should pay a total indemnity amounting to £67,500,000, in annual installments extending over a period of 40 years. The Taku forts were to be demolished so as to give access from the sea to the Peking legations in the event of another anti-foreign outbreak and permanent garrisons were to be established by the foreign powers both at the legations in Peking and on the route from Peking to the sea. A number of the leaders of the Boxer movement were executed, others allowed to commit suicide, and apologies were conveyed to Germany for the murder of her Minister.

There were a few further outbreaks of Boxer activities in 1901 and 1902, but they no longer had the sympathy of the government, and most effective measures were taken to suppress any activity against foreigners.

Russia's need for an ice-free port led to her designs to secure complete control of Manchuria. Her demands made shortly after the Boxer trouble amounted virtually to annexation and Chinese leaders urged the necessity of warlike preparations. In the meantime Japan, having her own plans regarding the development of Manchuria, grew tired of the vacillating policy of China and took action herself, dealing directly with Russia. The result of the breakdown of these negotiations was the Russo-Japanese War, in which Japan was the victor and took from Russia the special privileges which had been granted to that country by China in the southern part of Manchuria, including the lease of Port Arthur.

Through all the turmoil of the war with Japan, the Boxer trouble, and other stirring events which marked the close of one century and the beginning of another, the reform movement which in some places showed anti-dynastic tendencies became more powerful and the Manchus themselves began preparations for the adoption of a form of constitutional monarchy. Edicts were issued in 1906 promising this great change at some indefinite date. A few years later a more definite step was taken in a decree fixing the convocation of a parliament in the then safely remote year of 1917. The reformers were jubilant for they believed a genuine desire for change was felt in Peking.

Two months after issuing this decree, (1908) Emperor Kwang Hsu died, the death of the Dowager Empress occurring the following day. One of her last acts was to secure the accession to the throne of Pu Yi (Henry Pu Yi), the infant son of Kwang Hsu's brother, Prince Chung. Immediately on his accession to the throne Prince Chung became Regent and inaugurated a change in policy. He dismissed Yuan Shih K'ai, and other leaders of the conservative reform movement and nothing more was done to further the reform program.

In the few years following, revolutionary activities, secretly promoted by many leaders, grew so rapidly that in the early part of 1911 the leaders were unable longer to hold it in check. The plans of the Peking government to borrow money from foreign banks and nationalize all the railways of China led to riots in Szechuan, where the people objected to the government taking over a railway property they had promoted. There were other local complications which tended to accentuate the grievances of the people and Szechuan was in a state of open rebellion in September, 1911.

In the following month, the activities of the revolutionists in the cities of Hankow, Wuchang and Hanyang became so noticeable that the Viceroy took active measures to suppress them. He had thrown some agitators in jail and beheaded others when the accidental explosion of a bomb in the foreign settlement of Hankow revealed the location of one of the revolutionary headquarters. The Viceroy was informed of the discovery and at once a thorough search of Wuchang began, several suspected rebels being beheaded. The vigorous measures taken to suppress the movement compelled the revolutionists to take action at once. A small number of soldiers mutinied, were joined by others and within twenty-four hours the Viceroy and other officials had been compelled to flee while the rebels under the leadership of Li Yuan Hung took complete possession of the three cities.

Imperial troops from the North were sent against the rebels, but the anti-dynastic movement spread over all the country with surprising rapidity. The loyal troops were able to make some headway against the rebels at Hankow,

6

but the Republican army grew rapidly, and city after city in the South drove out the Imperial officials, declaring allegiance to the provisional Republican government. At many places the bitter race feeling led to bloody massacres of the Manchus, neither women nor children escaping.

Within a month after the outbreak of the fighting in Hankow, fourteen of the eighteen provinces of China had thrown off Manchu authority and sent representatives to the provisional Republican government. Dr. Sun Yat Sen who for years had directed the revolutionary movement from abroad arrived in China during the latter part of 1911 and was at once elected president of the provisional Republican government, the capital being established in Nanking. In the meantime two commissioners had been appointed to decide on the future form of government, Dr. Wu Ting-fang representing the Republicans and Tang Shao Yi the Imperialists. These negotiations ended on February 10, 1912, when an Imperial Edict announced the abdication of the infant Emperor and appointed Yuan Shih K'ai to carry out the formation of the Republican form of government.

Shortly after the publication of this edict, the Republican Assembly in session at Nanking accepted the resignation of Sun Yat Sen and elected Yuan Shih K'ai as president. The coalition Republican government was then established in Peking which has remained the capital, but with many changes of administration until the establishment of the National government with the capital in Nanking.

RELIGIONS OF CHINA

THERE are in China five religions—Taoism, Confucianism, Buddhism, Mohammedanism and Christianity. Of these Taoism and Confucianism are native religions, the others having been introduced from foreign lands. Buddhism and the two native religions are the most popular and though they contain conflicting elements many claim adherence to all, while the temples of each have borrowed many gods from the others. As many Chinese can see no objection to accepting more than one religion, no reasonable estimate can be made of the relative strength of the adherents of Confucianism, Buddhism and Taoism. One may "belong" to all three, just as in America one may be a Methodist, Mason and Democrat. However, in general it may be said that Confucianism is the belief of scholars and officials, while Buddhism and Taoism appeal to the masses. The followers of Mahomet hold aloof from the other religions and their temples or mosques contain no strange gods. Different authorities place their number at 9 to 15 million. Christian converts according to rough estimates number about two million.

TAOISM.

This religion was founded on the teachings of Laotze, a sage born in 604 B.C. in the present province of Honan. According to tradition he was an adult at birth, from which circumstance he derived his name of Laotze, or "old boy." He taught contemplation and retirement as a means of spiritual purification and the attainment of the *Tao,* or "correct road," a word which he used to signify the highest spiritual ideals of mankind. Laotze spent his life in study and teaching and about 500 B.C., old and discouraged at the failure of men to accept his doctrine, he determined to quit China and started on a journey to the West, to Tartary or Tibet. Many Taoists claim that he found his way to India and was really the founder of Buddhism, which, if a fact, would justify the Taoist theft of popular Buddhist gods. His teachings are incorporated in a profound book *Tao Teh King* which Taoists regard as the final authority in religious matters. According to one authority* "The pure Taoism of the *Tao Teh King* is as much quoted in every age of Chinese history, officialdom, and poetry as Shakespeare is quoted in the literature and speech of modern England; and though officially Confucianism is the orthodox official belief, it is Taoism, or rather the ancient natural religion as interpreted and expressed by Laotze, which really forms the character of the gentleman philosopher in China. The impassiveness, stoicism, democratic feeling, contempt for profuse luxury and vulgar show, patience, humility, calmness, deliberation, aversion from imperial puffery, boastfulness, and military glory which characterize the best Chinese minds are Shinto-Taoist rather than Confucian in spirit; and the fact that men in responsible positions only too frequently give way in fact to cupidity, sensuality and cowardice in no way prevents the same men in theory from honestly aspiring to, admiring and teaching their true ideals; just as with us, a man may be or try to be a convinced Christian gentleman, although occasionally he may take a drop too much, or yield to business frauds and feminine seductions."

Laotze's teachings are admirable but there is a great gap between them and the Taoism of the present day, which has incorporated into its temples local gods and beliefs and degenerated into low forms of mysticism and geomancy. The priests "live in temples and small com-

---

* E. H. Parker in "China and Religion."

munities with their families, cultivating the ground
attached to the establishment, and thus perpetuate their
body; many lead a wandering life, and derive a precarious
livelihood from the sale of charms and medical nostrums.
They study astrology and profess to have dealings with
spirits, their books containing a great variety of stories
of priests who have done wonderful acts by their help."*

"Taoist temples are built upon the same general plan
as the temples dedicated to the Buddhist cult. The
adherents of Laotze have borrowed from the Buddhist
bonzes the interior decorations of their sacred halls, as
well as the plastic representation of divinities, the worship
of idols, and many of their ritual ceremonies. The Buddhist triad is replaced by an imposing triad of supreme
deities called Shang Ti, who preside over the jade paradise
of the Taoist heavens; statues of Laotze and of the eight
immortals, called Pa Hsien, are posed in prominent places;
and there are separate shrines for the three star-gods of
happiness, rank and longevity, and for a multitude of
lesser lights of the faith whose name is legion. The
sacrificial vases, candlesticks and incense burners, as well
as the other ritual surroundings, bear distinctive Taoist
symbols and emblems."†

BUDDHISM.

Shakyamuni, the name by which Buddha is generally
known in China, was born in the fifth or sixth century
before Christ but it was not until the early part of the
Christian Era that his teachings reached China, where
they were destined to have a profound effect on Chinese
thought and to leave an indelible impression on art. In
the first Christian century a Chinese Emperor sent a
mission to the West for priests to teach Buddhism. The
mission found its way to India and returned to the
Chinese capital with the first of a great band of zealous
Buddhist missionaries who for more than a thousand years

---

* S. Wells Williams in "The Middle Kingdom."
† Stephen W. Bushell in "Chinese Art."

came to China both by the northern land route and the southern sea route. It has been suggested that the first missionaries were sent for because of some vague rumors of the teachings and death of Christ which may have reached China at that time. Buddhism rapidly gained popularity and to-day the Buddhist priests outnumber the Taoist. "Their demonolatry allows the incorporation of the deities and spirits of other religions, and goes even further, in permitting the priests to worship the gods of other pantheons, so they could adapt themselves to the popular superstitions of the countries they went to, and ingraft all the foreign divinities into their calendar as they saw fit. The power of Buddhism in China has been owing chiefly to its ability to supply the lack of certainty in the popular notions respecting a future state and the nature of the gods who govern man and creation. Confucius uttered no speculation about those unseen things, and ancestral worship confined itself to a belief in the presence of the loved ones, who were ready to accept the homage of their children. The longing of the soul to know something of the life beyond the grave was measurably supplied by the teachings of Shakyamuni and his disciples, and, as was the case with Confucius, was illustrated and enforced by the earnest, virtuous life of their founder."

It is probably not far wrong to say that pure Buddhism is unknown among the great mass of its followers. Though the sutras have been translated into Chinese the liturgies used in the temples have only been transliterated, Chinese characters representing the sounds of the original Sanscrit words. As the priests are unfamiliar with Sanscrit, the occasional Buddhist service one will hear is just as intelligible to the tourist as to the priests who perform it.

One of the interesting features of Buddhist teaching in China is a system of merits and demerits which allows one to keep books on his virtues and vices and at any time to strike a balance which will show his credit in heaven. Ten points are allowed for making a road or digging a well, thirty for the gift of enough ground for a grave. Against these credit marks, which are computed on an elaborate scale covering almost every possible good act, must be charged the demerits reckoned by an equally elaborate scale. Thus to level a tomb costs fifty demerits and to dig up a corpse one hundred.

The priests take a vow of celibacy and abstinence from meat and wine, wear no skin or woollen garments and shave the entire head. Begging, the sale of incense paper and charms, the cultivation of the temple grounds and fees received for the performance of funeral rites afford them a means of support. They are gathered in monasteries and temples, some of great fame because of the beauty of the surroundings, the magnificence of the architecture and the renowned history of the institution.

Most statistics of Buddhism are very much in error. It is often spoken of as having a greater number of followers (500 millions) than any other religion. This error arises from the supposition that all Chinese are Buddhists, forgetting that (not counting Mohammedans or Christians) there are few who could not with equal truth be called Taoists or Confucianists.

The Chinese Buddhist temple usually comprises a number of semi-detached halls, grouped about rectangular courts, with the principal building in the center. The entrance is guarded by a pair of carved stone lions and on festival days the wooden columns beside the entrance are hung with banners and lanterns. In the vestibule are always ranged the gigantic figures of the "Four Great Kings," while in the center are usually the images of Maitreya, the Buddhist messiah, and Kuan Ti, the god of war. Maitreya, better known by his Chinese name of Milo Fo, is a smiling and fat-bellied Chinese, while Kuan Ti is a mailed figure in ancient costume seated on a chair. In the Lama (Thibetan and Mongolian) temples, Maitreya is depicted as a dignified and commanding figure.

Buddha is always the central figure in the triad enthroned in the position of honor in the main hall, the other two being favorite disciples. Life-size figures of the eighteen disciples who attained emancipation from rebirth are ranged near by. Kuan Yin, the goddess of mercy, is usually enshrined in a separate hall behind the main building. She is the central figure of a group of three, the others being Wenchu, the "god of wisdom" and Pu Hsien, the "all good." In addition to these principal gods there are in the larger temples hundreds of idols ranged along the walls of adjoining halls representing lesser divinities and saints.

CONFUCIANISM.

Confucius, born 551 B.C. in what is now the province of Shantung, was a contemporary of Laotze and like him devoted much attention to the study of the old traditions of Chinese history. It was on the lessons taught by these traditions that both Laotze and Confucius based their teachings, though different, and in some aspects, opposing conclusions were reached. Laotze has been described as "a rugged, radical denouncer of the Jeremiah or Carlyle type. Confucius was a man of comfort, order, reverence and courtliness." Pure Confucianism cannot be called a religion, in the western sense, as it is only a system of ethics, based on the old Chinese legends and the court ritual. Confucius codified the five relations of Chinese life which embraced the duties of ruler and minister, husband and wife, father and son, elder and younger brother, friend and friend. He taught loyalty, faithfulness, filial piety, respect for seniority, and sincerity. His study was of the relation of man to man and he declined to discuss a future state of being. He was once asked about his belief in God and replied that as he had not been able to solve all the mysteries of earth he could not be expected to solve those of heaven. Again he said, "Heaven does not talk, and yet the four seasons come with regularity." Confucius differed from Laotze (and in that probably laid the foundations for the official adoption of his teachings) in that while Laotze was a sturdy democrat,

Confucius was always a courtier, whose teachings were designed to encourage obedience on the part of the people to their rulers. Laotze expressed some contempt for mere earthly relations, while Confucius made these his chief study. He devoted great attention to the perfection of rites and ceremonies, not only for the feudal court of Lu to which he was attached, but for the use of all his fellow countrymen. He gave minute attention to the nurture and education of children, the ceremonies of mourning the dead, and to all the smallest details of etiquette which in his teachings embraced all human relationships.

Confucius died in 479 B.C. at the age of 72 and it was not until about five centuries later that he became recognized as the great sage of China, a position which he holds officially and in the minds of most educated Chinese, though foreign students would be inclined to bestow that honor on Mencius, a later sage who followed and expounded Confucius. About the beginning of the Christian Era Confucianism was officially adopted, several Emperors paying visits to his tomb. His family was elevated to the nobility and to this day his descendant in direct line bears the title of Duke of Kung.

The orthodox Confucian temple is severely plain and contains, as the only objects of worship, the ancestral tablets of Confucius, Mencius and other sages, but this is often elaborated by the addition of an image of Confucius sometimes accompanied by images of his disciples.

ANCESTRAL WORSHIP.

Apart from the three religions previously mentioned, but sanctioned by all of them, exists the family cult commonly known as ancestral worship. Dr. S. Wells Williams,* to whom the writer is indebted for much that appears in these brief chapters on the religions of China, describes the cult as follows:

---

* In "The Middle Kingdom."

"In every household, a shrine, a tablet, an oratory or a domestic temple, according to the position of the family, contains the simple legend of the two ancestral names written on a slip of paper or carved on a board. Incense is burned before it daily, or on the new and full moons; and in April the people everywhere gather at the family graves to sweep them, and worship the departed around a festive sacrifice. To the children it has all the pleasant association of our Christmas or Thanksgiving; and all the elder members of the family who can do so come together around the tomb or in the ancestral hall at the annual rite. Parents and children meet and bow before the tablet, and in their simple cheer contract no associations with temples or idols, monasteries or priests, processions or flags and music. It is the family and a stranger intermeddleth not with it; he has his own tablet to look to; and can get no good by worshipping before that bearing the names of another family.

"As the children grow up, the worship of the ancestors whom they never saw is exchanged for that of nearer ones who bore and nurtured, clothed, taught, and cheered them in helpless childhood and hopeful youth, and the whole is thus rendered more personal, vivid and endearing. There is nothing revolting or cruel connected with it, but everything is orderly, kind, and simple, calculated to strengthen the family relationship, cement the affection between brothers and sisters, and uphold habits of filial reverence and obedience. Though the strongest motive for this worship arises out of the belief that success in worldly affairs depends on the support given to parental spirits in hades, who will resent continued neglect by withholding their blessing, yet, in the course of ages, it has influenced Chinese character, in promoting industry and cultivating habits of domestic care and thrift, beyond all estimation."

Mohammedanism.

In A.D. 755 a serious rebellion broke forth in China under a Turk or Tartar leader, and the Emperor of China in his helplessness asked for help from the Arabs. Some of these came overland, others by sea *via* Canton, in numbers varying, according to reports, from 4,000 to 100,000 and were quartered in garrisons in different parts of the Empire. When the rebellion was ended the Chinese Emperor gave permission to the Arabs to marry Chinese wives and become residents of the country. Thus Mohammedan colonists were found all over the Empire. Even before this time Mohammedanism had gained some foothold in China, for Arab traders had come to Canton and Hangchow by sea while others found their way overland to the western city of Sianfu. They do not appear ever to have increased by means of converts made through a religious propagandum, but mainly by natural increase of the original colonists.

To this is probably due the remarkable fact that "while the Chinese annals are clear about the Persian and Babylonian religions which came and went during a couple of centuries, none of their histories record a single word about the introduction into China of the Mohammedan faith." The Mohammedans have not translated the Koran into Chinese for they consider the book too sacred to be put into a foreign language. On this account they maintain many theological colleges, where Arabic is taught to the *ahungs*, the preachers who expound the Koran every Friday in their mosques. But they have a few standard works in Chinese, explaining the main principles of Islam, which they do not offer to outsiders, as they believe their religious literature too sacred for sale to the public.

No idols are found in the Mohammedan mosques which are severely plain in contrast with the Buddhist or Taoist temples. The mullah or *ahung* does not call the hours of prayer from a minaret but contents himself with shouting it from the front door of the mosque. Though he puts on special robes during the service, the *ahung* wears the ordinary Chinese garments at all other times. Mohammedans in China are supposed to number about 15,000,000.

CHRISTIANITY.

While Western Christians were hard at work converting Europe, the Nestorian Christians set about the conversion of Asia, at first from their original seat of Antioch; and soon they had established bishops in Syria, Babylon, Bagdad, India, Central Asia and China. There is good reason to believe that Nestorian missionaries had reached China as early as A.D. 500. Alopen, a Nestorian missionary, with a band of followers, one of whom was an Ethiopian, went to Sianfu, the then capital of China in 635. The presence of the Nestorian missions in Sianfu is attested by the Nestorian Stone, bearing an inscription of 3,500 words, consisting of a statement concerning the being of God, the sin of man, the coming and teaching of Christ and the work of Christian missionaries. When Marco Polo was in China six centuries after the arrival of the Nestorian missionaries he found many Christians and churches in all parts of the Yangtsze Valley.

The Franciscan mission began in China in the early part of the 14th century, when John of Monte Corvino was received by Kublai Khan and built a church in Cambaluc where he remained 36 years, and "converted more than thirty thousand infidels." Monte Corvino was an immediate disciple of St. Francis of Assisi and is regarded as the first Roman Catholic missionary to China.

Francis Xavier began his evangelical work in Japan, going there at the suggestion of a Japanese convert he had made in Malacca. In Japan he constantly met with the objection "If yours is the right religion why have the Chinese, from whom we get our civilization, not accepted it?" He took the hint and began to make arrangements for a mission to China, going first to Malacca to get letters of introduction from the Portuguese authorities. He returned to Macao and died on an island near Canton without having set foot on the mainland of China.

In 1538 the Jesuit Father, Matteo Ricci, brought clocks to China, a great novelty then, as presents to the authorities. On arriving at Peking he taught mathematics and science as well as Christianity, and was highly honored by all who knew him. He died in 1601 at the age of 58. Ricci was followed by Fathers Schall and Verbiest, both brilliant men, who were put in charge of the astronomical board at Peking and corrected errors in the Chinese calendar. It is interesting to note that they were responsible for the calendar in use to-day.

From the time of Ricci to 1735 the Roman church sent five hundred missionaries to China and the learned Jesuits gained high honors in the capital. At length a controversy arose between the Christians over the question of ancestor worship, some insisting that these rites were mere civil forms while others denounced them as redolent of idolatry and superstition. This dispute was carried to Rome and back to China again, the issue being finally decided against the rites. This was one of the main causes for the expulsion, about 1735, of all Christian missionaries and the systematic persecution of Christians. Though the Roman Catholic missionaries never definitely abandoned the Chinese field, their activities were limited until the opening of the treaty ports in 1842.

In 1807 Robert Morrison, the first British Protestant missionary to China, arrived in Canton. He was soon joined by Milne and together they translated the New Testament, and later the Old Testament, into Chinese. In 1823 Morrison's great Chinese-English dictionary in six volumes was published, and became the key by which Chinese literature was afterwards made known to the world.

In 1830 the first American missionaries, Bridgman and Abeel, came to China. These British and American missionaries soon founded hospitals and schools and distributed books and tracts wherever they went. As was the case with Roman Catholic missions, Protestant activity was limited until the opening of the treaty ports. Within a short time after this event, many of them, chiefly British and American, arrived and as soon as opportunity offered pushed into the interior.

Protestant and Roman Catholic missionaries are now found scattered throughout the country, and there is scarcely a city of any importance which does not contain a community of native Christians, nor are there many places of importance which do not possess schools, hospitals, dispensaries, orphans' homes and other worthy institutions maintained by the missionary societies.

SUPERSTITION.

Though not properly a part of any of the religions of China, geomancy and superstition play a very large part in the lives of the average Chinese. The native priests are not superior to the common people in this respect and divination has been for so long a part of their stock in trade that in the minds of the ignorant divination and religion are indistinguishable. A large part of Chinese popular superstitions is embraced in the belief in *fêng shui*, or "wind-and-water" rules.

"The principles of geomancy depend much on two supposed currents running through the earth, known as the dragon and the tiger. A skillful observer can detect and describe them, with the help of the compass, direction of the watercourses, shapes of the male and female ground, and their proportions, color of the soil, and the permutations of the elements. The common people know nothing of the basis on which this conclusion is founded, but give their money as their faith in the priest or charlatan increases."

In Chinese belief, the spirits which inhabit various objects of nature have a profound influence over the life of man. It is the function of the geomancers to discover and sell charms for these evil spirits, locate their haunts and guard against their attacks by the building of walls, the tearing down of buildings or even the deflection of the courses of streams.

The choice of a burial place is believed to affect the future of the surviving relatives and its choice is left to the geomancers. Malign influences will, it is believed, disturb the dead and cause his spirit to wreak vengeance on those who have failed to provide a more comfortable habitation. Thus great efforts are put forth to secure a grave site which will bring about the happiest results and some families spend large sums for the service of the best geomancers that they can secure. That the "wind-and-water doctors" themselves believe in their solemn nonsense is indicated by Dr. Wells Williams' story of one who "after having selected a grave for a family was attacked with ophthalmia, and in revenge for their giving him poisonous food which he supposed had caused the malady, hired men to remove a large mass of rock near the grave, whereby its efficacy was completely spoiled."

An electric light plant was located in an important Chinese city several years ago, the smokestack towering up some distance from the *yamen*, or office, of the chief official. The official suffered a period of illness and other misfortunes which convinced him that the *fêng shui* was not right, so he called in a geomancer. That worthy made a careful examination of the neighborhood and decided that the evil spirits flew into the *yamen* from the vantage ground of the smokestack. A request for the removal of the offending structure was refused by the unimaginative foreigner who owned it, so the old entrance to the *yamen* was carefully blocked up and a new one cut on the opposite side of the building. After that the spirits did no more harm.

Just inside temple and other doors will often be seen a screen larger in size than the door opening. This is placed there because evil spirits can fly only in a straight line and have not the power to go around the screen. For the same reason, the bridges which lead across artificial lakes to the teahouse in the center follow a zigzag course, and blank walls are often built in front of doors which otherwise would be exposed to the direct attacks of the spirits. This kind of superstition is to be found in everything. Many Chinese when ill, will send to the

Taoist priests for a charm, which consists of a piece of paper with mystic characters. The paper is burned, the patient swallows the ashes, and is better at once. When a baby is born, a piece of raw ginger is hung outside the house as a polite means of warning strangers not to come inside, as the presence of a stranger near an infant is supposed to have a very bad influence. One of the amusing features of Chinese superstition is the practice, rather common in some places, of dressing small boys as girls in the hope that evil spirits will be deceived thereby and will pay no attention to the supposed girl.

These superstitious beliefs prevail among nearly all classes of Chinese and many who laugh at them are at the same time careful not to do anything which would, according to popular belief, bring them ill luck. In former years every Chinese family purchased an almanac in which were listed the lucky and unlucky days and to a certain extent the actions of every member of the family were guided by the advice contained in this book. With the official abolition of the old Chinese calendar the publication of almanacs of this sort have been prohibited but a great many are clandestinely published and sold by "bootleg" methods.

THE FAUNA AND FLORA OF CHINA

By Arthur de C. Sowerby, F.Z.S.

HINA contains a very varied and very interesting fauna, one of the richest in the world. Naturally over such a wide area as that covered by China, there is a great range of different types of country, and working from north to south and from east to west we pass through several faunal zones or regions. Thus in the extreme north, the fauna of China is related to that of Mongolia, and is called Tartarian. Here, where the country is more or less arid, and in many places semi-desert conditions prevail, the mammals and birds are adapted to desert conditions; reptiles and amphibians are few and far between; fish, though fairly plentiful in the permanent rivers, do not show a great variety; and insects and other invertebrates, while numerous enough, are neither as plentiful nor as varied as in more southerly and humid areas. The flora of North China also responds to the climate and topographical conditions, and we find drought resisting plants in great abundance.

In the highlands of West China, including the provinces of Szechuan and Yunnan, and parts of Kansu, South Shensi, Honan, Hupeh, Kweichow, and Hunan, the fauna is Himalayan in its affinities, as also is the flora.

In South and South-east China, the fauna belongs to what has been called the Oriental Region, that is to say, it is closely related to the fauna of India, Malay, the Philippines and other tropical and semi-tropical countries of Asia; and through the Indian fauna to that of Africa. The flora is tropical in the southern provinces of China.

In East China the fauna appears to be somewhat of a mixture. For instance in Fukien and Chekiang provinces there are numerous distinctly Himalayan types, which keep to the higher mountainous areas; while in the low-lying area, the fauna is Oriental. Further north the Oriental and Tartarian types mix in the Yangtsze delta and on the plains and low hilly regions of Anhui, Shantung and Chihli, while throughout North-east China there is an infusion of European-Siberian faunal forms. A great part of Manchuria is purely Siberian in its fauna, with the exception of one or two forms. The Siberian fauna is, of course, very closely similar to that of Europe, and not at all like that of the rest of Asia.

The flora of East China and Manchuria again follows the same trend as the fauna, and we have a mixture in the provinces of the former, while in the latter we meet a plant life that will remind us strongly of that of Europe and even of North America. It is, in fact, what is called by scientists *holarctic.*

MAMMALS.

China has a very interesting mammalian fauna. Some nine orders are represented including the *Ungulata,* or hoofed animals; the *Carnivora,* or flesh-eating animals; the *Insectivora,* or insect-eating animals; the *Chiroptera,* bats; the *Primata,* monkeys and apes; the *Pinnipedia,* seals; the *Rodentia,* rats, squirrels, etc; the *Lagomorpha,* hares and pikas; and the *Edentata* with but one representative, the pangolin, or scaled anteater.

The anthropoid apes are represented in China by two or three species of gibbon, which occur only in the extreme south-west and south. The monkeys are represented by several forms. A large macaque is found in the Imperial Hunting Grounds, north-east of Peiping in Hopei. Other macaques are found in Anhui and further south. In West China the famous golden-haired monkey is found. This is a large species, characterized by the hair of the back being very long and of a golden colour, and by the presence of a distinct up-turned snout or nose. Another closely related species, in which the hair of the back is short, also occurs.

Numerous species of deer are found in China, amongst the most interesting being the sikas, or spotted deer, the wapiti, the now almost extinct* elaphure (David's deer) or *ssupuhsiang*, the roedeer (confined to the north), the sambur (confined to the south and west), the muntjac, the musk deer, the river deer and the tufted deer. The last three have no horns, the musk and river deer being armed with long tusks instead. The river deer is confined to the Yangtsze Valley, the musk to the high mountains of the west and north and to the great forests of Manchuria, in the extreme north of which country occur the moose and reindeer.

There are several forms of hollow horned ruminants, goats, sheep, antelopes and the like. The big-horned sheep is found along the Mongolian frontier in North Shansi. The blue sheep, or bharal, is found in various parts of Kansu from the Tibetan border on into North-west Shansi. Three species of antelope or gazelle are found along the Mongolian border; while several species of serow and goral, goat-like animals that keep to the highest mountain ranges, occur in various parts of the country. A peculiar animal known as the takin (*Budorcas*) is found in the highest mountains of South Shensi and Szechuan. There are two species. These animals are as large as oxen, but have all the agility and habits of the goat.

In Chinese Turkestan the wild ass, or *kiang*, occurs in large herds, as well as the wild camel and the wild horse, often known as Przewalski's horse after its discoverer. In Indo-China, the wild water-buffalo, the boar or seladang and the banteng, other large bovines, are to be found.

Wild pigs are plentiful all over China and Manchuria, except in the provinces of Chihli and Shantung.

---

* Now only known alive in capitivity, in the Duke of Bedford's collection in England.

The carnivores are well represented in the country. The tiger is found in the wilder, more forested parts of North China, while it is extremely common in certain parts of the south, notably in the province of Fukien. A large, light coloured, thick coated form occurs in the forests of Manchuria. The leopard is almost universally distributed, while there are a number and variety of smaller felines to be met with. Weasels, martens, minks, civets, mongooses, polecats, badgers, otters and the like make up a host of small carnivores that abound, while the dog family is represented by the wild dog, the wolf, foxes and the raccoon-like dog, all of which, except the wild dog, are well distributed over the country. A black bear related to the Himalayan black bear, is to be found in Szechuan, another in the Eastern Tombs area of Chihli, another in the Manchurian forests, and yet another in Formosa. A grizzly bear and a brown bear are found in Manchuria, while both grizzlies and brown bears occur on the Tibetan borders. The remarkable creature known as the giant panda, or cat-bear, is an inhabitant of the highest and most inaccessible regions of Western Szechuan and the Tibetan border: the little panda, which differs in being much smaller and in having a long tail, is also found in these parts and in Yunnan.

Sea lions and common seals are found off the coasts of East China and several species of whale, porpoise and dolphin in the China Sea. In the Tung Ting lake and Middle Yangtze a remarkable dolphin, known as the "White Flag Dolphin" has recently been discovered. It is of a peculiar greyish white colour, lives on fish which it digs out of the mud at the bottom of the lake, and is most closely related to a river dolphin of South America. The black river porpoise is also found in the Yangtze and in the estuaries of other rivers in the south-east and south.

Many species of shrews, moles and hedgehogs occur in China. A remarkable species is the tree shrew of Yunnan and South China, which resembles a squirrel in general form and habits. The Indian muskrat (or musk-shrew) is common in the south and south-east. Several peculiar forms of shrew-moles, and a hedgehog-shrew also occur.

China is rich in bats, the *Chiroptera* being the second largest order in the country. In the south large fruit-eating forms occur, as well as several leaf-nosed insectivorous forms; while a number and variety of smaller forms are found in the north.

The great order, *Rodentia*, is the best represented of all the orders in China, where chipmunks, squirrels, rats, mice and voles of every description are abundant. There are several species of flying squirrel, and other more remarkable forms, such as the molerats, the bamboo rats and the jerboas or jumping rats. The crested porcupine occurs in the central and southern provinces, and the brush-tailed porcupine in the south, centre and south-west.

Several species of hare and a great many forms of pika, little rabbit-like animals, are to be met with. There is no wild rabbit in China.

One of the most interesting mammals of China is the pangolin, or scaled anteater. This remarkable creature is devoid of teeth, has the body covered with horny scales instead of hair, and lives exclusively upon "white ants" and the larvae and eggs of ordinary ants, for securing which it is armed with a long sticky tongue. Powerful claws on the front feet enable it to get at its prey in partly decayed tree trunks or deep under ground. It can also climb well, while its long tail is prehensile. It belongs to one of the lowest orders of mammals.

BIRDS.

In the number of orders and families represented, and in the variety of genera and species, the birds of China greatly exceed the mammals.

China is the headquarters of the great pheasant family. Besides numerous varieties of the common ring-necked pheasant, so beloved by sportsmen, there are a great many even more beautiful and strange forms represented in this country. Of these the golden pheasant, the blood pheasant, Lady Amherst's pheasant, the Reeves' pheasant, the fire-back pheasant, the eared pheasants, the silver pheasant, the monal and the tragopans are all remarkable for their gorgeous plumage. The pucras pheasant or koklass is another handsome bird found in high mountainous regions. The partridges are represented by the bearded partridge and the chukar, or red-legged partridge in the north and the famous bamboo partridge, Rickett's hill partridge and the francolin in the south. In the highlands of the west are found the snow-cock and the snow partridge. The Chinese quail is a small brightly coloured bird confined to the south: the Japanese quail, closely resembling the common quail of Europe, is ubiquitous: while the button quail, characterized by having only three toes, migrates between Manchuria and Kwangtung, or Canton Province.

The grouse are represented in China Proper by Pallas' pin-tailed sand grouse, a Mongolian bird which appears in the north during severe winters, and the pheasant grouse and hazel grouse in the west. In Manchuria, we have the hazel grouse, the blackcock and the capercailzie.

Several species of dove are to be found. The rock dove occurs in huge flocks in the north and west in the valleys and plains, except during the breeding season, when the mating couples repair to the cliffs and old buildings to nest and rear their young.

The eastern great bustard, a bird that outrivals the common bustard of Europe, is prevalent throughout North China as far as the Yangtsze Valley except in summer, when it retires to Mongolia and Siberia to breed. A number of species of cranes are also prevalent during the migration periods.

Wild swan, several species of geese, ducks and teal, snipe, woodcock and innumerable shore birds, such as plovers, sandpipers, curlews, whimbrels, godwits, avocets, stilts, knots, green shanks, sandpipers, stints and the like, complete a very comprehensive list of birds that offer the fowler excellent sport.

Herons, egrets, storks, bitterns, spoonbills, ibises, grebes, divers, coots, moorhens, crakes, rails, cormorants, and pelicans swell the throng of aquatic birds that frequent marsh, lake and river; while the marine birds consist of awks, guillemots, puffins, skuas, petrels, albatrosses, gulls and terns. The lesser frigate bird has also been recorded from Chinese waters.

A large variety of birds of prey are also present in China, ranging from the golden eagle, the lammergier and the great black vulture of the north down to the tiny black and white falconet of the south. Other species worthy of note are the imperial eagle, the spotted eagle, the sea eagle, the serpent eagle, the white headed buzzard, the saker falcon, the peregrine, the hobby, the merlin, the kestrel, the red-footed falcon, the osprey, the kite, the goshawk and the sparrowhawk. Of owls the following may be mentioned: the great eagle owl, the wood owl, the Japanese hawk owl, the long and short eared owls, the little owl, the pigmy owlet, the scops and the screech owl.

By far the largest group of birds in China is that known as the passerines, or perching birds. It includes the crows, jays and pies, of which many interesting species are found in the country; the finches, too numerous to mention; the flycatchers, warblers, robins, thrushes and wagtails, soft-billed birds, mostly migrants; the tits; the larks; the shrikes; the drongoes; the orioles; the minevets; swallows; creepers; bulbuls, confined to the more southerly regions; and the laughing thrushes or babblers. Amongst this motley throng are the majority of our song birds, cage birds, and birds of beautiful plumage. There are hundreds of species belonging to this group, many of them being migrants or transient visitors, many others permanent residents.

Cuckoos of several species; the closely related so-called crow-pheasants; the hoopoe; swifts; nightjars; numerous woodpeckers; king-fishers, large and small; the brilliantly coloured oriental roller, bee-eaters and barbets, further enrich the avifauna of this ancient land. In the extreme south parrots are to be met with, while in Szechuan in the west is found the handsome Darwin's parakeet.

REPTILES AND AMPHIBIANS.

In these branches of animal life North China is comparatively poor. The number of genera and species, however, increase as we pass from north to south, till, in South China, there is a great variety of both types of animal.

The reasons for this are not far to seek, and may be summed up in the two words "climatic conditions." The severe winters and long periods of drought that characterize the climate of North China are inimicable to these cold-blooded vertebrates. Lizards and snakes cannot survive the long winters; while frogs, toads and salamanders are not suited to an arid climate. Only one poisonous snake, the pit-viper, is found in the north, while in the south we have a number of species of pit-vipers, including the gigantic and deadly Chinese viper, several smaller forms related to the common species of the north, and the equally deadly bamboo viper, whose brilliant green colouring renders it a beautiful creature to look upon. The great black cobra, identical with the Indian species, ranges as far north as Chekiang, as also does the deadly krait. Several species of marine serpent (banded yellow and black snakes that spend most of their lives in the open sea) are commonly found along the coasts of South and South-east China. These also are poisonous.

Of non-poisonous snakes there are half a dozen or so species found in the north, all belonging to a single family, *Natricidae*. The most beautiful is the common tiger snake, which is brilliant green with bright vermilion markings. It is commonly found in the vicinity of streams, rivers, creeks and lakes. Another very common species is the brown snake, whose range extends throughout Central Asia. In Manchuria a large species of water snake is very common. It reaches a length of well over five feet and is of a brilliant black and yellow colour.

In the south we have the python which reaches a length of upwards of 20 feet. The smallest snake is the little blind-snake (*Typhlops*), which is about four inches in length and looks much like an earthworm, whose underground habits it follows. Besides these there are a great many other non-poisonous species.

The same distribution applies to the lizards. The commonest in the north is the little gecko or wall lizard, that keeps mainly to human habitations. A few other species are found in the open country, one, the toad-headed lizard, being very common in the sandy wastes along the Mongolian border.

The *Japalura*, a tree-inhabiting species, is found in the south. The commonest form is the blue-tailed skink. Many other forms occur.

The mud-turtle is found in all the rivers in China, while two or three species of marine turtle occur in her seas. Land tortoises and terrapins are found in the south, one species of terrapin ranging as far north as Tientsin.

The most interesting reptile in China is the little Yangtze alligator, the only other alligator known to occur to-day being that of the Mississippi and Florida. Its home is in the marshes of the Wuhu district of the Lower Yangtze, whence it is sometimes carried down the river in flood time. The estuarine crocodile is found in the extreme South.

In South China occurs a great variety of frogs and toads, including some giant species almost as large as the American bullfrog. The smallest is the little toad known as *Microhyla*. A large tree-frog of a brilliant green colour with long legs and webbed toes, the tips of which are in the form of suckers, ranges as far north as Shanghai, where, however, it is not common. The little tree-toads (*Hyla*) are universally distributed except in the extreme north, though one species occurs in Manchuria, where also the beautiful fire-bellied toad is abundant.

The Asiatic common toad and the edible frog are very common. Radde's toad, a beautifully marked species, is common in the north, and is even to be found in the sandy deserts of the Ordos and Mongolia.

Several species of salamander and newt are prevalent in the country, the most interesting species being the giant salamander, which attains a length of from three to five feet. It is found in the mountain streams of the central, western and southern provinces and occasionally in large rivers in the east.

FISHES.

China possesses a very interesting and varied fish-fauna, the most predominating family being that of the carp (*Cyprinidae*). In fact, this country is looked upon as one of the headquarters and dispersal centres of this important group of fishes.

One of the most interesting species, the *huangchuan*, which looks like a salmon, attains a length of over five feet and a weight of as much as 150 lbs., and may be caught with rod and line with a spinner bait. Other species that reach a large size are the Chinese ide and the common carp, 40 to 50 lbs. being no unusual weight for these fish. Perhaps the most beautiful form is the rainbow carp, so-called on account of its brilliant breeding colours. The wild form of the common goldfish is prevalent everywhere, sometimes even red, white and red and white individuals being met with in a wild state.

The largest fish found in Chinese rivers is the sturgeon which reaches a length of upwards of 12 feet and a weight of 400 to 500 lbs. A very peculiar form is the Yangtsze beaked sturgeon, which has a flat, broad, sword-shaped snout almost as long as the head and body. This, too, attains a great size. The bass family is represented by the Mandarin fish, a well known table delicacy. The most highly prized fish for eating is the *samli*, a species of shad, that ascends the Yangtsze and other rivers in the late spring and early summer to spawn. A very predacious fish is the serpent head, whose flesh is of poor flavour. It, too, reaches a large size. Numerous forms of catfish are to be found, one, the wels, reaching a large size. The salmon family is represented by a spotted trout in the Imperial Hunting Grounds in the north, and a sort of sea-charr that ascends certain rivers in the east. The candle-fish (often called whitebait) occurs in the estuaries of the large rivers, being related to the salmon family. In Manchuria are several forms of salmonoid, including the spotted trout, several coregonoids, the greyling, and the migratory salmon of the genus *Oncorhynchos*, the same as swarm up the rivers of western North America to spawn. At times some of the larger rivers of Manchuria swarm with these salmon. Several forms of eel are prevalent throughout China.

A great variety of marine fishes are taken off the coasts of China, such as seabreams, mackerel, tunny, maigres, seabass, soles and other flatfish, herrings and anchovies, garfish, gurnards, scabbard-fish, sharks, rays— too numerous to mention, but forming a very valuable source of food for the inhabitants, a great many of whom are fishermen.

INVERTEBRATES.

The complete history of the Chinese invertebrates has yet to be written, though several branches, such as the butterflies and other insects, and the mollusks have received considerable attention.

China is extremely rich in insects—butterflies, dragon flies, grasshoppers, cicadas, beetles and bugs, not to mention more disagreeable kinds, abounding. Spiders, centipedes, scorpions, ticks and many other similar creatures are numerous, especially in the warmer areas.

Her molluscan fauna, especially of the rivers and seas is also very rich. Mussels, water snails, clams, and oysters are important as food. The pearl mussel of the southern rivers supplies the famous oriental pearl so beloved by the Chinese woman.

Crustacean and other marine invertebrate life is also very abundant. Some very fine species of prawn are the most valuable economically, though the fresh-water shrimp and prawn fisheries are very important. The famous and remarkable king-crab is abundant on the south-east coast.

A host of other lower forms of animal life fills the country, but it is impossible to deal with them here.

DOMESTIC ANIMALS.

The domestic animals of China are the horse or pony, the donkey, the mule, the ox, the buffalo, the camel, the sheep, the goat, the pig, the dog, the cat, the rabbit, the fowl, the goose, the duck, and the pigeon. The yak is used along the Tibetan border for packing, also for food and as a milk supplier. The reindeer is similarly used in north-western Mongolia and the more remote parts of Manchuria.

FLORA.

The flora of China is even more varied and interesting than the fauna; indeed, it is said to be one of the richest temperate floras in the world.

Though there are a great many species of valuable timber trees, including the oak, walnut, elm, poplar, willow, pine, spruce, birch, and fir in the north, and many purely Chinese forms, deciduous and conifereous, in the south, such as the *Cunninghamia, Tsuga, Pseudotsuga, Keteleeria, Fokienia,* and the like, China is peculiarly short of timber, owing to the way the once magnificent forests have been destroyed.

In Fukien in the south-east and in some of the central provinces, there still remain fairly extensive wooded areas, while in the higher mountain ranges of the north some very extensive forests occur. Notably is this the case in the mountains of West Shansi, in the Tsing-ling range in South Shensi, and in the highlands along the Tibetan borders of Szechuan and Kansu. Very extensive primeval forests occur in Manchuria. The Foochow pine (*Cunninghamia*) is largely exported from Fukien province to other parts of China, while timber is brought down the Yangtze and the Sungari and the Yalu (Manchuria) in considerable quantities. But it is practically all consumed in China and little, if any, goes abroad.

In the barren areas of Kansu, Shensi and Shansi, almost the only timber trees to be seen are poplars, willows and elms. The white-barked pine (*Pinus bungayana*) is found on the mountains of Shânsi, and is a favourite tree for decorating temple grounds. The maidenhair-fern tree (*Ginkgo biloba*) is indigenous to China, but is not now found in the wild state.

China boasts a great variety of fruit-bearing trees— apple, pear, apricot, peach, plum, mulberry, persimmon, grape, and jujube prevailing in the north; and orange, pomegranate, lichi, longan and loquat in the more southerly regions. Wild grape is abundant in Manchuria.

The wood-oil or varnish trees of China are famous, being very prevalent in the central and southern provinces. From these the valuable varnish oils are derived, forming an important item of export.

In the higher parts of Central and West China a great many species and varieties of rhododendron occur, often in regular forests, while everywhere from the Yangtze basin southward, magnolia trees abound.

It is impossible to give details here of the flowering plants of China, but it may be noted that this country is the headquarters of the primula family as well as of the azaleas and rhododendrons. Indeed, an enormous number of the garden plants of the West have been derived from China, especially such as belong to these three groups. In Yunnan a wonderful blue poppy grows in the mountains. Bluebells, violets, roses, lilies, daisies, snapdragons, vetches, clematis and a host of other beautiful species go to swell the floral wealth of a country often known as "The Flowery Republic." Nor is this wealth of flowering plants and timber trees in any way greater, proportionately, than that of economic plants. Cereals of all kinds, including wheat, oats, rice, sorghum, millet and maize, beans and peas in great variety, cabbages, kale, spinach, onions, leeks, garlic, peppers, eggplants, melons, pumpkins, marrows, and cucumbers, tuberous plants such as potatoes, sweet potatoes, yams, lotus-root, carrots, turnips, and the like, are all cultivated, besides a number of edible plants less known to westerners. One of the most useful plants known to the Chinese is the bamboo, hundreds of household utensils and articles of common use being made from the various kinds that grow in the country. The young shoots are eaten as a vegetable. Forests of the larger kinds and jungles of the smaller species clothe the mountain sides in the wilder parts of the south, and west, while cultivated varieties abound everywhere from the Yangtsze Valley southward.

Mushrooms, woodears and other fungi are also eaten, as well as numerous kinds of seaweeds.

It is hardly necessary to say that there is a great wealth of such non-flowering plants as ferns, mosses, lichens and fungi, not to mention the innumerable kinds of fresh-water and marine algae. Ferns are less prevalent in the dry northern areas than they are in the more humid south, however. Grasses, sedges, reeds and rushes line the creek and river banks everywhere, or spread thickly over the marshes. In the mountains of the South-east and south, the terrible sword-grass forms an almost impenetrable cover, except where it is burnt away to make room for cultivation or where bamboo or other forests occur.

ARTS AND INDUSTRIES

ORCELAIN.—Always ready to add to the glories of their ancient history, Chinese writers ascribe the beginning of their pottery to a very remote time. There is no reason, however, to believe that the art originated in China though the Chinese are the world's greatest potters and have produced the most beautiful and valuable porcelain known. The pottery of China went through the same process of evolution as in other countries. The first rude bricks, baked in an open oven, were succeeded by moulded and scooped out pieces, made in imitation of the forms of their bronze, which had been developed several centuries earlier. During the Chow dynasty (1122 to 249 B.C.), the potter's wheel was known and books of that period clearly describe the difference between moulded pottery and that made on the wheel.

From the very first knowledge we have of it, Chinese pottery was different from that of any other country, largely owing to the higher temperature at which it was fired, resulting in a hard, vitrified ware. To the same cause must be ascribed types of glaze unknown elsewhere, and so different were the results obtained by the Chinese that for several centuries after the introduction of the ware to Europe, its manufacture remained a mystery to the European potters, who thought it entirely different from the ware they were producing.

Somewhere about the beginning of the Christian Era glaze was discovered, the first mention of it being in the Earlier Han dynasty (206 B.C.—A.D. 22). This glaze was dark greenish, the ware being vitrified, and so hard that it could not be scratched with a knife. The Chinese were the first to discover that at a high temperature pottery could be glazed with powdered felspathic rock mixed with limestone or marble. Out of this discovery, and the constant use of a very high temperature, with great care in the selection and preparation of the clays used, the Chinese developed the porcelains which mark the highest development of the art. But the development was slow, and the thousand years following the discovery of glaze are included in the primitive period, the first of the five periods into which the chronology of Chinese porcelain is divided.

The primitive period ended with the Yuan dynasty (1368), and before its close great advancement had been made from the early brown pots, unglazed, and ornamented only with daubs of various colored clays. During the Tang dynasty, in the seventh century, the industry began to flourish and successfully compete with the much older bronzes for the attention of art connoisseurs. In the following Sung dynasty (960 to 1280), the industry was firmly established under royal patronage, an Imperial manufactory being established at Ching-teh-chen, this district remaining ever since the center of the industry. Contemporary writings describe the porcelain of that period as being "blue as the sky, fragile as paper, bright as a mirror, and sonorous as a plaque of jade stone."

Crackle is supposed to have been known during the latter part of this period. Its discovery was probably accidental, but the Chinese developed it to a high state of perfection. To produce this effect, the piece, while being fired, was exposed to a sudden drop of the temperature, which caused the glaze to contract more rapidly than the body of the piece, and break into innumerable crackles. So well did the Chinese potters understand this process that they were able to produce at will any size of crackle desired.

The second period of Chinese porcelain coincides with the Ming dynasty (1368-1644), which is considered by the

Chinese to have produced the most glorious products. The industry made much more rapid progress than in the preceding period. During the 14th century, the Chinese came in contact with Persian painted wares and at once began imitating them. But the only colors in the Persian paint pot which could withstand the fierce heat of the Chinese kilns were cobalt blue and copper. Floral designs came into existence at the same time. The early decorations were stamped, the designs being strongly silhouetted by raised outlines. The famous green porcelain known as *celadon* was produced about this time, probably being made in imitation of the highly prized jade stone. The Chinese place the highest value on the blue and white wares made during the reigns of Yung Lo, Suen Te, and Ching Hwa (1403-1488). This 15th century blue and white set the standard for all blue and white production of a later date. The magnificent *sang de bœuf* was first produced at this time. Another ware of this period was the eggshell porcelain, on some pieces elaborate designs being engraved before firing. Some of the designs are so delicate that they cannot be seen until held to the light. The yellow pieces of Hung Chi (1488-1505) and Cheng-te (1506-1521) are most prized.

Toward the end of the 16th century, China began to produce porcelain with colors fixed over the glaze. Previously the potters had been confined to cobalt and copper, results from the latter being very uncertain. In the new process, the pieces were refired after fixing the decoration. The first colors used were green, purple, and yellow; red over an underglaze of blue being added later. During this time, the production was enormous, and shipments to Europe began, by way of Portuguese trading vessels. This led to certain changes in design, to comply with what was thought to be European taste.

The most famous porcelain of the Ming dynasty was produced during the short reign of Suen-Te (1426-1436), the favorite design being pale blue flowers. The product of Ching Hwa (1465-1488) is most frequently copied.

8

The system of marking china by means of characters which show the reign under which the piece was made originated during the Ming dynasty, but only one piece of a set was marked. Decorations of this period are usually in five colors, green predominating, and hence such pieces are classed as *famille vert*. Other colors used were: blue under the glaze, red, yellow and deep purple over it.

The third period was introduced with the Manchu dynasty, 1644, and extended to the end of the reign of Kang Hsi, 1723. The Imperial pottery works were destroyed more than once in the 17th century as a result of rebellions and the Manchu invasion, but the early Manchu Emperors gave the industry their protection and their period saw the height of artistic production reached. Kang Hsi, the second of the Manchu Emperors, was the only ruler of China who remained on the throne for a complete cycle of sixty years, and during this time some of the most notable pieces were produced. Attempts were made to reproduce the green and blood-red glazes of former times, but the results were different, and in their attempts to imitate former wares were excelled by their achievements, for the *sang de bœuf* reached perfection. The blue and white pieces of the Ming dynasty were perfected not only with greater decorative skill but the cobalt blue was more brilliant and the purity and quality of the white glaze superior. Hawthorn ginger jars belong to this period. Many fine specimens of this period have no date marks at all, for a rather curious reason. In 1677 the superintendent of the factory gave orders that the name of the Emperor should no longer be used as a mark, because the accidental breaking of a piece of porcelain bearing his name would amount to an act of disrespect to the Emperor. Pieces marked with empty rings may be ascribed to the few years following 1677, during which the order was enforced, though this mark is very frequently copied. The three most famous monochrome glazes of the reign were: apple green, *sang de bœuf* and peach bloom. During the Kang Hsi period the *famille vert,* or five colored porcelain with a brilliant green usually predominating, were first perfected and are much sought after and highly prized by connoisseurs who also place a high value on what is termed "three-color Kang Hsi." Some of the specimens of the latter have sold at enormous prices, especially those with the black glazed background. The marks of the period vary but the most common are double circles and the fungus leaf.

Following this came the short Yung Chêng period, which lasted thirteen years, from 1723 to 1736. Short as it was, the period recorded many advances, largely because of the personal interest taken in the art by the Emperor. The drawing is better than that of any preceding period, and the designs were assigned to smaller spaces on the pieces, so that the porcelain itself could be admired. Owing to an inferior supply of cobalt, the blue was not so good as before, but to balance this defect, the rose color, from gold, was discovered, giving birth to the great rose family. The fine stipple work of Yung Chêng, distinguishes it from the broad, bold washes of color of the preceding period.

The Kien Lung reign (1736-1795) will always stand out as a distinctive period, the fourth in the cycle. It represents the highest technical skill and the perfection of not only quality but details and finesse. The beautiful *famille rose* was perfected and reached its highest stage of development. With the perfection of detail, however, a certain amount of the forceful character and strength which characterized the Kang Hsi period was lost. During the first part of the period of Kien Lung there were but few changes from the ware of the preceding reign. Then a new director of the Imperial pottery was appointed and further experiments in the rose color were carried out. The pink, ruby and rose eggshell plates and dessert services which were so popular abroad were produced during this reign. As this period was so much longer than that of Yung Chêng, the production was larger and for that reason the period is of more importance from the stand-point of the collector. However, there is little difference in the class of production, and it is difficult even for the expert to tell to which reign many pieces belong, unless authentic distinguishing marks are present.

The modern period of porcelain making in China extends from the close of the reign of Kien Lung to the present time and has been distinguished by no remarkable developments. The industry has suffered a great deal through rebellions and misrule, the works at Ching-teh-chen being destroyed by the Tapings. A few new types have been produced, but the potters have chiefly confined themselves to the reproduction of older masterpieces, to copying Wedgwood and Sèvres and making pottery in semi-European style to meet the demands of the Chinese living in treaty-ports. A poor quality of blue and white has been made for sale in Europe.

It is most difficult for any but the expert to determine the period to which specimens of porcelain belong, for the potters have always copied the best works of the preceding periods. As the mark has been copied also, it seldom means anything but an indication of the period to which the particular type of porcelain belongs. The collector will see nothing earlier than the Ming dynasty in the shops, which are to be found in every city of China. If there are any specimens of the Sung dynasty extant, they are in the great collections. The pieces offered in the shops to-day belong to a much later date, few of them being more than 100 years old.

References: "Chinese Porcelain," by W. C. Gulland; "Chats on Oriental China," by J. F. Blocker; "Chinese Art," by Stephen W. Bushell.

PAINTING.

China can boast of a succession of great painters for the past twelve centuries, with some worthy of note who lived and worked much earlier. Chinese writing being, in its earlier form, merely a kind of pictorial representation of ideas, writing and painting developed together, the distinguished penman usually being also a painter of note. By the end of the third century B.C. painting was a developed art, as distinct from writing, and since that time several schools have flourished and given place to later developments.

It is unnecessary to go into a history of the art, which followed about the same periods of advancement and decline as porcelain making. Developed without any outside influence, Chinese painting is entirely different from European, and foreigners, until they adapt themselves to the Chinese point of view, find in it much to be desired. Chinese painting is an art of lines, rather than of color, and one in which imagination and poetry are more important than technical details. Landscapes, the symbolic figures of Buddhism and Taoism and famous figures of Chinese history make up the principal subjects of the pictures. The painter always strives for harmony of composition and subtlety of conception. If a beautiful female character is to be portrayed, she must be surrounded by graceful animals, billowy clouds or swaying reeds. If it is a stern warrior who makes up the principal figure in the picture, the artist will probably paint massive mountain peaks in the background. The first thing the foreigner notices in Chinese paintings is the lack of perspective. The Chinese reply to this criticism is that it is unreal and therefore inartistic to represent space and distance on a flat surface where it cannot exist.

Although the best specimens of Chinese paintings do not command the prices paid for the best porcelains and bronzes, there are many which are valued at tens of thousands of dollars. Very often this value is determined not so much by the quality of the painting itself as by the history of the painting itself. It is the custom for owners of pictures to inscribe on the margins, poems or epigrams which the pictures have inspired. In a famous collection one will often see pictures which are embellished by the poems or comments of a half dozen

men famous in as many different centuries. Thus the
picture acquires a great value through historical
association. One may be able to vizualize this by
conjecturing the value of a Rubens painting which had
been in the possession of Queen Elizabeth, Shakespeare,
Washington, Napoleon and Queen Victoria and embellished
by the comments and autographs of each of the famous
owners.

All Chinese paintings are on silk or paper scrolls,
which are rolled and stored in cabinets. The affinity
between pictures and writing is exemplified again in this
for paintings are preserved like books. Instead of being
hung on walls as a part of the furniture of a house they
are put away and only brought out for the edification of
those who are especially interested. It is for this reason
that many fine Chinese paintings which are hundreds of
years old appear by the freshness of the colors to have
been painted but yesterday.

BRONZES.

Bronze represents the oldest form of art in China,
and the history of the development of bronze can be
traced with reasonable accuracy for more than 3,000 years.
The earliest specimens in the collections of to-day date
back to the Shang and Chow dynasties (1766-255 B.C.).
Bronze vessels of that period are chiefly of a ceremonial
type and the forms have been repeated in both bronze and
brass to the present day with but slight changes. The
older pieces display a savagery of design in contrast to
the delicacy and refinements of later Chinese art. Very
early in the development of the art, conventional designs
of real or fabulous animals were used as decorations.
The genuine early pieces are covered with red, green and
brown patina, and later pieces show excellent counterfeits
of these evidences of age. The artificial patina is often
put on with wax, but the deception is at once revealed by
scraping the surface with a knife, or by immersing the

suspected piece in boiling water.   Genuine patina is almost
as hard as the bronze itself.

In bronzes dating about 500 B.C. the highest development of the art is found.   Specimens were magnificently
decorated with gold and silver and the earlier crudities of
technique had disappeared.   The later pieces are more
elaborate and less austere in design.   More refinement of
form was shown after the second century of the Christian
Era, owing to the influence of Buddhism.   The art suffered
a decline in the Tang dynasty, was revived in the Sung
and later by the Ming, the highest excellence of the
renaissance being reached under the reign of Kang Hsi,
the great Manchu Emperor.

ARCHITECTURE AND MONUMENTS.

Throughout her history China has clung to the use
of bricks and wood as building materials with the result
that there are in the country but few buildings either of
great antiquity or of imposing structure.   One type of
architecture prevails now, as it has always prevailed and
one who goes to China today will see buildings but little
different from those in which Confucius lived.   There are
few structures in China more than two stories high.   The
crowded cities are almost entirely made up of buildings
of that elevation, and the narrow, dark streets give no
encouragement to architectural ambitions.   The effect of
the few fine façades is lost for the same reason.

With its elaborately curved corners, projecting eaves
and graceful sweeping lines the roof is the predominant
feature of the Chinese house.   The construction of Chinese
houses is singularly similar to that of modern steel
buildings, as the walls are not retaining walls.   The
structure is built up on a frame work of pillars, which
are later filled in with bricks and mortar.   Often the roof
is curiously ornamented with sharp barbs and points
which stick out in all directions, the object being to
impale any evil spirits which may be flying about.   For
a similar superstitous motive all important buildings must

face the south. In modern China many of the old superstitions have disappeared but the forms and conventions they inspired remain. Official buildings and pretentious residences are made up of a number of small buildings constructed around a series of courtyards and connected by passages.

The pagoda is the most striking type of Chinese architecture. There are several thousand of these structures in China, usually crowning the summit of a hill or the highest ground swell in a flat country, and it is a poor city indeed which does not boast of at least one. The erection of pagodas was often prompted by superstition. Some of them were put up by public subscription in order to propitiate the evil spirits and bring good luck to the town. Among the reasons for building of pagodas are: as monuments over the graves of Buddhist priests, as store houses for religious relics, as expressions of filial piety, to help a soul out of purgatory and to correct the *feng shui* or luck of a place. Most of them are of seven or nine stories, while some are thirteen stories, the number of stories being always odd, and therefore lucky. A Buddhist temple is usually found in the vicinity of a pagoda.

Often grouped in great numbers about ancient temples and scattered throughout every part of China will be found stone tablets, about six feet high and mounted on a turtleshaped base. These are known as *stupa* and the inscriptions they bear usually refer to some event they were erected to commemorate, or consist of transcriptions of the classics. The most famous *stupa* in foreign eyes is the Nestorian Monument, mentioned in the article on religions (page 83).

Not so numerous are the *pailous*, more commonly known to foreign residents as "widows' arches." These are stone arches erected with official permission to commemorate some distinguished or virtuous resident. From the fact that some were erected in honor of widows, foreigners have given them all the name of "widow's arch," though many are dedicated to scholars, warriors and officials. The *pailous* are probably more numerous in Western China than in any other part of the country but are to be found everywhere.

SILK.

Silk is one of the chief items by which China formerly maintained the balance of foreign trade, the annual exports of this article amounting to more than £13,000,000, while according to Chinese estimate twice that amount is used at home. The invention of artificial silk has seriously affected China's foreign trade but has not materially changed the native industry. Chinese history credits the invention of silk to Yuen Fei the consort of the Third Emperor, who, for that reason, has been deified and is worshipped as the goddess of the silk industry (literally: goddess of silk worms). It is certain that silkworms were reared about her time (2600 B.C.) and for many centuries the secret of the production of silk was jealously guarded by the Chinese. The methods were learned from China by Japan and the latter country now produces, for foreign sale, a larger amount of silk than China.

Great care is taken in the cultivation of the mulberry tree, the leaves of which form the chief food of the silkworms. These trees are planted in rows five or six feet apart and are carefully pruned down, seldom being allowed to grow to a height of more than six feet. The wild mulberry, which attains a height of forty feet, is also utilized, but all of the fine silk is produced by worms fed on leaves from the small domestic trees. The coarser kinds of silk, including *pongee*, are produced from worms which feed on oak leaves.

The eggs of the silkworm, carefully preserved during the winter, are hatched out artificially when there are enough mulberry leaves to supply food for the worms. In some places hatching trays not unlike poultry incubators are used, but many peasants hatch the worms by the heat of their bodies, or between blankets placed beneath the bed. The newly hatched worms are no larger than a hair, and about one-tenth of an inch long, one ounce of eggs producing about 30,000 worms. With their voracious appetites, the worms consume huge quantities of mulberry leaves, frequently moulting or casting their skins to make room for their rapid growth. The worms produced from one ounce of eggs will, in their short lifetime of one month consume a ton of leaves. They increase their weight 10,000 times from time of hatch to time of spinning their cocoons. During this time, the worms are carefully tended, the peasants observing many superstitious precautions regarding them. From the time they are hatched, the worms are supplied plentifully with leaves. At maturity, the worms are two inches long.

They then climb to the top of loose stalks of straw, which have been provided for their use and begin to spin the cocoons. At this time they are carefully watched to prevent crowding, which would result in double cocoons. A few threads are attached to the straw by the worm, which immediately begins spinning, moving its head round and round and building the silken sheath, in which it encloses itself. The spinning is completed in from three to four days, and if left undisturbed the moth will break through the sheath in another ten days. To prevent this, the cocoons are gathered, and the chrysalis killed within a few days after the spinning is completed. This is done either by heating and drying the cocoons, or packing them with leaves and salt in a jar which is buried in the ground.

The cocoons are sold to the filatures, a few uninjured ones being allowed to produce moths in order to supply eggs for the next crop. The cycle of the ordinary silk worm extends over the year, but some produce two to seven crops of cocoons annually. The worms which feed on oak leaves are not given such careful attention, but are merely placed on the trees, being removed to new trees as fast as they exhaust the leaves. They also spin their cocoons on the trees, from which they are later gathered.

Of recent years large steam filatures have been established with foreign machinery in Shanghai, Canton, Hangchow, Hankow, Soochow and other places, and these to a great extent have replaced the more primitive methods of silk manufacture. However, the hand reels and looms still produce enormous quantities of silk. Many beautiful varieties are made by these primitive methods. Each silk-producing city is famous for the manufacture of one or more kinds of silk, the finest white cloth coming from Wusih and the richest brocades being made at Soochow, the satins coming from Nanking. Certainly the best stocks in the country are to be found in Shanghai.

CARVING.

The patience and industry of the Chinese artisans make them excellent carvers, though their work is distinguished by the tedious care with which it is produced rather than by its artistic qualities. Ivory is one of their favorite materials, and such is their skill and patience in working with this material that it is difficult to believe that the carved ivory balls, one inside another, sometimes to the number of twenty, can be produced without recourse to some trick. But this is the kind of work in which the Chinese carver delights. The outside ball is carved and through holes in the surface, tools are introduced and the inside balls carved one at a time. All are then covered with minute designs. Elaborately carved and gilded pieces of wood are used to decorate the fronts of shops and sometimes in private residences. Small images are carved from ivory, jade, soap stone, or seeds. A favorite material is gnarled roots, which are carved into fantastic shapes of fairies and gods, polished and varnished. Under the training of foreigners, the Chinese produce some magnificent wood carving. At Siccawei, a suburb of Shanghai, the Jesuit missionaries maintain a furniture factory where they train and employ orphan boys. Some of the productions of this place have been used in decorating the palaces of Europe, and many travellers carry home one of their

carved camphor wood or teakwood boxes as the richest
trophy of a trip to the Orient.

JEWELRY.

Few travellers return from China without some piece
of characteristic jewelry, usually either jade or a piece
of gold or silver of distinctive design. The Chinese rank
jade as the most precious of stones and one who attempts
to purchase a piece of the color particularly prized by
connoisseurrs will find it as expensive as a diamond of
equal weight. The favorite and most expensive color is
a fine apple green. Other shades of color, not so popular
among the Chinese, satisfy foreign tastes at more
moderate prices. Much artificial jade is made in Europe
and chrysoprase from Siberia is sold to the unwary as
jade. Some of the carved ornaments offered as jade are
made of a greenish white soapstone. This particular
fraud may be easily detected, for real jade is too hard to
be scratched with a knife, while soap stone is very soft.
Defective pieces of jade are frequently filled with wax
and thus made to pass muster as perfect specimens.

Very fine pieces of filigree work in both gold and
silver are produced by Chinese jewelers. The beautiful
kingfisher feather work is peculiar to China. Some of
these pieces are of striking beauty but they are not
durable. The turquoise tinted side plumes of the feathers
are gummed on thin metal plates and quickly wear off.
The colors of kingfisher feathers are often imitated in
enameling, an art in which the Chinese are very
skilful.

Many imitations of precious stones are sold in China.
Very rarely will the beads on "mandarin chains" be of real
stones. The jade is glass, the turquoise enamel and the
amber made of resin which will crumble into dust with
age.

It may be useful to know that the goldsmith as well
as the silversmith stamps the name of his shop inside any
piece of gold he sells and thus binds himself to repurchase

the piece at any time by weight without questioning the
quality of the metal.

CLOISONNE.

Peking is the center for the manufacture of cloisonné
and one is advised to postpone any purchases of this
beautiful ware until he reaches the former capital. The
prices in Shanghai are fairly satisfactory, but as a
general rule Peking prices are far cheaper than those
quoted in any other part of the country and a greater
variety is offered.

In the manufacture of cloisonné, a process which can
be seen any day in the factories of Peking, the design is
outlined on a copper base with thin flat wires, sometimes
of gold and silver, but more often of copper. These wires
are soldered on and when this process is completed the
cells are filled with enamel colors in the form of paste.
The piece is then fired and the process of filling with
enamel and firing is repeated until all the cells are
completely filled. The enamel is then ground to a smooth
surface with pumice stone, polished and the wires
gilded.

In the Peking factories one may have any design
copied. It should be remembered that the wires are only
gilded and that on any piece, such as a cigarette case,
which will receive much wear, this gilding will soon wear
off. Vases and other purely ornamental pieces are not
so likely to tarnish.

LACE.

Lace making was unknown to the Chinese before the
coming of the missionaries, but is now quite important
among the minor industries. As lace making has been
taught by missionaries coming from all parts of the world,
the visitor will find almost every variety of lace produced
by the Chinese and at prices which cannot be duplicated
elsewhere. But care should be observed by the purchaser,
for with labor so cheap, there is a tendency to use cheap
materials even in the most elaborate pieces.

EMBROIDERY.

The same qualities of patience and industry which have made the Chinese such excellent carvers of wood and semi-precious stones have made them equally good at embroidery. This is an art which they share with other people of the East, but the earlier development of the silk industry in China gives Chinese embroidery a longer history than that of any other country.

Developed locally, there are many different styles of embroidery, varying both as to the stitch and the colors employed. One of the most famous of these is the Peking stitch, made by twisting the thread around the needle, the result being similar to the French knot, but much finer. The high esteem in which the Chinese hold all ancient products is more justified in embroidery than in many other things, for with the recent introduction of aniline dyes, and attempts to copy foreign patterns, the harmony and beauty of the older pieces is not to be found in present day productions.

The richest examples of modern embroidery are to be seen in theatrical costumes, for no producer of America or Europe ever lavished on his theatrical costumes one half of the expense that is borne by the actors themselves in China. One costume worn by an actor will have required the labor of ten or twelve women for five years, and during the performance he will appear in many different garments. Naturally, fashions in these expensive gowns do not change rapidly.

A great deal of embroidery is produced now for export by the women and girls in mission schools and the traveller will be able to secure fine pieces at but a fraction of the cost of a similar piece at home. A large quantity of mandarin robes and other Chinese products are offered for sale at the curio shops, often at prices which barely cover the original cost of the material. With the establishment of the Republic, these elaborate ceremonial costumes have been abolished for plainer dress, and there is no longer any Chinese demand for them.

LACQUER.

The Chinese very early learned the uses of products of the *lac* tree which is cultivated throughout central and southern China. From it centuries ago they made wonderful pieces of lacquer ware which are not excelled by the present products of Japan. The sap of the *lac* tree is drawn when the tree reaches the age of seven years, being collected in middle and late summer for the use of the lacquer workers. The wooden article to be lacquered is carefully polished and covered with layers of paper or silk. Over this is placed a layer of *lac* covered with a mixture, often of emery powder, red sandstone and vermillion, though other mixtures are made up of different materials. The piece is then dried and the whole process repeated from three to eighteen times. When pieces are to bear a design, it is drawn on heavy paper and marked with fine pin pricks. The design is transferred to the piece by powdered chalk, and drawn with a needle. Carved lacquer is very expensive and is now seldom produced. In its manufacture, a dark paste, in which powdered egg shells have been mixed, is applied to the wood and allowed to dry. The piece is then carved and several coats of *lac* applied.

The whole process of lacquer making is tedious and its many processes requires a long period of time. Foreign purchasers have been unwilling to give the Chinese workmen enough time to complete pieces ordered and as a result inferior methods of manufacture have become prevalent. The work is done in dust-proof rooms, and not without a good deal of physical suffering, as the raw *lac* is very irritating to the skin, and will cause small boils. Its effect on the skin is similar to that of the American poison oak or poison ivy. The oldest specimens of lacquer ware in the shops belong to the Ming dynasty. The finest present-day products come from Ningpo and Foochow though Canton produces large quantities of an inferior quality for export.

THE GOVERNMENT OF CHINA

Y an Imperial Edict, following a successful anti-dynastic revolution, the Manchu imperial dynasty abdicated the throne of China and acquiesced in the establishment of a Republican form of government. The abdication edict was dated February 12, 1912, and at the time this is written, although twenty years later, it is too early to discuss the Republican government, which has gone through many vicissitudes and in spite of obvious progress has many unsolved problems before it. The system of government which it replaced had existed unchanged for several thousand years, for although the Chinese have often rebelled against tyrannical rule, they were content with the form of government to which they were accustomed. Much of the old system will doubtless survive, tempered by a constitution, elected legislative bodies, and a new sense of individual political rights and duties. Since the establishment of the Republic radical local reforms have taken place; and there have been administrative changes in the capital, but the machinery of government of necessity remains much the same as it was under the rule of the Manchus and preceding dynasties. What follows is a description of the foundation on which the Republican government of China may be built and at the same time a description of the form of government under which Chinese art and culture developed. What part of it may be incorporated into the future governmental system of China remains for future generations to weigh and measure.

Theoretically the ancient government of China was an absolute monarchy, strengthened by the political fiction that the Emperor was the "Son of Heaven," who offered sacrifices direct to the divine powers, leaving his subjects to follow any religion they liked so long as their worship included the worship of himself. This fiction had behind it many centuries of Chinese custom and tradition and was doubtless the model of governmental machinery copied so successfully by the Japanese.

In theory, the Emperor was supreme, held the power of life and death over all subjects, could regulate their lives down to the humblest detail, was not amenable to any earthly authority and from his decisions there was no appeal. Though surrounded by boards of councillors and advisors, it was not necessary for him to follow their advice, or even to pretend to do so. His rule was by divine right and he was subject only to the displeasure of heaven, manifested by floods and famine when his rule was unwise, or by rebellions when tyrannical. If rebellions were successful they were as naturally inspired by heaven, but if unsuccessful they showed the fate of rebellions in other countries and were classed as the acts of traitorous rebels of evil inspiration.

The ancient Chinese system of government was a curious and interesting growth from primitive clan rule. The unit of administration was the village, which usually consisted of a single hamlet of several dozen related families with its surrounding farm land, although in the larger cities several villages might be included within the walls. The chief officer of the village was the *Tipao* or village head-man, who was selected by the villagers and then received official recognition or sometimes the practice was reversed and he was nominated by the local magistrate and confirmed by the villagers. He was the representative of his fellow villagers in all official capacities and in ordinary times was the only official with whom they came in contact. He attended to the registry of deeds and the

9

collection of taxes, was responsible for the enforcement of law and acted as constable and coroner.

This democratic form of selecting officials ended, however, when the *Tipao* and all others in the country received their appointment and their power direct from the official oligarchy in the capital. Leaving out of consideration the numerous boards and councils which surrounded the Emperor, the chief administrative official under him was the Viceroy, appointed as Governor-General over one or more provinces, each of which may or may not have had its own Governor. Among Chinese the Governor was known as Inspector, a name which survived his former status, when he made periodic visits to the provinces to see that the provincial officials were properly attending to their duties. Later he became a permanent resident and enjoyed supreme authority in his own province, but subject to the check of the Viceroy. Other provincial officials were the Treasurer, Judge, and Commissioner of Education, the latter being a modern addition to the list.

Within the province, the unit of government administration was the county or district which might contain a score of villages in addition to the county seat. A few districts formed a prefecture, while two or more prefectures formed a circuit, under the jurisdiction of a *Taotai*. The *Taotai* was an assistant to the Governor, having charge of military operations and civil administration within his own circuit. The *prefect* was a means of communication between the lower officials and his superiors, rarely exercising any executive powers, but acting as a court of appeal from the District Magistrates, when the resources of the litigants enabled them to enjoy the luxury of an appeal. The District Magistrate was the lowest in rank of all of those appointed by the court and the representative of the throne who came in closest contact with the people.

It would be very difficult to find, in any other government, officials whose duties corresponded to those of any Chinese official of the old order. In theory he was able to undertake any task, no matter how technical or involved with political complications. If troops were to be provided, tribute paid, dikes or canals built, and, in later days, railways projected, the Viceroys and Governors were ordered to perform the various tasks, the government at Peking rarely going any further in its commands than to demand that certain results be accomplished, leaving the manner of accomplishment entirely to the discretion of the official who received the Imperial Edict. In practice, each official always shifted the task to his immediate inferior and in this constant shifting of work, most of it finally reached the District Magistrate, who was last on the list and had to satisfy his superiors that the work had been done. The source of power, the gradations of rank and the shifting of tasks, were usually indicated in the proclamations of the District Magistrate, a typical one beginning:

"The Magistrate has had the honor to receive instructions from the Prefect, who cites the directions of the Taotai, moved by the Treasurer and the Judge, recipients of commands of their excellencies the Viceroy and the Governor, acting at the instance of the Foreign Board, who have been honored with His Majesty's commands." Then follows the command and the signature of the magistrate who indicates again the sources of the command which in theory came from the Emperor, although it might concern nothing more important than the discontinuance of a tax-collecting office or the promotion of an official.

Within his own district the magistrate or mayor was the supreme official. He tried all cases, was judge, jury and executioner, jailer, coroner, famine commissioner, tax collector, road and bridge superintendent, treasurer, commissioner of education, and chief of police, and assumed all the duties usually attended to by the entire staff of officials found in a county or town of another country. The annual salary of this busy official amounted to $120 to $360 with an allowance of a larger sum granted "for the encouragement of integrity among officials." But the salary was no indication of the emoluments of the office, which might be and often were a hundred times the amount. He was equipped with a large number of subordinates, yamen runners, messengers, jailors, clerks, and tax collectors, for all of whom he must provide and all of whom must, to the extent of the opportunities offered by their delegated powers, provide for him.

Although possessor of supreme authority in his territory, the magistrate was careful in all of his official functions not to offend public opinion or to presume too much on his power. His one aim was to serve his three years' term of office with no disturbances in his district which would attract the attention of his superiors. The people always knew very effective methods of embarrassing an over-officious magistrate. When the tax collectors made unusually heavy demands, the country people rioted and set fire to the official yamen. In the cities the guilds declared a cessation of trade, which is a strike, lockout and boycott combined, thereby effectively cutting off all the incidental revenue of the officials and soon attracting attention from the superiors of the magistrate. In extreme cases they seized the magistrate, bound him and carried him to the governor's or the *taotai's* yamen with the announcement that they would have no more to do with him. These small rebellions against misused authority have been going on constantly in China for centuries and formed a very effective means of counterbalancing the despotic power of the Emperor no matter what the dynasty.

In the old imperial days official advancement was obtained by literary ability only, and the prefect with his other duties was charged with conducting the examinations in his prefecture. Success at these examinations carried with it the privilege of taking part in the provincial examinations. These examinations were usually attended by many thousand students, of whom only a few hundred would succeed. The successful ones, again, were entitled to compete in the great metropolitan examination held at Peking. Out of several thousand competitors at this examination, probably half would be successful and the names of these were placed on a list from which all official appointments were made, except those awarded to sons of old and faithful public servants and to students who had failed to pass the examinations but had made frequent attempts. Chinese literature is full of stories of students who grew old and grey in their efforts to pass the examinations, finally succeeded, and died enjoying the dignity and wealth of official life.

During the last century of Manchu rule this ancient civil service was corrupted and in its place was substituted a rather open system of selling official positions. Under the later years of the last dynasty this system was highly developed and practically every official, before receiving his appointment, was squeezed of enormous sums, only a small part of which ever found its way into the government treasury. Secret as these transactions presumably were, Chinese generally knew the sums paid for various offices. For instance, a cabinet position was supposed to cost about $200,000 and the responsible post of *Taotai* of Shanghai was worth $100,000 for each year the incumbent held office. In addition to these lump sums, the prospective official was compelled to oil his way to those in power by liberal gifts to all the hangers-on of the important officials, and to the eunuchs in the Forbidden City of Peking.

This purchase price of the office was an investment which the office holder soon regained by similar deals for official positions included in his patronage, and it was customary for the relatives and friends of an aspiring and competent young man to finance him for the purchase of an office, confident that he would soon be able to repay the amount invested.

With the offices purchased outright, the incumbent named for only three years, and with practically no supervision from the capital it was natural that bribery and extortion should develop in all official dealings. The viceroys and the governors bought their offices at high prices from the court and high officials and they naturally expected to regain the price paid and a good profit during their term of office, and also to recoup themselves for the frequent presents it was necessary to give the authorities in Peking in order to make their official lives endurable. The same system extended throughout the official line to the district magistrate who was always careful to employ good tax collectors, but paid little attention to the repair of roads or bridges in a district which would be his home for only a short time, and under circumstances which made everything spent on repairs reduce his private income.

The transportation of tribute rice (the annual present of rice to the Imperial Court) offered a good example of the means whereby government officials regained the amount paid for their appointments. This tribute rice, coming from the southern and Yangtsze Valley provinces, was formerly shipped by the Grand Canal, each provincial governor through whose territory the shipments passed being allowed certain sums for the expense of transportation. In addition to this, each governor was charged with the maintenance of the canal and for this was given a specified allowance. Finally, with the partial filling up of the canal and the establishment of coast steamship lines, it became much cheaper to transport the rice in steamships than in the canal barges. Practically all of the shipments were made in this way in the last years of the Manchu dynasty but in theory the rice was still hauled over the Grand Canal and for this purpose a fleet of imaginary barges was maintained at great official expense. At frequent intervals this fleet was theoretically destroyed by a storm and was theoretically rebuilt, all of which added to the income of a body of enterprising and inadequately paid officials.

The deterioration of official life in China extended to all classes during the latter part of the Manchu rule. The sale of an appointment to one high official soon spread the corruption through all the lower ranks of officialdom, through his efforts to recoup himself, and at the beginning of the present century the term "Chinese official" was a synonym for inefficiency, corruption and tyranny. The outward respect accorded the average official was measured chiefly by the fear he inspired and when one, by his tolerance, public spirit and comparative honesty, gained the good will of those over whom he ruled, his name was linked with the names of the local heroes.

With the overthrow of the Manchu *régime* in 1911 China became a Republic in name but in reality a military dictatorship. Among the forces which overthrew the monarchy there were rival factions while not a few of the monarchical adherents, by a quick change of front, managed to ride in on the popular tide of republicanism. As a result the republican administration has been beset by factional difficulties which have made the organization of a permanent and stable government difficult. Owing to these difficulties no permanent constitution has been adopted, the government being carried on under the provisions of the hastily adopted provisional consitution of 1912.

Since the overthrow of the Manchus there have been two abortive attempts to restore a monarchical form of government, one by Yuan Shih Kai who sought to found an imperial line, and after his death, an attempt on the part of the reactionary Chang Hsun to restore the Manchu line. On both these occasions the opposition of the Chinese people was so determined and outspoken as to indicate that the old form of government is gone forever and that the political future of China will be worked out along modern and Western lines rather than the ancient and Oriental. This does not involve such radical changes as one might think for the Chinese people have for many centuries of their long history enjoyed a form of local self-government more liberal, perhaps, than that afforded in any other country. According to the theory of at least one school of political economy the Chinese government was the best because the individual Chinese subject was amenable to fewer laws and had less taxes to pay than the citizen or subject of any other civilized country.

SHANGHAI AND THE YANGTSZE
VALLEY

ENERAL INFORMATION.—Distance from London by sea 11,000 miles; from San Francisco, 5,000 miles; from Hongkong, 850 miles. Local time is 8 hours in advance of Greenwich. When it is 12 o'clock noon in Shanghai, it is 11 p.m. of the preceding day in New York, and 4 a.m. of the same day in London. Shanghai lies in 31° 14' N. Latitude and 120° 29' E. Longitude, being on the same parallel as Cairo and New Orleans.

Greater Shanghai is made up of several municipalities including the International Settlement, the French Concession and the Chinese administered Municipality of Greater Shanghai. The population of the International Settlement is 1,023,330, the French Concession 478,552 and the Chinese Municipality 1,702,130, a total of 3,204,012, making Shanghai the fifth city in the world in point of population.

It is exceeded in population by London, New York, Berlin and Chicago but is ahead of Paris, Los Angeles, Rome and Boston.

The population, both foreign and Chinese, is strikingly cosmopolitan. No less than forty-seven nationalities are numbered among the foreigners, while Chinese from every province are represented in the Chinese population. In the foreign population of Shanghai, the following are the principal nationalities represented: Japanese 18,804; British 10,747; Russian 9,532; American 3,667; Portuguese 1,784; French 1,565; German 1,474; Danish 334; Italian 326; Polish 343; Swiss 223; Dutch 190; Spanish 241; Greek 190; Czechoslovakian 153; Norwegian 164. These figures do not include several thousand foreigners who live outside the two foreign settlements, and approximately 200 nationals from many of the smaller central European and South American countries.

Arrival.—Although one of the world's great seaports, Shanghai is not on the sea but on the Whangpoo River, 13 miles from Woosung, an undeveloped port at the mouth of the river. All important passenger steamers proceed up the Whangpoo and tie up at docks or buoys which are in easy reach of the principal hotels. Passengers by train arrive at the North Station of the Nanking-Shanghai Railway, near the edge of the International Settlement. Representatives of all hotels meet the steamer or train and take charge of baggage.

Hotels.—Astor House, Burlington, Cathay, Metropole, Palace, Plaza. All hotels are on the American plan. The Great Eastern, Yih Ping Shang, Oriental and many other hotels, under Chinese ownership and management, serve foreign style meals and are patronized by some foreign travelers.

Consulates.—Austria, Belgium, Brazil, Czechoslovakia, Denmark, Finland, France, Germany, Great Britain, Italy, Japan, Netherlands, Norway, Portugal, Spain, Sweden, Switzerland, Union of Soviet Socialist Republics, United States of America.

Telegrams and Cables.—Domestic telegrams and radio messages can be sent by the Chinese Telegraph Administration, corner Foochow and Szechuen Roads. Offices of foreign cable companies located in the Cable Building, 4 Avenue Edward VII, near the Bund, also at 3 Peking Road. The Japanese Telegraph is at 5 Seward Road. Radio messages may be sent abroad by the Chinese Government Radio Administration in the Sassoon House (Cathay Hotel) on Jinkee Road. Domestic telegrams in local currency; cable rates are based on gold currency, but, at a fixed rate in local currency which is changed each quarter in accordance with exchange fluctuations.

Railways.—Nanking-Shanghai Railway, from Shanghai to Nanking, 193 miles, connecting by steam launch or train ferry across the Yangtsze with the Tientsin-Pukow Railway; Shanghai-Hangchow-Ningpo Railway, from Shanghai to Hangchow, 125 miles. The latter line will eventually be extended to Ningpo.

Transportation.—Ricshas, 20 minutes, 20 cents; half-day $1; whole day, $1.70. Motor cars $3 to $6 per hour; minimum fare of $1 per 20 minutes.

Newspapers.—Daily English: The China Press, the North Daily News, the Shanghai Times, the Evening Post and Mercury; French: Journal de Shanghai; Russian: Shanghai Zaria, Slovo. In addition there are many daily papers published in the Chinese and Japanese languages and many weekly and monthly periodicals published in English and other foreign languages.

Steamer Routes.—Shanghai is a port of call for nearly all the trans-Pacific and European steamship lines, as well as the steamers which run from Japanese to Australian ports. It is the most centrally located of all the Far Eastern ports and frequent sailings can be had to all points on the China coast, to Japan, the Philippines or other countries of Eastern Asia. In point of tonnage entering and leaving, Shanghai is the second largest port in the world.

Travel by Air.—The China National Aviation Corporation provides daily mail and passenger service by airplane from Shanghai to Hankow by way of Nanking, Anking and Kiukiang. Planes take off every morning except Sunday at 8 o'clock and reach Hankow at 3 o'clock the same afternoon. Connection is made at Nanking with a similar airplane service to Peiping and at Hankow with a service to Chungking.

Currency.—The old standard currency of Shanghai was the Mexican dollar, but in recent years Chinese dollars of the same value have come into general circulation. The small coins, ten and twenty cent pieces and coppers, are always depreciated. The dollar is usually exchanged for about 120 cents. Local money exchange shops are licensed and strictly regulated by the municipal authorities.

Shanghai, the commercial metropolis of the China Coast and of Asia, is the most important of the treaty-ports of China, and one of the most diverting and cosmopolitan cities in the world. Popularly termed "the Paris of the East" by observant tourists, it is an interesting mixture of East and West, for while the dominating business interests are largely western, the greater part of the population is Oriental. In the teeming streets every day it is not unusual to see almost every national costume, and although the Chinese form the bulk of the population, they and their dress are nearly as varied as the foreigners and their assorted costumes, for the Chinese population is made up of representatives from every province in the country. Japanese and Russians comprise the largest part of the alien population. In the Hongkew section are to be found extensive Japanese settlements, where many of the shops deal in nothing but Japanese merchandise. Here one may find anything from dainty lacquer boxes and gaily flowered kimono to heavy leather goods of expert workmanship. Although here and there will be found shops which deal exclusively in Indian, French, British, American and Russian goods, the Hongkew district is predominently Japanese. On the other hand, the Russians have appropriated a great stretch of Avenue Joffre and the adjoining blocks as their own particular territory. Avenue Joffre, the principal street of the French Concession, is a phenomenon of the post-war period. Since the Russian Revolution, thousands of "White" Russians, their property confiscated and their lives endangered by the Soviets, have fled to the comparatively secure havens which the larger cities of China afford. In large numbers they came to Shanghai, selecting the French Concession as a place to start anew. And from a placid residential street, Avenue Joffre was gradually transformed into a gay and bustling thorough-fare that bears many resemblances to streets in the larger continental cities. Here are to be found the clever modistes who smartly gown more than half the chic women of Shanghai, and side by side are the milliners and shoemakers who provide the accessories. Here, too, are the tiny cafés serving the delicious cream cakes and thick chocolate of which the Russians are so fond, the florists and delicatessens, the cosmetic and barber shops, and even an occasional pawn shop, where, if one is an astute shopper, an ancient samovar or a bit of strange jewelry may be unearthed.

Shops of almost every other nation are scattered throughout the rest of the strangely conglomerate city. More than forty distinct nationalities have found their way to Shanghai, and with every nation in Europe represented here, it would seem that there is scarcely a nation in the world which has not helped to make up the cosmopolitan community. Malays, Parsees, Sikhs, Japanese, Koreans, Annamese, Brahmins, Hindus, Singalese, Persians, Turks and Javanese are only a few of the many races to be seen on the streets.

The international nature of Shanghai's population may be judged from the great number of national clubs established here. In addition to many national associations, there are the American, British, French, Japanese, German, Portuguese, Swiss, Italian, and Jewish clubs. The schools also show the international character of the city. Not long ago one school gave a program which included recitations in twenty-two different languages by students of the same number of nationalities. So cosmopolitan is the population of Shanghai that it has acquired the name of "a miniature League of Nations."

The native city, which gives its name to the now important port of Shanghai, is of no great importance commercially. It was only a small village when it was first known in the kingdom of Wu, the feudal State of which Soochow was the capital. When Shi Hwang-ti, who built the Great Wall of China, captured the delta, he made Shanghai a *hsien*, or district, and during the Sung dynasty the name of Shanghai began to be used,

the first mention being chronicled in A.D. 1075. Before
the foreigners came and developed it into China's largest
port, it was only a small fishing port enclosed by a sturdy
wall to protect it against the inroads of marauding
Japanese pirates, and could boast of no more importance
than that of being a port of call for seagoing junks and
the home of a fishing fleet of about four hundred vessels.
When the Treaty of Nanking was signed in 1842 between
China and Great Britain, Shanghai was included as the
most northern of the five ports to be made open to foreign
residence and trade. It is no longer considered to be a
part of North China, although the earlier geographical
division is perpetuated in the name of the oldest
newspaper, the North China Daily News. The settlement
was formally opened on November 17, 1843, and at first
grew very slowly. At the end of the first year as an open
port, Shanghai had but 23 foreign residences, one consular
flag, 11 business firms and two missionaries. To-day there
are approximately 700 foreign firms engaged in foreign
trade in Shanghai, employing about 9,000 foreigners and
60,000 Chinese.

The site which had been selected for a British
Settlement was little more than a reed-covered marsh,
intersected by many small canals—what is now the
famous and imposing waterfront boulevard called "The
Bund" was then only a foot-path used by the trackers who
towed the boats. The settlement limits were marked by
what are now Peking Road, Avenue Edward VII, Honan
Road and The Bund. One of the first tasks of foreign
residents was to make this place habitable. How well
that work has been accomplished can only be appreciated
by a visit to this modern and progressive city. Six
years after the British Settlement was marked out, the
Chinese government gave territory to France for a
settlement between the Chinese city and the British
Concession. In the late fifties Americans leased ground
on the north of the British Settlement, although the
so-called American Settlement was never formally taken

over by the American government. Later the British and American Settlements were combined as the International Settlement, while that of the French remains separate. Thus there are three distinct municipalities in Shanghai the Chinese municipality of Greater Shanghai which includes the cities of Nantao and Chapei, the French Concession and the International Settlement. These cities are separated only by streets so that the newcomer and many old residents pass from one city to another without knowing it.

Of these the International Settlement is the most important. A single self-governing community, it unites the subjects and citizens of many different nations under a municipal constitution of a popular character and the administration of an elected representative body, the Shanghai Municipal Council. The Council is composed of fourteen members in all, of which nominally five are British, two American, two Japanese and five Chinese. This body of public-spirited men, none of whom receives any remuneration for his services, has controlled the activities of the community since 1854. In that year the Settlement established a representative governing body and provided for the organization of a police force because of the large increase of Chinese population due to civil uprisings and rebellion throughout the land, and also because the Chinese authorities in 1853 were unable to afford protection to the Settlement against the dangers resulting from rebellion and civil war.

The activities of the Council are manifold. In the International Settlement taxes are uniformly and without discrimination imposed and collected in accordance with the requirements of the municipality. Thus the necessary revenue is provided which enables the Council to maintain its several departments. Of these, the Police Department provides an excellent police force and administers the jails and reformatories which it has established. The control and supervision of municipal cemeteries, the administration and maintenance of municipal hospitals, the examination of water, milk and ice-cream, the providing of clinics for vaccination against smallpox and the maintainance of public sanitation are only a few of the duties of the Public Health Department. The Public Works Department superintends the construction of roads, bridges, municipal buildings, bundings, parks and sewers, while the Education Department provides six municipal schools for foreign children and seven schools for Chinese. In addition to these departments, the Council maintains the Shanghai Fire Brigade, and the Shanghai Volunteer Corps, which, including the Light Horse, the American Troop, the Field Artillery, the Engineer Company, the Armoured Car Company, the Infantry Units, the Unit Reserves, the Special Reserve and the Russian Detachment, totals about 2,000 members in all, and has been called, by competent military authorities, "the most complete and efficient small army in the world." Since the close of the World War, it has undoubtedly seen more active service than any other army.

The International Settlement has the right to take active measures for its own protection against invasion or attack, the right to maintain an attitude of armed neutrality during Chinese wars, and the right to require all Chinese commanders, including commanders of Chinese government forces, to respect its neutrality by keeping their forces outside the Settlement limits. The years 1913, 1924, 1925 and 1927 are memorable in the history of Shanghai, for during these stirring times, the Settlement Volunteer Corps and police force, together with foreign naval and military re-enforcements which had come to their aid, had to resort to desperate measures to prevent the entry into the Settlement of Chinese military forces engaged in civil war on its borders. Justice is administered in the Settlement by fifteen national courts of fifteen different countries, and in addition to these there is also the Court of Foreign Consuls, which is an international court exercising jurisdiction in cases in which the Shanghai Municipal Council is the defendant.

Thus, under the long and honourable administration of the Council, this section of Shanghai has become known the world over as "The Model Settlement." Its modern buildings, clean, paved streets, and its prosperous air of business activity usually surprise the visitor who expects to find a Chinese city rather than one which has all the aspects of a Continental metropolis.

The French Concession, adjoining the International Settlement on the south, is administered by the French Consul-General and the French Municipal Council, which consists of four French councillors, elected by French electors, four foreign councillors, belonging to at least three different nationalities, elected by foreign electors, five Chinese councillors and three French councillors nominated by the Consul-General and the Commissioner for Foreign Affairs. At a first glance it might easily seem that the power and authority of the French Municipal Council is similar to that of the Shanghai Municipal Settlement. Upon closer inspection, however, it is of a very different type—the real powers of government are vested in the French Consul-General, the Council merely serving as an advisory body.

The Chinese areas, Chapei and Nantao, adjoining the Settlement and the French Concession, constitute the Chinese Municipality of Greater Shanghai, and are independent of district or provincial administrations, being under the direct control of the Central government at Nanking. They are administered by a mayor, appointed by the National Government and the directors of various administrative bureaus, and a chief secretary, also appointed by the government.

Shanghai is built on the low banks of the Whangpoo, a muddy river which flows with a deceptive lethargy into the great mouth of the Yangtsze, near the sea. In reality, it is a river of amazingly swift currents. The navigability of the Whangpoo, upon which the growth and prosperity of commercial Shanghai have been greatly dependent, was achieved through the enterprising efforts of the Whangpoo Conservancy Board, which consists of the Commissioner of Customs, the Harbor Master and a member appointed by the Chinese Government. In 1905 the river had two narrow channels of 8 and 10 feet, and a bar at the mouth of 15 feet at low tide. Since that time the Board has superintended the dredging and widening of the river, training walls have been built in many places by means of piles, brushwood mattresses, caissons and stone, so that now the Whangpoo has a navigable depth of 24 feet at low tide, and 32 feet at high tide, enabling large ocean steamers to make their way up-river to the docks conveniently situated near the center of the business district.

From the banks of the Whangpoo River the surrounding country extends for miles into a monotonously level plain, which, because of its fertility, is the garden spot of China. The great productiveness of this region, as well as the commanding position of Shanghai in the trade of the Yangtsze Valley, have combined to make it the most important business center of the Far East. Its trade territory embraces the great Yangtsze Valley with a population of about 200,000,000, or half the population of China.

The visitor coming up the Whangpoo sees but little that suggests China or the Orient. The river is crowded with shipping, the waters dotted with large and small steamers and freighters, tugs, lighters and barges. Here and there, it is true, he may see small brown sampans, their sails taut, scampering before the breeze, and occasionally a junk fleet putting out to sea; but more than likely this native craft is the only means he has of reassuring himself that he is in Chinese waters. The smoke stacks of many factories form a business-like pattern against the blue background of the sky, just as they do in London, or New York or any other of the larger cities throughout the world. On the shores there are huge ship-building plants, warehouses, cotton mills, silk filatures, oil tanks, docks and a busy line of railway, the branch of the Nanking-Shanghai line from Shanghai to Woosung. This was the first railway to be constructed in China, it being built from Shanghai to Kiangwan by a British firm in 1876. For a short time the road was run successfully, but soon there developed native opposition based on superstitious grounds, railways being thought to offend *feng shui* (spirits of wind and water), which grew to such serious proportions that the Chinese government bought the line. The rails and rolling stock were shipped to Formosa, then a Chinese possession and dumped on the beach there to disappear in rust. The present line was built many years later.

The traveler who arrives on a trans-Pacific steamer is usually landed at the Customs Jetty on The Bund, the principal street, which marks the waterfront of Shanghai. It is shaded and inviting, and behind the trees are the proud buildings of the city's largest banks and business houses. That strange mosaic which is Shanghai is well illustrated by the medley of vehicles which crowd The Bund at all times. These include tramcars, motor buses, carriages, motor cars, bicycles, ricshas, handcarts and wheelbarrows, all contending for the right of way.

The northern end of The Bund is marked by the Garden Bridge which spans Soochow Creek. It may be interesting to the newcomer to know that until a few years ago the slope over this bridge was the steepest to be found on any Shanghai road, and that motor cars which could negotiate it had achieved the most gruelling hill climbing test Shanghai could offer. The Szechuen Road bridge two blocks west now has that distinction, its grade being a few degrees steeper. The river life as seen from the Soochow Creek bridges is always amusing. The creek is usually crowded with native boats, for much of the cargo discharged from vessels anchored in the stream is brought up this creek for storage in warehouses and godowns along Soochow Road. The public garden on The Bund at the junction of Soochow Creek and the Whangpoo River is largely made ground. A small vessel was wrecked near the center of the garden and mud collected around it. The surrounding marsh, formerly a part of the grounds of the British Consulate, was ceded to the Settlement by the British Foreign Office, and here the handsome garden was built. In the garden and on The Bund lawn are a number of monuments. Just inside the southwest gate of the garden is a monument to the foreign officers of the "Ever-Victorious Army" who fell in attacks against the Taiping rebels.

At the termination of Nanking Road is a statue of Sir Harry Parkes, British Minister to China, 1882-1885. Before going to Peking as British Minister, he had served as British Consul at Canton, Amoy and Shanghai, and as Minister to Japan and Korea. Near by, at the front of and facing the Customs Building, is a statue of Sir Robert Hart, who was for so many years Inspector-General of the Chinese Maritime Customs, and to whom much of the credit for organising that efficient service is due.

Many of the finest business buildings in Shanghai are located on The Bund. In the early days of the settlement, all of the business houses were on this waterfront. Land was cheap, and pioneer firms provided themselves with liberal sites. With few exceptions, they have kept their original locations, so that here, as elsewhere on the China coast, a Bund address has come to signify age and stability. Among the notable buildings are those of the Hongkong & Shanghai Bank, Jardine, Matheson & Co., Chartered Bank, Customs House, North China Daily News, Yokohama Specie Bank, Glen Line, Yangtsze Insurance and the Sassoon House. The British Consulate occupies a large area near the Garden Bridge. At the junction of The Bund and Jinkee Road is a striking building of German architecture, formerly the German Club, now the premises of the Bank of China. Near the junction with Avenue Edward VII, the street which separates the International Settlement from the French Concession, is the Shanghai Club, the oldest and most important organization of its kind in the city, famous

for the possession of what is reputed to be the longest
bar in the world.

Second in importance and in interest to The Bund is
Nanking Road, on which will be found the large foreign
and Chinese shops, the retail shopping street of the city.
A few years ago it was, except for a few blocks near
The Bund, composed almost entirely of two-storey native
shops. Now most of these have been replaced by what
has aptly been described as buildings of the "comprador-
esque" style of architecture. But the most striking buildings on the road are three great Chinese department stores
located at and near Chekiang Road crossing. Each store
is under Chinese management, and each, in addition to its
varied merchandise, maintains a modern hotel, roof garden
and restaurant.

Foochow Road, famous all over China for its restaurants, is decidedly worth visiting, especially at night
when it is ablaze with electric lights in huge, fantastic
signs. Here the epicure picks his way past shops of every
description, through the crowds gathered about fortune
tellers and street peddlers, to one of the restaurants for
which the Foochow Road tradition is so justly famous.
Since Shanghai is one of the most cosmopolitan of cities,
there are no restaurants serving food that can be said
to be characteristic of Shanghai. There is as much
difference between the food and cookery of Peking and
Canton as there is between that of Germany and Italy
and in fact there are numberless schools of cookery in
China, each with a definite following. Hence if one is
in search of the delectable Cantonese food, he goes to
Hang Fa Lau, at 526 Foochow Road. Da Ya Loo, at
231 Foochow Road, has an enviable reputation for its
Peking food, while only a block north, Toa Loo Chuen, at
243 Hankow Road, and Siao Yu Tien, at 148 Hankow
Road, tempt ones appetite with savory dishes of Szechuen
and Fukien fare. The average dinner at any of these
restaurants consists of four cold dishes, corresponding to
hors d'ouvre, four preliminary hot dishes, ten main courses,

four kinds of dessert, two of which are sweet, noodles, four dishes of meat or vegetables to accompany rice, and some kind of sweet gruel, generally made from almonds. There is one Cantonese restaurant on Nanking Road which serves a dinner costing $600. This provides food for the usual table of six persons and must be ordered days in advance. Apart from the fact that the courses appear with a regular frequency that is apparently endless, each dish of this veritable banquet is an epicurean delight in itself. To ensure accommodation at these restaurants, it is always best to make reservations in advance. No visitor who spends any length of time in Shanghai should forego the interesting experience of dining in a Chinese restaurant.

To the casual visitor in Shanghai, however, it is the infinite variety and number of cafés and restaurants that prove the measure of Shanghai's cosmopolitan nature. Glittering and gay, hushed and restrained, dozens of them beckon enticingly. In picturesque little Japanese houses one may have sukiyaki, eaten with chop sticks of course, and saké, served by charming little figures in bright flowered kimono. At various Russian restaurants hours slip by in the endeavor to survive and surmount those innumerable strange but delicious courses beginning with *zakouska* and the inevitable vodka, and ending with *plombier*, that triumph of Russian culinary art. Hidden away in one of the oldest sections of the city is an Italian restaurant where those with a zest for spaghetti and chianti and Verdi may indulge their particular weaknesses. German, French, Spanish, Austrian and Turkish restaurants or cafés are to be found, to say nothing of American restaurants which advertise ham and eggs and freshly percolated coffee. Each of these places, the visitor discovers, has retained its own peculiar identity—those singular qualities which set it apart from the others just as one country uniquely contrasts another.

Thibet Road marks the end of Nanking Road, for from that point on, the continuation of the street is picturesquely known as Bubbling Well Road, an avenue which once boasted

the finest residences of Shanghai and which is still one of
the most famous streets in the Far East. A mile from The
Bund at the junction of Bubbling Well and Nanking Roads
is the Public Recreation Ground. The presence of this
fine race track and recreation ground in the heart of the
city is a striking evidence of the rapid growth of Shanghai,
for in the sixties, when this magnificent piece of land was
acquired, it was barely on the outskirts of the city. Here
the semi-annual race meetings are held in spring and
autumn, and Shanghai maintains an old custom of its
sailing ship days by taking a half holiday on race days.

The races are held in the first week in May and November of each year on Saturday, Monday, Tuesday, Wednesday
and Saturday afternoons. The entries are all "China
ponies," that is, native Chinese ponies imported from
Mongolia. The riders are amateurs. Many of the more
prominent business men of the city not only maintain
stables, but ride in the races as well. The betting on the
races, which runs into large figures, is all on the pari-mutuel
basis; all the money wagered, except for a commission
charged by the Race Club, being divided among those
fortunate enough to pick the winning ponies. The feature
of each race meeting is the championship race, and the
lottery sweepstakes which accompany it. Each year
thousands of sweepstakes tickets are sold at $10 each, so
that the purchaser of a $10 ticket who is fortunate enough
to draw the winning pony will win approximately $200,000.
There are large second and third prizes as well. The Race
Club makes large profits, all of which are devoted to the
support of charitable organizations, hospitals and schools.
In addition to the racing oval, the grounds contain a golf
course, tennis courts, a polo field, baseball and cricket fields.

No visit to Shanghai would be complete without a drive
through the residential portions of the city. Formerly the
most pretentious residences were grouped about Bubbling
Well Road, but now there are many streets able to compete
with the older thoroughfare. The French Concession in
recent years has become the residential center for the

rapidly growing American and British communities, and
many delightful houses set in spacious gardens are found
on Avenue Haig and west of the shopping district on
Avenue Joffre. Recently many large modern apartment
houses have been built throughout the city. Nor should
one fail to drive around the Rubicon Road. From any hotel
the round trip can be made in leisurely fashion in an hour.
The road takes one out of sight and sound of the city and
affords an excellent opportunity to see the Chinese countryside. Other interesting motor roads lead to Woosung, Minghong and Liuho.

To list the parks, clubs, public buildings, etc., of
Shanghai would be as tedious a task as to list similar things
in any large commercial city of Europe or America.
Shanghai is a foreign rather than a Chinese city. In spite
of their great bulk, Chinese residents are more or less under
foreign influence. Anyone who studies China from the
point of view of Shanghai is sure to carry away wrong
impressions. Because of the size of the place and the
importance of the local foreign communities, Shanghai is,
to most Shanghai residents, sufficient unto itself. If the
traveler wishes to see Chinese life, or to study things
Chinese untouched by foreign influence, he must go elsewhere.

Shanghai is essentially a commercial city, as is evident
to the visitor as soon as he arrives. And although it is the
most important manufacturing city in China, it is still
comparatively young, for the first cotton mill was established only so long ago as 1890. The stretch of the
Whangpoo from Woosung to The Bund is always the
anchorage for dozens of ocean-going steamers, while on
both sides of the river are wharves, factories and warehouses. The Bund foreshore is usually crowded with boxes
and bales which coolies transport by means of long bamboo
poles on their shoulders, invariably smiling and keeping
step to the sounds of shrill, long drawn-out cries. The
customs revenue is more than three times that of any other
port in China, and amounts to 45 per cent. of the total for

all of China. The principal imports are cotton cloth, iron and steel, tobacco and mineral oil, while the most important exports are silk, tea, skins and wood oil. There are in Shanghai 61 cotton spinning and weaving works, 66 silk filatures, 34 iron foundries, 68 cigarette and tobacco factories, and, in addition, many soap, match and paper factories. Public utilities include the large Shanghai Power Company, the Shanghai Telephone Company, the Shanghai Electrical Construction Company, the Shanghai Omnibus Company, the Shanghai Gas Company and the Shanghai Waterworks Company.

Shanghai is also the publishing center of China. The largest and most important of Chinese newspapers are published here. One of them, the Shun Pao, occupies a structure which would do credit to any western city. Here, too, are located the large mission publishing houses and the headquarters of the bible societies which each year distribute thousands of bibles printed in the vernacular. Among the Chinese publishing enterprises worthy of note are the Commercial Press and the Chung Hwa Book Co., large establishments both, employing thousands of skilled Chinese workmen. Kiukiang Road near Avenue Edward VII is lined with dozens of smaller printing and book shops, where one may find anything from sheet music to bright colored scroll and calendars. These and other concerns turn out a constant stream of Chinese books, pamphlets and magazines, many of them consisting of translations of foreign books.

Until very recently the Chinese city known as Nantao remained unchanged by the proximity of the foreign settlements, and up to the time of the establishment of the Republic was still surrounded by walls which were first put up in the fourteenth century, and had been repaired and replaced many times. With the establishment of the Republic, the Chinese officials have shown more energy in cleaning up the streets, although much remains to be done. It is typical of the older type of Chinese cities, the narrow streets being crowded with small shops where all kinds of curios and Chinese goods may be purchased. Near the center of the city, in a small artificial lake, and reached by the zigzag bridges so common in China, is a famous tea-house, called the *Wu Sing Ding,* often pointed out as the original of the tea-house pictured in the famous willow pattern porcelain. This is a mistake, however, for the story of the willow pattern plate is older than this tea-house, which is only about 300 years old. In China there are many tea-houses of this type. There is nothing of particular interest to be seen in the building, but from the top a sweeping view of the tiled roofs of the city may be obtained. The city contains a number of temples, buildings and gardens of interest to the visitor. The *Doo Ka Say,* or Big Mountain Garden, now the headquarters of the Rice Guild, and the Mandarin's Garden, a pretty spot with its many old grottoes, rockeries, pavilions and an enchanting lotus pond, are not far from the tea-house. The Mandarin's Garden was given to the city a century ago by a rich official who had spent much time and money developing this as his private garden. It is a glimpse of old, peaceful China, in a city almost totally westernized. A few yards from the "willow pattern" tea-house is the city temple where thousands of Chinese, especially during Chinese New Year, go to burn incense and ask for good luck.

One of the most interesting points is the section given over to bird dealers, extremely well patronized. Nearby is a tea-house, where the patrons take their feathered pets and listen to their songs while they drink tea. Guides, not more than usually avaricious or untruthful, are always to be found loitering about the approaches, but more trustworthy ones may be secured from the hotel, or from travel agencies. The stranger is apt to lose his way in the narrow, crooked lanes, as in other Chinese cities, if he ventures into the city alone.

The finest Chinese shops are to be found in the International Settlement, where the fixed price system generally prevails and it is unnecessary to bargain for purchases. The best Chinese jewelry is to be found on Nanking Road, although the smaller places on the side streets ask much lower prices. Those in search of silks and furs should go to Honan Road, where they will find the largest and greatest variety of shops. Yates Road is famous the world over for its dainty feminine lingerie of embroidered *crepe de chine* and lace. Curio shops are to be found all over the city, for Shanghai, next to Peking, offers the richest stocks of curios to be found in the country. Finely drawn and embroidered table linen and old embroideries may be obtained at almost any of the Chinese shops on Nanking Road. One of the most interesting curio centers is in the native city, near the "willow pattern" tea-house. Here the small dealers spread their wares on the tables of a teahouse and await customers, meanwhile trading among themselves. Here, however, shrewd business acumen must be employed by the visitor or he will be charged excessive prices.

Siccawei Road leads to the settlement of that name established by the French Jesuits in 1847. The name of the place (literally Zi-Kai-Wei) means "Homestead of the Zi Family," recalling the famous Shanghai resident Zi Kwang-chi, a cabinet minister of the 16th century who became a convert of the Jesuit priest Matteo Rici and was a valuable ally of the early Christian missionaries. The Zi family have been Christians for more than 300 years. The settlement consists of a number of interesting buildings, in which useful missionary work is carried on. One of the principal groups of buildings is used as a convent, where Chinese girls are taught embroidery and lace-making. Many of these girls have been given to the convent by their impoverished parents. From year to year these inmates number several thousand. A short distance from the convent is the furniture and brass shop, maintained in a similar style for Chinese boys. Beautiful intricately carved teakwood furniture is their most famous production.

Established in 1873, one of the most complete meteorological observatories in the world is maintained here by the Jesuits. Its service covers all of the coast of China. Weather predictions are locally sent out twice daily, while typhoon warnings are sent to all the ports in the Far East. This service, as complete as the government weather services in other countries, saves many lives and thousands of dollars worth of shipping annually. It is maintained entirely at the expense of the Jesuits. They also provide, with the assistance of the municipal councils and shipping firms, a semaphore station on the French Bund where weather signals are displayed.

Shanghai is an important center for the administration and practical work of many Christian missionaries, as well as the business headquarters of a great number of missionary enterprises. Several societies have established offices in Shanghai, where the number of missionaries and allied workers is very large. The head office of the China Inland Mission, and the head office for China of the American Bible Society are here, as well as the headquarters of the Christian Literature Society and several similar organizations. St. John's University, one of the leading schools of China, established by the American Episcopal Mission, occupies its beautiful and spacious grounds on the outskits of the town. Among the other notable enterprises are St. Luke's Hospital and St. Elizabeth's Hospital for Women (American Episcopal Mission), the Hospital of St. Marie (Sisters of Charity), the Margaret Williamson Hospital for Women (Women's Union Mission), McTyeire High School for Chinese Girls (Methodist Episcopal Mission, South), and the Door of Hope with its several industrial schools. A large number of smaller schools, chapels, orphanages and nursing homes are to be found in all parts of the native cities and the two foreign areas. In addition to the schools maintained by the municipalities for China and foreign children, there are a great many public, private and semi-private schools, including the French School, the Jewish School, the American School and the Japanese School.

It is in Shanghai that the visitor will find his best opportunity to visit a Chinese theatre. Until a few years ago, the drama in China occupied about the same position as the Mediaeval drama of Europe. The plays were mostly of a religious or historical character, and were performed on appropriate anniversaries by strolling bands of players in temples or in the courtyards of large residences. Usually the players were paid for the performance by a guild, by a private individual, or by public subscription. With the growth of the large Chinese population in the foreign settlement of Shanghai, western ideas made great changes in the drama of China, so that now there are in Shanghai several pretentious Chinese theatres conducted on western lines. Within the past few years, there have been a number of foreign plays translated into Chinese, and others have been written about foreign characters. Formerly actors were placed at the bottom of the social scale, along with barbers and beggars. But the Empress Dowager did a great deal to put an end to the social ignominity of actors, for she was very much interested in theatricals and received many famous actors at the palaces and the old prejudice against actors has disappeared. The Chinese actor realizes that his attraction and the value of his reputation is enhanced by his inaccessability and the rareness of his appearances. But even if one has not the fortune of seeing one of the nationally famous actors, it is decidedly amusing to attend at least one performance. During the course of an evening (the usual program starts at eight and continues until well past one in the morning) several short plays and sketches are presented, very much in the manner of foreign vaudeville.

Shanghai is famous for its night life which supports dozens of cabarets, cafes and night clubs. These are to be found in all parts of the city and range from places which cater to soldiers and sailors to rather exclusive establishments. The dancing partner is a Shanghai institution and is to be found in most of the cabarets. The visitor who spends a night visiting these places will naturally wonder how the Shanghai resident manages to get any work done after staying up most of the night. As a matter of fact, there is always a very large transient population in

Shanghai and it is the visitors who give Shanghai night life its colour and support.

Included in the attractions of night life in Shanghai are dog racing and Hai Alai. Regular meets where greyhounds pursue the mechanical hare are held at the Canidrome in the French Concession and are attended by thousands. As in the case of horse racing, the betting is on a pari-mutuel basis and large amounts of money change hands at every meeting. The Basque game of Hai Alai is played at the Auditorium located near the Canidrome and the spectators have an opportunity to place bets on their favorite players. This is one of the few places in the World where this difficult and interesting game can be seen.

At Sungkiang, 25 miles southwest of Shanghai on the Shanghai-Hangchow Railway, is the grave of General Frederick Ward, the American who fought against the Taipings and who organized the "Ever Victorious Army" taken over by General Gordon after Ward's death. The cemetery, which contains also the temple erected by the Chinese in honour of Ward, is outside the West Gate of Sungkiang. Ward was severely wounded in an engagement in Chekiang province, September 20, 1862, and died the next day. His body was brought back to Sungkiang, where he had recruited his Chinese volunteers. A tablet at the tomb sets forth his praises as follows: "An illustrious man from beyond the seas, he came 6,000 *li* to accomplish great deeds and acquire an immortal fame by shedding his noble blood. Because of him Sungkiang shall be a happy land for a thousand autumns. This temple and statue shall witness to his generous spirit." Every year at Easter time the local Frederick Ward Post of the American Legion makes a pilgrimage to the tomb around which are many graves of Chinese soldiers killed in the civil war of 1924.

There are any number of interesting trips to be made in and about Shanghai—short ones for the traveler who has but a few brief hours to spare, and longer ones for those who have the time to really see something of this fascinating country. With the building of motor roads many short excursions into the surrounding countryside are possible, as well as longer trips to famous places like Hangchow and Nanking. Comfortable ferry boats provide pleasant excursions on the Whangpoo River. Interesting cities such as Soochow and Sungkiang can be reached in a few hours by rail and of course there are houseboats available for those who have time to avail themselves of this very comfortable and interesting method of seeing the Chinese countryside.

Among the trips which may be made from Shanghai are the following:

Shanghai to Kaochiao, via Hsitu, Ching Ning Hsih and Tungkou.—The Shanghai city government maintains a fleet of well equipped ferry boats connecting places of importance on both sides of the Whangpoo River. The trip from the Nanking Road Jetty to Kaochiao ferry Jetty, stopping at Hsitu, Ching Ning Hsih and Tungkou, may be made in one hour and twenty minutes. From the Kaochiao jetty a motor bus may be taken to the village from where it is about an hour's walk to the sandy beach on the Yangtsze shore. Here the bathing is popular in the summer months, while not far away is a quaint village. There is a foreign style hotel at Kaochiao.

Shanghai to Woosung.—This trip may be made by motor car, past the Hungjao Golf Club, and the Chinese Military Aerodrome by way of the new Chung Hsan Road, past the Kiangwan Race Course, and from there along the tree-lined road following the Whangpoo to Woosung Forts at the junction of the Yangtsze and the Whangpoo Rivers. Lunch may be obtained at the Woosung Forts Hotel, after which the afternoon may be spent in visiting the walled village of Paoshan and leisurely returning to Shanghai.

Shanghai to Minghong.—An interesting trip taking only a half-day, the excursion to Minghong is made by motor car through the French Concession, through the charming countryside dotted with tiny villages. Here the traveler may see the far-famed river scenes so typical of China.

Shanghai to Liuho.—Another of the shorter trips which the visitor should not forego, this is made by motor car through the country to the interesting village of Liuho, 20 miles north of Shanghai on a tributary of the Yangtsze and totally untouched by the influences of western civilization. The trip may easily be made in a half-day.

Shanghai Hills.—Fully a whole day is required for this excursion into the pleasant Shanghai Hills. Leaving the hotel at 6 a.m., the traveller proceeds by motor car to the intersection of Hungjao Road and Rubicon Creek, continuing from there in a houseboat by way of Siccawei Creek to Zosé, lying at the foot of one of the group of Shanghai Hills. After lunching, visit the famous observatory established by the Jesuit fathers at the top of the hill and the pretty Catholic Church, and then continue by houseboat south to Sunkiang, where the tomb of General Frederick Ward may be visited. A train to Shanghai may be taken at 5.58 or at 9.18, arriving at the North Station at 7.30 and 10.38 respectively.

Shanghai to the Loonghwa Pagoda.—The visitor who cannot visit any other city in China should see the Loonghwa Pagoda, easily reached in an hour by motor car through the French Concession and the adjoining countryside. The pagoda is by no means a fine one, but it is typical of this peculiar type of Chinese architecture. A climb to the top gives an excellent view of the surrounding country.

Shanghai to Hangchow to Wusih and Soochow, via Taihu Lake and including Mokanshan.—One of the most interesting of trips, this may be made in three days. Leaving Shanghai by train at 6 p.m., the visitor arrives in Hangchow at 10.15. After a night spent at the Lakeview Hotel, a chair trip may be made through the city, stopping at the North Mountains, the monasteries and caves, visiting the tomb of Yao, the Cave of the Purple Cloud, the Cave of the Yellow Dragon, the Gem spring of the Dancing Fish, the Monastery of Ling Yin, and the Monastery of Secluded Light. The afternoon may be spent in a motor car visiting other temples and monasteries, or on the lake in a boat visiting Liu's Villa, Waung's Villa, Island of Three Pools of the Moon's Reflection, Pavilion of the Lake's Heart, and the grave of Su Hsiao Hsiao. The next morning Hangchow is left by motor car for Mokan-shan, a quiet mountain resort famed for its beauty. After driving through interesting Chekiang villages and towns along canals, where one sees the picturesque cormorant fishing, and after passing through delightful bamboo groves, the car arrives at Yue Chung at the foot of Mokan-shan Mountain. Here it is necessary to transfer to sedan chairs for the ascent of the steep mountainside, at the summit of which a popular summer resort was started by missionaries many years ago. Here nestling bungalows are protected by dense bamboo groves, and here one may have a sweeping view of the fertile Chekiang plains. Lunch at the Railway Hotel, operated during the summer season by the Shanghai-Hangchow-Ningpo Railway, and then return to Yue Chung by a different route. From here continue to Huchow by motor car, and there spend the night in the Chinese hotel. The next morning Huchow is left by steamer at 6 a.m., proceeding through interesting canals and crossing the beautiful Taihu Lake to Wusih, an ancient walled city on the north shore of Taihu Lake. After luncheon, Wusih is left by rail, arriving at Soochow at 2.58 p.m. At Soochow either a hurried visit of the city may be made, or the night may be spent there at one of several hotels. If possible, the traveler should remain to make a leisurely tour of the Great Pagoda, the Twin Pagoda, the Beamless Temple, Tiger Hill Pagoda and the City Temple, as well as various other spots for which Soochow is so justly famed.

HOUSEBOATING AROUND SHANGHAI.

House-boating in China can be divided roughly into two categories, the first being confined to Chinese and fore'gn house-boats without motive power and those with motive power. In Shanghai are to be found large numbers of house-boats belonging to both categories. Of the former the majority are privately owned, but there are also a considerable number available for hire. With the exception of a very few, all power driven house-boats are privately owned; most of those available for hire are owned by one of the ferry-boat companies. The so-called discomforts invariably connected with house-boating in the old days by some people have largely disappeared, and it is now possible to purchase for a very low price or to hire for a reasonable rental boats with or without power embodying practically all the comforts found in a modern home. This is particularly the case with the power boats.

The ordinary old fashioned (*yuloh*) house-boat used by foreigners usually contains two or more comfortable bunks, a saloon, kitchen and pantry with a large sized kitchen range, adequate lighting, either by electric plants, or acetylene or kerosene lamps. Lighting sets are being used more and more, and they add greatly to the comforts available, particularly as it is also possible to instal in addition a small refrigerator service, which does away with the necessity of carrying ice. Suitable accommodation is provided on all boats for the crew, who are completely segregated.

It is not unusual for the ordinary house-boat to have a small motor boat tender to tow it along tideless creeks at a speed of anything from 4 to 8 miles an hour, and thus enables large distances to be covered, usually at night. In the absence of a motor boat tender the old fashioned house-boat is propelled by a *yuloh* (a very large stern oar) and should it be desired to reach places situated any distance from Shanghai it is necessary to take a tow from one of the many steam launches operating between Shanghai and practically all important towns within a radius of 150 miles. The launch trains which are used for this purpose are restricted to seven house-boats or cargo boats and they usually leave Shanghai round about 4 o'clock in the afternoon and, traveling all night, reach their terminus anything from 80 to 150 miles away either in the early hours of the morning or before tiffin the next day according to the distance involved. Traveling in tow of the launch train is extremely comfortable; the house-boat glides along without sound or motion and it has the great merit of rendering the covering of great distances possible without breaking into daylight hours, which trippers naturally like to use tramping the countryside and sightseeing. Towing charges are very reasonable.

Having reached the terminus of the launch train, the house-boat then travels under *yuloh* to its final destination. In the Soochow and Wusieh district it may be the neigh-bouring hills or the Taihu Lake; at Hangchow and Huchow the beautiful well-wooded hills in the neighbourhood of Mokanshan, or Chapoo with its rambling hills and sea beaches along the Hangchow Bay. There is game in abundance in practically all places.

The *yuloh* house-boat can be taken along any creeks with a minimum depth of 2 feet and it is possible to reach the most beautiful and otherwise inaccessible spots by this means. They may be rented for Tls. 10 to Tls. 15 per day, according to size and accommodation.

Motor house-boats are invariably more elaborately fitted than *yuloh* house-boats and in all cases they are fitted with electric light and most other modern comforts. They have the great advantage of making it possible to travel long distances at will, but certain restrictions are imposed by their draft, which usually exceeds 3 feet and it is not therefore possible for them to reach many of the numerous backwaters which are available to *yuloh* house-boats. In order to overcome this drawback, however, it is usual for each motor house-boat to have a tender in the form of a shallow draft motor sampan, by which means the tripper is able to navigate all waters.

When hiring *yuloh* or motor house-boats it is almost invariably necessary to pay the wages of additional coolies over and above the permanent crew which are essential on most trips. These charges work out at approximately $1 per day per man including food. On the *yuloh* houseboat

11

six additional coolies are carried, in the motor house-
boat probably two, over and above the permanent crew.
It is also necessary to take personal servants in the way
of cook and boy, but usually one servant is sufficient and,
of course, all provisions have to be provided by the hirer.
This latter can more easily be arranged by the uninitiated
through hotels or restaurants or arrangements can be made
through a travel agency.

Favourite trips are as follows:—

Shanghai Hills—(Zosè). Actually 15 miles from
Shanghai as the crow flies, but 6 or 8 times that distance
by the Whangpoo River or Soochow Creek. The former
route is the most attractive, as one passes through the
neighbourhood of Sungkiang with its beautiful creeks and
backwaters. At Zosè is situated the Observatory of the
Jesuit Fathers and Observatory Hill holds many attractions.

Seetai Lakes situated 60 miles from Shanghai up the
Whangpoo River. A beautiful series of fresh water lakes
reaching almost to Soochow, with abundant game in the
season.

Chapoo, Haiyen, Kanpu, all on the Hangchow Bay from
80 to 120 miles from Shanghai, providing hill scenery,
beaches and an abundance of game.

Huchow to the south of the Taihu Lake, 120 miles from
Shanghai, from which it is possible to reach the most
beautiful hill scenery within many hundreds of miles of
Shanghai, and an abundance of game.

Soochow, which can be reached either by the Soochow
Creek (about 80 miles) or through the Seetai Lakes, which
is a considerably longer distance but provides a more
beautiful journey. Within easy reach of Soochow are:—
53 Arch Bridge, Sanfangse (9 Arch Bridge), Seeke and
Kuanfoong (on the Taihu Lake, known as the Garden of
China).

The above are but a few of the many beautiful places
within reach of the house-boat and in the event of visitors
desiring to reach certain of the places mentioned with the

least possible delay so as to have more time available at the resort visited, it is possible to send the house-boat ahead and reach it by train at, say, Hangchow, Soochow or other stations in the neighbourhood of the resort to be visited.

HANGCHOW.

This city with a population of 524,012, is located on the Shanghai-Hangchow-Ningpo Railway near the Ch'ien T'ang River, 125 miles southwest of Shanghai. Several first class trains run daily between Shanghai and Hangchow, a journey of about five hours. The trip by motor road from Shanghai can be made in about the same time. Several Chinese hotels serve foreign style meals but the Lakeview Hotel is especially recommended. Motor cars are available at the station.

Among the renowned cities of China, Hangchow, the capital of Chekiang Province, holds a most important place. Few other cities have played such an important part in the dramatic history of the country and few others are as picturesque, though most of its ancient glories have disappeared and the city is only a fraction of the size it was in its prime. In point of historical interest Hangchow is second only to Peking, while for the beauty of its surroundings it is second to no other city in China.

The earliest notes we have of the site of Hangchow date back to the time of the great King Yu, about 2198 B.C., who organized the river systems of China and stopped the floods. In his travels he is said to have landed here, hence the original name of the city, Yu Hang, the "Place of the Boat-landing by Yu."

About 210 B.C., the first emperor of the Ch'in dynasty came to the foot of the hill where the Needle Pagoda now stands and moored his boat to the large rock now known as the Great Buddha. Evidently even at that time the plain of Hangchow was flooded by the sea. From early times to considerably later than the Christian era the present City Hill and what is now known as Phoenix Hill were occupied by fishermen.

In A.D. 606 Yang Su built the first city walls and changed the early name to the present name of Hangchow. The walls he built are said to have been 36 *li* and 90 paces in circumference. In 893, Ch'ien Liu, before he became the first of the famous Wu-Yueh Kings, rebuilt the walls of Hangchow with the circumference enlarged to 70 *li* or about 23 miles.

Then under the famous Wu-Yueh Kings, A.D. 900-980, four in all, there came Hangchow's golden age of building, when most of the famous monasteries, temples and all the pagodas were built. It was during this period that the first dyke walls were built, by Ch'ien Liu, about A.D. 910 and since then his name has ever been associated with this great work of engineering, in spite of the fact that many subsequent alterations have been made. These dykes were built to hold the tidal wave or bore within certain reasonable shore and river limits.

The second golden age in the history of Hangchow came in the times of the Southern Sung Dynasty, 1130-1278. Hangchow became the center of foreign trade in China. "Here the Parsee could be seen worshiping the rising sun or bowing at his fire altar, or carrying a corpse to the Tower of Silence: here the Jew intoned his law and rested on the Sabbath: here the Christian, who had come overland from Persia, read his Syriac Bible: here too the Moslem built his mosque, whence the muezzin chanted five times daily the sonorous call to prayer."

In 1278 great Mongol hordes invaded and captured Hangchow, demolished its splendid walls and took vengeance on its inhabitants. Great libraries, both public and private, for which the city was renowned, were confiscated and burned. Thousands of families were utterly annihilated and their estates confiscated.

Marco Polo visited Hangchow, following the Mongol invasion, and his description of the city shows that much of its ancient grandeur had remained and some of it had been restored. Even then, in art, literature and commerce it was the Queen City of the Orient, the center of Oriental fashions and gaiety. Hither came merchants, travelers, missionaries and adventurers to view the place and enjoy its material delights. The account that Marco Polo gives reads almost like the stories of ancient Rome in regard to the sensual indulgences of the people.

Friar Odoric, who visited China in 1324-1327 wrote of it as follows: "Departing thence I came unto the city of Cansay, (Hangchow), a name which signifieth the City of Heaven and 'tis the greatest city in the whole world, so great indeed that I should scarcely venture to tell of it, but that I have met in Venice people in plenty who have been there. It is a good hundred miles in compass, and there is not in it a span of ground that is not well peopled. And many a tenement is there that shall have ten or twelve households comprised in it. And there lie also great suburbs which contain a greater population than even the city itself. This city is situated upon lagoons of standing water, with canals like the city of Venice and it hath more than 12,000 bridges on each of which are stationed guards, guarding the city on behalf of the Great Khan. But if any one should desire to tell all the vastness and great marvels of this city, a good quire of stationery would not hold the matter, I trow. For 'tis the grandest and noblest city and the finest for merchandise that the whole world containeth."

After the Mongols were driven out, about 1359, Chang Shih Hsin rebuilt the walls and his admiring biographers say that because of the great military emergency which existed the work was completed in three days and three nights, a record which might well shame our engineers with modern ideas of efficiency. The walls were thirteen miles in circumference and thirty feet high. The record states that in order to build the walls in this short space of time it required 540,000 stone masons, 50,000 carpenters, 360,000 plasterers, 6,675 metal workers and 4,500,000 coolies. The stone for this work was quarried from near the site of the present Needle Pagoda.

In 1651, Emperor Shun Chih of the Ch'ing Dynasty

built the wall of the recent Tartar City, which wall has been torn down since the Revolution and the entire section has been made into the present modern city. In this same Ch'ing or Manchu Dynasty, Hangchow was honored by several visits from two of China's greatest emperors, K'ang Hsi and Ch'ien Lung. Many evidences of the visits of these emperors exist to-day in temples, tablets, and in specially constructed roads.

In 1860 and again in 1862 the Taiping Rebels came to Hangchow and in a few months reduced nine-tenths of the city to ashes and utter ruin. It is stated that four-fifths of the inhabitants were massacred, or committed suicide, while the remainder were driven from the city. According to local chronicles the canals were so full of the bodies of those who had committed suicide that those later wishing to end their existence could not find sufficient water in which to drown themselves. Even the West Lake was so filled with dead bodies that one could walk out on them for a distance of a half *li*.

Since the establishment of the Republic Hangchow has made notable civic progress. The Tartar City section is one of the finest of its kind in all China. In few other cities in China will one find finer or broader streets. The provincial authorities have kept pace with the municipal development with the result that Hangchow is now the center of a net work of fine motor roads by which it is possible to reach such distant places as Nanking and Shanghai. Hangchow has always been famous for its beauty and has been a favorite resort for Chinese of the wealthier class. Probably no other city of its size in China has so many hotels and restaurants. The city abounds in pleasant little gardens and parks and altogether has the air of the pleasure resort that it is.

A variety of industries are carried on in Hangchow. Like Soochow it has been noted for centuries for its silk manufacture which in recent years, through the introduction of hand-looms, has had a marked revival. Among the ancient industries which have survived is the manufacture of "joss paper," made from paper and tin foil. Even this industry has become modernized for they now make imitations of silver dollars rather than the former clumsy representations of the silver sycee.

The most famous fan shop as well as the most famous drug shop in China are to be found in this city. One wall of the fan shop is covered with certificates of awards received at foreign expositions. The drug shop is uncontaminated by modern ideas and dispenses nothing but remedies approved by the Chinese pharmacopeia. Attached to the establishment are a large number of deer kept in cages. Every part of the deer is used in making medicine. The medicine made from the horns is considered by the Chinese to be especially efficacious as a tonic to prolong life. That made from the very tips of the horns sells at $100 an ounce. A modern electric light plant, two cotton mills, six silk filatures, a soap factory, match factory, and other institutions, are among the enterprises which mark Hangchow's participation in the industrial development of China.

The Needle Pagoda or "Prince Shu's Protecting Pagoda" with the other famous pagodas of Hangchow date back to the great building period of the Wu-Yueh Kings, approximately A.D. 1000. There are two accounts concerning this one. The first account is that it was originally built by one of the Wu-Yueh Kings, and later that it was rebuilt by a Buddhist priest. This priest was stricken with blindness for the recovery of which he took a vow. On his recovery he fulfilled his vow by rebuilding the pagoda. The other account is that the last of the Wu-Yueh Kings, went to the capital to offer his allegiance the Sung Emperor. He feared he would not live to return and made a vow that if his fears proved groundless he would build a pagoda as a token of gratitude. As he was cordially received by the Emperor and permitted to return to Hangchow in peace he built this pagoda which commemorated his divine protection while absent from home.

On the opposite or southern side of the lake are the

ruins of the Thunder Peak Pagoda, also called the White Snake Pagoda. This structure was given its peculiar name because of a legend built up about it. An enchantress called White Snake, who could change her form and often appeared as a beautiful woman, was buried under this pagoda by the Goddess of Mercy to make atonement for her past and to prepare her for the immortals. Her story fills a large volume and is one of the most famous of Hangchow legends.

It is also interesting to note that of the ancient structures in Hangchow this was the only one consisting of red bricks and built long before red bricks were made in Chinese kilns. About four centuries ago the coast was infested by Japanese pirates. They regarded the pagoda as a point of vantage for spying upon them in their approach from the sea so they built a great fire around it and for three days and nights it was burned, until all the outside framework was destroyed and the outer bricks were burned red. The bricks at the core retained their original bluish colour. There has long been a superstition that the dust ground from the bricks of the pagoda, if scattered upon the rice fields, would insure good crops and if steeped in tea it had peculiar medicinal properties. At every pilgrim season quantities of brick were chipped from the base and carried to the country districts. This had been done to such an extent that for a quarter of a century the base has been too slender to carry the huge bulk above and the ruin of the pagoda had been predicted. In September 1924 the prediction was fulfilled, and this much loved and admired memorial with its romance and legend fell in ruins.

In digging among the debris it was found that many of the bricks were hollow and into some of them were sealed rolls of Buddhist prayers and portions of Buddhist sacred books written on silk. It has been suggested that this was the method used to preserve to future generations the sacred Buddhist literature. While most of these copies had disintegrated beyond recognition, some were well preserved and sold for very high prices.

The Six Harmonies Pagoda is located on the Ch'ien T'ang River about a mile from the terminal railway station Zahkou. In China "the six harmonies" means "everywhere," that is, the four points of the compass plus up and down. This pagoda was built to harmonise the geomantic influence of these six points. Another reason for its erection was to stay the force of the Hangchow Bore which in ancient times was more violent than it is to-day. It was built in the times of the Wu-Yueh Kings by a priest whose name meant "The Prolongation of Life." It differs from the other pagodas mentioned above in that it has an outside superstructure. The others have only the original core. The inner core of stone and brick consists of thirteen stories while the outer superstructors has seven stories. This wooden portion was built in 1895 at a cost of $175,000. It is one of the largest pagodas in all China.

Approximately the year A.D. 260 a Buddhist monk, came from his home in India to the beautiful valley where the Monastery of Ling Yin or "Soul's Retreat" is located. The scenery was so similar to his native haunts that he named the hill to the left of the present main road the "Peak that Flew Over (from India)." In proof of his testimony he called forth from a cave some distance from the real entrance, two small white monkeys. In the "Peak that Flew Over" are some of the oldest relics of Hangchow, carved Buddhas that date back to as far as A.D. 600. In front of this peak is also a small pagoda which marks the tomb of the Indian monk. Passing two pavilions one enters "The Temple of the Kings of Heaven" in the center of which is the Laughing Buddha who welcomes the incoming pilgrims and who smiles upon all, whether good or evil. At his back is Wei T'o who is Commander in Chief of the Four Heavenly Kings. These latter are in the four corners of the hall, and form the temple guardians. Beginning with the nearest figure on the right going from east to south, north and west the first deity has a kind of mandolin, the purpose of which is to rectify with music the hearts of men. The second has a sword to destroy evil spirits.

The third has an umbrella to cover and to give protection and the fourth has a snake wherewith to overcome all evil. This arrangement of images is to be found in almost all Buddhist temples and monasteries in China.

In the main hall of the monastery are immense figures the central one being that of Buddha. The main figure at the beholder's right is Yao Shih, a physician who represents the future ages. The one at the left is A Mi T'o who represents the ages of the past and the intermediate figure on the left is A Nan, both of whom were disciples of Gotama. On the sides of this main hall are the principal Lohan or disciples of Gotama. At the back of the main group is a large image of the Goddess of Mercy (Kwan Yin). This is one of the most important of Buddhist deities and is here represented as the guardian of the sea. About her on the water and in the clouds are her attendants and lesser deities who are under her control. This particular representation at Lin Yin is of special interest because of its magnitude and workmanship. To the left of the main hall is the "Hall of the Five Hundred Lohan," also disciples of Gotama, among whom can be seen what some believe to be the image of Marco Polo who visited Hangchow about 1280. The man hall was built in 1911 at a cost of $200,000. Most of the lumber used in its construction is of Oregon pine. The erection of some of these huge pillars by primitive methods is a wonderful example of Chinese engineering.

The Upper Monastery of India is farther up the same valley in which the Ling Yin Monastery is located and dates back to A.D. 940 when a priest saw here a gleaming log of wood and carved from it an image of the Goddess of Mercy. In the three main halls of his monastery which is dedicated solely to the goddess, she appears under different forms and names, the inner temple being dedicated to her as a goddess who grants children. There are many imposing tablets in the main hall, testimonials to her prayer-answering power.

The Monastery of Manifest Congratulations was built

about A.D. 967. It is especially noted for its "Altar of the Oath" which is in a hall at the rear of the grounds. Here it is that men take their vows as priests and have the markings on the crowns of their heads burned in with incense, each mark registering one vow they have taken. In the main hall the principal figures are covered with the old fashioned official umbrellas, a sight not common to-day.

The principal points of interest on the West Lake are the Imperial Island, called Ku-Shan (Solitary Hill) by the Chinese, also the lake dykes or causeways. About A.D. 821 a lock was built on the lake so as to store up water and deliver it at will for the irrigation of the country to the north-east. In A.D. 1090 the great Hangchow poet Su Tung P'o deepened the lake and built the causeway named after him on the western margin. About 1130 and later the lake and Imperial Island were made famous by the residence of the Southern Sung Emperors. In 1700 and later the great Manchu Emperors K'ang Hsi and Ch'ien Lung built their palaces on Imperial Island. In addition to visiting the various memorial halls and the very interesting provincial museum on the island one should visit the public park, originally the site of one of the palaces of Emperor Ch'ien Lung. From the upper part of the park one can get a fine view of the lake.

A sr ler island is known as Island of the Three Pools and the _loon's Reflection (San T'an Yin Yueh). In the times of the Wu-Yueh Kings there was a pond here for the "Preservation of Life." Near the shore of the island are to be seen three small iron pagodas in the lake. When the poet Su was commissioned to dig and to improve the lake it is said that here there were three pits occupied by evil spirits. He caused three pagodas to be built over these pits and thus locked up the spirits so that boats could pass without fear. The original pagodas are not to be seen to-day but are replaced by more modern structures. On the island is the "Bridge of Nine Windings." There are also some memorial halls and pavilions for the pleasure of guests.

The "Pavilion of the Lake's Heart" is the name of a small island where was once a monastery which was destroyed in the Ming Dynasty because of the ill-repute of its priests. The small temple now on the island is dedicated to the worship of the Dragon King.

If one has the time it is worth while to visit the Mohammedan Mosque built in the T'ang Dynasty. This mosque is one of the ancient landmarks of Hangchow. If possible, it would also repay the tourist to visit the City Hill and from there get a view of the city, the bay and the Ch'ien T'ang River, also the lake and the surrounding hills. It is a view of picturesque beauty uncommon in China.

CHEKIANG PROVINCE.

Chekiang is the smallest of the eighteen provinces of China proper, containing 36,680 square miles, with a population of 22,043,300. Though it is known in a general way to travelers, few realise how much scenic beauty it contains.

Rice is the principal crop of the province, practically all of the country being intersected with natural streams and artificial waterways used for irrigating the rice fields. The silk industry is also important and in Hangchow, the capital, the finest guild hall of the city is that of the Silk Guild. Many parts of the province are covered with forests of mulberry trees so dense that one can easily lose one's way in them unless previously acquainted with the general direction of the little paths that run through them.

Tea is largely grown in the hill districts and that cultivated near Hangchow is famous, especially that which is called "Dragon Well" a variety of green tea from the Dragon Well Valley which was served to the old Imperial Household previous to the founding of the Republic. Fishing is an important industry on the rivers and canals and along the coast, and in the country around Ningpo may be found many ice houses, virtually huge straw huts, where ice is stored to be used for the preservation of fish caught by the fleets of boats when at sea.

From an historical standpoint, few provinces are more interesting than Chekiang, which was for many centuries the southernmost part of China, all to the south of this province being given over to barbarian tribes. The ancient Emperors Shun and Yü are frequently mentioned in the annals of the province, which also mention the visits of the first emperor of the Chin Dynasty (255-206 B.C.) and K'ang Hsi and Ch'ien Lung of the Manchu line. Chang Tao-ling, the "pope" of the Taoists, was born 34 A.D. in this province. Chekiang was overrun by the Taiping rebels who took all of its principal cities and laid most of its territories waste.

The principal cities are Hangchow, the capital, Ningpo and Shaohing. The latter place is much older than Ningpo, while Hangchow is comparatively modern. There is evidence that Shaohing existed as far back as 2200 B.C. and that the great Yü held court there after the flood. His tomb is situated in the country not far from the city of Shaohing and constitutes one of the famous sights of Chekiang.

By way of the port of Haimen 80 miles south of Shanghai one can visit the T'ien-Tai monasteries which are famous throughout China. They are built on mountains from three to four thousand feet above sea level and have long constituted a center for higher Buddhism, sometimes visited by Japanese and Korean priests. They date from the visit of an Indian monk who came there over a thousand years ago. In connection with one of the monasteries are 108 hermitages, running along the bank of a lovely mountain stream, in the midst of thick woods. The begging bowl of the Indian founder, is also shown. There are fine virgin forests, beautiful streams and many striking waterfalls.

Indeed some of the finest temples and monasteries in China are to be found in this province, which may have been the birthplace of Chinese Buddhism. Among the

many famous monasteries is Tien Dong, in the region of
the Ningpo lakes.

Chekiang province has led all others in the construction
of modern motor roads and it is because of the initiative
of the Chekiang provincial authorities that Hangchow is
now connected by motor road with Shanghai, the commercial
metropolis and Nanking, the capital of the country.

The Hangchow Bore, a natural wonder of this province,
is described elsewhere.

CH'IEN T'ANG RIVER AND RAPIDS.

Houseboating is a popular diversion at Hangchow,
particularly on the Ch'ien T'ang River. Unfortunately
there are no adequately equipped houseboats for hire on the
river and those who make the trip must be prepared to
use native boats with the customary discomforts and in-
conveniences. A railway connects Zakhow and Lanchi,
and many make the trip to Lanchi by rail and return by
boat. Enjoyable as it may be to the old resident of
China this is not a trip to be lightly undertaken by the
inexperienced traveler.

The Ch'ien T'ang is one of the most beautiful rivers
in China. Its tributaries drain the eastern portions of
Anhwei and Kiangsi and flowing over rapids and through
the picturesquely beautiful hills of Chekiang, its clear
waters reach the sea below Zahkow.

It traverses the entire length of Chekiang Province, a
distance of some 800 *li*. It is different from most other
streams in China because its waters are particularly clear.
Especially is it crystal clear as one ascends above Tunglu.
Its flow is over small rapids which can only be negotiated
up stream by the smallest of craft when towed by trackers.
The largest craft that participate in the trade of the
Ch'ien T'ang often have tows similar to those seen in the
Yangtsze Gorges.

At places the river bottoms are under perfect agricultural cultivation and again the hills tower above the
stream. At all times the varied beauty is wonderfully

attractive. On one or both sides are two paths which the pedestrian can use with comparative comfort. In spring time azaleas cover the hillsides and the reflection in the clear water is as attractive as is the natural beauty of the hills. The beauty of the autumn foliage and flowers cannot be exaggerated. In the autumn the houseboater finds, in easy distances from the stream, game in abundance. On the lower reaches pheasants, partridges and snipe are plentiful, while further up owing to the abundance of acorns wild boar are numerous. It is a favorite resort for wild pig hunters.

The places of chief interest after leaving Zahkou, which is a suburb of Hangchow, are Tunglu with a population of 95,000; Yenchow, 138,000; Lanchi, 128,000; Fenshui, 33,000; and Fuyang, 136,000. One of the most interesting sights is the famous parapet of Yenchow.

The people along the river are not very familiar with the sight of foreigners. Their attitude is peculiarly one of friendly curiosity and it is certain that there is the kindest feeling displayed at all points. A traveler says that one gains the impression that the people are healthier, happier and more prosperous than those living in the environment of the large cities of Shanghai and Hangchow.

The journey to Lanchi may be made by houseboat or by rail. From Zahkou to Tunglu the houseboat may be towed. Beyond that steam launches are rare and it would be difficult for them to negotiate the rapids. It is possible to make the trip from Zahkou to Lanchi and return a distance of 360 *li*, in seven days. This gives only the minimum of time to see the various places of interest and no time for sport.

MOKANSHAN.

This is the favorite summer resort for the lower Yangtsze Valley. It is situated on a mountain top thirty miles north-west of Hangchow, 2,500 feet above sea level and is famous for its beautiful mountain scenery and bamboo groves.

The Mokanshan Summer Resort Association maintains sanitation, roads, tennis courts, swimming pool, kindergarten, medical service, dispensary, etc. Several hundred foreigners and an increasing number of Chinese enjoy the privileges and the refreshment of the resort each summer.

Transportation to the mountain, including buses, passenger autos, sedan chairs and carriers, for which fixed charges are maintained, is under the supervision of the Chekiang Highway Administration. A good highway leads to the foot of the mountain from Hangchow so that with the completion of the motor highway between Shanghai and Hangchow, it is possible to go by motor car from Shanghai to Mokanshan. As a visit to Mokanshan really is a side trip from Hangchow, most travelers will go there by motor car from the latter place. The ascent is made by sedan chair or on foot. Several hundred houses dot the sides of the hills, and the village has a number of provision stores, a post office, telegraph office, and a branch of a Shanghai bank. A modern, foreign-style hotel is conducted by the Shanghai-Hangchow Railway, and is open the year around.

Travel agencies in Shanghai offer round trip tickets to Mokanshan, which includes railway fare, motor car hire and chair transportation to the top of the mountain. For a small sum baggage is taken care of and delivered at Mokanshan.

SHAOHING.

This important but little known city of Chekiang is 70 miles west of Ningpo and 35 miles east of Hangchow. It may be reached from either Hangchow or Ningpo by motor road, steam launch, sedan chair or native houseboat. Being off the usual routes of foreign travel it should not be visited except by those who have special business there and who are willing to make the necessary preparations. From Shanghai the Ningpo route though longer is more attractive as it takes one through some beautiful mountain scenery. Population about 300,000.

The records of Shaohing go back to the beginning of China's history, for places in the district are intimately associated with the great Emperor Shun (2255-2205 B.C.). His mother is said to have been a native of the Shaohing district. Shun's successor, the great Yu (2205-2197 B.C.) is buried in the hills three miles east of the city. The fine system of water-ways for which the fertile Shaohing plain is famous are attributed to him. The city which is now known as Shaohing was built in 480 B.C. The day after the completion of the city it was discovered that a new hill had appeared during the night, which was given the name "Flying Hill" as it was said originally to have been an island off the coast of what is now Shantung and through some species of magic flew several hundred miles South to commemorate the completion of the new municipality.

In 1862 the city like many other places in Chekiang province suffered severely at the hands of the Taipings, but it made a quick recovery. To-day it is a busy market, famous throughout China for its silk and satin, spirit money, wine, and vessels of brass and pewter. The largest of the Chinese bells on exhibition in the British Museum was cast just outside a gate of the city. But the best known product of the city is its men. A Chinese proverb says there are three things which are found everywhere under heaven "bean curd, sparrows and Shaohing men." The Shaohing men are to be found in every corner of the country and are famous as government clerks. Another class have, in many places, dominated the business of carrying chairs. Nearly all the chair coolies of Hangchow are from Shaohing.

POOTOO, THE SACRED ISLAND.

Fifty miles east of Ningpo—off the north-eastern coast of Chekiang and accessible by means of steamers either from Shanghai or Ningpo, is the sacred island of Pootoo, one of the Chusan archipelago, notable for two reasons. Among foreigners living in Shanghai it is known as the nearest accessible bathing beach; to Chinese Buddhists it is

12

the most sacred place in East China. During the summer occasional excursion steamers run direct from Shanghai to Pootoo, enabling one to spend the week-end there. The Sacred Island does not maintain a hotel and those who go there except by the excursion steamer, will find lodging in one of the many temples. As the island is a Buddhist sanctuary no animal may be killed on it and no animal food can be served. However, there is a Chinese hospital and under the pleasing fiction that all foreigners and other non-Buddhists are ill, eggs, chickens and other forms of animal food are available. Those who go to Pootoo to spend a holiday should remember that as in other parts of China the hospitable temple means bare walls and floors with, usually, an equally bare bed.

Pootoo is about four miles long and very irregular in shape, ranging in width from three miles to a few hundred yards. It is known to the Chinese Buddhist as one of the four sacred hills, a distinction which its geography justifies by the possession of a hill nearly 1000 feet high. Owing to the nearness to the outlets of the Yangtsze and Ch'ien T'ang rivers, the water surrounding Pootoo is slightly muddy. The bays on the eastern side are bordered with beaches of yellow sand on which heavy breakers roll. The landing place is a well-built jetty on the extreme southern part of the island. From here well-paved roads, kept in good repair, lead to all the principal temples with smaller roads branching off in all directions to the various grottos, shrines and smaller temples. The full name of Pootoo is Putoloka, the name of the mythical sacred hill from which Avalokitesvara, one of the most important of Buddhist gods, looks down on the world. With the spread of Buddhism to Thibet, a second Putoloka came into existence at Lhasa, and Pootoo is the third. Because of the natural beauty of the place it was famous in Chinese mythology long before the advent of Buddhism and in fact it did not become a Buddhist shrine until A.D. 847 when a Buddhist pilgrim from India saw in the mists of a cave a vision of the goddess Kwan Yin. Other pilgrims visited the place and there were other miraculous manifestations which accordingly to Buddhist lore have continued to the present time. The powers of the goddess, however, were not strong enough to prevent the depredations of Japanese pirates, who during the Ming dynasty, destroyed most of the religious settlements and in 1387 drove most of the monks to the mainland. For a century Pootoo was nominally deserted and its history a blank. The work of rebuilding started in the early part of the sixteenth century, but 150 years later, in 1665, Dutch pirates driven from Formosa, plundered and burned the temples. In 1688 the monks returned and since that time they have lived in comparative peace and prosperity.

The island contains about one hundred temples and monasteries and is the residence, normally, of more than a thousand monks. Almost all of the temples and monasteries, with their neighboring shrines and grottos, are intimately connected with the miraculous happenings of the island, or with the visits of the many famous pilgrims who at various times have visited the place.

The nineteenth day of the eleventh month of the old Chinese calendar is regarded as the birthday of the Kwan Yin and this event is celebrated on Pootoo with special stately ceremonies. The number of regular monks is greatly increased while thousands of laymen come from all parts of China. Interesting as these ceremonies are, it is a time to be avoided by the foreign traveler who does not want to undergo the discomforts of crowded travel.

Most of the buildings on Pootoo date from the early part of the eighteenth century when repairs and reconstruction were undertaken by Emperor Yung Cheng. Of these structures the most important are the Southern and Northern monasteries, located on the island as their names imply. These two establishments divide the honors in the ordination of monks, performing the function in alternate years. Each monastery is a triumph of Chinese architecture and each contains treasures which have been accumulated during the centuries. The story of each is a story not only of Pootoo but of Buddhism itself and of the history of China because every change in the ancient Empire was reflected here and recorded in the local annals.

As might be supposed, many fabulous stories are told —and believed—about Pootoo. It does not, like another island, boast of the absence of snakes for they are numerous here, but, according to the monks, all are harmless. Among the many miraculous happenings connected with the history of the island, none is more interesting to foreigners than the story of the loss and recovery of the great bell of the Northern Monastery. The story is told by R. F. Johnston in his *Buddhist China*, a book which all students of Chinese Buddhism should read.

"This bell was cast by the founder of the monastery, Ta-Chih, in the last quarter of the sixteenth century. The Red-hairs carried it off as part of their loot, and succeeded in safely conveying it to the gateway of their capital in ' the country of Europe.' There, however, it fell down, and, owing its great weight, was left lying where it fell. Gradually sinking into the soft ground, it at last disappeared altogether, and was forgotten. But in 1723 a sound like the rolling of thunder was suddenly heard coming from the ground; whereupon amazed people of the neighbourhood dug up the ground and discovered the bell.

"Somehow or other these events came to the knowledge of the monastic authorities. The abbot of the monastery at the time of the discovery of the bell was one Fa-tse, who happened to be a native of Fukien, and was acquainted with many merchants who were engaged in foreign trade. Through these merchants negotiations were opened with ' the country of Europe ' with a view to the recovery of the long lost bell. The negotiations ended successfully, and in the year 1728 it was brought back to China and landed at Namoa Island, near the port of Swatow, in the Canton province. Difficulties as to its reshipment were not overcome till 1733, which by a happy coincidence was the year which witnessed the completion of a restoration of the monastery under the auspices of

K'ang-hsi's son, the emperor Yung Cheng. To the great joy and wonder of the monks the bell was finally disembarked at Pootoo on the thirtieth day of the tenth month, at the very time when a solemn service was being held in the great hall of the monastery to celebrate his Majesty's birthday.

"There is no reason to doubt that the story as thus told in the annals of the monastery is substantially true; but it seems improbable that the monks were correct in their belief that the bell had actually been conveyed to Europe. The Chinese of those days had very vague ideas of geography, and the monks of Pootoo had evidently no very distinct knowledge of the political divisions of the ' country of Europe." Perhaps the bell did not make quite so long a journey as they supposed. The suggestion may be hazarded that its resting place during the period from 1665 to 1723 was no European town, but Batavia, a city of the Dutch East Indies, and though its old ramparts no longer exist, it was a strong walled town in the seventeenth and eighteenth centuries. Possibly the Chinese story of the fall of the bell at the gates of the city, and its subsequent disappearance until its presence underground was revealed by a sound like rolling thunder, is based on the historical fact that in 1699 Batavia was visited by a destructive earthquake. Thus the real course of events may have been something like this: the bell was carried from Pootoo to Java in 1665; it was suspended in a tower on the wall of the city of Batavia; it remained there till 1699, when the wall was destroyed by an earthquake; it lay buried under the ruins of the wall until 1723; and in that year, after it had disappeared from view for almost a quarter of a century, the removal of the *debris* restored it to the light of day. The inscription on the bell, we may suppose, was read by Chinese residents in Java, who learned thereby the name of the monastery to which it originally belonged. Through them the story may easily have come to the ears of the Chinese merchants of Fukien, who at that time controlled a large proportion of China's foreign trade.

"The joy of the monks at the return of their founder's bell was tempered by their discovery of the melancholy fact that it was no longer in a fit condition to serve its proper purpose. It had been cracked and injured to such an extent that before the hearts of monks and pilgrims could again be thrilled by its mellow tones it had to be put through the process of recasting. Their work was not carried out for nearly a hundred years. It hung silently in its tower till 1825, when a wealthy pilgrim named Hsu having interested himself in its history, undertook to defray the cost of having it recast. It is the bell of Ta-chih, originally cast before the year 1592, but re-cast in or shortly after the year 1825 by the pilgrim Hsu, that hangs to-day in the bell-tower of the Northern Monastery."

The highest point on the island is near the Northern Monastery and is reached by a pathway from that establishment. From the summit there is a magnificent view of the Chusan Archipelago.

Only recently have foreigners come to appreciate the natural beauties of this place, one of the prettiest in the country, and its many advantages as a place for an outing. It is always possible to secure rooms in one of the temples or monasteries, but bedding, food, supplies, and cooking utensils should be taken on the trip. One should be careful not to visit the place when the pilgrimages are at their height as at that time boats, inns and monastery quarters will be crowded.

Throughout China the anniversary of the "goddess crossing the sea" is celebrated at Buddhist temples on the 19th of the sixth moon, commemorating the crossing of the image of Kwanyin to Pootoo with the Monk Agaku.

CHUSHAN ISLAND.

This island, the largest of the Chushan Archipelago, lies off the coast of Chekiang Province, forty miles east of Ningpo. The largest city is Tinghai which is regarded as suitable for a Chinese naval base. The island is noted for the fact that most of the turkeys on the markets of China are reared there. Turkeys are not native to China and it is said that they were first introduced into this part of the country by early British traders. The climatic conditions of the island are suitable for the rearing of fowls of all kinds.

HANGCHOW BORE.

The Hangchow Bay derives its name from the fact that the city of Hangchow lies practically at the end of an extensive gulf and on the mouth of the Ch'ien T'ang river. The port and suburb of Hangchow is Zahkou, lying directly on the shores of the Ch'ien T'ang.

The bay has become known to navigators and the general public more because of its inaccessibility to power craft than from the standpoint of a port. Its inaccessibility is due to a tidal phenomenon known in different countries as *bore, eager, mascaret, pocaraca,* etc., which usually takes place in a bay or estuary which has extensive mud flats, dry at low water and where the tide frequently rises with such rapidity as to cause the wave to break in the form of a vertical wall of water. The bore of the Ch'ien T'ang is not a tidal wave. There are no regular undulations of the surface. Particles of wood have been seen borne along on or immediately behind the crest of the bore—retaining their relative position with respect to the crest of the bore for long distances.

The ocean tide, breaking as it does at spring tide into a vertical wall of water running up the river, is the result of several influences acting simultaneously and may be described as follows. The conformation of the bay may be likened to an enormous funnel. At its entrance it is approximately 60 miles wide, narrowing down to a width of nine miles at Kanpu, 70 miles inland, a contraction of 51 miles in 70 miles. At Zahkow 30 miles further inland it has a width of two miles. The entrance is traversed by a chain of islands, the Chusan Archipelago, which occupy about sixty per cent. of the width; a natural promontory projects into the bay from the northern shore at Kanpu, and another promontory, probably the result of silting and reclaiming, projects from the southern shore opposite Hsiao Hsi San.

The depths at the entrance of the bay and as far as Kanpu are fairly uniform ranging from four to five fathoms. Occasional deep holes appear along the Chapu bay. Near Kanpu the sand bar practically extends across the bay suddenly reducing the depth in the channel to one or two feet and from here up the river to Zahkou the depths never exceed two feet at lowest low water.

The ocean tide has a rise varying from six to sixteen feet and enters the bay through the narrow passes between the islands. This tide advances rapidly into the bay, causing a piling up of the waters in the vicinity of Kanpu, the rise here in the spring being 28 to 32 feet. The rise during the first and second hour of flood at Kanpu is twelve to fourteen feet.

During this rapid rise at Kanpu the water is rapidly falling above Kanpu; two hours before the wave breaks into a bore there is a difference of level of nine to twelve feet between Chapu and Kanpu—and a similar difference between Haining and Kanpu, the slope of the water surface being towards Kanpu from both directions. The rise at Kanpu is very rapid and when it is low water at Haining, the water has risen so that the slope from Kanpu is reversed and the difference between Kanpu and Haining is twelve feet; when this condition becomes critical the wave breaks and runs up the river in the form of a bore.

The sand bars and the natural channel of the river cause the currents to divide near Kanpu; one current is deflected towards the southern shore and the other runs up the channel. The current running towards the southern shore is again deflected to the northern shore and comes against the sea wall at right angles to the current coming up the channel. These meet about thirteen miles below Haining and run up the river as one wave. The bore passes Haining practically as the moon crosses the meridian.

The height and force of the wave depend primarily upon the tide. As a general rule the bore is highest at the equinoxes and when it is new or full moon, with the moon in perigee. The height however is greatly affected by the wind, the fresh water discharge of the Ch'ien T'ang and the position of the sand bars opposite Kanpu. The position of the bars change with every tide but seem to be shifted back and forth across the river according to the season. When the bars are forming along the northern shores or are reduced by the river's flow, the bore is less. At low river they are built up again and the bore is again higher.

At Haining (on the Shanghai-Hangchow motor road) the roar of the rising water may be heard from 45 minutes to an hour before the bore arrives at the Pagoda. It first appears as a long white streak across the horizon, alternately, rising and falling. Shortly after the bore arrives in sight, junks riding in on the after rush may be seen. The front seems to grow higher and higher. The wave from the south-east superimposes itself on the wave from the east about ten miles below Haining, reaching its maximum height near the Haining Pagoda; from here it begins to fall away.

The front advances at about fifteen knots at spring tide and from eight to ten knots at neaps. After the vertical front has passed, the water rises rapidly—eight to ten feet in one hour—and the tidal stream runs from four to six knots; the duration of the rising tide is about three hours and of the falling, nine hours.

During the first two hours of falling water the tidal stream runs about four to six knots; and the water falls about four feet in the first hour, while during the last two hours of falling water the change in level is hardly perceptible.

Haining is an important market for charcoal which comes down the Ch'ien T'ang river. Junk harbours or shelters have been constructed to protect the junks from the force of the bore. These junk shelters are elliptical buttresses about 1000 feet apart, built out some 30 to 40 feet from the sea wall. Between the buttresses junk shelves from six to eight feet high and extending along and out from the sea wall about 20 feet have been built. The junkman comes alongside at high water, lashes his strong hawsers on shore and when the tide goes out the junk is resting on the shelf. The vertical face of the bore seldom reaches the top of the shelf for the buttress has broken the force of the wave—and he rides up clear on the after rush.

The wall at Haining is about 26 feet high; the bore and after tide seldom reaches the top of the sea wall. However an earthen dyke four to six feet high, and eight to ten feet behind the sea wall provides additional protection in case of higher tides.

Various mythical accounts of the cause of the bore are related. The most generally told myth is that a general being unusually successful against the enemies of the emperor and thereby having become very popular with his people, excited the jealousy of his sovereign who caused him to be assassinated and thrown into the Ch'ien T'ang, and his troubled spirit sought ever after to avenge its wrath by flooding the country. Many pagodas, temples and smaller places of worship have been erected along the sea wall and thousands proceed here yearly to offer sacrifices.

The best place to observe the bore is at Haining—a small market town about 40 miles from Hangchow. Haining may be reached by motor road from Shanghai or Hangchow.

The usual supposition that the bore only occurs at the equinoxes is wrong. The Chinese have made it a custom to go at this season, but the bore may be seen at any time; probably the best is at new or full moon.

The author is obliged to Mr. E. C. Stocker for the above description of the Hangchow Bore.

NINGPO.

This city which was so closely associated with the development of foreign trade in China is 150 miles south of Shanghai, connected with that port by daily steamer service. Population about 260,000; with the suburbs, another 150,000. It was opened as a treaty port in 1842, and for many years was an important center of foreign trade. This trade has now been diverted to Shanghai and the foreign population of Ningpo is negligible.

With the history of Ningpo is associated the earliest attempts of Europeans to establish themselves in China, for the Portuguese traders settled here in 1522 and soon established a properous colony, which numbered more than a thousand twenty years later. At that time trouble arose between the Portuguese and the Chinese, and as a result the settlers, who refused to obey the laws of China, were ordered to be expelled. The colony was attacked by Chinese troops and 800 Portuguese massacred. In the latter part of the 17th century, the East India Company established a post near Ningpo on the island of Chusan, but the trade did not prosper and the place was abandoned. Ningpo was one of the first five ports thrown open to foreigners and though the center of a large foreign trade at one time, has since declined in importance.

Ningpo was a city of great antiquity at the time these European adventurers came. The present city, 1,200 years old, was built near the site of a much older city which was mentioned in the time of Yü (2205 B.C.) It is situated fifteen miles from the sea on the Yung River whose branches water the fertile Ningpo plain. A good view of Ningpo's magnificent surroundings can be secured from the top of the Heaven-Invested Pagoda, built in 696, and one of the oldest in China. The hills which form the easternmost portion of the Chekiang mountain range enclose the plain in a great natural amphitheater in a grand sweep of more than 100 miles.

Ningpo is the commercial metropolis of Chekiang province and although the foreign trade is not now what it was forty years ago, owing to the opening of other ports, the Chinese trade shows a steady increase. A great deal of household furniture is made here, and it is a center for the manufacture of "joss paper." Ningpo is second only to Foochow in the production of lacquer, and is famous for carved work in white wood.

Shallow draft ocean steamers are able to navigate the mouth of the river and anchor at Ningpo, maintaining a daily service with Shanghai. Steam launches ply farther up the river, enabling the traveler to visit the interior. A railway connects the port with Pah-Kwun, fifty miles distant and will eventually connect with the railway to Shanghai by way of Hangchow.

The approach to the port is through the islands of the Chusan archipelago, and the scenery which they form has been often likened to that of the most beautiful parts of the Inland Sea of Japan. The banks of the river, from its mouth to the city are lined with huge straws huts, which are used for the storage of natural ice. Ningpo is the greatest fishing port and the greatest fish market in China; to this fact the existence of the ice-houses is due. With the coming of the cuttle-fish season each spring, great fleets of boats move down the river to the sea, and for weeks afterwards the pervasive odor of drying cuttle-fish is wafted on nearly every breeze that blows over the town.

The river is spanned by two bridges made of big barges lashed together, which rise and fall with the tides. Life on the bridges from month to month is almost that of a little world in itself. There are of course hucksters and fortune tellers and beggars of every description. Just across the principal bridge is a pyramidal structure of stone some twenty or more feet high, which is a monument erected to the memory of the sailors and soldiers, French and British, who perished at Ningpo in the troubles of the Taiping rebellion. Half a mile up the river is the little Catholic cemetery, where several French officers, also victims of those stirring times, are buried. Inside the city is a residence of the Church Missionary Society where they preserve with care a hole in the wall, and the cannon-ball which madè it, the result of fire from a British gunboat at the same period.

The pagoda is in the care of the priests of a monastery next door. No census of the temples of Ningpo has been made but the casual visitor soon comes to the conclusion that Ningpo is much what St. Paul said Athens was—very religious. There are of course the regular temples to the city deities. There is the Foochow guild temple, with its remarkable carved stone pillars. There is a fine old Confucian temple, which with its attendant buildings makes a group that can only be compared to foreign college building groups. The temple itself, however, is used only for the semi-annual sacrifices. Ningpo is the seat of a vigorous Buddhist movement, for which the neighboring monasteries of Pootoo, the sacred island, and one of the five great Buddhist centers in China, is largely responsible. The Buddhist religion is decadent in many quarters of China but not here or in other parts of Chekiang province. The Buddhists support an excellent orphanage and other benevolent institutions.

The most interesting street for the stranger to visit is the main shopping street which extends from the east gate a distance of two miles to the opposite west gate. This magnificent thoroughfare is a little difficult to find, for the entrance is narrow and is approached through shops crowded on the valuable land just outside the gate. Some years ago the first half mile of the street was a fine example of the old style Chinese street of the better sort, with splendid old signs whose calligraphy was much admired by scholars. But one fire after another has destroyed most of the old architecture. Fire walls at intervals of about two hundred yards through the business portion of the city confine the fires, but there have been enough of them to change the character of that part entirely, and now the visitor will walk past Anglo-Chinese

architectural abominations for a long distance, resplendent
in gilt and black, and in red brick, and lit with sun-bursts
of electric lights, till he will wonder what sort of creature
conceived this style of renaissance building. Fortunately
the goods within are not the same, and should he wish to
buy silks and satins, furs, or linen, or pearls or jade, or
what you will, here is the chance. The furniture which
has been alluded to is made in a quarter not far away,
which is decidedly worth a visit. The inlaid bone work
is a speciality of Ningpo, not made elsewhere, and the
bone work on a Chinese bed-stead, the size of a whole
room, will make the visitor gasp, when he realizes the
amount of artistic labor involved.

Mention has been made of some of the ancient
worthies who come from Ningpo and its neighborhood.
To that number should be added the philosopher Wang
Yang-ming called the Chinese pragmatist who was born
in the city of Yuyao and has his temple there still; to his
writings many Japanese ascribe the origin of the spirit
which has made their nation a first-class power. Many of
the great merchants of Shanghai are Ningpo men.

The long-time resident of Ningpo comes to learn that
the people are not very progressive, in spite of the fact
that they have electric lights and telephones and other
modern improvements. But in general the town is
unfriendly to new ideas. The proximity of Shanghai
has drained the town of just the class that is forward-
looking, for Shanghai is filled with Ningpo men. The
slower and more cautions element is left at home; hence
the orthodox conservatism of the old city.

Around the Ningpo Lakes a few hours journey from
Ningpo, are many places of great historical interest and
natural beauty which can be reached by house boat,
including a number of famous monasteries and temples
built on the sides of wooded hills. The visitor may be
certain of a welcome at the monasteries and if he takes
provisions and bedding with him will be very comfortable.
Owing to the narrowness of the canals and the many low

bridges they must pass under the Ningpo houseboat is rather small and a party of four, in order to travel in comfort, will need three boats, two for passengers and a third for baggage, provisions and servants.

Yui Hwang lies in an easterly direction from Ningpo, distant about 15 miles, proceeding by boat to the landing place Pao-Dzaung, one has about one mile or less to walk before reaching the temples. Ching-Ho-Za (or Golden Monastery) is situated at the end of the Wan-Chi Valley at the bottom of the mountain in the midst of a beautiful bamboo grove. The distance from Ningpo by boat -to Wan-Chi is some thirteen miles. From there one has to walk or proceed by chair a distance of eight miles before reaching the temple. This temple has been visited by foreigners for many years. Tunghu or East Lake lies about twelve miles south-east of Ningpo. The scenery there is regarded by some as more lovely than that of West Lake at Hangchow. The lake is surrounded on all sides by richly wooded mountains, the scenery is really picturesque. The lake formerly was famous for its duck shooting in the winter, but owing to the large number of Chinese sportsmen who visit there, very few bags of any importance have been made within recent years. Tzu-Chi is situated about thirteen miles to the north of Ningpo. This beauty spot can be reached either by boat or train. There are several temples in the immediate neighbourhood and a very ancient pagoda one mile west of the city. Snowy Valley (Shih Doa Zu) is forty miles to the south-west of Ningpo. Visitors proceed by boat to Siao-Wong-Miao about twenty-five miles, then by chair about thirteen miles to the temple. The famous Tien Dong Monastery, one of the largest and most famous in this part of China may be visited as a part of the itinerary of any Ningpo Lake trip. The best time to spend a holiday in the Ningpo district is during the spring or autumn months, preferably the former, as the mountains and hills are then ablaze with flowers, principally azaleas.

NANKING-SHANGHAI RAILWAY.

This railway runs through one of the most thickly populated sections of China, connecting Shanghai and Nanking, with an extension from Shanghai to Woosung. The length of the Shanghai-Nanking section is 193 miles. With the ten miles constituting the branch to Woosung the total mileage is 203. Construction of this road was begun in 1904 and the work was completed four years later at a total cost of Tls. 18,718,000. The funds for construction were secured from a British loan. At Nanking the road connects, by means of a train ferry across the Yangtsze with Pukow the southern terminus of the Tientsin-Pukow line, making possible a rail trip from Shanghai to Peking, or by the Trans-Siberian and other lines from Shanghai to Paris. The railway makes it possible for the visitor with only a short time in the country to see some of the most interesting places in China at small cost. Although the night express is comfortable, sightseers should make the trip between Shanghai and Nanking by day because of the very interesting country traversed. It is one of the most fertile and intensely cultivated sections of China and throughout the growing season nearly every square foot of the countryside is planted. The trip between Shanghai and Nanking may be made in seven hours by express.

Important points on the line are:

Miles from Shanghai		Miles from Nanking
0	Shanghai	193
32	Kunshan, a seaport 2,000 years ago...	161
53	Soochow	140
80	Wusih	113
150	Chinkiang	43
193	Nanking	0

SOOCHOW.

This famous old city is 53 miles west of Shanghai, on the Nanking-Shanghai Railway and 40 miles from the

Yangtsze River; a treaty port opened in 1896. Population between 700,000 and 800,000. Several comfortable hotels for foreigners are maintained here under Chinese management. As these hotels have their ups and downs it is best to ask the advice of a Shanghai travel agency.

On arrival at the Soochow railway station the traveler will find himself besieged by the proprietors of carriages, ricshas and donkeys, representing the three competing transportation systems of the city. The carriages can be used only so far as one of the city gates for with a few exceptions the principal streets inside the walls are too narrow for anything but donkeys and ricshas. The hotels are outside the walls and can be reached by carriage in five or ten minutes.

The many canals which intersect the rich and beautiful city of Soochow have given it the name of "The Venice of the Far East," while the very high standing which its scholars have always enjoyed has made it "the Athens of China." It is one of the oldest and most famous cities of the country and the admiration of the Chinese for the place and for its rival in fame, Hangchow, is expressed in the familiar quotation "Heaven above, and below Hangchow and Soochow." The history of the city covers more than 2,500 years. In about 525 B.C. only 250 years after Rome was founded, a prince of the Kingdom of Wu, one of the feudal kingdoms which existed at that time, ordered his prime minister to build a city for him to serve as his capital. The instructions were to build a large and influential city where his subjects could dwell in time of danger and where his government stores could be protected from the enemies that constantly menaced his kingdom. The official decided on ambitious plans. The city was to have eight water gates, like heaven, and be square like the earth. The total length of the outer walls aggregated 47 li, about fifteen miles. Inside were two inner enclosures, the larger one enclosing the Forbidden City, for the palaces and yamens, and the smaller enclosure for the personal use of the prime minister and other important officials.

The city became the capital of the kingdom and grew in importance, but about A.D. 591 a new city was built for the reason that the old one was full of organized robbers, rebels and thieves, who were so strong that it was impossible to drive them out. The walls of the new city were of wood, and the honest people who moved there to escape their rascally neighbors lived within these insecure enclosures only a short time, moving back to the old city during the first years of the Tang reign. In the year 876, a band of robbers captured the city and again a new enclosure was built for the protection of the honest people. The new city took a rough wedge shape. Within the walls were many canals and 300 streets. The walls thus constructed were allowed to fall into disrepair and were restored several times.

The most recent restoration of the city walls was in 1662, under the renowned Manchu Emperor, Kang Hsi. A Manchu garrison was quartered here and the town refortified. Battlements were added, rising to a height of six feet above the wall, which is 28 feet in height and 18 feet thick.

The walls as they stand to-day have been frequently repaired but are much the same as in 1662. During recent years new gates were cut in the walls to give readier access to the city from the railway station and the " horse road." Although the walls are regarded by Chinese and foreigners alike as a relic of ancient history, it is interesting to note that as recently as 1925 the walls of Soochow proved of great value in protecting the civilian population during the local civil wars. The walled city is about four miles long from north to south and about three miles broad having a total circumference of about fifteen miles. A walk along the broad well-paved top of the wall is delightful, far away from the noise and crowds below and yet giving an excellent view of the whole city. A moat 50 to 100 yards wide surrounds the city and is used as a canal, connecting with the narrower intersecting canals inside the city all of which connect with the Grand Canal, which runs along the city wall and parallel to the railway.

Approaching Soochow from any direction, tall pagodas first come into view. There are five of them inside the city and three crown the near-by hills. The pagodas of Soochow are intimately connected with the city's history and are an interesting feature to travelers. They are, indeed, characteristic landmarks. Soochow and its immediate vicinity has eight famous pagodas, one of which— the Great Pagoda seen near the city wall from the railway station,—is one of the most famous in China. It consists of nine stories, 250 feet high and is a marvel of proportion. Sixty feet in diameter at the base, it is 45 feet at the top, each storey being proportionately shorter, each balcony narrower, each door and window smaller. The whole is of massive construction and carries well its age of 700 years. From the upper stories an excellent view of the interesting surrounding country can be obtained. In the vicinity are beautiful hills and lakes, the latter connected by innumerable small canals. To the east is a level plain broken only by the groves which surround the many prosperous villages. Five million people live within the radius covered by the eye from the top balconies of the pagoda. From few other places can one view the habitations of so many of his fellow men.

The Tiger Hill Pagoda, the "leaning tower" of Soochow, was first built in A.D. 601, burned down in 1428 and the present structure was built ten years later, eight years before the birth of Columbus. The Twin Pagodas, known also as the Two Pen Pagodas, stand near the site of the old Examination Halls, and to their good influence is attributed much of the fame which has come to Soochow through her scholars. Near these is the Ink Pagoda. "A scholar built the Two Pen Pagodas to attract the good luck required to insure good scholarship to the town; but as most of the candidates kept on failing afterwards, he consulted the geomancers, and they showed how absurd it was to provide two pens but no ink. The omission rectified, the candidates passed." Soochow University, an American missionary institution, is located near the Ink Pagoda. Soochow, for many centuries, sent more honors men to the great Metropolitan Examinations at Peking than can be claimed by any other city and it rivals Hangchow in the space it occupies in the literature of China. The History of Soochow, a compilation begun 1,000 years ago by one of the city's most famous men, has grown to 150 volumes, through the contributions of generations of scholars.

The City Temple is one of the show places of Soochow. Within its enclosure are fourteen separate temples, containing more than two hundred principal images. Within the city walls there are several hundred temples, nunneries and monasteries. There is one large Confucian temple at which the provincial officials formerly worshipped and a smaller one where the district magistrate worshipped before going to worship at the large temple. Near the large temple, to the east and south, are a normal school, a college, a middle school and an industrial school, all run and financed by the government. To the west are the Horticultural Garden and the Beamless Temple. This famous building is of two stories, built about A.D. 1572 and without any timber at all. There is no wood in any part of the building, the roof being supported by arches made of specially constructed brick. The roof is covered with beautifully colored tiles.

The Temple of Scrolls is full of scrolls of all kinds and a walk through it gives one some idea of the various tendencies of Chinese art to run to commercialism. It is said that only countrymen go there to buy scrolls, as the best artists do their work upon order or exhibit it in private shops. On the east side of this large temple there is a smaller one that has very interesting representations of the lower regions with its varied tortures and also of saints seated upon clouds in heaven.

To the south of the customs house (which is at the opposite end of the horse road from the railway station and near the southeast corner of the city) is a magnificent bridge called the Precious Girdle Bridge. It consists of 53 arches and is built entirely of granite. This and many other beautiful bridges in the vicinity are well worth the time taken to see them. The bridges of Soochow are famous throughout China.

The gardens of Soochow could provide an interesting day's outing in themselves. There are several inside the city, but the two largest are the Loen Yoen and the Si Yoen (*yoen* means garden). Loen Yoen was formerly owned by a high Manchu official. The property was siezed by the Republican government and is now open to the public. They are both located outside of the northwest gate (Chang Mung) of the city and may be reached by carriage from the railway station or by ricsha from any of the hotels. A small entrance fee is charged and one may wander at leisure through the many walks and rockeries. The Loen Yoen is one of the finest examples of a Chinese garden open to travelers.

To the west of the city are a number of hills, a few hours journey by boat and within easy reach by donkeys. There one may tramp through many shaded spots rich in historic lore. The hills afford good climbs and excellent views. The fields of yellow rape and patches of purple clover in the early spring are well worth seeing.

Soochow has regained much of what it lost because of the Taiping rebellion which devastated this as well as many other famous places and is again the rich and cultured city of old, with a very large class of idle rich. In addition to its fame as the birthplace of many scholars, Soochow is also widely known in China as the home of the most famous sing-song girls. Soochow women are noted for their beauty and the pleasing softness of their dialect and as a result fashionable women from other parts of China ape the Soochow accent. The place has not held its own, commercially, with other cities of the neighborhood, but retains its reputation as a center for the production of high grade silks, maintaining many thousand looms for the production of brocades.

"The silken goods which form the staple export are the glory of the place, and the Imperial household formerly got its chief supplies from here. It is strange to see the primitive surroundings, a little hut with an earthen floor in which they are produced, with their exquisite designs and perfect workmanship."

To the west lies the Great Lake (Tai Hu) one of the most beautiful bodies of water in China. Its beauty has been celebrated by Chinese poets for many centuries and it has been the scene of outings by residents of Soochow for the past 2,000 years. It should be included in any houseboat trip. It can be made a part of the itinerary from Shanghai by houseboat, or Chinese houseboats may be hired in Soochow. In ancient days the shores of this lake came to Soochow, but the lake has receded and the land filled in and reclaimed.

WUSIH.

To the north-west of Soochow on the Nanking-Shanghai Railway is Wusih, a progressive walled city with a population of more than 500,000. Formerly a place of small importance, Wusih is now growing rapidly and next to Shanghai is the most important industrial city in the province. It has supplanted Soochow as a transfer point for goods destined for Shanghai and with the introduction of modern methods is also supplanting that city as a silk center. Evidence of the city's industrial importance is offered those who do not stop to visit the place, for many tall factory chimneys may be seen from the train.

There are several foreign style hotels under Chinese management in Wusih, about five minutes from the station by ricsha or carriage.

The industrial development has been carried out by Chinese themselves, but with foreign machinery and a certain amount of expert foreign assistance. Among the enterprises of Wusih are: 45 modern steam filatures,

5 large flour mills, 9 cotton mills, 18 textile weaving plants, 2 cotton seed and bean oil mills besides wood oil, soap and other factories. A great many other enterprises of this nature are either under construction or are being promoted. The surrounding country is famous for the production of silk and Wusih is one of the most important centers for the marketing of cocoons.

Though the building of the railway has made great changes in the transportation of goods, Wusih remains a very important boat town and most of the boatmen between Shanghai and Nanking call it their home. The city is intersected by many canals, which are wide and filled with clear water, in contrast to the muddy streams seen in the neighborhood of Shanghai. The canals cover 150 miles in the city and suburbs.

The people of Wusih are very progressive and there are many evidences of municipal enterprises. A good paved road leads from the station to the city gate and many good ricsha roads have been built into the factory districts. One of the remarkable institutions of the place is a public library of 170,000 volumes, all of which have been collected since the Republican Revolution.

An interesting and curious minor industry of the district is the manufacture of clay images, which are well-modeled and artistically decorated. The images are small and represent everything under the sun from the human figure to beasts and birds. They are to be found in Chinese homes all over the land.

An hour distant by boat is the Weidzien spring, with a hill near by on which are located temples, a monastery and a great number of ancestral halls. All are kept in good repair, are clean and surrounded by fine gardens and courts. From this place there is a good view of the Great Lake. The approach to the spring is through a canal lined by fine trees. On the left is to be seen a regular mound 60 to 70 feet high, surmounted by a ruined, ivy-covered pagoda. Many motor boats and a superior style of native houseboat are on hire.

CHINKIANG.

Located 150 miles from Shanghai by rail Chinkiang is at the intersection of the Yangtsze and the Grand Canal, is the provincial capital and one of the most important stations on the Nanking-Shanghai Railway.

The town is about 2,000 years old and has borne its present name for half that time. The population is estimated at about 300,000. The port was opened to foreign trade in 1861. "Chinkiang is undoubtedly the prettiest place on the river below Hankow. The Silver Island Pass with its narrow and difficult channel, its great rush of water, its overhanging cliffs and bristling forts is justly called the 'Gate of the Yangtsze.' Silver Island itself, with its ancient temples, its fine trees and magnificent view, is one of the most attractive spots in China. From the summit of the hill a good idea of the neighborhood can be gained. On the north a low-lying plain interspersed with trees stretches to the horizon, and on a clear day the pagoda of Yangchow (a city associated with the name of Marco Polo) may be discerned. To the eastward lies a labyrinth of islands and waterways, all of which appertain to the Yangtsze, the main stream of which bends to the southeast, passing the entrance to the southern portion of the Grand Canal at Tant'u. On the right bank classical Kanlushan, with its newly restored temple and the remains of its famous iron pagoda, juts sharply up. The native city and foreign settlement, overshadowed by hills, line the water's edge, and Golden Island with its temples and pagodas forms a weird background to the harbor and shipping."

Golden Mountain, or Golden Island, is a place of more than usual fame, partly because of the visits paid to it by the renowned emperors, Kang Hsi and Ch'ien Lung, and partly because of the many beautiful spots, peaks, rocks and grottoes, each one connected with some legend dear to the Chinese. Emperor Kang Hsi visited the place in 1703 and gave names to a number of points on the hill. About fifty years later his successor the Emperor Ch'ien Lung came, occupying a temporary palace, which had been erected for him on the summit. Here his prolific poetic muse was inspired and he wrote a number of poems in praise of the beauty of the place. On five subsequent visits he added a great many more poems, thus setting the style for all the literati who followed him, with the result that Golden Mountain could be hidden under the reams of paper inscribed with poems in its praise. The Buddhist temple on the hill was first erected in the sixth century, was restored in 1021 and endowed by the imperial court.

According to Marco Polo, Chinkiang was at one time a stronghold of the Nestorian Christians. He says: "The Grand Khan, in 1278, sent there one of his barons, Marsarghis, who was a Nestorian Christian, to be governor of this city for three years. And this is what he did: in the three years of his residence there he built two Christian churches. And they have remained since then, for before were none."

The city is a center for the sale of what is known locally as "Yangtsze mud ware" which is made at Yang-chow. Many kinds of small objects, especially trays and boxes, are made of wood and covered with mud and *papier maché* which, when baked, presents a hard, glossy, black surface, a rather crude imitation of black lacquer, or inlaid ebony. Mother-of-pearl ornaments are laid in the mud, forming some very handsome designs. The ware is serviceable and will last a surprisingly long time, even when in daily use. It is very cheap and only a few dollars should be paid for the most elaborate piece.

The British fleet anchored off Chinkiang in 1842, after silencing the Chinese forts, but since that time the channel of the river has changed so much that the spot on which the fleet anchored is now covered with villages.

Fifteen miles to the north of Chinkiang, on the banks of the Grand Canal, is Yangchow, famous for the wealth of its men and the beauty of its women. It is the city where Marco Polo served as governor for three years. A daily launch and water service connects the two cities. According to some authorities Yangchow gave its name to the Yangtsze River. It was formerly the capital of the Yang Kingdom, which comprised the territory around the mouth of the Yangtsze and in that way the river acquired the name of the city.

NANKING.

Nanking, the ancient and more recently re-established capital of China is on the left bank of the Yangtsze River, about 200 miles north and west of Shanghai (Latitude 32°5', about the same as Charleston, S.C.) It may be reached by train on the Nanking-Shanghai Railway by river steamers or by airplane from Shanghai. Hotels: Bridge and Yangtsze, both near the railway station and steamer landings. The southern terminus of the Tientsin-Pukow Railway is at Pukow, across the river from Nanking, a launch and train ferry service connecting the two places.

Nanking (southern capital) owes its name to the fact that it has served several times, as at present, as the capital of the country. The last emperors of China to reside in Nanking were the early Mings, but the third Ming emperor, Yung Lo, deserted it for Peking, as a means of keeping more secure control over the north, threatened as it was by the Tartar and Mongol tribes. Previously Nanking had been the seat of a kingdom on seven different occasions during the long and turbulent history of China. It was the residence of the King of Wu and later, for 120 years, the capital of Eastern China. For 800 years before the Ming dynasty, it was a city of great political importance, though not the capital of the country. Under the name of Nanking, the city dates only from the beginning of the Ming dynasty (1368—1644), but the city which was built as the capital of this dynasty occupied the site of other cities which have figured in the history of China for more than two thousand years under different names. The ancient city was known as Kin-ling, but several centuries before Christ the name was changed to Tan-yang, and later to Kiang-nan and Sheng Chow.

Modern Nanking being developed as the capital of China, is in the making as this is written. The program of development embraces an ambitious city beautifying scheme, the building of roads, public parks, restoration and improvement of ancient buildings, etc. Enough of the program has been carried out to make Nanking one of the show places of modern China. The most impressive sight in the city and indeed one of the greatest architectural achievements of modern times is the Sun Yat Sen mausoleum, a gigantic structure which covers the southern slope of Purple Mountain, scene of the decisive battle in the 1911 revolution. This is the tomb of the great Chinese patriot who is looked on as the father of modern China and it is the objective point of many patriotic pilgrimages. Designed by a young Chinese architect Lu Yen-chi, who died before his work was finished, the tomb cost more than $2,000,000 and took five years to complete, although it was almost completed when Dr. Sun was buried there in 1929. Climbing the several hundred steps to the tumulus where the Chinese patriot is buried, somewhat after the fashion of Grant's Tomb in Riverside Drive (New York), the visitor obtains a marvellous view of the countryside stretching as far away as Anhwei province. The tomb is the central feature of the Mausoleum National Park where many beautiful temples, pagodas, and buildings are being erected and where the new national athletic stadium, accommodating 60,000 persons, is located. An interesting feature is the Beamless Temple, a restored Ming dynasty building which is being converted into a Hall of Revolutionary Heroes following the style of the Pantheon in Paris. In visiting the mausoleum the visitor is advised first to apply to the Ministry of Foreign Affairs, which will provide a guide if necessary.

Nanking has been a walled city since the 5th or 6th century, the present walls being built about 500 years ago. Surrounded by hills and facing the Yangtsze river, Nanking is very advantageously situated for defense and has been the vantage point striven for by many of the leaders of China's numerous rebellions. Probably a deciding reason why the great pirate Koxinga failed to unseat the Manchus and restore the Ming dynasty to the throne of China was because he failed to capture Nanking. He subjected it to a twenty day's siege in 1657, but on the twentieth night those in the city made a savage sortie, killing several thousand of the pirates' retainers and forcing the others to retire. The Taipings captured the place and held it against a siege for eleven years (1853-1864), it being the Taiping capital during that period. More recently the Republicans captured it (1911) and made it the capital of their provisional government. It was here that Dr. Sun Yat Sen took his oath of office as President of the Republic of China, on January 1, 1912, and here that he remained during his brief tenure of office. At the present time, Nanking is the official capital of the country, though most of the foreign diplomats remain in Peiping.

The present walls of Nanking are among the finest in China, being 40 to 60 feet high, 20 to 40 feet thick and 26 miles in circumference. They enclose a vast area, a large part of which is vacant land, covered with bamboo groves or utilized by farmers. A number of stone bridges crossing streams in the middle of fields, and unused for hundreds of years, indicate the location of streets which existed at a time when Nanking was many times its present size. The population inside the walls once numbered more than a million. The population is now 600,000. During the occupation of the Taipings, practically all of the monumental works of an older period were destroyed, but enough remain to indicate the glories of Nanking at its prime, which was during the early Ming period.

Outside the south gate of the city lies the only remaining remnant of the great Porcelain Pagoda. It is the bronze cupola of the pagoda, now overturned, forming a basin. That world-famous pagoda, the most beautiful in China, was destroyed during the Taiping Rebellion. It was built in the early part of the fifteenth century by the Emperor Yung-Lo to commemorate the virtues of his mother and was encased in the finest white glazed brick, while overhanging eaves were covered with green tiles and more than 100 porcelain bells hung from the ornamented cornices. A few of the tiles from this pagoda are treasured by the Metropolitan Museum of Art in New York.*

In spite of the fact that Nanking has been the capital of the country for several years and is of increasing commercial and political importance, it has by no means equalled its past glories as will be seen on any drive through the city. In many places there are a few scattered houses and a few small groups of residences, and only an occasional ruin indicates that it was ever more populous than at present. Indeed, in places it is difficult for one to believe that he is not in the open country, but in a city, which, in its zenith, was second to none. The circumference and solidity of the Nanking walls indicate the importance of the position it formerly held. Near the center of the walled city is one of the historic land marks, the Drum Tower. This massive

---

* Longfellow celebrated this wonderful pagoda in his poem "Keramos."
"And yonder by Nanking, behold
The tower of porcelain, strange and old,
Uplifting to the astonished skies
Its nine fold painted balconies.
With balustrade of twining leaves,
And roofs of tile beneath whose eaves
Hang porcelain bells that all the time
Ring with a soft melodious chime:
While the whole fabric is ablaze
With varied tints all fused in one
Great mass of color like a maze
Of flowers illumined by the sun."

structure was first erected in A.D. 1092, just 400 years
before the discovery of America by Columbus. The
present structure was built by Emperor Hung Wu of
the Ming Dynasty in preparation for a battle against
a force of rebels. He beat the large drum, which could
be heard at a great distance, and served as a signal
to his soldiers in attacks against the enemy. The Drum
tower was also used as a place for the study of
geomantic influences. The earliest European visitors to
China made note of this tower. Marco Polo spoke of
it in 1274. So did Xavier in 1552 and Ricci in 1581,
though Xavier never visited it. In 1867 Mr. Duncan, the
pioneer Protestant missionary to Nanking, took up his
residence within the tower because the anti-foreign feeling
in Nanking was so intense that no one would rent him a
room.

Three roads branch off from the Drum Tower.
Turning to the right the gate of the Japanese Consulate
is seen, and beyond that the campus of the University
of Nanking, an American missionary institution of high
repute, which stretches beside the road for more than half
a mile. Since the capital of the National Government was
established in Nanking an ambitious city development
plan has been inaugurated, an important feature being the
building of Chungshan Road which bisects the city and
leads to the Sun Yat-sen mausoleum. Along this road
many fine Government buildings, in modified Chinese
style, have been erected and will form the administrative
heart of the capital. Notable buildings are the Ministry
of Railways, Ministry of Communications, Overseas
Chinese Hostel, and the Officers Moral Endeavour
Association, revealing the renaissance of Chinese
architectural forms. Outside the Chungshan, or East
Gate, is the "Pink House" of China, overlooking an
extensive system of barracks. The fine new avenue which
bisects Nanking passes near the Drum Tower and brings
the visitor to the southern portion of the city, where
resides the bulk of the population. This road leads out

of the East Gate of the city now known as Chungshan
Gate and across the plain to the famous tomb of the
first Ming Emperor.

Here in the side of a mountain the Emperor was
buried in 1398, and around the site of the tomb are
grouped walls and buildings which for more than five
hundred years have stood witness to the grandeur of the
beginnings of the last purely native dynasty to rule over
China. Leading to the tomb itself is a long avenue,
bordered by huge stone figures of animals and men, the
whole being similar to the earlier Han tombs near Sianfu,
and the later burial places of the Manchu rulers. The
tombs suffered from the visits of the Taipings and have
never been restored; the buildings are roofless. This is
also the burial place of Empress Hsiao and Prince Piao,
Emperor Hung Wu's consort and son, both of whom died
before him. Hung Wu came of a humble family, living
at Feng Yang Hsien, about 100 miles to the north of
Nanking, and served there as a servant in a Buddhist
temple. After his accession to power, one of his first
acts was to confer posthumous titles of emperor, king
and queen, on his father, grandfather, great grandfather,
uncles, mother, aunts, etc., and to surround their graves
with monuments befitting their implied rank. Many other
interesting ruins in or near the city include what remains
of Hung Wu's palace which was occupied by the Mings
for fifty years. It is inside the city walls and can be
reached by the road leading east from the old Tuchun's
Yamen.

Other spots which may be of interest to the visitor
are the Mint, one of the largest in the world; the beautiful
Lotus Lake and various temples. In a small temple not
far from the Drum Tower is one of the largest bells in
existence, said to owe its peculiar tone to the fact that
the daughters of the maker threw themselves into the
metal while still molten. Effigies of the daughters are
preserved to testify to the authenticity of the story which

is told of many other bells in China. The same interesting story is told of two bells in Peiping.

Outside the South Gate is the Precious-Stone Tea-house, built on a small hill. According to an ancient legend, a priest in the reign of Wu Ti, of the Liang dynasty, chanted the sutras of Buddha and showers of flowers came down from heaven and turned into colored stones. The soil of the hill is full of gaily colored pebbles which are disclosed every time a heavy rain falls and are sold at the tea-house. From the top of the hill a good view may be obtained.

Nanking was made an open port for foreign trade by the French treaty of 1858, but it was not formally opened until 1899. In 1908 the Nanking-Shanghai Railway was completed, while the Tientsin-Pukow Railway was opened four years later. The railway station and steamer landing are in Hsia Kwan, a suburb of Nanking, north of the city walls.

Nanking was an early field for the work of foreign missionaries and is to-day one of the most important missionary centers in the country. Probably the most note-worthy achievement of missionary work in Nanking has been the establishment of several union enterprises. The University of Nanking is under the joint management of four different denominations. The Union Bible School is conducted by five denominations and students attend from a larger number of communions. The Union Bible School for Bible women is supported by a number of different societies having work in the Yangtsze Valley and a training school for nurses is supported by the different societies working in Nanking. Besides three hospitals for Chinese the missionary community maintains a hospital for foreigners only.

KIANGSU PROVINCE.

The province of Kiangsu has an area of 38,610 square miles and a population of 33,786,067, being the most densely populated province with a population of 875 per square mile. "Its name is derived from the two cities Kiangning (Nanking) and Soochow." With the exception of a few hills which were once islands off the shore of the mainland, almost the whole of the province consists of flat and very fertile land, formed of the sediment deposited by the Yangtsze and the Yellow River, and is only a few feet above the sea level. In addition to the many natural waterways which traverse the province, there are hundreds of canals, marking the boundaries of almost every large land holding. The land is so intensely cultivated, especially in the southern part of the province, that the whole country has the appearance of a garden and is particularly beautiful during the growing season. It is one of the richest agricultural provinces in China. The silk which is produced is the best that is raised anywhere in the world. The province also contains the most important cotton district in China, extending from the coast near Shanghai along the Yangtze river west to Kiangyin, including the famous cotton district of Nantungchow. Rice and silk are the principal summer crops and wheat and rape are the principal winter crops. In the northern part of Kiangsu peanuts and beans are the most important summer crops. The important cities are Shanghai, Nanking, Soochow, Chinkiang and Wusih. Nanking and Soochow have for centuries been looked upon as among the most cultured cities in the country, while Shanghai holds first place in commerce. No other province has such a large population of foreigners and probably in no other are there so many Chinese who have been educated abroad, or are graduates of modern schools in China. All of these things go to make Kiangsu the most cultured, the wealthiest and among the most progressive of provinces.

THE YANGTSZE RIVER.

No trip to China would be complete without a voyage on the Yangtsze, one of the longest and most important rivers in the world. Rising in the highlands of North-

14

Central Thibet not far from the place where the Yellow River suddenly turns north-west between mountains 20,000 feet high, the Yangtsze flows into the ocean near Shanghai, some 3,200 miles from its source. From the Thibetan plateau, the river runs eastward through the arid regions of Eastern Thibet, bends southward to the borders of Western Szechuan where it runs parallel with the Mekong and Salween, the three rivers cutting through the eastern extension of the great Himalayan range, forming deep narrow gorges with high dividing ridges. Still running parallel with the Mekong in a southerly direction, the Great River or *Ta Kiang*, as it is usually called by the Chinese, enters the province of Yunnan where it follows a circuitous course, flowing eastward and then northward, forming for a few hundred miles the boundary between the provinces of Yunnan and Szechuan. In the latter province, the Yangtsze is joined by several large tributaries, continuing on an eastward course until it flows into the ocean near Shanghai.

With its tributaries, the Yangtsze drains approximately 756,000 square miles, and is navigable from the sea to Sui-fu in South Szechuan, 1,600 miles from the mouth. The headwaters of the river are fully 16,000 feet above sea level. Much of the torrential stream between Sui-fu and the headwaters is unexplored. For the first 400 miles, beginning at its source, the river has a fall of only 200 feet as it runs on the high Thibetan plateau, and then there is a drop of 6,800 feet in 150 miles as the stream descends to the Szechuan plain where there is a steady fall in the course between Chungking and Ichang.

Between the Thibetan border and Sui-fu, the river is known as the Chin-sha Kiang or Chin-Ho, the "Golden River," and has one big tributary, the Ya-lung. At Sui-fu another important tributary, the Min, enters. This, being rather more navigable, was formerly considered the main stream. From Sui-fu to Ichang, the river varies greatly in width, passes through numerous gorges and has many dangerous rapids. Two large tributaries enter it, the

Kia-ling and the Kung-tan. The former is important as being the main stream of the Szechuen plain, and at its junction with the Yangtsze there is the important treaty port of Chungking. Downward, from Ichang, which owes its importance to its position at the emergence of the river from the gorges, navigation is normal and continues throughout all seasons of the year, whereas between Chungking and Ichang, the great variations in the water level make that section difficult and dangerous both at low and high waters.

Like the Yellow River, the Yangtsze rises annually, due to the melting snows in the Thibetan highlands and over-flows its banks in many places, the annual rise being from 70 to 90 feet at Chungking, and from 40 to 50 feet at Hankow and Kiukiang. At Chungking there is a difference of 100 feet between the average mimimum flood level and the average maximum flood level.

At Ichang the river begins its more or less peaceful course to the sea. Fifty miles down stream from Ichang the dykes appear and are continued with a few breaks in the hills to the ocean. Steamers of ordinary construction but of shallow draught are able to proceed from Hankow to Ichang. At Yochow, a treaty port about 200 miles below Ichang, a large volume of water enters from the Tung-T'ing Lake and its feeders. The important city of Changsha is served by this water connection. Next comes Hankow, some 600 miles from the mouth, at which place the Han River discharges into the Yangtsze. From Hankow to the sea, navigation is possible at all times of the year for shallow draught steamers and in summer when the water is high, for large ocean-going vessels. At Kiukiang another lake and its feeders pour into the river. This is the Po-yang lake around the shores of which most of the population of Kiangse province dwells.

At a comparatively recent geological period, all of the present Yangtsze Valley was under the sea, and the land has been built up by the sediment carried down by the Great River. At the present time this amounts according to the calculations of engineers to 6,428 million cubic feet a year—enough to deposit a layer one foot thick over an area of 230 square miles. The country around the mouth was formed recently, as indicated by the fact that Kunshan (Quinsan) at one time was on the seacoast. This delta land is the most fertile in China.

The volume of water in the Yangtsze is 675,800 cubic feet per second at Ichang, and at Hankow, 360 miles down stream, it is one million cubic feet per second, the increase being due to the influx from tributaries. For comparison, it may be noted that the volume of the Thames River at its mouth is 2,300 cubic feet per second.

Important points on the Lower Yangtsze are:—

Miles from Shanghai		Miles from Hankow
0	Shanghai	600
112	Chinkiang	488
205	Nanking	395
255	Wuhu	345
355	Anking	245
458	Kiukiang	142
600	Hankow	0

WUHU.

On the south bank of the Yangtsze, about 50 miles from Nanking, is Wuhu, a treaty port opened in 1877. It has a population of about 500,000. Rice is grown in great quantity near Wuhu, which is the principal rice distributing center in China.

One of the important industries of the city is lumber. Here the great Yangtsze timber rafts are broken up and smaller ones formed to be sent into creeks and estuaries. The foreshore of the city is usually lined with wood and timber rafts. Figures for a recent year show total annual imports and exports of all commodities amounted to Tls. 66,000,000. The principal export items were: rice, 534,000 tons; and iron ore, 400,000 tons. As Wuhu is at low water the head of navigation for deep draught steamers, its commercial importance will doubtless grow. The principle industries of Wuhu are its large cotton mill, employing more than one thousand, and its flour mills. Its close proximity to coal and iron deposits indicate that the city will become an industrial center in the future. The articles of native manufacture for which Wuhu is noted are its scissors, the art of making metal flowers from iron, and the making of white copper filagree over red earthenware.

Among several interesting temples in the city is one built in memory of Li Tai-po, the popular Chinese poet, who flourished in the eighth century. For a long time his great talent was unappreciated, for, according to legend, the poet was so constantly and continuously under the influence of liquor that no one dared present him to the Emperor. At length he agreed to reform, was received at court and prospered in the receipt of royal favor. But one night while crossing the Yangtsze near Wuhu, after a rather convivial dinner, he attempted to embrace the reflection of the moon which he saw in the water, fell overboard and was drowned.

About midway between Wuhu and Anking, 25 miles to the south, the passenger on a Yangtsze river boat can see the Nine Lotus Flower Mountain made up of a number of sharp and rugged peaks. This mountain is one of the four sacred mountains of Buddhism in China and on it are located many temples of more than usual fame, as well as the burial places of some of the greatest saints, both real and imaginary, of past ages. Each autumn the mountain is visited by thousands of pilgrims who come for hundreds of miles to pay their devotions.

ANKING.

On the Yangtsze River, 150 miles from Nanking and 355 miles from Shanghai, is Anking, the capital of Anhui province. At the close of the Sung dynasty (1280) it was founded by refugees who fled from other parts of the country to escape the conquering Mongols. Its high elevation, with water on three sides, made it easily defensible. It has a population of about 85,000, being one of the smallest and least important of China's provincial capitals. With the exception of one or two buildings, the pagoda and the walls, the city was completely destroyed by the Taipings and has been rebuilt since that time. Some of the Taiping trenches and embankments remain in the vicinity. The Great Pagoda, outside the Eastern gate, built in 1580 is the finest in the Yangtsze Valley, and in the fanciful ideas of the Chinese, serves as a mast to the city, which is thought of as a boat. To heighten the illusion, two large anchors are fixed in the walls. The pagoda is seven stories high and on each tier are hung many small bells (formerly of gold) which tinkle in the wind. In conformity with its character as a mast, it is reputed to be elastic and to sway in the wind. For a similar reason, there was for many years a popular local superstition against the appointment of men with the names of Peng, "sail," or Chang, "oar," to important local offices as it is believed that if this were done the city would float down the river. Another fancy is that the pagoda is the head of a dragon because of its position relative to the hills on which the city is built.

Anking is a center for the sale of so-called Indian ink, which is manufactured in the province. Oil lamps are lighted in closed rooms and the soot which collects on walls and ceiling is removed and compressed into cakes of ink.

ANHUI PROVINCE.

The area of the province of Anhui is 54,826 square miles and its population is 19,832,665. The Yangtsze divides the province, one-third being south and two-thirds of the area north of that river. The southern part is mountainous, fertile, has many fine forests and abounds in beautiful scenery, while the northern part is a plain, subject to drouth and flood and is practically deforested.

The soil in this part of the province has been greatly impoverished by the deposits of sand from floods of the Yellow River, made before that erratic stream adopted its present northern course. It is one of the famine regions of China and has been the scene of many disastrous famines. Very large sums have been spent on famine relief and also in preventive work such as the building of dikes and levees. During the famine of 1921 about 100 miles of motor roads were built in the northern part of the province. That part of Anhui province which lies south of the Yangtsze is prosperous. There are a number of lakes in Anhui, the largest being the Hongtsze in the northeast and the Chao in the center; all abound in wild fowl, and provide the winter homes of wild geese. Probably the best hunting section is near Taiping where leopards, boar and big deer are to be found. Hweichow is a city of the province famous for its bankers, who are so wealthy and have such a monopoly of the business in some districts, that there is a popular saying: "It is impossible to do business without a Hweichow man." The city of Tienshan, 30 miles west of Anking, on the old high road from Canton to Peking, was once the capital of the ancient principality of Wan (Hsu), while Tungcheng claims, with many other cities, the distinction of being the most famous in China for scholarship.

KIUKIANG.

This city, "The City of Nine Rivers," is on the Yangtsze, near the outlet of the Poyang Lake, 142 miles from Hankow and 458 miles from Shanghai. Population about 100,000. River steamers usually stop long enough at Kiukiang to allow a trip through the city.

Kiukiang has great fame as having been one of the most fruitful fields for the propagation of Buddhism when that religion was introduced from India. The beautiful Lushan mountains (4,000 feet high) surrounding the place are covered with famous temples and are visited by thousands of pilgrims every autumn. Kiukiang was occupied by the Taipings in 1853 and was almost completely destroyed. Since the opening of the place to foreign trade in 1862 it has slowly built up, but the present city has not regained its old-time importance.

The Monastery of Benevolence, a sacred place of great fame, is located in Kiukiang. More than a thousand years ago, a celebrated abbot had a dream in which Buddha told him that on a certain day a divinity would come down the Yangtsze from Tibet. At the appointed time, the abbot and many others were on the banks of the river watching, when a boat made of stone arrived, occupied by a majestic being, who was immediately escorted with great pomp to the shrine appointed for him and Buddhists came from far and near to offer their devotions. A life-size image of the divinity was made of iron, in order to perpetuate his good influence, and the temple remained the object of the devotion of thousands for several centuries.

After the Taiping rebellion, the old abbot's successor returned to Kiukiang to find his famous temple destroyed and no vestige of the iron god, which had brought it so much fame and prosperity. Discouraged and despondent he was walking across the fields one day, when he stumbled over an object which protruded from the ground. This proved to be the iron god, minus an arm, and suffering from other mutilations at the hands of the sacrilegious Taipings. These defects were soon remedied and the idol restored, with a fresh coat of gilding. It may now be seen in the monastery, while the stone boat in which the deity arrived is in the courtyard. The idol is in a glass case in the rear of the grounds. In the temple is a bell which is continuously tolled, every stroke sending a flash of light into the Buddhist *hades*. The pagoda near by was constructed by the literati of Kiukiang who had for several years failed to pass the official examinations. The spirits were so propitiated by the erection of this pagoda that thereafter the local scholars, according to legend, were almost uniformly successful.

Kiukiang is one of the most noted centers in China for

the sale of both porcelain and silver-ware. The former is brought to Kiukiang from Ching Teh Chen, where all the imperial pottery was made for centuries, Kiukiang being the port from which it was shipped abroad and to other parts of China. The silversmiths' work is very interesting to the tourist not only because of the primitive methods employed but also because of the exquisite results attained. Much silk is made in and about the city and on the shelves of the local shops may be found roll upon roll of luxurious brocades, and satins of every shade and many patterns.

This city boasts of the largest and oldest girls' school in Central China—Rulison High School—which was founded in 1873 under the auspices of the Woman's Foreign Missionary Society of the Methodist Episcopal Church. William Nast College is maintained by the same mission.

KULING.

This Yangtsze Valley summer resort which each year grows more popular with foreigners living in Central China is 15 miles south of Kiukiang in the Lu Shan mountains at an altitude of 3,500 feet. The climate here is temperate, rarely falling below 15° in winter while the mean maximum of the summer is about 75°. During the summer season when hundreds of visitors come to Kuling from all parts of the Yangtsze Valley, special arrangements are made for transportation from Kiukiang. Motor cars, carriages and chairs have been used with varying success. Information as to the best means of transportation available at the time of one's visit can always be obtained at Kiukiang. Head coolies, wearing "Kuling Estate" hats and bearing distinctive numbers are employed at Kiukiang, the foot-hills, and Kuling to assist travelers. At Kiukiang they meet steamers and trains to take charge of baggage.

Kuling is admirably situated for a summer resort and is surrounded by many points of interest, which can be reached by short excursions. The White Deer Grotto, one of the most famous of these, has the more or less romantic reputation of being the oldest university in the world. During the ninth century, Li Pu, an illustrious poet, made this place his study, living in the artificial grotto which he built. He was always accompanied by a tame white deer and in the 14th century an image of the deer was carved by one of his followers and placed in the grotto. Owing to the fame of Li Pu, the grotto became a favorite resort for scholars, especially during the troubled period following the end of the Tang dynasty, when there were many contenders for the throne and the accompanying civil wars. A school was opened here at that time and buildings erected. In A.D. 960 the school was raised to the rank of a university and the attendance greatly increased. The university was enlarged during the Sung dynasty but of late years the buildings have fallen into decay. It is still frequented by students, who congregate there in great numbers during the summer.

NANCHANG.

To the south of Poyang Lake, on the Kan River, is Nanchang, with a population estimated as from 750,000 to 1 million, the capital of Kiangsi province. It is connected by rail with Kiukiang and intending visitors should take the rail route though it is possible to go by boat across the lake. Nanchang is not a treaty port, but has a semi-foreign hotel and a few foreign residents.

Nanchang is unique in that its fine walls, 22 miles in circumference, have never been scaled by an enemy during the 900 years of their existence. It is the only large city in Central China which the Taipings were unable to take and during the revolutions and civil wars it suffered little damage. In the minds of Nanchang residents credit for this remarkable record is due to the town's great deified saint, Hsu Chin Yang who at one time saved the province from flood by killing a dragon snake which was threatening to make the province a part of the Yellow Sea. Hsu cast the dragon into a well and as a result he was in A.D.

200 deified by the Taoists and made " Universal Lord of
Happiness." Many temples in all parts of China are
dedicated to him.

Located 120 miles from Ching Teh Chen, the great
pottery and porcelain center, Nanchang as well as
Kiukiang is an important point for the distribution of
these wares. Local grass cloth is specially famous. Other
important exports are tea, cotton, hemp, tobacco, paper,
indigo, camphorwood chests, lumber, and wood carving.
The stock of curios and works of art are perhaps more
numerous than in most cities because the place has never
been looted. The city is located on the old " Ambassador's
Route " which led directly from Canton northward through
Kwangtung and Kiangsi provinces to Kiukiang. It was
over this route that the MacCartney Embassy passed in
1793 on its way to Peking. Later, in 1816, the Amherst
Embassy returned by the same route. Long and glowing
accounts of the journeys through the Meiling Pass and
down the Kan River to Nanchang and out into Poyang
Lake are given in the records of these missions.

Nanchang is a very conservative, proud, and wealthy
city. It still looks with suspicion upon the innovations
brought in by the foreigner and Western influence has not
yet penetrated the city to any noticeable extent. Foreign
goods are exceedingly scarce and western methods of doing
business have not been adopted by the local merchants.
China is a country of contradictions, and conservative
Nanchang is most progressive along some lines, for there
were electric lights here some years before this modern
innovation was seen in Nanking. Compared with other
Chinese cities, sanitation is quite well taken care of. A
health department does considerable in the way of street
cleaning and food inspection.

The first object of interest that one notices on his
approach to Nanchang is the "Pagoda of the Gilded Ball,"
a pagoda surmounted by a ball which is said to be of pure
gold. One of the unique features of interest is the pavilion
called Tung Wen Kou, built in honor of a twelve year old

boy of marvelous ability. He was a poet and essayist and possessed a remarkable style which has been copied by thousands of scholars.

To see Nanchang in its entirety and in its natural geographical setting, one has only to climb the steps of the fire tower. Here from a height of nearly three hundred feet one can pick out every point of interest that makes the name of Nanchang so famous among Chinese.

KIANGSI PROVINCE.

The province of Kiangsi has an area of 69,498 square miles and a population of 24,466,800. One half of the province is mountainous and hilly while there are a few large tracts of flat land which are given over almost entirely to the cultivation of rice and ramie. Tobacco, sugar cane, hemp and lumber are among the less important productions of the province. In many places the land is so fertile and the climate so favorable that with good seasons four crops a year may be raised. There are extensive orange groves in several of the prefectures especially in Van Fung where the sweetest and the smallest orange in China is grown. Probably the finest tea in the world comes from the famous valleys of Wuning and Ningchow, most of the production formerly going to Russia, where it commanded a high price. The mineral resources of the province are extensive but, as in other parts of China, are inadequately developed. A large part of the coal used in the great steel works of Hanyang comes from the Pinghsiang mines. A railway extends due west from the mine and connects with the northern section of the Hankow-Canton railway (in construction). There are also iron mines and a few unimportant washings for gold. The finest porcelain in China is manufactured in this province. The only forests in the province are in the southeast and southwest. Kiangsi is very rich in skins and those found on the market are leopard, wolf, tiger, wild cat, oppossum, raccoon, badger, deer, otter and fox.

THE WU-HAN CITIES.

At the junction of the Han and Yangtsze Rivers, 600 miles from the the sea (Woosung) are located the three cities of Hankow, Wuchang and Hanyang, commonly grouped under the name of "The Wu-Han Cities." Of the three cities Hankow is the most important, though Wuchang is capital of the province of Hupeh, and in Hanyang are located great steel works and a government arsenal and powder works. The total population of the three cities is about 1,300,000. The foreigners, most of whom live in the foreign settlements of Hankow, number about 2,000.

The Chinese city of Hankow and the French, and Japanese foreign settlements and the former German, British and Russian settlements occupy the north bank of the Yangtsze, east of the Han. A fine Bund fronts the various settlements, extending for two miles along the river. Each settlement has its own local government. The port was opened to foreign trade in 1861, when the site of the British concession was marked out. At the same time the French and Russian concessions were granted but the French did not take possession until 1896. The German and Japanese concessions were granted in 1895. In 1920 following the Great War, the Chinese government took possession of the German concession and the Russian concession was taken back in 1925. The British concession was later voluntarily returned to China. The great commercial growth of the port dates from the completion of the Peking-Hankow railway in 1906. West of the Han is Hanyang, and south of the Yangtsze, which is two miles wide at this point, is the city of Wuchang.

Hankow is connected with Peking by the Hankow-Peking railway (768 miles), with Shanghai by a number of river boats and during the high water period of summer and autumn ocean steamers sail for European ports. Daily air mail and passenger service to Shanghai.

When China's railway system is complete, Wuchang will be connected with Canton by rail and the three cities will then be at the junction of the biggest railway artery in the country (the Peking-Canton railway) and the Yangtsze and Han rivers. At present, Hankow is linked with south China as far as Changsha through the Wuchang-Changsha section of the Canton-Hankow Railway which is now in operation. From Changsha, the railway extends to meet the Chuchow-Pinghsiang Railway, also in operation, thus bringing the coal of the Pinghsiang Colliery into connection with the trunk line. Another much desired railway, the Szechuan-Hankow line, still remains in abeyance due to lack of funds to continue the construction work. The Szechuan-Hankow Railway when completed will add materially to the prosperity of Hankow by bringing it into access with the vast natural resources and products of Szechuan, the richest province of China. Hankow is at present connected with the various ports of Szechuan by shipping through the gorges of the Upper Yangtsze. But, as shipping on this route is at best slow and precarious, the Szechuan-Hankow Railway would play a unique role in improving communication in the interior. Hankow has already assumed great commercial importance and is Shanghai's most serious competitor for the trade of the Yangtsze valley.

Hankow was formerly regarded as only a suburb of the ancient city of Hanyang, but has outstripped that city, its growth being especially rapid since the establishment of the foreign concessions. There is little here of interest to the tourist.

A visit to the great steel works in Hanyang should be made, it being advisable to secure permission for the visit from the head office in Shanghai. The plan for the steel works originated with Chang Chih-tung who, as Viceroy of Canton, memorialized the throne on the need of railways built with Chinese capital and material. Accordingly he was sent to Hankow where 5 million dollars were spent on the works without much success. The plant represents a strange mixture of Chinese progressiveness and superstition for, while it contains what was at the time of its construction the latest and best machinery, it was located on the direction of geomancers, with the result that expensive and unnecessary trans-shipments of coal and ore add to the expenses of operation. The iron ores are mined at Tayeh, 50 miles southwest and the coke comes from the colliery at Pinghsiang more than 300 miles distant. Hanyang is also the location of a large government arsenal.

The city of Wuchang is surrounded by a wall seven miles in length and is cut into two almost equal parts by Serpent Hill. The principal street of the city, lined by 1,000 shops, runs north of the hill. Wuchang, before 300 B.C. was the capital of the Kingdom of Chu and from A.D. 25 to 589 was the capital of Wu. As has been mentioned, it was around the three Wu-Han cities that the principal battles of the Republican Revolution were fought. On October 9, 1911, the accidental explosion of a bomb in the Russian concession, revealed the headquarters of the local revolutionists. On the following evening a small section of the troops at Wuchang mutinied. Others joined them and before dawn they had driven the Viceroy, the imperial commanders and other officials out of the city. The fighting began about a week later, the interim being occupied with preparations on both sides.

The actual engagements between organized forces on each side began on October 27, when Imperial troops opened fire on a village north of Hankow where a number of revolutionists were encamped. With short lulls, the fighting continued for a month, the imperialists slowly driving the revolutionists along the rear of the foreign concessions to the Chinese city of Hankow. Failing to dislodge them from the streets, the city was fired by the imperial commanders and practically all was burned. The great majority of the population had fled to the country before this and few lives were lost in the flames. The local fighting ended on November 27, when the Imperialists, after a battle of five days, crossed the Han river and took Hanyang. Immediately thereafter, Nanking was taken by the Republicans, and an armistice brought an end to the fighting.

HUPEH PROVINCE.

This province has a population of 27,167,244 and an area of 71,428 square miles. The western part of the province is hilly and mountainous, while there are numerous lakes and swamps in the two valleys (Yangtsze and Lower Han) into which the province is divided. A very small part of the total area is arable land and the population is concentrated in the central and eastern section, these being well watered and fertile regions. Timber is scarce except in the hills and mountains of the west, which are 7,000 to 10,000 feet high. Marco Polo spoke of the thick woods on the plains but these forests have disappeared as have so many other forests of China. Iron and coal mining are among the principal industries, large quantities being mined in the Tayeh and Ping-hsiang districts. The principal crops are cotton, wheat, rice and tea. It produces no rice for export and the exportation of tea has declined. In the mountains immense quantities of mushrooms which grow on the bark of trees are gathered and are sold in all parts of the country. Besides the Wu-Han cities, the principal towns are Ichang and Shasi.

CHANGSHA.

Population 300,000. Foreign and Chinese steamers run between Hankow and Changsha, a distance of 200 miles. The railway from Wuchang to Changsha was opened in 1918. This is the northern section of the proposed Canton-Hankow railway, projected in 1898 and financed by a loan of G.$40,000,000. The original American interests were taken over in 1905 by the Chinese government with a payment of G.$6,750,000 for the title to the road as then constructed. Little has since been done toward completion of the line but with the British loan of 1933 it appears that construction may be resumed. The steamer service is irregular from about the middle of November to the middle of February because of low water. A semi foreign-style hotel is located outside the South Gate and it sends a small boat to meet steamers. Frequently those who visit the city make the round trip on the steamers, which generally go on to Siangtan where an afternoon and night is spent.

Changsha is the provincial capital of Hunan and was one of the last cities in China to hold out against the demands of the foreign merchant and missionary for entrance. Until the Boxer movement in 1900 less than a score of foreigners had ever been able to get inside the city and most of these were expelled as soon as their presence became known to the authorities. In 1901 the missionaries were permitted to come into the city and in 1903 the place was opened as a treaty port. Foreign business firms have established agencies and living quarters on an island which is a stone's throw from the city where their Chinese employees live. Frequent sampan and launch service makes this very accessible. The foreign residents number more than 100.

The famous city wall has been torn down and a part of the site is now covered by a boulevard. According to local tradition the first wall was built by Prince Wu Jui about 202 B.C. The only relic of this famous " King of Changsa " is found in the Chia I temple on Taiping Road, where there is a marble bed on which his great adviser, Chia I, once slept. In 1637 the city was captured by rebels and ten years later the walls were entirely rebuilt by the Manchu rulers.

Changsha, like the mountainous province of which it is the capital, is even more famous for the men it has produced than for any of its manufactured or natural products. Many families of the city are able to boast of having in the family tree the names of viceroys, governors and famous generals, and the city abounds in temples and arches which honor the local heroes. " The celebrated Dragon Festival, observed with the greatest éclat on the fifth day of the fifth moon throughout China, owes its origin to the suicide by drowning near Changsha of an

15

early statesman and poet, Chio Yuan, author of the interesting elegy, the Li Sao." Changsha was one of the few places which successfully withstood attacks of the Taipings, though it was besieged for eighty days. Because of this, it earned the title of " The City of the Iron Gates."

The city is on the eastern bank of the Siang, the largest of the three rivers which flow into Tungting Lake. On the western bank is Yolu Shan, a celebrated hill said by geomancers to be under the influence of the literary star. A university which has been in continuous existence for 700 years is located on this eminence. On the hill is a stone monument recording the mastery of the floods by the great Emperor Yu. This monument is but a replica of the one on Ke Lo Feng, a mountain peak Hengchou a hundred miles south of Changsha, which though said to to have been placed there by an order of Yu Wang in 2205 B.C. is generally believed to be a forgery. The characters on this monument, in imitation of the old tadpole style of Chinese writing, would appear to indicate a great age. The hill is much frequented by residents and visitors because of the interesting Buddhist temple and the magnificent view of the surrounding country side.

The streets of Changsha have always been cleaner than those of the average Chinese city and are almost universally flagged with granite blocks but most of them are so narrow that rischas cannot operate so that walking is the only method of getting about the city.

A distinctively local industry is outline embroidery in black and white, on silk and satin. Linen, or China grass cloth, is produced in the neighborhood and is exported in large quantities. Changsha is also noted for its white brassware and pewter teapots. The local bamboo workers produce beautiful boxes and other articles made of this useful plant. At the bazaar on White Horse Lane all articles of local manufacture are exhibited for sale. Many firecrackers are manufactured here as in Siangtan and neighboring towns; most of those used in the United States coming from this part of China.

A railway line is in operation with daily through trains between Changsha and the Ping-hsiang collieries, the trains having accommodation for a few passengers. The portion of the line between Changsha and Chuchow will be made a part of the projected trunk line from Canton to Hankow. A military highway 25 feet in width runs up the east bank of the Siang river 30 miles to Siangtan. Regular motor service is now carried on and the trip can be made in a little more than one hour. From Siangtan to Siangsiang the Chinese-Foreign Famine Relief Committee constructed a motor road on which regular motor service is maintained.

Graduates and students of Yale University (New Haven, Conn.) have established in Changsha an institution popularly known as "Yale in China." The purpose of this institution is to provide for Chinese students in their own country thorough medical education and hospital training.

HUNAN PROVINCE.

The picturesque mountainous province of Hunan is sometimes described by the Hunanese as containing three-tenths mountain, six-tenths water and one-tenth plain, but a more accurate estimate would be six-tenths mountain, one-tenth water and three-tenths plain. Its area is 83,398 square miles and its population 28,443,279. One of the most interesting geographical features of the province is Tungting Lake which covers about 4,200 square miles in the high water of summer, when the water sometimes rises thirty or forty feet above winter level. In the winter it dwindles to a vast area of mud flats between which run the channels of rivers. It abounds in wild fowl.

In recent years large areas on the north side of the lake have been reclaimed for cultivation, most notably the whole region now composing Nan Ting Chou. Various projects have been discussed for dredging part of the lake, making it fit for navigation, and reclaiming still other parts for cultivation. However, it has been found that floods have been more disastrous since the building of the great dikes reclaiming land, and very serious questions are involved in this project.

In addition to Changsha other important cities of the province are: Ch'angteh, west of the Tungting Lake, the leading trading center; Siangtan, south of Changsha, a great trans-shipment center; and Yochow, celebrated for its cloth manufactures and the fact that it is the strategic military center of the province.

Hunan is noted for its rice production, the region round the Tungting Lake and the plains bordering and extending back from Siangtan leading in this crop. It is also in this region that the most famous tea of the province is grown. Green leaf for the imperial family was produced for centuries on Chunshan Island near Yochow. Changsha is an important center for the production of antimony in which China leads the world, exporting large quantities annually to foreign countries. The ore is brought to Changsha by boat from numerous sections of the province. Coal is mined for use at the iron works and river ports. Gold, lead, zinc, tin, copper and arsenic have been mined in small quantities.

Most of the lumber used in Central China and as far down the river as Wuhu comes from Hunan province. Large areas are still under forests in the south and west. Great rafts representing hundreds of thousands of taels in value are constantly being floated down the Yuan River from Western Hunan across Tungting Lake to the Yangtsze River. The annual exports amount to about Tls. 10,000,000, the greater part of this consisting of fire wood. Oil is also one of the most valuable exports. Many tons of fine rice-fed pork are exported annually by a company which maintains a pork-raising farm between Changsha and Siangtan.

In ancient times the territory which is now included in Hunan formed a part of the " Kingdom of the Three Aboriginal Tribes." Members of these non-Chinese tribes exist to the number of several thousands to-day, mostly in the hills of the southern and western parts of the province. The great Emperor Shun died while on an expedition against these tribes and on Chunshan Island in Tungting lake is the grave of his two wives, the daughters of Yao, who were on their way to nurse him and drowned themselves in the lake when they received news of his death.

During the Taiping Rebellion, when the rebels had driven out most of the civil authorities in the province, the Hunanese gentry came to the aid of the Governor, assisting him in organizing military expeditions which restored the machinery of government. The men who drove out the Taipings followed up their success to lasting advantage. The great Tseng Kuo Fan, a native of Changsha, was the leader in these military operations and it was under him with the assistance of General " Chinese " Gordon that the Taiping Rebellion was finally put down. The Hunanese gentry never till the end of the Manchu rule relinquished the advantage they gained through this. Government officials in Hunan always acted with the committee of the gentry, which was usually more powerful than the officials themselves.

There are many mountain peaks in Hunan, those of the Nan Yo or Hengsheng Mountain being the most famous. The Nan Yo is one of China's sacred mountains; it rises to a height of 4,500 ft. Its sides are covered with temples and are well wooded and it is a place of regular and crowded pilgrimage.

YANGTSZE RIVER GORGES.

Five miles above Ichang the famous Yangtsze Gorges begin and a trip through them is well worth the time and expense. Ichang, 1,000 miles from the sea, is only 130 feet above sea level, but Chungking, 350 miles farther inland is 630 feet above. This rise of 500 feet in a distance of 350 miles is accomplished through a series of gorges unsurpassed for their beauty and grandeur. The most famous of the gorges are between Ichang and Kweifu, a distance of 140 miles.

Passage through this part of the Yangtsze, where the great river has cut a channel for itself through deep mountain passes, would appear to be impossible. But it is the only means of transport for the great province of Szechuan, with a population nearly half as large as that of the United States, and millions of dollars' worth of cargo are hauled over the rapids each year. This is accomplished by means of trackers, who pull the boats up stream against the swift current with long ropes made of bamboo splints, the coolies climbing over the rocks alongside, or using steps which were cut into the sides of the cliffs centuries ago.

In places the river passes between ledges of solid rock which rise to heights of 4,000 feet. A steamer upward bound enters the first of the gorges almost immediately after leaving Ichang. This gorge, sixteen miles long, is known as the Ichang Gorge and is one of the most interesting of the series. Steamers usually leave Ichang at day-break and are in the gorge at sunrise. The Wushan Gorge is the longest on the river, its length being thirty miles and its width 1,800 feet at the maximum. In some places the mammoth cliffs which border the river have a smooth surface, while at others erosion has performed strange feats of carving on the stone face.

Here and there through the gorges, caves may be seen hundreds of feet up the precipices, and the river people have made places of abode out of these holes in the rock and various sorts of structures have been built in the cave entrances overlooking the river. These cave houses and numerous huts dotting the face of the cliffs are most picturesque in appearance. The mountain people cultivate the thin soil in almost impossible places on the sides and tops of the bluffs seen along the river. The scenery is delightfully diverse—here a gorge, now the stream widening into a lateral valley with a tributary stream pouring into the great river. The Yangtsze and its tributaries have seasons of heavy flood, and this explains the tremendous variation in the water level. In summer the water level in the gorges climbs at certain points 175 feet up the cliffs from its lowest midwinter mark.

While steamer traffic through the Gorges is comparatively new, navigation on the Upper Yangtsze is centuries old. Native boats are pulled up-stream by hand-power, and this has been the practice since ancient times. The river people are a distinctive type. Thousands of men are employed on junks and in the industries connected with the junk traffic. The occupation of a tracker is a most perilous one. In many places in the gorges the men are forced to walk along narrow footpaths carved in the face of the cliff, and often they must climb over huge boulders and make dangerous turns. At the rapids these men may be seen crawling on hands and feet, straining their muscles to the utmost and clawing in the crevases of the rock to move a loaded junk up-stream against the strong current.

The large number of junks in operation along the river explains the presence of scores of villages and settlements of various kinds which furnish supplies and labor for the river traffic. Some of these villages are most picturesque with their pagodas, temples and shrines. A Buddhist shrine a short distance below Chungking is known as the " Chungking Harbor Master." The steamers slow down as they pass it, and the Chinese passengers light firecrackers.

Mrs. J. F. Bishop, one of the first foreigners to visit this part of China, wrote of it as follows in her book *The Yangtsze Valley and Beyond.*

" We were then in what looked like a mountain lake. No outlet was visible; mountains rose clear and grim against a dull grey sky. Snowflakes fell sparsely and gently in a perfectly still atmosphere. We cast off from the shore; the oars were plied to a wild chorus; what looked like a cleft in the rock appeared and making an abrupt turn round a high rocky point in all the thrill of novelty and expectation, we were in the Ichang Gorge, the first and one of the grandest of those gigantic clefts through which the Great River, at times a mile in breadth, there compressed into a limit of from 400 to 150 yards, has carved a passage though the mountains.

" The change from a lake-like stretch, with its light and movement, to a dark and narrow gorge black with the shadows of nearly perpendicular limestone cliffs broken up into buttresses and fantastic towers of curiously splintered and weathered rock, culminating in the Pillar of Heaven, a limestone pinnacle rising sheer from the water to a height of 1,800 feet, is so rapid as to bewilder the senses. The expression ' lost in admiration ' is a literally correct one.

" With a strong fair wind our sail was set; the creak and swish of the oars was exchanged for the low music of the river as it parted under our prow; and the deep water (from fifty to a hundred feet), to a striking bottle-green color, was unbroken by a swirl or ripple, and slid past in a grand, full volume. The stillness was profound, enlivened only as some big junk with lowered mast glided past us at great speed, the fifty or sixty men at the sweeps raising a wild chant in keeping with the scene. Scuds of snow, wild, white clouds whirling round pinnacles and desolate snow-clothed mountains, apparently blocking further progress, added to the enchantment. Crevices in the rock were full of maidenhair fern and on many a narrow ledge clustered in profusion a delicate mauve primula unabashed by the grandeur and the gloom. Streams tumbled over ledges at heights of 100 feet. There are cliffs of extraordinary honeycombed rock possibly the remains of ' potholes ' of ages since, rock carved by the action of water and weather into shrines with pillared fronts, grottoes with quaint embellishments—gigantic old women gossiping together in big hats—colossal abutments, huge rock needles after the manner of Quiraing, while groups of stalactites constantly occur as straight and as thick as small pines supporting rock canopies festooned with maidenhair. Higher yet, surmounting rock ramparts

2,000 feet high, are irregular battlemented walls of rock, perhaps twenty feet thick, and everywhere above and around are lofty summits sprinkled with pines, on which the snow lay in powder only, and ' the snow clouds rolling low ' added to the sublimity of the scenery.

" It was always changing, too. If it were possible to be surfeited with turrets, battlements, and cathedral spires, and to weary of rock phantasies, the work of water, of solitudes and silences, and of the majestic dark green flow of the Great River, there were besides lateral clefts, each with its wellsided torrent, with an occasional platform green with wheat, on which a brown roofed village nestled among fruit trees, or a mountain, bisected by a chasm, looking ready to fall into the river, as some have already done, breaking up into piles of huge angular boulders over which even the goat-footed trackers cannot climb. Then, wherever the cliffs are less absolutely perpendicular, there are minute platforms partially sustaining houses with their backs burrowing into the rock, and their fronts extended on beams fixed in the cliff, 'accessible only by bolts driven into the rock, where the small children are tied to posts to prevent them falling over, and above, below, and around these dwellings are patches of careful culture, some of them not larger than a bath towel, to which the cultivators lower themselves with ropes, and there are small openings occasionally, where deep-eaved houses cluster on the flat tops of rocky spurs among the exquisite plumage of groves of the golden and green bamboo among oranges and pumeloes with their shining greenery, and straight stemmed palms with their great fanlike leaves."

Ichang.

Formerly a walled city, about 60,000 inhabitants, opened as a treaty port in 1877. The encircling walls were torn down a few years ago and replaced by a road. It is important chiefly as the gateway to the gorges above, an important point for the trans-shipment of goods and the supply of provisions and labor for the river traffic. A small foreign colony of less than fifty live here. The hilly and mountainous country so characteristic of the Upper Yangtsze begins about 40 miles below Ichang, the low hills gradually increasing in height until at Ichang the surroundings are mountainous. "In the vicinity of the town the hills are pyramidical in outline, with prominent cliffs nearby; north, south and west of the town the country is much cut up, forming an archipelago of peaks 2,000 to 4,000 feet high, the peaks themselves being offsets from spurs attaining altitudes of 7,000 to 9,000 feet, situated some days distance beyond. These pyramidical hills around Ichang are very interesting and never fail to attract the attention of travelers."

Oranges, lemons, persimmons, rice, wheat and bamboo are grown in the vicinity. The only export of importance is opium, which, as contraband, is smuggled and does not appear on the customs returns.

Ichang is the terminus of a projected railway line to connect this port with Chungking, and the troubles which arose over the construction of the line are credited with starting the revolution of 1911. In order to prevent the construction of the proposed railway by foreign capital a local company had been formed and about £2,000,000 raised. Of this amount less than one-third had been voluntarily subscribed. By the terms of the Hukuang loan agreement, signed in May, 1911, the Chinese government agreed to take over the shares in this line. Violent opposition to this plan arose, and the disturbance in Chengtu precipitated the revolution. When the revolution halted work, 16 miles of track had been laid and preliminary work completed for 60 miles. It is estimated that the construction of the line, which passes through an exceedingly mountainous country will take from 10 to 15 years. The rails which had been laid have been removed but a little of the grading remains.

CHUNGKING.

Chungking occupies the end of a bold and rocky bluff at the confluence of the Kialing and Yangstze rivers 1,350 miles from the sea. It is surrounded by a stone wall five miles in circumference built in 1761. There is a difference of nearly 100 feet between low water and high water levels here and hundreds of rudely carved stone steps lead up from the low water level to the city gates. Half surrounded by a range of hills 1,000 feet in height, the situation of the city is one of great beauty although restricted for convenient expansion. The Chungking hills afford a pleasant and easily accessible summer resort.

Like Wanhsien, Chungking forms a terminus for the trip to the provincial capital of Chengtu, formerly 10 days' journey distant by chair but now more easily accessible by motor car. There are now many steam and motor boats on the upper river so that cargo and passengers are carried all the year round as far as Luchow and during high water to Kiating. From Chungking also the traveler leaves the river for the overland journey to the province of Kweichow.

Chungking is known as the " Great City " of West China and was opened to foreign trade in 1891. The annual volume of imports and exports now amounts to ￥35,000,000 being equally divided. Formerly native junks were used exclusively for carrying on this trade, but now numerous foreign steamers ply the Yangtsze and its tributaries, carrying cargo for transhipment here. The larger foreign vessels have increased the dangers of navigation for the junks, and it is said that the jealousies of the owners of the latter have been partly responsible for the firing on foreign craft and other outrages which have been committed against foreigners in the upper Yangtsze. It is from Chungking that foreigners conduct trade with Thibet, Szechuan Province and other distant regions of Western China. Several foreign powers have consulates in the city, and usually the gunboats of these and other nations lie at anchor there for the protection of trade and the interests of their respective citizens. The crowds seen on the streets of Chungking always are cosmopolitan and picturesque. In the shops may be found

Szechuan silks and brocades, and sometimes Thibetan tapestries and jewelry which make rare possessions. In spite of revolutions and banditry which constantly disturb Western China, the trade at Chungking has increased steadily. Cargoes carried by foreign vessels and native junks include silk, skins, wood oil, cotton goods and drugs. The drug trade is of considerable importance. As Chengtu is the political and literary center of Szechuan, so Chungking is its commercial *entrepot*, and it is a fascinating place for the tourist. Foreign visitors travel about the city in sedan chairs or on the backs of Chungking ponies, noted for their agility and ability to climb steep inclines. Tourists usually live on board the boat that brought them, but it is possible to obtain accommodation at the homes of foreigners or at the missions.

Chungking and Kiangpeh, a walled town on the opposite bank of the Kialing, have a combined population estimated at 600,000. The foreign population exclusive of the contingents on the gunboats numbers several hundred.

CHENGTU.

It is only through the Yangtsze gorges or by a more difficult trip through the narrow passes of the mountains separating the province of Hupeh from Szechuen that it is possible to reach Chengtu from the Yangtsze Valley. Formerly the traveler had to traverse the distance between Chungking and Chengtu by sedan chair, a long and tedious journey which has now been greatly shortened through the building of motor roads. This city is the capital of the province of Szechuan and one of the oldest and most important cities in China. It was once the capital of the independent kingdom of Shuh. Population, about 600,000. It is situated in the center of the famous Chengtu plain, covering an area 120 miles by 40, the population of which is estimated to be 1,200 to the square mile. The soil is rich, the climate mild, and the excellent system of irrigation devised more than 2,000 years ago by Li Ping, China's great irrigation engineer, insures

water at all periods of the rice season. The farms of the
plain are valuable, and are so intensely cultivated that they
resemble small garden patches rather than farms. It is
possible to raise a winter as well as a summer crop and
four seasons of garden vegetables. Famine has been
unknown for two thousand years.

The city is unique as being the only old and important
city in China without a pagoda. It is surrounded by a
massive wall nine miles in length and over 40 feet broad,
which being splendidly paved forms a favorite promenade
for the citizens. The citadel and enclosed place of residence of the ancient emperors still exists dating from
A.D. 221-265. It is used as a normal school.

In few other places in China can such a contrast in
architecture be seen, for while the Chinese who live here
cling to the standards of South and Central China, the
Manchus as persistently duplicated the old styles of Manchuria and as a result architectural types both of Peking
and Canton can be seen. The population of Szechuan
province and of Chengtu is comparatively modern. The
independent Szechuanese refused to accept the rule of the
Manchus and it was necessary for the Manchu troops
almost to depopulate the province before the anti-dynastic
rebellions were put down. The invading Manchus liked
the country so well that they stayed on as permanent residents. Little remained of the ancient Szechuan population
and the rich province was filled up with immigrants from
South and Central China. These sturdy settlers have
produced a race as independent as the more ancient Szechuanese, as evidenced by the fact that one of the first
outbreaks which heralded the revolution of 1911 was in
this province.

The streets of Chengtu are noted throughout China
for their width and cleanliness, all being paved by wide
stone slabs and well policed. Some of the older streets
are 30 to 40 feet wide with side-walks on each side. On
the principal Great East Street are many silk stores.
Szechuen is one of the most important silk provinces of

China and is famed for the excellent weave of its various silks and satins.

A large number of Moslems are found in the Chengtu plain. They have lived in China for many generations and are nearly indistinguishable from the native Chinese, but still persist in regarding themselves as foreigners. They are the cattle merchants and butchers of Chengtu and its neighborhood. Chengtu is quite a missionary center. Eleven missions are represented and two Bible societies. There magnificent hospitals have been erected. A Christian Union University has been established in the south suburb.

To the south of Chengtu, on the banks of the Min river, are found many rock-cut tombs. They contain stone and burnt-clay coffins together with fragments of grave goods belonging to the times of the Han dynasties and the period of the Three Kingdoms (206 B.C.—A.D. 265). The entrances to them are occasionally finely carved. They vary much in size but the larger ones measure from 40 to 100 feet deep and 6½ feet high, with an equal breadth. In the sides are niches for the placing of coffins and the *hades* images and articles.

The road between Chengtu and Chungking (260 miles) passes through the densely populated heart of Szechuan province, touching eight walled cities. The return journey to Chungking can be made by boat. The traveler can delay at Kiatingfu to visit Mount Omi, 30 miles distant, the famous Buddhist mountain, nearly 11,000 feet high. A stone path runs all the way to the top, where, on a clear day, an excellent view can be had of the snow-topped mountains of Tibet. Lodging can be secured at any of the many temples by the wayside.

Visitors to Mount Omi are often able to see the strange apparition which made Omi famous as far away as India. This consists of a rainbow floating in space one to three thousand feet below the precipice, and, in the center, what appears to be a colossal human figure. The rainbow is formed by the sun and the mists while the figure is the shadow of the observer. In the time when Buddhism exerted a stronger influence than at present, this phenomenon excited such awe that many devotees threw themselves from the cliff, expecting to be caught in the arms of Buddha. Among the many temples on the mountain, those most worthy of a visit are: Ta-wu-su, Chiu-lau-tong (famous for its caves), Kinting (on the summit) and Wan-yansu.

SZECHUAN PROVINCE.

The area of the province of Szechuan is 218,533 square miles and its population is 49,782,810; its name, "four streams," is derived from the fact that four rivers, the Kialing, Ching, Min and Yulong flow through the province into the Yangtsze. The province is peculiarly isolated from the other parts of China, for it not only lies in the remote western part of the country, bordering on Thibet, but its mountainous boundaries make communication difficult, even with the provinces immediately adjoining it. The hills rise to great heights on the Kweichow boundary and the northeast corner, bordering on Hupeh, is mountainous. The gorges here are almost inaccessible and are said to be more impressive than those on the Yangtsze. The fact that the province is so densely populated testifies highly to the agreeableness of the climate, the fertility of the soil, and the efficiency of the ancient system of irrigation. The most important parts of the province are (1) the "Red Basin," in which lies the plain of Chengtu and many small valleys, all of them about 1,000 feet above the sea level, (2) the famous salt-well region lying in the triangle between the cities of Kiatingfu, Fuhsuenhsien and Luikianghsien; and (3) the country around Chungking. All the valleys and even the hills are intensely cultivated, the province being " dotted with farmhouses, hamlets, villages, and market towns, many of them larger and more important than ' cities ' in other parts of China." The whole of the province has a climate peculiar to itself. There is rarely any frost or snow in winter and the average maximum summer heat is 92°.

Eastern Szechuan is often cloudy in winter but in Western Szechuan it is not uncommon to have long spells of the brightest sunshine in December and January. Two harvests are reaped in the year, the first of wheat, pulse and rape seed in April and May and the second in August and September of rice, maize, potatoes, etc. The high mountainous region of the west, bordering on Eastern Tibet, is the paradise of the botanist, the ethnologist and the sportsman. Traveling in Szechuan in spring and autumn·is a pleasure no visitor ever forgets. The climate is ideal, the scenery unsurpassed for beauty, food is always plentiful, coolie hire is not expensive and the people if treated rightly always show the utmost friendliness.

The Chinese race is predominant throughout Szechuan, but their features vary somewhat; and some, especially in regions near to the western mountains, are of mixed blood. " The varieties result from the position occupied by Szechuan, it being the limit and border land where widely different races come into contact with each other. Revolutions have also largely modified the population of the country. Among those upheavals, we must mention the great massacre which took place there at the close of the Ming dynasty. Three-fourths of the inhabitants are said to have been exterminated.. To repeople the province, a large number of immigrants flowed in towards the middle of the 17th century. Traces of this immigration are still met with at Chungking, where the local Council of the Gentry is called Pasheng (the 8 provinces), alluding thereby to the eight provinces to which the members of the Assembly originally belonged. The predominating element of the population is said to have a striking resemblance to the aborigines of Yunnan, the Kachyns (Burmese ' wild men ') who inhabit the Burma-Chinese frontier, and whose principal characteristics are: a triangular face, large, obliquely-set eyes, light hair, and extremely short stature (4 ft. 8 to 5 feet). In the east, a portion of the population is made up of families that came from Hunan.

" The people of Szechuan are shrewd, active, quarrelsome, but nevertheless very polite. They are also hospitable, and migrate easily from their homes, being found in Kansu, Shensi, Kweichow, and even upon the lofty table lands of Yunnan." *

TATSIENLU.

Tatsienlu, 8,349 feet above sea level, is an exceedingly interesting and politically important little city between Szechuan proper and Eastern Thibet. It is situated in a narrow valley amidst vast mountains through which runs the main road from Chengtu to Lhassa. The former is 12 stages or 267 miles distant, the latter 66 stages or 1,506 miles. Official estimates give the population of the place as 700 Thibetan and 400 Chinese families, but besides it has a numerous floating population of merchants, soldiers and visitors.

Being at once a Thibetan and a Chinese capital, as also a commercial and a missionary center, travelers to West China, if they have time at all, generally make it a point to visit Tatsienlu. Here are administered the Chinese affairs of the whole of Eastern Thibet and here come long caravans of merchandise from the interior returning with tea, cotton, and metal goods. Though only at the threshold of Thibet, the Thibetans come and go in such numbers that they can be seen here in all their quaint, free, happy ruggedness of character. Eight lamasaries are to be found in or near the city. Prayer flags fly from the houses, large prayer wheels are driven by water power on the banks of the streams, cairns of sacred inscribed stones rise from the wayside. On all sides are the snow-topped mountains. A day or two to the west the snow line on the highway can be reached at a pass 13,923 feet high. Bear, leopard, wild cow, wild sheep and goat, deer, pheasant, pigeon, etc., can be shot in the neighborhood. The country is one of mountain, forest, tableland

---

* Richard's " Comprehensive Geography of China."
16

and rushing river; grand, free, bracing, fascinating, the fitting home of its hardy sons and famous dogs.

From Chengtu to Tatsienlu the traveler can ride a pony or hire a sedan chair while coolies carry his luggage, 70 catties per man. Each coolie costs 50 to 60 cents per day. From Tatsienlu westward all luggage is transported on the backs of pack animals. These are provided by the Thibetan system of " Ula," the hire of each animal being about 50 cents for one day.

From Tatsienlu two roads run westwards into Thibet, called the North and South roads. The first is the business route, and proceeds by way of Dawo, Kantsze and Derge; the second is the official route and proceeds by way of Hokow (where French engineers have erected a steel bridge over the Yalung river), Litang, Lamaya, Batang, Kiangka and Chiamdo. At Chiamdo the Chinese postal service has its most western post office.

On the official route the distances are as follows: Tatsienlu to Hokow, 120 miles; Hokow to Litang, 88 miles; Litang to Lamaya, 46 miles; Lamaya to Batang, 117 miles; Batang to Kiangka, 120 miles; Kiangka to Bhiamdo, 274 miles. A stage or day's journey may be roughly reckoned at 18 to 25 miles. The full distance from Chengtu to Lhassa is 1,646 miles.

From Batang a road runs to Derge; the traveler can thus, when the political situation is quiet, proceed by the north road and return by the south or *vice versa*. Southward from Batang an important road leads to Yunnan, from which the route can be followed on into Burmah. The distance between Batang and Talifu in Yunnan is about 600 miles or 31 stages; Batang to Yentsing, 6 stages; Yentsing to Atensze, 7 stages; Atensze to Talifu, 18 stages.

Between Tatsienlu and Ningyuanfu a road can be pursued which also leads into Yunnan and Burmah. The chief interest of this is that it passes through the Nosu or Lolo country. The Lolos are a race of aboriginals whom the Chinese have failed to subdue. Driven out of the Kienchang or Ningyuanfu valley they have maintained their independence in the mountains. From Tatsienlu to Fu-lin it is four stages; from Fu-lin to Yue-shi-hsien, four stages; from Yue-shi-hsien to Ningyuanfu, four stages, twelve in all. Mode of travel: sedan chair, horses, coolies. From Ningyuanfu to Hui-li-chow, five stages, from Hui-li-chow to Yunnanfu, twelve stages.

There is another road from Ningyuanfu to Yunnan which is chosen by those who wish to go to Talifu. Ning-yuanfu to Yenyuenhsien, five stages; Yenyuenhsien to Talifu, twelve stages.

HANKOW *to* PEIPING.

Hankow is connected with the former capital by the Peiping-Hankow, or Ching-Han Railway, 753 miles.

Important points on the line are:

Miles from Hankow		*Miles from Peiping*
0	Hankow or *Han k'eou* *	753
109	Cross Mu Ling mountain by a tunnel 1,115 feet long, leaving the basin of the Yangtsze for that of the Yellow River. The country between Hankow and the Yellow River was formerly divided between the three kingdoms of Chu, Chin and Wei and this is the scene of many stirring adventures of that period.	644
112	Hsin-tien or *Sin-tien*. Three miles east at an altitude of 1,980 feet is Chi-kung-shan, a summer resort frequented by Hankow residents.	641
236	Yen-cheng Hsien or *Yen T'cheng Sien*. Cross the Sha Ho, a tributary of the Yellow River.	517

---

* The French spelling of Chinese names is used on this railway. Both the official and the French spelling are here given, the French in *italics*.

Miles from Hankow		*Miles from Peiping*
295	Hsin-cheng Hsien or *Sin T'cheng Sien*, a very old town which was captured by the state of Cheng (806-375 B.C.).	458
323	Chengchow or *Tcheng Tcheou*. Railway connections to Honanfu and to Kaifeng. Cross Yellow River.	430
581	Shai Kai Chwang or *Shih Chia Chuang*. Branch line to Tai Yuan-fu 151 miles distant.	172
663	Pao-ting-fu.	90
701	Kao-pei-tien. A branch line 25 miles long leads to the Western Tombs.	52
722	Liou-li-ho. Sixteen miles distant are the famous grottoes, Yuan-shui Tung.	31
733	Leang-hsiang Hsien. Ten miles distant are the burial places of the ten monarchs who ruled China from A.D. 1115 to 1234. The tombs are in ruins.	20
753	Peking or Peiping.	0

CHI-KUNG-SHAN.

This summer resort is on the Hupeh-Honan border, about three and one-third miles from Wushinkwan, the gateway between Central and Northern China. It also is about the same distance from Sintien station on the Peking-Hankow Railway, the latter station being 115 miles from Hankow, or a journey of five and one-half hours by express train and seven hours by ordinary train.

There are about one hundred bungalows at Chi-kung-shan. The settlement has a church and a public hall and schools for foreign children. The supply of drinking water is taken from wells. The temperature in summer is about 80 degrees, while in winter it goes down below zero.

KAIFENG.

The 40 miles by railway from Chengchow to Kaifeng is traversed in 2½ hours, bringing the traveler to Kaifeng

(population 230,000), capital of Honan province. This
city has been the capital of the country on several
occasions. The northern Sung dynasty reigned here when
the place was known as Pien-liang, from 960 to 1129. It
was also the eastern capital of the Mongols and has been a
center of great wealth. " At one siege Kuan Li-pu demanded an indemnity of five million ounces of gold, ten
thousand horses and as many oxen. While this enormous
exaction shows the wealth of the capital, the fact that it
was paid explains the rapid decline afterwards and the
one reason why it was abandoned as the capital in favor
of Nanking."

Owing to its central location and political importance
it has been the scene of many fierce battles. Under the
Mings Kaifeng was destroyed by robbers and floods, but
rebuilt. The city was captured in 1642 by the rebel-
brigand Li Tze-cheng, whose later victories at Sianfu and
Peking led to the overthrow of the Ming dynasty and the
establishment of the Manchus as the rulers of China.
Kaifeng at that time withstood a long siege, but was at
length subdued when the rebels cut the embankments of
the Yellow River, thereby flooding the city. One hundred
thousand people perished. Later there were many
disastrous fires which seriously affected the importance of
the city. The population is now much reduced and except
for a few ancient temples, Kaifeng has few places of
interest. One of the famous pagodas of China is located
here, the so-called " Iron Pagoda," built largely of glazed
tiles and porcelain. It is one of the few remaining pagodas
of this style of construction. The old throne room of the
Sungs can also be seen.

Kaifeng is noted as the location of a now extinct
Jewish colony, which has attracted a great deal of
attention from students of history. It is known that the
Jews settled in China during the Han dynasty, and " it is
supposed that the settlement took place soon after A.D. 34
at which time a terrible persecution of the Jews took place
in Babylon. No less than 50,000 were then massacred.

Others hold that the settlement took place 35 years later, after the fall of Jerusalem. It is quite possible that the Jewish colony in China may be of even older date—Is. 49: 12: 'And these from the land of Sinim.'" When the great Jesuit missionary, Matteo Ricci, was in Peking, he was visited by one of the Kaifeng Jews, who was familiar with the tenets of his religion and told of a large congregation of Jews with a synagogue in Hangchow, as well as large Jewish populations in other provinces. Other Jesuits at later dates made copies of inscriptions on stone tablets at Kaifeng, giving isolated details of the history of the colony, and also translated some of the inscriptions found in the synagogue.

From these inscriptions as well as from the writings of Jesuits and of Marco Polo, it is evident that the Jewish colony at Kaifeng was at one time large and important and supported a fine synagogue. As late as the first part of the eighteenth century the colony was still vigorous and the members distinguishable from their neighbors by their Hebraic features. In the flood of 1642 many of the Hebrew manuscripts were destroyed and the fragmentary records of the colony tell a pathetic story of the efforts to repair and revise the damaged sacred papers which remained. The synagogue was rebuilt, apparently for the last time, in 1653. Two centuries later when the Jews of Europe began to be interested in the colony it was rapidly declining. A letter from European co-religionists was sent to the Kaifeng Jews, and the reply received in 1870 told a pathetic story of the colony's plight. The teachers were all dead and no one remained who could read Hebrew, a knowledge they had preserved for almost 2,000 years, while isolated from all others of their race. "Daily with tears in our eyes we call on the Holy Name; if we could but again procure ministers, and put our house of prayer in order, our religion would have a firm support." At that time only seven of the seventy Jewish clans remained, the colony consisting of about 200 persons. The Kaifeng Jews are now indistinguishable from their Chinese neighbors, with whom they have intermarried, though a few still persist in calling themselves Jews. Only in abstinence from pork do they exhibit any knowledge of the beliefs of their religion. The synagogue itself has disappeared, but its site and a number of important relics have been preserved.

HONAN PROVINCE.

The area of Honan is 67,954 square miles and its population 30,831,909 or an average of 454 per square mile With the exception of the mountainous western parts, the whole of the province is a remarkably flat and fertile plain, crossed by a number of rivers which connect principal market places of the province with Chinkiang, Hankow and Tientsin. Roads from principal centers cross the province and unite at Honanfu. The central part of the plain is buried in sand brought down from the Yellow River, but the remainder is fertile, "dotted over with cities, towns and villages, and crossed in every direction with brown earth roads, wide in the north and center, and narrow and paved in the south, teeming with a hardy farming population." The province is probably the most treeless region of China, even the bamboo being very scarce. In its absence the fences are built of *kaoliang* stalks or of mud. The houses are mostly built of mud and stone. The climate of the province shows great extremes, the winters being cold and bracing, with a temperature which often drops below zero, and summers with a maximum temperature of 100°. There are extensive coal mines in the province, in many of which modern mining methods have replaced the former primitive Chinese methods. "The Honanese . . . do not care for travel. Their view of the world is limited by their own horizon. The majority are farmers, somewhat rude and uncouth in manner, easily roused to anger, quick to take offence. They are of an independent turn of mind and will not brook reproof; very conservative, they do not welcome foreign innovation."

Honan has occupied an important place in the history of the country, having been the seat of the government more frequently than any other province. As early as 2,180 B.C. Taikang was the capital of the Hsia dynasty, while 400 years later Kweitehfu was the capital of the Shang rulers. Honanfu and Kaifeng have also served as the capital on several occasions.

Ten miles to the south of Honanfu is the famous mountain defile, Lung Men, decorated with many huge carvings, which include statues of Buddha over sixty feet high. The Lung Men is an artificial river channel cut through a limestone mountain, the work, according to tradition, being done by Emperor Yu, with the aid of a dragon. In the seventh century hundreds of temples were quarried into the limestone sides of the defile, and thousands of images carved, chiefly depicting Buddha and his disciples. Hot springs in the neighborhood add to the interest and fame of the region. To the south of Honanfu is the sacred mountain of Sung Shan, 7,000 feet high. In the south-eastern part of the province, in the district of Kwangchow, is the Shwang-ho Shan, a mountain of considerable interest as the inhabitants of the district believe it is the dwelling place for the souls of the departed. Because of this belief, they have gone to considerable expense to build hundreds of rooms and dwelling places for the souls of departed friends and relatives.

HONANFU.

Before the Chinese people moved far from their cradle in the valley of the Yellow River, Honanfu was an important city, well located in the rich valley of the Loho, and at the crossing of the two great high roads to Sianfu. From a military point of view it is of great strategic value, commanding the entire western section of the Lunghai Railway, which connects at Chengchow with the Pekin-Hankow line. A railway runs west from Honanfu to Tungkuan, a distance of 160 miles, and thence is building to Sianfu.

The city is of great historical interest, having served as the capital of the country under four dynasties: Chow,

781 B.C.; Eastern Han, A.D. 25; Tsin, A.D. 280; and T'ang, A.D. 904.

CHENCHOW.

Chenchow, which is not to be confused with the near-by city of Chengchow,* is one of the oldest, if not the oldest city in China. According to the annals it was in existence as long ago as 3,000 B.C. when it was the residence of Fu Hsi, the legendary first ruler of China, who is supposed to be buried at the place. Shên Nung, the "Divine Plowman," also lived here. The burial place of Fu Hsi is at a temple about a mile from the city, visited by many thousand pilgrims each spring when the festival in his honor is celebrated. According to Chinese mythology, Fu Hsi began all things. "He discovered the use of salt, under the influence of which men lost the gills and hair with which their bodies had previously been furnished. He taught them how to hunt and how to split wood for firing and therewith to cook what they took in the chase and from the streams. He taught them the care of flocks and herds, too, and how to twist silken threads and produce harmonious sounds therefrom. He found family life matriarchal; he instituted marriage and so produced the patriarchal type which has nowhere persisted so strongly as in China. Men in those days kept their records by means of knotted cords, similar probably to those Cortez found in use in Mexico. Fu Hsi superseded them by written characters and introduced a calendar." At the tomb in Chenchow there is a circular raised platform, on which the signs of the Pa-kua are inscribed in stone. In the center is placed the Lung-ma, or dragon horse on which has been marked the sign of the elemental principles according to Chinese theory—the T'ai-ki-t'u. The dragon horse is supposed to have emerged from the Yellow River at the command of Heaven, to aid Fu Hsi in his task of civilizing the earth; the figure of the T'ai-ki was found on its back, and from it Fu Hsi deciphered the Chinese

---

* Spelled Tcheng Tcheou on the railway time-tables.

system of written characters. " According to Chinese history Fu Hsi lived about the time of the flood, and some Europeans think that probably Noah is really the character referred to. However that may be, a very interesting and curious thing about these diagrams is that they represent father, mother, three sons and three daughters, thus exactly coinciding with the number and relationship of the family of Noah."

PEIPING (PEKING) AND
NORTHERN CHINA

P EIPING, lies on a plain a few feet above sea level, eighty miles west of Tientsin, and within ten miles of the foot of the Western Hills, which in clear weather are visible from the. city. Three main railways enter the city—the Peking-Mukden Line connecting with Shanghai by way of Tientsin, Pukow and Nanking, and from Mukden in the north likewise by way of Tientsin; the Peking-Hankow Line from Hankow and central China; and the Peking-Suiyuan Line from Kalgan and the more intermediate station at the Nankow Pass where the Great Wall can be seen. The Peking-Mukden Railway makes connection with the Trans-Siberian route by way of Changchun and Harbin.

Arrival.—Passengers from Tientsin over the Peking-Mukden line arrive at the Chien Men East Station, inside the Chinese City and just south of the Tartar City Wall, within a few minutes ricksha ride of the Legation Quarter and the hotels. Passengers coming from the south over the Peking-Hankow Railway arrive at the Chien Men West Station directly opposite the East Station and equally near the Legations and hotels.

Hotels.—Grand Hotel de Pekin, Grand Hotel des Wagons-Lits, du Nord, Central, Astor and Palace. All hotels send motor busses to meet trains.

Post Office.—On Chien Men Street just north of Legation Street is the new Central Post Office, attended by an English speaking staff and a foreign member of the Chinese Maritime Customs.

Telegraphs and Cables.—The main office of the Chinese Telegraph administration is on Tung Chang An Chieh and messages can be sent to any part of the world at approximately the same rates as from Shanghai.

Transportation.—Rickshas twenty-five cents first hour and twenty cents subsequent hours. Motor cars may be hired at $4.00 for each hour or part of an hour. For trips outside the city such as to the Summer Palace, the Great Wall, etc., fixed charges are made, depending on the distance traveled rather than the length of time the car is retained.

Guides.—English speaking guides may be hired at the rate of $3.00 per day from hotels and travel bureaus.

251

Churches and Missions.—American Bible Society, American Board, American Presbyterian, Church of England, London Missionary Society, Methodist, Episcopal, Mission Catholique de Peking, Russian Orthodox, Salvation Army, Y.M.C.A., Y.W.C.A., British Legation Chapel (Church of England), Union Church, St. Michel, etc.

Legations.—American, Belgian, Brazilian, British, Cuban, Danish, French, German, Italian, Japanese, Mexican, Netherlands, Norwegian, Peruvian, Portuguese, Spanish, Swedish, and Mission of the Russian Soviet Republic. Most of these Legations occupy substantial compounds within the Legation Quarter and those of America, Britain, Netherlands, Japan, France and Italy maintain small military guards.

Foreign Theatres.—Pavilion, Chen Kwang, Kai Ming and Capital.

Tourist Bureaus.—American Express Company, Thomas Cook & Son, China Travel Service and Japan Tourist Bureau.

With China a republic, and the capital of the Nationalist government removed to Nanking, Peiping is no longer an imperial city, but the change in the form of government and the removal of the capital to Nanking has not detracted from its interest to the visitor. In fact, it is even more interesting now since many of the most important places were, under the old regime, forbidden to the eyes of the foreigner, who now has access to everything of interest in the city. For nine hundred years under various names, Peiping has been the capital of China, with short intervals during which the capital was removed to other places. During these centuries of imperial residence, the city has been beautified by the erection of many buildings, temples and altars, most of them typifying the barbaric splendor and wealth of the Tartar rulers of China. Foreign influence and the establishment of the Republic have made few changes in it and the city remains the same mysterious, picturesque, interesting place it has been for centuries. The whole history of China is told by the bricks and stones and plaster walls of Peking. On every hand are mementos of conquests and dynastic changes, and evidences of the influence of Jesuits, Mohammedans and Persians. The changes which have been brought about by modern influences and by the new form of government are trivial and superficial. With slight changes the Peiping of the twentieth century might well be the Peking of five centuries ago. The soul of the city

has remained unchanged and the modern dramas of political intrigue and treachery, cruelty and conquest are played to-day in a setting of the Middle Ages.

Located on a flat, sandy plain and surrounded by high walls, Peiping from a distance looks much like a giant box and the scarcity of habitations on the plain makes it difficult for the approaching traveler to vizualize the busy life within the walls. Nothing can be seen to indicate the presence of the many temples, pagodas and palaces inside for it is a city chiefly of one storey houses and of those of more pretentious dimensions few are as high as the walls. The city occupies the northern extremity of the great alluvial delta which stretches in broad, flat perspective to the south for 700 miles, broken only by rivers, canals and a few hills.

Peiping is on the same parallel of latitude as Madrid. The climate is dry and bracing, there rarely being any rain between October and April, while there may be several feet of ice in the rivers in January. The short period of hot weather, lasting six to eight weeks, comes during July and August. The thermometer climbs high and the heat is often more annoying than in points farther south. The annual range of temperature is from 104° above to 10° below zero.

While they are most prevalent in the spring, if one remains in Peiping long enough, he will not escape one of the famous Peiping dust storms. "On some sunshiny days it is noticed that the rays of the sun appear to be less powerful than usual. Presently they are obscured. No cloud is to be seen, but a dull haze of dark brown hue becomes more and more pervasive, until the dust settles down quietly from above, or the wind which has arisen arrives in swirls, speedily enveloping everything, so that on the worst occasions it may be necessary to light the lamps in the middle of the day." The clouds of dust arise from the dry sandy plain of the Gobi Desert and at times cover all of North China. They have even been known as far away as Shanghai and to have been visible far out at sea.

As long ago as 1200 B.C. a city was built on the present site of Peking and later became the capital of the Kingdom of Yen, which was overthrown by the Ch'in dynasty (222 B.C.) and the city reduced in rank. It was taken in 986 by the invading Kitan Tartars who established themselves there and called the place Nanking (Southern Capital) to distinguish it from their more northern seat. The Chinese drove out the alien invaders and recaptured the city in the early part of the 12th century, changing the name to Yen Chau-fu. A few years later the "Golden" Tartars succeeded to the city, restored it to its former imperial rank, and gave it the name of Chung-tu (Central Capital). When Genghis Khan, the great Mongol leader, began his conquest of China, this was one of the first places he captured and it was occupied as the capital by his renowned successor and grandson, Kublai Khan. In the latter part of the thirteenth century, he rebuilt the city, and gave it the name of Khanbalik (City of the Khan). It was under this name, corrupted into Cambaluc, that the most important city in China became known to Europe. Some ruins of the mud walls of this ancient city may be seen outside the An Ting Men, near the Bell Temple, while the Bell Tower and Drum Tower are two surviving monuments to the architectural pretensions of the period.

For a short time at the beginning of the Ming dynasty the capital of China was located at Nanking, but the third Emperor of the dynasty, Yung-lo, removed to the northern city and in order to distinguish it from the southern capital he had deserted, gave it the name of Peking (Northern Capital). The location of the capital under the Mings and their successors the Manchus was always an unhappy one, being far removed from the southern and most prosperous part of the country, but its selection was dictated by what was considered to be sound politics. The Chinese Emperors found it necessary to locate the capital in the north in order to keep watch on the restless Tartars and Mongols, while the later Manchus naturally preferred Peking to any other location because of its proximity to their ancestral home and political associates in Manchuria. With the removal of the seat of the National government to Nanking, the name of the city was changed to Peiping to signify that it had lost its rank as a capital.

Peiping is built in the form of an exaggerated Gothic letter **T**, with the lines of the letter so thickened and the top so shortened that it resembles a rectangular oblong. The northern part is almost exactly square and is known as the Tartar City. This part was restored by Emperor Yung-lo, the walls being completed in 1437. The walls are 50 feet high, 60 feet thick at the base and 40 feet thick at the top. They have been kept in good repair, although the guard houses which surmount them are in a dilapidated condition and brush and weeds have been allowed to grow on top. The walls are faced on both sides with brick and filled in with dirt. After the Tartar City was built, the Chinese population used the ruins and debris of the older city on the south to build up a large suburb. A hundred years after the completion of the walls of the Tartar City, the suburb was enclosed in walls and has since been known as the Chinese City. The walls around the Chinese City are 30 feet high, 25 feet wide at the base and 15 feet at the top. Square buttresses surmounted by guard houses are built at intervals of 60 feet. The two walls enclose an area of about 20 square miles and are 30 miles in circumference. There are nine gates in the Tartar Wall, namely, Hata Men, Chien Men and Shun Chih Men on the south, Ping Chi Men and Hsi Chih Men on the west, Teh Sheng Men and An Ting Men on the north, and Tung Chih Men and Hwa Men on the east. In the Chinese city wall there are seven gates, being Tung Pien Men at the north-east corner, Sha Wo Men on the east, Chiang Tso Men, Yung Ting Men and Nan Hsi Men on the south, Chang Yi Men on the west, and Hsi Pien Men at the north-west corner. A railroad circles the Tartar City wall. It takes about two hours to make the trip with stops at various stations.

When the Manchus captured Peking in 1644, the Tartar City was taken over by them for residence. Here they settled Manchu soldiers, together with the Chinese troops who had aided them in their conquest, each of the eight Chinese troops (banners or divisions) being assigned to a certain section of the city. From that time until the overthrow of the Manchu dynasty in 1912, these men and their descendants existed on tribute rice sent to Peking by the provinces. The original inhabitants were Chinese, Mongols and Manchus, but it is now difficult to distinguish the races, except for the Manchu women who can be recognized by their large distinctive head dress and rouged faces.

The Tartar City is intersected by six main thoroughfares, three running north and south from the principal gates, and three running east and west. These streets are broad and kept in a fairly good state of repair. Unlike other Chinese cities farther south, Peking has a great deal of wheeled traffic—springless Peking carts drawn by mules—while the city's proximity to the sandy deserts of Mongolia is shown by the presence of many double humped Bactrian camels which carry freight over long distances. The street life of Peking is fascinating and a visit to the city would be well worth while even if one never got behind the gates and walls and saw nothing except from the seat of a ricsha. Peking funerals are famous throughout China. In this, as in other things, royalty set the fashion and lesser families followed the standard of the impressive royal *corteges* as far as their purses allowed. In the large funeral processions there are dozens of musicians who get strange and unearthly sounds out of instruments unlike anything heard or seen elsewhere. The hired mourners may run into hundreds while the priests in their gaudy embroidered robes will be numerous enough to staff a fair sized temple. The foreigner unfamiliar with the technique and ritual will be unable to tell whether the procession he is viewing is in celebration of a wedding or in observance of a funeral until the latter part passes him and he is able to see whether it is a coffin or a bridal chair being carried. Wedding ceremonies, like funerals, follow the old imperial precedent. The Peking carts may be seen in many parts of North China but it is only in the former capital that one finds these vehicles in the apex of their glory, with varnished sides, silver trimmed harness and silken hangings. Formerly the color of the cart hangings as well as the richness of the harness trappings were severely regulated as belonging to certain classes, but there is more laxity now and any one who wants to use silver harness buckles may do so. In the old days all officials traveled by Peking carts or sedan chairs, those being the only conveyances of sufficient dignity, but to-day the automobile is the vehicle preferred and the use of the sumptuous Peking cart is confined to the conservative and old fashioned.

Leading from the main thoroughfares are smaller streets, usually very narrow and crooked, which are known as *hutungs*. A trip through any *hutung* will give the visitor no idea of the really beautiful homes which are concealed by the mud or plaster walls which surround them. As in other parts of China, the magnificence of the home is always prudently concealed from the street, and the finest residence may be hidden by the meanest wall. These Peking residences usually cover large areas, and are valued more for the spaciousness of their courtyards than for the buildings. Many foreigners have rebuilt and refurnished these houses, and while still maintaining the Chinese formal style have made them remarkably comfortable and attractive.

Occupying the center of the Tartar City, and taking up about two square miles, or one-sixth of its total area, is the Imperial City, surrounded by a pink wall 20 feet high. Formerly there were four entrances, each pierced with a triple gateway, and until the downfall of the Manchu line, the middle gateway was opened only for the

17

Emperor.   However, there are now many entrances cut in
the old wall and part of the east section has been entirely
torn down.   Inside this Imperial City, and surrounded by
its own reddish pink walls, is the still more exclusive
Forbidden City, for centuries a mystery to the outside
world, for until the victory of the foreign troops following
the Boxer trouble in 1900 no foreigners were allowed to
enter it.   Within it were the palaces, the royal residences,
and the quarters for the hundreds of eunuchs and
servants attached to the imperial family.   Indeed, it was
a city in itself, with a population of several thousands.
The present palaces occupy the site marked out for the
palaces of Kublai Khan in the thirteenth century.   In fact,
the spot has served as an imperial residence for about ten
centuries, for the Liaos had a palace here at the end of
the tenth century and their successors a few centuries
later began the construction of the series of artificial lakes
which have been elaborated into the present system.
However, the rulers of the Ming dynasty deserve credit
for the beauties of the Forbidden City, and their successors
the Manchus added little to it.   When the Manchu rulers
returned to Peking after their flight from the Allied
armies in 1900, one of the measures of conciliation which
they adopted toward foreigners was a slight relaxation
of their rigid policy of exclusion and for the first time
foreign ladies were entertained within the sacred precincts
of the Forbidden City.   With the establishment of the
Republic, additional parts of the palace have been opened,
until now it is possible for the traveler to visit all of the
interesting buildings and the place is forbidden in name
only.

The best general view of the two sections of the city
can be gained from Chien Men, the tower on the south wall
of the Tartar City reached from the Legation Quarter by
a ramp on Wall Street just west of Canal Street.   To the
north of this point of vantage may be seen the greater
part of the Imperial and Forbidden cities, the brilliantly
colored tile roofs of the palaces, temples, and pagodas, and

the busy life of the streets below combining to form a picture which cannot be duplicated elsewhere and is seldom forgotten. One can understand after a view from this ancient wall, why Peiping has a population of less than one million despite the large area it occupies. For a long time this city was believed by European geographers to be the largest in the world in point of population. But such a great part of its space is taken up with temple and palace enclosures and the average Chinese house of the better class occupies such a generous amount of ground space that the population per square mile is probably lower than in any other large city.

To the south, from the Chien Men, the Chinese City offers a less imposing view but one which is full of interest. The tiled roof of the Temple of Heaven can be seen from here, and is one of the most conspicuous landmarks in Peiping. From the summit of these great walls the human life below looks strangely small and insect-like. This portion of the wall between Chien Men and Hata Men overlooks the nearby Legation Quarter. It was from this section of the wall that the Chinese Boxer troops bombarded the Legations in 1900 and later it was from here that the guns of the foreign forces shelled the imperial palaces. Under one of the provisions of the Boxer Protocol, this portion of the wall was handed over to the foreign powers not only as a retributory measure but also as a means of securing protection to the Legations from similar attacks. At the Chien Men end are the towers of the American wireless plant rising one hundred and fifty feet above the street. This plant is operated by the American Marines as a precaution against ever again being cut off from communication with the outside world as suffered by the foreign legations in Peking at the time of the Boxer trouble. While the whole wall is well paved, brambles are permitted to grow on most of it so that walking is bad, but the section from Chien Men to Hata Men is well looked after.

Aside from the sights of Peiping, the city is a fascinating center for the purchase of Chinese curios and art works of all kinds. In variety of curios, no other city surpasses it and those who intend doing shopping of this kind should resist the temptation to purchase elsewhere unless it be at one of the larger shops in Shanghai. For many centuries the finest products of the weaver, porcelain maker, jeweler, artist and other craftsmen, came to Peiping either as tribute to the ruling family or were brought here to add to the collections of rich officials. In addition, there may be found many European jewels which somehow or other have found their way into the Peiping shops. The city has been looted many times and from year to year one hears that the stocks of embroideries or porcelains are diminishing. But the sources of supply, the treasures of prominent families which fall on evil days, seem to be inexhaustible. The types of porcelains and embroideries found elsewhere may be purchased in Peiping, but the local shops offer many things not usually found in other cities. Among these are Thibetan and Mongolian brass and Mongolian carpets and rugs. Among the modern manufactures in which Peiping leads are cloisonné, lanterns and jewelry. Peiping is also a center for manufacture of the woolen rug which has become known to foreigners as the Tientsin rug, though most of them are made in Peiping.

The sights of Peiping are so numerous that one can spend several weeks and leave without having seen all of the important ones. The Temple of Heaven would probably head any list of attractions, with perhaps the Lama Monastery (commonly known as the Lama Temple) coming second, but few will ever agree as to the relative interest or importance of the dozens of others. In addition to these places inside the city, there are many others outside: the Great Wall, Ming Tombs, Summer Palace, Yellow Temple, the Western Hills with their numerous temples, and so on. No attempt is made in this book to arrange any set itinerary. The travel agencies or the hotel management can give all the necessary information on that score.

Like most of modern Peiping, the Legation Quarter dates from the time of the Boxer trouble, for since that time a definitely marked and adequately protected quarter has replaced the old group of legations which were separated by Chinese residences and official buildings. In spite of the fact that the seat of government has been removed to Nanking the foreign governments still maintain their legations in the former capital. Adjoining the southern wall of the Tartar City, the quarter is separated on all sides from the city itself by walls and wide open spaces. On the south side is the Tartar Wall patrolled by foreign troops, and on the north side the wide *glacis* on which no permanent structures are allowed to be erected. By the terms of the Boxer protocol no Chinese are allowed to reside in the Legation Quarter and on the other hand no foreigners except missionaries are supposed to live outside. However, in times of stress and political uncertainty the quarter is filled with Chinese refugees, while as the Quarter is small and inadequate, foreigners reside in many parts of the Tartar City and all but one of the hotels are located outside of the Quarter. The Legation Quarter is controlled by an Administrative Council made up of representatives of the foreign powers.

Though the Quarter is quite modern, its history goes back two hundred years, for the church in the Soviet Legation was erected in 1727 for the use of Russian missionaries, while the site of the Soviet Legation was the residence of several of the Russian embassies and special missions which visited China in the latter part of the seventeenth century.

However, the British Legation is actually the oldest, having been established soon after the negotiation of the Treaty of Tientsin. It was formerly the residence of the thirty-third son of Emperor Kang Hsi and was leased to the British government. The original form of the buildings has been retained as far as possible. More recently the sites of the Han Lin College and of the Imperial Carriage Park were incorporated in the legation grounds. The Imperial Carriage Park was formerly used to stable the elephants sent as tribute from Annam which was then ruled by China. Although the fiercest fighting in the Boxer siege was at the French Legation, the British compound sheltered the greatest number of refugees and almost every foot of the soil was stained with blood. A portion of the old wall just within the north gate of the Quarter on Canal Street, is still preserved with its bullet and shell holes and marked with a sign "Lest we forget."

The French Legation was established soon after the British and occupies its original site, though some additional land has been acquired. The other legations are more modern.

FAIRS AND BAZAARS.

Peiping's fairs offer not only a good chance to observe Chinese customs, but also to make unique purchases. The most famous fairs are those held in temple grounds in various parts of the city on regular days of the Chinese calendar. Leading all others is the one held at Lung Fu Ssu, close to the Tung Ssu P'ai Lou off north Hatamen Street, about fifteen minutes by ricksha from the Hotel de Pekin. The fair gets in full swing early in the afternoon and abounds in curios, brass pieces, small pieces of blackwood, beads, semi-precious stones, Chinese toys and hair ornaments. It caters to foreigners more than any other of the fairs. It must be remembered by visitors that bargaining is the rule of the Chinese fair and the first price asked is much more than what will be accepted.

Other fairs are Tung Yueh Miao outside Chi Hua Men, twice each Chinese moon; and Hu Kou Ssu near the Hsi Ssu P'ai Lou, every fifth day.

In addition to these more frequent bazaars, there are famous fairs which are held at certain festival times. The best of these is the one popularly called Liu Li Chang, which is held at the Huo Shen Miao, just off the street Liu

Li Chang in the Chinese city west of Chien Men. There from the first to the fifteenth of the first Chinese month, people flock by the tens of thousands to buy antiques, curios, jewels and other articles. A short distance to the east, at the same time is held a fair where stones, jewels and ivories sometimes of immense value are exposed for sale. Some of Peiping's most valuable art works are shown at that time and the visitor is astounded to pick up a piece of jade, crystal or a precious stone, only to find the owner places a value of many thousand dollars upon it.

Pai Yun Kuan ('White Cloud Temple'), outside of the Hsi Pien Men, holds a fair that is very popular with the Chinese, from the first to the nineteenth of the first Chinese month. This is of interest to the foreigners merely as a spectacle as the Chinese participants erect large tea houses, hold horse races and display fine lanterns.

P'an T'ao Kung, which lies outside of Hatamen gate along the canal at the Tung Pien Men, is the scene of a large fair and religious festival from the first to the fifteenth of the third Chinese month. Nothing of value to the foreigner is sold there but it is worth a visit merely to see the crowds.

There are a number of permanent markets and bazaars of interest. Included in these is the so-called "old clothes market" or more properly "Heavenly Bridge market," east of the bridge on Chien Men Street en route to the Temple of Heaven. Here are found bargains in old embroideries, old silk coats and the like. The Jade Market springs up along the east end of Ssu T'iao Hutung outside of Hatamen shortly after daylight and closes before eight-thirty in the morning. The "Thieves Market" as it is commonly called, offers a general variety of goods for sale, some of which are of little value. It takes its name from the supposition that the wares offered for sale have been stolen.

There are two night fairs—one held along both sides of Hatamen Street every third day of the foreign calendar, beginning on the third of each month, and the other outside of Chien Men, held every four days of the foreign calendar, beginning on the first of each month. An artificial flower market is held on Ssu T'iao Hutung outside of Hatamen on the 4th, 14th and 24th of the Chinese month. The largest permanent curio and jewel bazaar is that housed in a large modern three storey building on Lang Fang, Tou T'iao Hutung, commonly called Lantern Street by foreigners, while the Tung An Bazaar, off North Morrison Street, presents an opportunity to see and buy the everyday things of China, such as foods and delicacies, flowers, chop sticks, seals, stationery, toys and the like.

TEMPLE AND ALTAR OF HEAVEN.

In the southern extremity of the Chinese City is the Temple of Heaven and nearby is its accompanying sanctuary, of lesser importance and interest, the Altar of Agriculture. They are reached by following Chien Men Street through the Chinese City from its northern terminus, the Chien Men, quite near the Legation Quarter. The Temple of Heaven is surrounded by a wall 3½ miles in circumference. The spacious grounds are filled with gnarled old cypress, fir and pine trees and formerly served as a pasturage for the oxen sacrificed in the annual worship by the Emperor. No permit is needed to enter the grounds but an admission fee is charged.

For centuries during the existence of the Empire of China the Emperor worshipped at this shrine semi-annually, with special prayers during times of famine, drought, or other calamities which threatened the peace and happiness of the nation. The ceremonies were most imposing, the Emperor being accompanied by thousands of the highest officials and they in turn by many minor officials, all escorted by many thousands of soldiers and servants, the entire company being gorgeously clad in eleborate gowns which indicated the rank of the wearer. The great pageant composed of these thousands of officials and courtiers formed at the palace in the Forbidden City

the day before the ceremony and proceeded to the temple
along Chien Men Street. All the houses along the route
were closed during the progress of the procession and no
one was permitted to view it. The Emperor spent the
night on the grounds in prayer and fasting and the
ceremony was held the following morning at dawn. The
worship of Heaven at the altar by the Emperor or "Son
of Heaven" was the survival of an ancient nature worship,
much older than Taoism or Confucianism. The worship
was not alone to Heaven, but also to the tablets of four
imperial ancestors, also to the sun, moon, clouds, rain, etc.,
though these were looked upon as minor deities. Separate
temples for the sun, moon, and patrons of agriculture are
erected.

The principal structure within the enclosure is the
Altar of Heaven (Tien Tan), the most sacred object in
China. "It consists of three circular terraces with marble
balustrades and triple stair cases at the four cardinal
points to ascend the upper terrace, which is 90 feet wide,
the base being 210 feet across. The platform is laid with
marble stones in nine concentric circles and everything is
arranged in multiples of the number nine. The Emperor,
prostrate before Heaven on the altar, surrounded first by
the circle of the terraces and their railings, and by the
horizon seems to be in the center of the universe, as he
acknowledges himself inferior to Heaven, and to Heaven
alone. Round him on the pavement are figured the nine
circles of as many heavens, widening in successive
multiples till the square of nine, the favorite number of
numerical philosophy, is reached in the outer circle of
eighty-one stones."

In the northern part of the upper terrace is a seat
where Shang-ti, the Ruler of Heaven, was supposed to sit
during the ceremony, beside it being shrines of the "wit-
nessing saints," ancestors of the Emperor. No foreigner
ever witnessed this ceremony, though some have seen
the place as prepared for the visit of the Emperor when
it was decked with lanterns and standards and many

ornaments and decorations of archaic significance.* No priest of any religion ever officiated and the elaborate ceremonies were carried out by Chinese court officials who in preparation for it underwent months of training and instruction.

Near the altar in one corner of the enclosure is the furnace of green tiles where the sacrificial bullock was placed at the time of worship. "The sacrifice was a calf without blemish and of uniform color." The eight metal braziers which partly encircle the altar were used for the burnt offerings of silk cloth and also for the written prayers of the Emperor after they had been formally read to the sacred tablets. The black tiled building near the altar was used for the storage of the tables and other paraphernalia of worship.

North of the Altar of Heaven is a smaller altar of the same design known as the Altar of Prayer for Grain (Chi Ku Tan). The approach is very impressive, over a raised marble tile avenue, with groves of evergreen on either side. About midway may be seen the platform provided for the Emperor's resting tent. On the upper terrace of this altar is the building known as the Temple of the Happy Year (Chi Men Tien). The building, 99 feet high, is the highest in the enclosure, and its roof can be seen from the south wall of the Tartar City. The triple roofs supported by massive pillars are covered with blue tiles, blue being the symbolical color for the worship at this temple, which took place each spring, the Emperor being the chief ritualist. The sacrificial vessels used on this occasion were of blue glass, and all who took part were robed in a similar color, the color effect being heightened by the fact that the windows were decorated with Venetian blinds made of rods of blue glass. This building is a very modern structure, for the older one was struck by lightning in 1889, because, according to local legend, an impious and foolhardy centipede climbed to the gilded ball

---

* The ritual itself has been described by Dr. John Ross in "The Original Religions of China."

at the top. When rebuilt every care was taken to reproduce the older building in all details but it was impossible
to find native timbers strong and long enough to support
the massive roof. Oregon pine was transported from
Portland at great expense. A few unimportant and dusty
pieces of furniture is all that can be found inside the hall.
One object which seems strangly out of place is an electric
light fixture. The place was lighted in the early days of
the Republic for the convenience of the Committee for
Drafting the Constitution who thought to give this
document an added sanctity by making the Altar its
birthplace. The buildings around the temple are uninteresting, consisting of guard rooms, places for the
storage of paraphernalia, provisions, etc.

Near the principal entrance to the grounds, and
usually the first building shown to the visitor, is the
Palace of Abstinence, surrounded by a moat, where the
Emperor on the occasions of worship spent the night in
fasting before the ceremony. The place formerly contained a throne and handsome furniture but these have
been removed.

Every conqueror of China took to himself the privilege
and responsibility of worshipping at the Altar of Heaven,
and the chief functionary has at various times been of
Chinese, Mongol or Manchu blood. But though custom
and tradition would allow this elevated station of chief
ritualist to be transferred, even to one of another race,
they would not brook a change in government. When
Yuan Shih-kai assumed the dictatorship of China, under
the title of President, he sought to prepare the way for
his imperial program by assuming the functions of the
Son of Heaven. One may safely presume that this astute
politician made every preparation to assure the success
of the ceremony but it was a flat failure. The idea was
repugnant to the Chinese and there was no second attempt.
Under the Republican form of government the place is
of no religious or political significance and is only a
beautiful and interesting relic of the past.

TEMPLE OF AGRICULTURE.

This Temple is situated across the avenue from the Temple of Heaven and is known in Chinese as Shen Nung Tan, *i.e.* "Altar dedicated to Shen Nung." Shen Nung is the mythical emperor who ruled China about 3000 B.C. and who is credited with the invention of the plow, the institution of markets and the discovery of the value of herbs.

It was here that in former days the Emperor, on the first day of the spring season, worshipped the tablets of Shen Nung and at the same time paid tribute to the respect in which the Chinese hold the useful vocation of a farmer. Attired in a peasant's garb of imperial yellow the Emperor plowed three furrows from east to west, being attended by officials who flourished whips, held the seeds, etc. The officials then finished the field which was carefully cultivated and the crop kept for use in special sacrificial ceremonies. Similar ceremonies were observed at the same time in all the provinces, the ritualists being the provincial governor and other officials.

The imperial plow, the costume worn by the emperor and many other objects of interest were formerly on display here but the halls in which they were kept have been closed and sealed.

Originally the Temple of Agriculture was much like the Temple of Heaven but attempts to modernize it have greatly changed the character of the place. Upon the altars are now erected pavilions of a semi-modern type, used as band-stands and tea-houses. On holidays this place becomes an ordinary Chinese fair and is thronged by thousands of visitors. One portion of the grounds has been converted into a modern pleasure park where there are Chinese theaters of the old and new variety, moving picture shows, bowling alleys, roller skating rink, endless restaurants and tea houses.

LAMA MONASTERY.

This famous show place of Peiping, commonly known as the Lama Temple is on Hatamen Street near the north wall of the Tartar City, easily reached by ricsha from any hotel. Although an admission fee is charged and notices urgently request visitors not to give tips, they may expect to be annoyed by the impudent Mongol monks and beggars.

There are several temples in Peiping devoted to this interesting form of Buddhism but this monastery is the most important Lama and Mongol center, being the official residence of a Living Buddha, although he does not actually live there. It is known to the Chinese as Yung Ho Kung, or "Lamasery of Eternal Peace." Originally the residence of Emperor Yung Cheng, before he came to the throne, that monarch stored up merit in the Lama heaven and at the same time strengthened his hold on the loyalty of his Mongol and Tibetan subjects by dedicating the property to the Lamas. According to old Chinese imperial regulations no building once occupied by an Emperor could ever be used as a dwelling place and there are many instances of property used for that purpose being given to temples. Since the days of Emperor Yung Cheng many emperors have used this monastery as a means of controlling Thibetans and Mongols, for the abbots of the establishment hold important places in the elaborate and complicated hierarchy of Lamaism. Many of the valuable articles the monastery contains are imperial presents. Even the republican government takes particular pains not to offend the monks who make this their home. However, republican support is not so munificient as was that given by the monarchy. Money grants have been cut off and the monastery is no longer the recipient of its former opulent revenue. Perhaps that is one of the reasons why foreigners, once so rigidly excluded, are now welcomed because the admission fees they pay as well as the tips they give, eke out a scanty income. Formerly the place was difficult of entry and many travelers had disagreeable experiences, for the ill-favoured monks would surround and threaten them in what was usually a successful attempt to extort illegal fees. Conditions are better now and it is only in the more secluded places that one is annoyed and then, usually, by an impudent neophyte. It is interesting to note that these monks, who are all Mongol or Thibetan, have scorned to learn Chinese, but many of them have picked up a little pidgin English.

The monastery grounds are quiet and secluded, and shaded by ancient trees. On entering, one passes through a long wide avenue which traverses the living quarters of the monks. These poorly ventilated cells have accumulated the filth of centuries and have doubtless furnished the setting for many a weird plot connected with the church politics of Lamaism. Like most Buddhist structures in China, the monastery consists of a series of semi-detached buildings grouped about courtyards. The buildings though in a sad state of decay, are decked with wonderful carvings and the courtyards are paved with fine flagstones. The equipment of sacerdotal paraphernalia is said to be the most complete in China.

In the first courtyard to be entered is a pair of bronze lions worthy of more than passing attention because they are remarkable examples of casting. In another courtyard is a huge stone monument inscribed on its four sides with the history of Lamaism in the Chinese, Manchu, Thibetan and Mongol languages. Prayer wheels, which the devout may turn, and thereby acquire the merit of having said a thousand prayers, are numerous.

The principal object of interest in the monastery is the huge image of Maitreya, the Buddhist redeemer, over 70 feet high, which stands in a building in the northern part of the enclosure. The temple attendants say this image is " seventy elbows high," that being the height the pious lama is supposed to reach in his reincarnation. They also assert that the image was carved from a single tree trunk and brought from Thibet. The giant idol passes through several successive stories of the building it occupies and around it is built a staircase which the devout may climb in order to gain merit. A huge praying wheel in the same building is almost as high as the image. It is curious to note that this stern Lama image of Maitreya represents the same god that Chinese Buddhism depicts as a fat-bellied smiling creature.

The monastery abounds in objects which are held in high esteem by Lamas. In one of the principal halls is an inconspicuous and somewhat crude and ugly image of Buddha. The story goes that Emperor Chien Lung dreamed of the existence of this image in a temple on the borders of Thibet. A monk was sent to bring the image to Peking and after several miraculous experiences succeeded in finding it and started to return with the image tied on his back. But he had to travel through Russian territory and the monk had a great deal of trouble finding his way as he did not speak Russian and failed in his attempts to learn the language. But the image encountered no difficulty about understanding Russian and acted as interpreter throughout the long trip. The visitor will usually have this image pointed out to him as soon as he enters the building. It can be distinguished from the other gods by its distinctive yellow silk cape and hood.

The many objects of greater or lesser interest in the monastery are too numerous for detailed description. They include a golden model of paradise, a replica of the great lamasery in Lhasa, images of the two hippopotami which made a murderous but unsuccessful attack on Emperor Chien Lung and of the two grotesque servants who saved their royal master.

In a side hall not often visited by foreigners but accessible to those who are persistent, is a group of strange and often obscene images which depict the grosser forms of Lamaism, which were associated with an older Phallic cult.

Visitors should plan to see the Lama Monastery either early in the morning or late in the afternoon for then they may have an opportunity of seeing and hearing the very interesting matin or vesper services in which many of the monks take part. Clad in their yellow, orange or brick red costumes the monks file into the hall and kneel about the abbott or chief ritualist who by lifting a bunch of peacock feathers gives the signal for the service to begin. There is a burst of cymbals, drums and conch shells, a weird harmony which sounds like nothing else on earth. A chant follows in which a prayer is recited time after time and meanwhile the monks make strange gestures, mysterious to the stranger and perhaps obscure to most of the worshippers for the lamas have always been more scrupulous about carrying out the forms of their religion than about learning the spirit which the forms represent.

Those who visit Peiping in the right season may be fortunate enough to see the famous Lama " devil dance " which is held annually in the latter part of the first Chinese moon. This is largely attended by Chinese for although no Chinese is a Lama, many have some belief in the efficacy of Lama superstitions. " After a long period of waiting, patiently endured, several beings half human, half devil, suddenly hurl themselves into the very midst of the expectant throng. Their costumes are weird, resembling those of Red Indian medicine men. Death's head masks cover their faces, red painted flames lick their limbs from foot to knee, and in their hands they carry fearsome-looking long-lashed whips to be used in clearing a space for the dance. With demoniacal yells they dash about pushing back the crowd and beating the unwary till they have made sufficient room. Then from the temple emerges a strange procession of dancers. They also wear strange vestments of many colors and huge ghastly masks of bird or beast. To the slow and measured cadence of unmelodious music, to the sound of hand drums and great drums, small flutes and great flutes, and pandean pipes of form unknown to Western Pan, they advance in fours bowing and circling, their heads lolling from side to side with the time and movement of their bodies. The performance, which lasts for hours to the immense delight of the crowd, who, regardless of the attentions of the long whipped devils, draw closer in an ever diminishing circle, culminates in the cutting up of an effigy of the Evil Spirit." *

* " Peking," by Juliet Bredon.

TEMPLE OF CONFUCIUS.

The Confucian temple is located in the grounds of the Kuo Tzu Chien, the old national university of China in the northern part of the Tartar City and a short distance from the Lama Monastery. Here on the 6th day of the second month and on the 10th day of the eighth month, the Spring and Autumn sacrifices to Confucius are observed. These ceremonies are conducted by high officials of the government and take place just at dawn. While it is not possible for a visitor to attend the actual ceremony, passes can be obtained to witness the dress rehearsals which take place on the afternoon before.

The chief object of interest in the large hall of the temple is the ancestral tablet of the great sage enshrined in an alcove. Tablets of four sages and disciples flank the tablet of Confucius, while tablets of many other disciples are placed in the hall. Before the alcove stands the conventional "sacrificial set of five," an incense burner, two candlesticks and two flower vases. The table in front is for the sacrificial offerings. Above the alcove are four Chinese characters meaning "The Model Teacher of a Myriad Ages," a tribute paid to Confucius by Emperor K'ang Hsi. The tablets on the roof are also in praise of Confucius, and were presented to the temple by various Emperors.

There is more of interest in the courtyard, where will be found ten roughly chiseled boulders inscribed with a description of a great hunting expedition which King Shan, ruler of the Chow dynasty, undertook nearly three thousand years ago. The stones are known as the "stone drums of the Chow dynasty." It will be noticed that one of the drums has been cut off and hollowed out as a mortar, thus destroying a part of the inscription. Grief over this mutilation is expressed in several famous poems. The stones were discovered in the seventh century A.D. and 800 years ago they were considered such valuable antiquities that a special palace was built for their exhibition at the then capital of Honanfu and the inscriptions were filled with gold. When the Tartars captured Honan they dug out the gold and carried the stones to Peking. So many rubbings have been taken that the inscriptions are now indecipherable. Stone tablets in the courtyard bear the names of all those who for five centuries received literary degrees. Huge monuments, standing on carved stone tortoises in the main courtyard, are covered with inscriptions telling of the successful wars undertaken by the Manchu emperors.

HALL OF CLASSICS.

This structure, called the Pi Yung Kung, adjoins the national university in which the Temple of Confucius stands and may be entered from the temple grounds. The hall is of a pure type of Chinese architecture being modeled on ancient lines, though the present building was erected by Emperor Chien Lung. " It is a lofty square building with a four sided roof covered with tiles, enameled imperial yellow, and surmounted by a large gilded ball, encircled by a pillared verandah under a second projecting roof of yellow tiles. The four sides consist, each one, of seven pairs of folding doors with tracery panels. It is surrounded by a circular moat with marble balustrades crossed by four bridges leading to the central doors." Along the main courtyard sheltered by buildings stand three hundred stone *steles* covered with inscriptions comprising the complete texts of the nine classics. This was done in order to prevent their possible destruction, as was attempted by Emperor Shih Hwang-ti. The characters are disposed in page size so that rubbings taken could be conveniently bound up in book form.

It was formerly the custom for the Emperor to come here on state occasions, and, seated on the throne provided for the event, expound the classics. The throne building contains tablets to the memory of several well known emperors. A magnificent porcelain *pailou* stands in one part of the courtyard, displaying a dedicatory tablet. The *pailou* is constructed of marble and tiles and is one of the finest structures of the kind in China.   An interesting old sun-dial stands in the main courtyard.

DRUM TOWER.

In return for a small tip, the keeper of the Drum Tower several blocks west of the Hall of Classics will allow the visitor to climb to the top of the structure. This is reached by means of 75 rather uncomfortable steps, which lead to a height of 130 feet, where an excellent view of the Tartar City is obtained.   The tower is one of the landmarks of Peiping as it can be seen from nearly all parts of the city.

The hours of the watch were once marked here by a *clepsydra*, an instrument which measured time by the trickling of water, but a clock is now in use.

BELL TOWER AND TEMPLE.

Between the Drum Tower and the northern wall stands the Bell Tower, containing one of the five great bells ordered to be cast by Emperor Yung-lo, who built the famous porcelain pagoda of Nanking.   The bell stands on a platform 130 feet above the street level.   According to local tradition the casting of the bell was attended by considerable difficulty and several attempts resulted in imperfect specimens.   The Emperor finally became angry and announced that another failure would result in the execution of the maker.   The beautiful daughter of the bell maker visited a shrine to pray for her father's success and was later told in a dream that the bell would be a success only if a life was sacrificed in the casting. When the molten metal was turned into the mould, she jumped into it, and the bell was a success.   Credulous visitors who believe the story are still able to hear low moans of pain proceeding from the bell.   Others who are sceptical will hear the bell only at 8.30 at night, when the watch is changed, and its deep tones can be heard in all parts of the city.

Having told this story it is only fair to state that it really applies to another and more remarkable bell to be found at the Buddhist temple, Ta Chung Ssu, or "Big Bell Temple" 2½ miles west of the Tartar City. The bell at this temple is the most famous of the five cast for Emperor Yung-lo and the legend told above as well as the dimensions and the description, has by many writers been applied to the more accessible bell in the tower. The bell in the Big Bell Temple is 14 feet high, 36 feet in circumference and weighs 60 tons. It is said to be the largest suspended bell in the world and is certainly the most remarkable. Both the inside and the outside of the bell as well as the mechanism with which it is suspended are covered with Chinese characters, consisting of extracts from Buddhist classics. These characters are not inscribed, as is usually the case, but were cast with the bell. The bell was cast about 1408 where it now stands and the ground excavated from beneath it. In 1578 a temple was built over the bell. The bell in the tower, though quite remarkable for its size and workmanship, is in both respects inferior to the one in the temple.

ASTRONOMICAL OBSERVATORY.

This famous institution is in the south-eastern part of the Tartar City, adjoining the eastern wall. The observatory formerly marked the south-east corner of the Mongol capital under Kublai Khan, but when the capital was rebuilt for the occupancy of the Mings, the southern wall was carried further to the south. It is the oldest astronomical observatory in the world, having been built by Kublai Khan in 1279 and equipped at that time with bronze instruments made by a celebrated Chinese astronomer. It was not until almost three hundred years later that Europe had its first observatory, founded by Frederick III of Denmark in 1576. However, the building is not so ancient as the site on which it stands for in the early part of last century the original structure was replaced and the present building is even more modern.

The principal instruments are on top of the tower, about ten feet higher than the city wall from which there was formerly an entrance, but the premises cannot now be entered from the wall but through the buildings below, where some of the instruments are to be seen. Visitors are supposed to be admitted only on certain days and on presenting cards from their legations, but those who go are rarely turned away.

Most of the instruments now in the observatory were made under the direction of the Jesuit priest, Verbiest, who was placed in charge of the observatory as head of the Imperial Board of Mathematics. Verbiest was in charge of the observatory until 1688 and taught the Chinese astronomical science as known to Europeans. The instruments Verbiest had constructed were copies of older Chinese models, except that the circles were divided into 360 degrees instead of 365¼, which was the old Chinese system, allowing one degree for each day in the year. One of the instruments was presented to the Emperor of China by Louis XIV of France. When Peking was looted by the foreign troops in 1900 some of the finest instruments from this observatory were taken by the Germans and sent to decorate a terrace in Potsdam. The looted instruments were replaced by copies half the size of the originals. As one of the provisions of the Treaty of Versailles Germany agreed to return the originals which are now on view.

ART MUSEUMS.

The first museum was established in 1914 during the presidency of Yüan Shih-k'ai who authorized the removal to Peking of the art objects which had been taken by the first Manchu emperors to the Mukden and Jehol palaces. Its control was entrusted to a special bureau in the Board of the Interior. It is generally known as the Government Museum. There are two entrances to it, one on the east by the Tung Hua Mên and one on the west by the Hsi Hua Mên. The Museum is housed in two courtyards. Entering by the Tung Hua Mên the visitor will find the courtyard called Wên Hua Tien on the right and in this palace are exhibited paintings and writings. Immediately

to the rear of this palace is the Library (with green roof)
built by the emperor Ch'ien Lung to store the great
encyclopedia which had been prepared under his orders
by a large group of scholars.

Passing by the main entrance to the palace and in
front of the five bridges which lead to the Three Great
Halls, which were the center of the Forbidden City and
should be seen, the visitor will find the second courtyard
called Wu Ying Tien. Here is shown a varied collection
of cloisonnés, porcelains, jades, writing brushes, inks,
ink-palettes, carved ivories, enamels, wall vases, carved
roots, textiles, bronzes and clocks. At the side in a
detached house is the bathroom of the Mohammedan
princess Hsiang Fei whose portrait may be seen on the
wall.

The Government Museum is open from 8 a.m. till
6 p.m. There is a small entrance fee at the gate and
another fee for admission to each of the two courtyards.
Rickshas or cars carry visitors through the outer entrances
direct to the entrances to the two courtyards.

Writing in 1918 of the Government Museum Dr. John
C. Ferguson in his "Outlines of Chinese Art" said that
it "is unique among the museums of the world. In
architectural design and detail and in historical surroundings, as well as in the examples of art products
stored within its walls, this museum is exclusively and
characteristically Chinese. The bronzes and jades, paintings and manuscripts, pottery and porcelain, inks and
writing brushes, all owe their common origin to the genius
of the Chinese race. This museum has not needed to
borrow from other nations examples of an earlier art, out
of which its own development has directly or indirectly
sprung; on the contrary, the art spirit which found its
expression in these various forms during the historic
period joins hands even with the earliest mythological and
legendary traditions of the country."

The second museum to be opened was under the
auspices of the Board of Education. It is known as the

Historical Museum and is located in buildings over the Wu Mên which is the main entrance to the Forbidden City. In this museum are exhibited neolithic potteries and many objects chiefly of historical interest. The days on which it is open to the public must be ascertained by enquiry at the time of a proposed visit.

The Old Palace Museum was opened in 1927 after the expulsion of the Young Emperor who was the last of the Manchu rulers. The entrance is through the Shêng Wu Mên opposite Coal Hill. It is open daily except on Tuesdays. It is divided into Eastern, Central and Western sections each of which is open on two days each week. The western section is the former residential quarters of the retired emperor and the rooms have been left just as they were when he and his court were expelled by the orders of General Fêng Yü-hsiang. In this section is a courtyard specially devoted to Thibetan Buddhism where small images of the Thibetan pantheon may be seen. The eastern section contains the palaces built by the emperor Ch'ien Lung for himself after his retirement from the throne. There is a beautiful rock garden at the back of these palaces. The theatre and an exhibition of theatrical robes are also interesting.

The central section, open on Thursdays and Sundays, offers chief attractions to visitors. After passing the entrance through massive wooden gates one sees a huge mass of fantastic rocks surmounted by a charming pavilion. This is the corner of the imperial garden which was the favorite spot of the old Empress Dowager. To the left are courtyards in which there are special exhibitions such as paintings, porcelains of the Sung, Yüan and Ming dynasties, porcelains of the Manchu dynasty, ancient bronzes, jades. Any one of these exhibits furnishes subjects of study for many days. Retracing steps through the garden one passes through the central gates into a series of halls and palaces in which screens, fans, weapons, inks, ink-palettes, textiles, jades, lacquers and furniture may be seen. Most impressive of all that strikes the eyes of visitors is the magnificent architecture of the buildings and their arrangement.

PEI HAI (WINTER PALACE).

The Pei Hai or " North Sea " is one of the San Hai or " Three Seas," or group of palaces and grounds just west of the Forbidden City and inside of the Imperial City walls, and known as the Winter Palace. All three are open to visitors for a small fee.

In the Nan Hai or "South Sea " are various palaces built by the late Empress Dowager and in one of them Kuang Hsu died a prisoner. In the Chung Hai or "Middle Sea " was, before the removal of the capital to Nanking, the official residence of the President of the Republic of China, his state reception room and general reception room.

The entrance to the Pei Hai is just opposite the marble bridge, which unfortunately has had a wall built bisecting it and preventing a view of the two lakes to the south. It does, however, afford a magnificent view of the Pei Hai and its clustered bright tile roofs.

The Pei Hai is famed for its imposing monument, the great " White Dagoba " rising on a high hill close to the entrance gate. It was built in 1652 as a mark of respect to the Dalai Lama, a visitor to Peiping at that time. It represents the common Mongolian and Thibetan Buddhistic type of reliquary, symbolizing the five elements of earth, water, fire, air and ether in its five component parts of base, body, spire, decorated rims and topmost ball.

The walk around the lake or boat trip across it is filled with views of temples and other buildings. The large tile "dragon screen" attracts the most attention in the trip about the Pei Hai and is itself well worth the visit, being regarded by many as one of the best of Peiping's many pleasing sights. This screen stands in front of the Wan Fo Lou or Buddhist temple, which was formerly sacred to the Mongols and is located in the north-west corner of the grounds.

COAL HILL.

Just to the north of the Forbidden City and enclosed by a wall which forms its northern boundary is an artificial mound 210 feet high variously known as Coal Hill, Prospect Hill or City Mountain—one of the most interesting spots in Peiping. According to local tradition, the mound was partly formed during the Mongol dynasty by huge stores of coal when revolution threatened, and later covered with earth. If this be true there are no evidences now of the store of fuel for the place is covered by grass and trees, the whole forming an attractive park. There are many theories as to the reason for building the hill which is quite obviously artificial, the most generally accepted being that it was built of earth taken from the moats and canals. The hill terminates in five summits, on each of which a temple has been built. The last Emperor of the Mings hanged himself on one of the trees in the enclosure, when the capital city was taken by rebels, a short time before its occupation by the Manchus.

Several holes have been bored into the hill at different times, but no coal was ever found. According to superstitious Chinese belief, the hill serves a very useful purpose of *feng shui*, warding off from the Forbidden City the evil influences which come from the north.

CENTRAL PARK.

A pleasant and interesting half hour's ricsha ride is that going west from the Hotel de Pekin on the Tung Chang An Chieh, which presently becomes the Hsi Chang An Chieh. After passing the north wall of the British Legation on the south side of this street, the road runs along the south of the Imperial City wall passing the Tien An Men with its two high guardian white marble cloud pillars, the entrance to Central Park, the Hsin Hua Men, which is the entrance to the President's Palace, later the Ministry of Finance, Ministry of Communications and finally the little temple with its two pagodas rising out of a most prosaic business block.

Central Park, which lies between the Forbidden City and the San Hai, was once the pleasure grounds of the Imperial family and has now been opened to the general public. Hundreds of vehicles waiting outside attest the popularity of this great garden with the Chinese and for the visitor it is probably the best spot in Peiping where one can see the upper class residents at leisure. Wonderfully dressed ladies accompany their silken clad men folk. It is very often the gathering place of large meetings and in the numerous tea houses and restaurants, the politicians of the former capital foregather to talk things over.

Upon entering, the eye is caught by the blue tile-roofed marble arch, which has become historically famous. Originally it stood across Hatamen Street just opposite Tsung Pu Hutung, having been erected by the Chinese Government as a memorial to Baron Von Kettler, the German Minister who was murdered at that spot in June 1900 when going to call on the Tsungli Yamen (Foreign Office). An inscription in Chinese, Latin and German formerly bore witness to the folly of evil doing. In the flush of the Allied victory after the armistice, the monument was taken down and re-erected in its present position and the revised inscription in Latin and Chinese, attests the victory of right over might.

The park is beautifully arranged with long walks bordered by old trees, artificial lakes and hills, flower beds, collections of gold fish and a few animals and birds. The main attraction, however, is the Altar of Harvests, which lies to the north of the entrance. This circular altar is built up in three marble tiers, the floor of the top tier being of five different colored soils, yellow, black, red, white and blue, which curiously enough, correspond to the colors of the first Republican flag which has been supplanted by the present flag of red, white and blue. This earth was transported from different parts of China.

Bordering the north side of Central Park runs the moat across which is the Forbidden City. It is possible to pass out of the park from this side and enter the Hsi

Hua Men or west entrance to the Forbidden City and the National Art Museum.

PEKING UNION MEDICAL COLLEGE.

This American institution is variously known as Yu Wang Fu, the name of the property it occupies, and the Rockefeller Hospital, having been built with funds donated by the Rockefeller Foundation through the China Medical Board. This hospital is equipped with every modern medical device and the architecture has established a precedent and set an example in China by utilizing the typical Chinese features of roofs and general outline to multi-storied western buildings. It has some very beautiful Chinese touches and is well worth a visit. The auditorium is particularly pleasing to the eye.

ALTAR OF EARTH.

The Ti Tan Miao or Altar of Earth is located just outside of the north wall of the Tartar City and to the east of the An Ting Men, being separated from the Lama monastery and Confucian temple only by the city wall and moat. The Altar of Earth is square, instead of round like the Altar of Heaven, it being the ancient belief of the Chinese that heaven was round and the earth square. The main altar is composed of two terraces 106 feet across, and the enclosure is surrounded by a moat. The structure is chiefly of white marble, while owing to the use of tiles the predominant color is yellow, not because yellow was the imperial color, but because it is the symbolical color for earth, just as blue is for heaven, red for the sun, greenish-white for the moon, etc.

Worship at this altar was conducted by the Emperor as at the Altar of Heaven but the ceremony, conducted during the summer solstice, was on a smaller scale. Offerings of bullocks, etc., were made at the Altar of Heaven, but here they were buried in the ground instead of burned. The present altar dates back to Mongol times.

Ti Wang Miao.

This, the Walhalla of China, is on the avenue leading to the west gate of the Tartar City. It is a collection of halls wherein the tablets of all the monarchs of China from the remote ages were worshipped. The rule for admission to commemoration in this hall of fame was to accept all rulers save the vicious and oppressive, those who were assassinated and those who lost their kingdoms. This memorial temple was opened in 1522 by the dynasty of that day and was continued by the Manchus. The Manchus generously admitted some of the Tartar rulers of the Kin and Liao dynasties, raising the total number of tablets to nearly three hundred. "It is an impressive sight, these simple tablets of men who once ruled the Middle Kingdom, standing here side by side, worshipped by their successors that their spirits may bless the State. The selection of the good sovereigns alone recalls to mind the custom in ancient Jerusalem of allowing wicked princes no place in the sepulchres of the Kings." Distinguished statesmen of all ages, called by the Chinese *Kwoh-chu* or "pillars of state," are associated with their imperial masters in this temple, as not unworthy to receive equal honors.

Mohammedan Mosques.

There are about 40 small Mohammedan mosques in Peiping, but the most important one is to be found on the street outside the south-west wall of the Imperial City. The principal building of the mosque was burned several years ago and has not been rebuilt, the services being conducted in a small side building, where the Mohammedans assemble every Friday for prayer. The most interesting object it contains is a great stone monument dedicated to the mosque by Emperor Chien Lung. The inscriptions are in Persian, Manchu and Chinese. Other stones about the place bear inscriptions in Persian and Arabic, which languages are spoken by many of the Chinese attendants.

BOTANICAL AND ZOOLOGICAL GARDENS.

These are in one large enclosure a few miles directly west from the Hsi Chih Men, the gate from which the trip to the Summer Palace is made or the station of the Kalgan Railway reached. The gardens are connected with the city by a good motor road and the visit could be made at the same time as the trip to the Summer Palace.

The Empress Dowager spent a great deal of money and care on these gardens. The pleasure boats she used can still be seen here and other pleasure boats are for hire and thus trips around the garden or the moat can be taken in comfort. The gardens have been modernized. An entrance marked by three fine buildings graces the frontage.

The gardens as a whole are kept in fine condition and with their winding paths, camel back bridges, pavilions of many styles, tea houses, etc., the place has become a pleasure resort for the people of the city who care for a day amidst trees and flowers.

The Zoological Gardens are also well worth seeing and are likewise well kept up.

YELLOW TEMPLE.

About two miles north of the An Ting Men (gate) is the great Yellow Temple (Hwang Kung) composed of two main buildings erected in 1651 and 1722. One was intended as a place of residence for the Dalai Lamas on their visits to Peking and the other for the entertainment of Mongol princes when they came to the capital with tribute. The grounds cover a vast area and the buildings still show evidences of their former magnificence though they are now neglected and are fast falling into decay. The idols in the grounds and various enclosures are more of the Thibetan or Indian type than of the Chinese. This was formerly a celebrated factory for the production of religious paraphernalia for the temples of Mongolia and Thibet. Many of the curious Thibetan prayer wheels, incense burners, etc., offered for sale in local curio shops were produced at this temple.

The chief glory of the place is the white marble dagoba built by Emperor Chien Lung in memory of the Panchan Bogdo, the Grand Lama of Tashilhunpo, who died there of smallpox on November 12, 1780. His robes were buried under this *stupa*, although his cremated remains were carried back in a gold casket to Thibet. "The *stupa* is modeled on Thibetan lines, adhering generally to the ancient Indian type—but differing in that the dome is inverted. The spire or *toran*, composed of thirteen steplike segments, symbolical of the thirteen Buddhist heavens, is surmounted by a large cupola of gilded bronze. It is mounted on a series of angular plinths, posed upon a solid base of octagonal form. On the eight sides are sculptured in high relief scenes in the life of the deceased lama, including the preternatural circumstances attendant on his birth, his entrance into the priesthood, combats with heretics, instruction of disciples, and death." This *stupa*, one of the best examples of modern Chinese sculpture, was multilated in 1900 by the foreign troops quartered in the temple during the Boxer uprising.

The temple is the scene of an interesting ceremony on the 13th day of the first Chinese moon, when the evil spirits are driven away by exorcisms and incantations, many of the Lamas appearing hideously disguised as black and white demons. The ceremony, accompanied by strange dances, terminates at noon when a painted statue of a demon is placed on a pile of straw and burned.

There is no admission fee to the Yellow Temple but the priests and gate keepers insist upon acting as guides and demand payment for their services.

SUMMER PALACE.

A macadam motor road leads from the Hsi Chi Men (north gate in the west wall of the Tartar City) to the famous Summer Palace, 8 miles distant. There are really two summer palaces near Peiping, and as they are equally famous and are located near each other, they are very frequently confused. The Old Summer Palace was the inspiration of Emperor Kang Hsi, who built here a summer residence. His renowned successor Emperor Chien Lung, added many improvements, securing the aid of Jesuit priests and the best of Chinese architects and landscape gardeners. Many of the pavilions were built in semi-European style under the direction of the Jesuits. Within the grounds were about thirty places of residence for princes and officials and many small villages for the residence of servants and eunuchs. Father Beviot, writing of the place 170 years ago, said, " To form any idea of its beauty one must drift into the regions of fairy land, such as described by imaginative writers." This summer palace was practically destroyed by the English and French troops in 1860, and the stone work and marble has been removed from time to time, so that to-day it is practically impossible to find where the old buildings stood and nothing remains except mounds and lakes. Before setting fire to the place, the foreign troops looted it. Many of the wonderful examples of Chinese art in European museums or private collections were taken from this palace at the time.

The present Summer Palace was built by the Empress Dowager just to the west of the older palace. In its construction she lavished the money which had been appropriated for the establishment of a modern navy for China. Like the older palace it is built on a series of hills and contains many pavilions and bridges.

" The grounds are lovely, a beautiful clear lake spanned by a white marble bridge lying in their midst, like a diamond sparkling in a setting of green. The palace itself is like all other Chinese houses, a succession of one storied halls, built around central courtyards, and each one divided inside into three, by tall beautifully carved blackwood partitions. These halls are raised upon stone terraces, and approached by a flight of broad steps. Their curling roofs are tiled with imperial yellow or bright green and each corner is bestridden by half a dozen curious little devils, from six to eight inches high, made of porcelain and representing dragons or phoenixes, their position there being in some way connected in the Chinese mind with the *feng shui,* or occult influences affecting the prosperity of the inhabitants. The eaves supporting the roofs are painted and decorated by hand with a multitude of gay scenes from Chinese life, treated with the utmost brilliant coloring of greens, blues and vermilions, the ubiquitous Chinese dragon appearing over and over again under a hundred different aspects. Some fine bronze birds and beasts stand sentinel at the chief entrances. A creeper overgrown 'covered way' meanders through the grounds, skirting the lake and leading from the palace to a group of temple buildings scattered on the side of the hill which backs it." One of the most interesting objects in the grounds is a white marble summer house built in the shape of a boat and apparently floating on the surface of the water. Chinese wags say this was built by the Empress Dowager to represent the Chinese navy.

During the monarchy the summer palace was open to foreign visitors on certain days of the month when the court was not in residence there, admission being secured through application to foreign ministers. The palace is now open daily to both foreigners and Chinese.

TSING HUA COLLEGE.

This well known educational institution is also known as the American Indemnity College because it was built from Boxer Indemnity funds which the United States returned to China to be used for educational purposes. It is a short distance east of the Old Summer Palace and accessible by a good motor road. Here in an absolutely foreign setting, Chinese students are given a western education preparing them for advanced study in America. While the college has a Chinese president, there is a large American staff.

Jade Fountain.

This fountain gushes forth in the surroundings of a beautiful park three miles west of the new Summer Palace on the motor road to the Western Hills. Its three pagodas are prominent landmarks from any point on the road outside of Shih Chi Men. From the pagoda built by Emperor Kang Hsi, perched on a high hill, there is a remarkable view of Peiping, the Western Hills with Pi Yuan-Ssu and the Hunting Park nestling against them, and the countryside far below dotted with rice fields. The second of these pagodas is constructed of white marble, the third of tiles.

For over seven centuries this spot has been beloved by the Imperial family as its name testifies—"The Garden of Peaceful Brightness." The clear water from the fountain runs into the Summer Palace lake, thence several miles to the three Sea Palaces in the Imperial City and finally into the Grand Canal by way of Canal Street through the Legation Quarter.

Western Hills Temples.

On the road to Pa Ta Chu from the Jade Fountain just at the foot of the hills and accessible by motor car, is Wo Fu Ssu, or the Temple of the Sleeping Buddha. Passing under the bright colored tiled *pailou* and through several courts, the Hall of the Buddha is reached where on a great couch reclines the fifty foot figure of Buddha. His feet are bare and it is to cover them that the large number of shoes, big and little, which can be seen in this temple, are brought by worshippers.

Wo Fu Ssu is one of the oldest monasteries in the Western Hills. The Peiping Y.M.C.A. has rented it as summer quarters and so there is now a mixture of Buddhism and Christianity. A short tramp over the hills from this temple brings one to the Black Dragon Pool which is fed by springs and used as a swimming pool.

Pi Yun Ssu is on the motor road continuing from Wo Fu Ssu. This " Monastery of the Azure Clouds " is

19

the most beautiful in this region. It is built on the side of a hill with courtyards and temples gradually climbing up until all is surmounted by the marble *stupa*, which rises high above the valley and eighty feet from its own base. This climb is hard but it affords a magnificent view of the countryside between the temple and Peiping.

Many of the pavilions of Pi Yun Ssu have fallen in ruin with roofs tumbling down upon the gods. The small figures representing the comparative joys and dreads of the Buddhist heaven and hell are still preserved, however. Another chamber houses the "Five Hundred Gods." These are all larger than life size and no two are alike in facial expression.

IMPERIAL HUNTING PARK.

Not far from Pi Yun Ssu is the old Imperial Hunting Park with its walled enclosure. This is known as the Hsiang Shan or "Perfumed Mountain." Built by the rulers of the Ching dynasty, it fell into disuse during the late Manchu period and to-day it is lovely in its wildness. Part of it is utilized by an orphanage conducted by philanthropic Chinese. It is thickly wooded and provides a most pleasant walk over its hills and valleys.

PA TA CHU.

This locality takes its name from the eight temples which dot the hill above the valley here. It has, however, become the center of summer homes for foreigners in Peiping. It is on a good motor road and the temples rented from the monks make a restful week-end possible for those living in the former capital. Two foreign style hotels have been built here and the traveler may stop there or visit them for tiffin or tea. The hills in the vicinity are filled with shrines and temples and the atmosphere is pleasant and healthful.

T'AN CHEH SSU.

This prosperous and quaintly situated monastery can be reached by taking the train from Hsi Chih Men station and leaving it at the end of the line, Men Tou Kou. From there it is necessary to take a donkey or chair, or to walk over a range of hills a trip which will take about three hours. It is possible to make the return trip in a day but that means rather fast traveling and the sights are too rare to spoil by hurrying. The best plan is to take your bedding, supplies and a servant and spend at least one night in the guest houses which the monks provide for Chinese and foreigners alike.

The name of this temple is translated as "Monastery of the Oak Pool" and, dating from the fifth century, is probably the oldest of its kind in these hills. There are many monks here and religious services are regularly held. It has a large income and on the whole provides a good example of Chinese monastic life. The trees outlined against colored tiled roofs, water spouting down the hill side and into pools and the periodical chanting of the services, amply reward one for having made the journey.

CHIEH T'AI SSU.

The "Monastery of the Ordaining Terrace" can be reached from the Men Tou Kou station in two hours by walking, donkey or chair, or may be reached in a three hours' journey over mountainous paths from T'an Cheh Ssu. It is the best plan to spend one night there also. The monastery is wealthy and well maintained and dates back to the seventh century. Like T'an Cheh Ssu, it has enjoyed imperial patronage, Emperor Chien Lung having left behind many inscriptions on the stones testifying to his satisfaction with the scene. It is still a strong center of the Buddhist faith.

MOTOR TRIPS.

There are roads open to motor cars about Peiping totalling some several hundred miles in length. Most of them are merely dirt surfaced but they are constantly used by motorists. The longest one is that connecting the capital with Tientsin, about eighty-two miles.

The favorite drive from Peiping is the Western Hills road which goes out of Hsi Chih Men past the Summer Palace, Jade Fountain, Wo Fu Ssu, Pi Yun Ssu, the Golf Course and back by way of Ping Tze Men. It is thirty miles long and there is a toll station at either end where a fee of one dollar is collected. However, it is only necessary to pay at one of these stations in traversing the road. There are several branch roads from this, namely the one going to Tsing Hua College, to T'ang Shan, the Race Course, and Pa Ta Chu.

The motor road to T'ang Shan Hot Springs branches to the north from the Summer Palace road before the Western Hills are reached and covers 28 miles through very pretty and interesting country. Rooms and meals can be had at the foreign style hotel there and many Chinese and foreigners go there for the hot baths.

Running directly south by way of Chien Men Street and through the Yung Ting Men of the Chinese City wall, is the motor road to Nan Yuan, covering 15 miles of good dirt road. It is kept in repair by the troops stationed there and is the route to the aviation field.

The road to the Race Course goes outside of Hsi Pien Men for 15 miles with small branches to the different bungalows which the foreigners have built there for summer use. A side road connects this one with the Western Hills road to the north.

There is another long road in north China available for motor use, namely the Tientsin-Paotingfu road, which is 122 miles long. This is a dirt road and connects the provincial capital with the military capital of Hopei.

MING TOMBS.

The Ming Tombs and the Great Wall are visited from Nankow, about two hours' railway journey from Peiping. The railway station at Peiping is outside the north-west corner of the Tartar City. By taking the morning train, one can reach Nankow before noon and the Ming tombs can be visited the same day, spending the following day on a trip to the Great Wall and to the Nankow Pass, the great gateway on the road beween China and Mongolia. Hotels at Nankow afford stopping places for travelers. Of course the most popular method of visiting this point of interest is by motor car.

The beautiful valley in which the tombs are located is six miles long, and the tombs, each in a separate enclosure, are on the slopes of the wooded hills which enclose the valley. The Chinese name of the place is Shih-san Ling or "Tombs of the Thirteen (Emperors)," that being the number of rulers buried there.

Approaching the tombs from Nankow one comes first to an enormous white marble *pailou* of five arches, marking the entrance to the "Holy Way." This is three miles distant from the tombs. The inscription on the *pailou* enjoins on all visitors a feeling of reverence for the holy places about to be visited.

On each side of the avenue are large images carved of blue limestone. "The military mandarins, six in number, have mailed coats reaching down below the knees, close fitting caps hanging over the shoulder, a sword in the left hand and a marshal's baton in the right. The civil officials have robes with long hanging sleeves, tasseled sashes bound with jade-mounted belts, embroidered breastplates, and square caps. The animals which follow, facing the avenue, comprise two pairs of lions, two of unicorn monsters, two of camels, two of elephants, two of *hi-lin* and two of horses, one pair being represented standing, the other seated or kneeling." In the building of these tombs as well as those at Nanking the Mings merely copied the styles set by the earlier dynasties. There has been a great deal of wanton destruction of the monuments and arches on the Holy Way, which in places is difficult to follow. At one time this avenue was magnificently paved and stretched through a beautifully wooded country. It was then the scene of many gorgeous processions when the later Ming Emperors offered sacrifices to their ancestors. Much of the paving has been torn up, the trees cut down for fuel and the fine bridges allowed to fall into disrepair. The country now has a bare and forbidding look.

At the end of the avenue is the semi-circle of thirteen tombs and in the center the great temple or sacrificial hall dedicated to Emperor Yung-lo. The large hall 200 feet long by 90 feet wide contains 40 red lacquered columns, each consisting of an enormous *Persea Nanmu* tree trunk, over 60 feet high and ten feet in circumference at the base. The columns reach to the true roof under which there is a lower ceiling. The *Persea Nanmu* is a fragrant wood and these old columns still exhale a faint odor. In the hall is the ancestral tablet of Emperor Yung-lo, before which sacrificial offerings are regularly placed. The fine building has remained intact for five hundred years. It is probably the largest ancient building in China and certainly one of the best preserved.

In the rear of the hall after passing through beautiful courtyards one comes to the tomb, and a subterranean passage leads to the top of the tumulus. This is a half mile in circuit and has the appearance of a natural hill, though it is really artificial. According to tradition the coffin was carefully suspended in a pit so that no water could touch it and all of the requirements of good *feng shui* be complied with. One feature which will always impress the visitor is the absolute silence of the spot for it is seldom that even the cry of a bird will be heard.

The twelve other tombs are constructed on the same general design, though the dimensions are different. They are rarely visited. Of the sixteen monarchs of the Ming dynasty, thirteen are buried here, while the founder, Hung Wu, is buried in Nanking. The second sovereign was obliged to fly from Peking in disguise when Yung-lo seized the throne. Emperor Ching-tsong (1450-1457) ruled only while his brother was held in captivity by the Tartars and on his death was not accorded imperial honors. Guides and donkey drivers, in order to save time often take the visitor from Nankow direct to the sacrificial hall. The trip should be made as described above, approaching the tombs by the "Holy Way."

THE GREAT WALL.

The trip from the village of Nankow to the Great Wall and Nankow Pass is made on a train which leaves Nankow in the early morning or the entire trip can be made by motor from Peiping. The Peiping-Kalgan railway extends to Paotaochen, a distance of 500 miles with an extension which will ultimately be completed to Urga, replacing, as a means of transportation, the many camel trains which now cross Mongolia. The railway line is especially interesting as being an enterprise successfully carried out by Chinese without foreign aid. It was built by Chinese engineers, who successfully solved many difficult problems of construction, and has always been under purely Chinese management. The engineering difficulties were greatest at Nankow Pass, where the grade is steep and many sharp curves were necessary. Between Nankow and Pata Lin, a distance of ten miles, the railway rises to an altitude of 1,600 feet, a difficult piece of construction. Four tunnels were necessary at this point, one of them, which reaches to the summit of the pass, being 3,000 feet long. The building of this section of the line took four years.

The Great Wall of China which for centuries has fired the imagination of men surpasses all other physical human undertakings in the daring of its plan and the industry and patience required for its execution. The construction of the wall was begun in the third century B.C. by the great Emperor Shih Huang Ti as a means of consolidating the established Chinese Empire and as a barrier against invasion by the Tartar warriors of the North, and for centuries it successfully served its purpose. History does not record how long the wall was under construction but it is known that the section from the Eastern terminus to the Yellow River, about one-third of the entire length, took ten years, a feat which could only have been accomplished by the use of a tremendous number of workmen. In fact it has been estimated that more than a million different laborers shared in its construction while practically the entire population of China was called on to contribute materials or labor. The work must have been completed in a comparatively short time because its inception naturally aroused the hostility of the Northern Tartars. There are many legends recounting the cruelty of the task masters who flogged the workers to such desperate efforts that many of them died and their bodies were thrown into the earthworks.

The Eastern terminus of the wall is at Shanhaikwan, on the Gulf of Pechili, now a station on the Peiping-Moukden railway marking the boundary between Manchuria and China proper. Running eastward and north of Peiping, the wall turns South and East through Shensi to the Yellow River and thence to Kaiyukuan where it comes to an end on the precipitous banks of the Great North River, the distance in a straight line from one terminus to the other being about 1,150 miles. However, the wall twists and turns throughout the whole distance and it is estimated that the main structure is 1,700 miles in length. There are many subsidiary walls and loops and if these are taken into consideration, the total length is more than 2,500 miles. An Englishman who saw the Great Wall in 1790 estimated that it contained more brick and stone than were to be found in the United Kingdom and a later visitor said that the material employed was sufficient to build a wall eight feet high and three feet thick that would encircle the globe at the equator.

The design of the wall is uniform throughout its length except where lack of materials necessitated changes in the original plan and the substitution of loam and tiles for the more substantial and permanent masonry. Starting at the sea level at Shanhaikwan the wall traverses plains and mountains being at some points 4,000 feet above sea level. The height is 20 to 50 feet, the base is 20 to 30 feet thick and the summit 12 feet. The retaining walls are of well tamped earth. The summit throughout is well paved and so constructed as to ensure perfect drainage. " The mortar employed is snowy white and, after standing for centuries, still binds the masonary in an adamantine grip. It is believed that the mixing of such mortar is a lost art. Some Chinese claim that the ancients employed rice flour with the lime after some forgotten formula." It is worthy of note that the granite blocks are as carefully dressed and the whole structure finished with as nice a regard for architectural details as if it had been built in a capital city instead of through a country so wild and forbidding that it is easy to imagine that sections have not been seen by the eye of man for centuries.

At intervals of 150 to 200 yards throughout the length of the wall there are defense towers which are about 20 feet higher than the wall itself and project about 15 feet beyond the outside edge of the wall. These towers provided vantage places for archers who could sweep the entire outer edge of the wall with their arrows. Authorities who have made a study of the matter say that these towers were obviously built first as a means of protection during the preliminary work of construction and the wall built later to connect them. Some of the towers are two storied and contain rooms for the storage of provisions and as a shelter for the guard. In the days when bows and arrows formed the only weapons used by armies the wall provided such a perfect line of defense that not more than a dozen men were needed for each mile.

In later years cannon were mounted along the wall and various Emperors made repairs and improvements. But it has now been almost three hundred years since the wall was used for defensive purposes and the garrisons of guards who formerly peopled it have all been withdrawn except for a few at important gates. The dust of centuries has covered the summit and provided soil from which great trees have sprung; in many places the walls are broken and the bricks and stones have been pilfered but the wall remains to-day as it has been for more than twenty centuries the only work of man that is visible from Mars.

WESTERN TOMBS.

Some of the Emperors of the Manchu dynasty are buried at the Hsi Ling or "Western Tombs," west of the town of Yi Chow. To reach the place, take the train on the Peiping-Hankow Railway to Kao Pei-tien (52 miles) and from there a branch line of 25 miles to Liang-ko Chuang, about one hour's journey from the tombs. The branch line of the railway was built to enable the Emperor to visit the tombs of his ancestors. As on a visit to Jehol or the Eastern tombs, one must make arrangements through his legation for a permit. Bedding and servants must be taken from Peiping.

The tombs are all in a park enclosed by a wall about 20 miles in circuit. The burial place is a natural amphitheatre formed by the Hsi Shan, and in a general way, is much like the Ming Tombs or the Eastern Tombs, though more beautiful because of the fine park. The Imperial Tombs are the burial places of: Yung Cheng (1723-1735), Chia Ch'ing (1796-1820), Tso Kuang (1820-1850), and Kwang Hsu (1875-1908). This is the burial place of many others of the Imperial family, including the 20 wives of Yung Cheng and 14 of the 17 wives of Chia Ch'ing.

EASTERN TOMBS.

This burial place of some of the Manchu rulers may be visited in a trip of 10 days to two weeks from Peiping. It is reached by way of the railway from Peiping to Tungchow (15 miles) and a journey on donkeys for the remaining 210 *li*. After leaving the railway at Tungchow, one passes through the following villages: Yen-chiao, 6 miles; Ma-chia-fa, 9 miles; Pai-fu-tu, 18 miles; San ho-hsien, 21 miles; Tuanchia-ying, 26 miles; Pang-chun, 32 miles; Chi-chow 40 miles; Lin-ho-chuang, (crossing the Lin Ho), 55 miles; Shih Men, 59 miles. The journey is through mountains and forests and is very beautiful and interesting. The traveler must stop at native inns.

The Eastern tombs comprising seven separate cemeteries bear a striking resemblance to the Ming tombs near Nankow, and the other important burial places in China. The cemeteries are located in a great natural amphitheatre of mountains 20 miles in extent. The tombs are widely scattered and it would take several days to see them all. The imperial graves number 54, in which lie the bodies of emperors, princes, princesses and concubines. The principal groups are approached by long roads bordered with stone images of animals and men similar to those at the Ming tombs. Among the sovereigns buried there are: Shun-chih (1643-1661), Kang Hsi (1662-1722), Chien Lung (1736-1795), Hsien Feng (1850-1861), T'ung-chih (1862-1875). The tombs are more magnificent than those at Nankow. One of the finest is that of the Empress Dowager, Tsu Hsi, finished in gold leaf and gold plate. It cost more than $10,000,000. The tombs were looted by soldiers in 1930 and jewels of fabulous wealth stolen.

JEHOL.

This old summer residence of the Emperors of China is 144 miles northeast of Peiping, connected by a motor road. An efficient interpreter is necessary for the success of the journey. Chinese inns are to be found at convenient points along the route. It is important before leaving Peiping to secure the necessary permission to visit the Imperial palaces, etc.

The town of Jehol derives its name from an abbreviation of the name of the stream, Je-ho-erh, " hot river," on which it is located. This river, a tributary of the Luan Ho, is really barely lukewarm. The site of the city is beautiful, on a bend of the stream and surrounded by mountains which shelter it from the north winds in winter and afford a means of escaping from the heat in summer. Emperor Kang Hsi began the construction of the Summer Palace in Jehol in 1703; his successors, Emperors Yung Cheng and

Chien Lung further beautified the spot and it was occupied
as an Imperial summer residence until September 2, 1820,
when Emperor Chia Ch'ing, while staying there, was struck
by lightning. This was considered an evil omen and the
place was abandoned for forty years, until 1860, when
Emperor Hsien Feng fled there at the time Peking was
occupied by the Anglo-French troops. He died in less than
a year after reaching Jehol and this event proved to the
Imperial Clan the correctness of their previous conclusions
regarding the evil influences of the place, so that in 1900
when the allied troops advanced on Peking the Court did
not flee to Jehol but to Sianfu instead. For the same
reason the Court refused to consider taking refuge there
during the Republican Revolution of 1911.

The principal entrance to the Imperial estates is about
an hour's walk north of Jehol. The park is enclosed by
high battlemented walls six miles in circuit, the entrance
gate being guarded by the usual stone lions. It was at the
Imperial residence in this park that the embassy of Lord
MacCartney was received in 1793 by Emperor Chien Lung.
The residences and other buildings are now in disrepair
and generally in a dilapidated condition, though this is not
apparent from any distance. The view from any vantage
ground is delightful; gilded domes of kiosks, brilliantly
painted bridges, pagoda towers, and many colored buildings,
rising in tiers on the lower slopes of the hillsides, are to
be seen through the shining greenery of the cedars. The
phœnix and the dragon are represented over and over again
in the architectural designs, while massive pink lions guard
each highly ornamented terrace. The lake covered with
beautiful islands is fed by shaded creeks and lead into many
canals crossed by fantastic foot bridges. The imperial
residence itself is composed not of a single building but of
more than thirty structures scattered about the park, all
located with a fine regard to the beauty of the whole
scheme, no matter from what point it is viewed. As is
usual in Chinese parks and gardens, there are many laby-
rinthine walks and grottoes constructed of artificial stone.

There is nothing remarkable about the villas themselves, though they contain many interesting mementoes of the sovereigns who occupied them, the walls of some being almost covered with inscriptions by Chien Lung and other Emperors.

Among the features of the place is a nine-storey pagoda, completed in 1764, and containing inscriptions in Chinese, Manchu, Mongol and Thibetan, recording the fact that the structure was erected in commemoration of the conquest of Zungari. The Imperial theater, surrounded by balconies, is reached by a handsome marble bridge. Two richly endowed Buddhist monasteries were built in 1770 and 1779 as replicas of famous Thibetan convents located at Lhasa and Chigatse. One of the temples bears a striking resemblance to the Temple of Heaven in Peiping. Each is occupied by hundreds of Lama priests.

Returning from Jehol the traveler may follow the same route as that by which he came, or go to Peiping by way of the Tung Ling or Eastern Tombs. Another route is by boat as far as Luanchow which is on the railway between Tientsin and Shanhaikwan. The boat journey will take from two to five days.

KALGAN.

The building of the Peiping-Suiyuan Railway has brought this city located on the edge of Mongolia within easy reach of travelers. Hotel-Kalgan, 5 minutes from the railway station. The railway between Peiping and Kalgan traverses a distance of 124 miles and is completed as far west as Paotaochen, a Yellow River port on the edge of Mongolia.

Kalgan is among the cities open to foreign trade and quite a number of foreign concerns are established there. It is the gateway to Mongolia and the center for the developing trade of that great territory. It was long an important caravan station for the shipment of tea to Russia and Mongolia and the meeting place of many camel trains traveling between Peiping and Urga. The railway

will eventually be completed to Urga, 728 miles, now
distant a five days' journey by motor. Before the building
of the Trans-Siberian railway the tea trade with Russia
passed through here and the very extensive compounds,
with their high mud walls, which at that time were the
centers for tea transportation, are still to be seen in the
western part of the city.

SIANFU.

At Chenchow the traveler to Western China leaves
the present terminus of the Lung-Hai railway for
more primitive conveyances for the journey to the ancient
city of Sianfu, the capital and most important city of
Shensi, and the most interesting city, historically, in all
China. Sianfu is about 30 li from the Wei River, a
tributary of the Yellow River, and about 250 li from the
Yellow River proper. This upper part of the Yellow River
is not navigable, and Sianfu has acquired its present
importance by overland trade, exporting cotton, wool, skins
and hides. The population of the city and suburbs is
about 150,000. It has no foreign hotels and the foreign
residents number about 30.

Sianfu or a neighboring city was the capital of the
country on several occasions, and it was near here that,
according to some authorities, the founders of the Chinese
race first settled, spreading out from here to all parts of
Eastern Asia. The city was in its prime as the capital of
the Tang dynasty, when it was known as Siking. Under
the name of Ch'ang-an, it was the capital of the empire
from 206 B.C. to A.D. 605 when the capital was moved to
Honan. It was near here that the books of the country
were burned by Shih Hwang-ti (240-209 B.C.). As late as
1900 the city served as the capital of the country, for the
Empress Dowager and Emperor Kwang-Hsu fled here
during the Boxer troubles.

" Sianfu was the starting point of all those religious
movements which have influenced in any degree the immo-
bility of the Chinese nation. Here Mohammedanism found
its entrance, first success and permanent hold. Here a

colony of the sons of Israel came to their perpetual banishment among the sons of Han. Here Buddhism, under royal patronage, first established its real sway. Here six hundred years later when the Greek Emperor Theodosius, the princes of Central Asia and the rulers of India and Persia were sending their envoys with presents to the Imperial court in Sianfu, came the apostles of Nestorianism to propagate the Christian creed."

The walls which surround Sianfu are about ten miles in circuit, and thirty feet high, surmounted by watch towers of equal height. They are visible for many miles across the loess plain on which the city is built. The present walls date from the reign of the founder of the Ming dynasty, Hung Wu (1368-1399), who also gave the city the name it has since retained. The towers were added in 1526. The four gates are built at the cardinal points of the compass and the Tartar City is separated from the Chinese City by a wall. Soon after the outbreak of the Republican revolution, the Chinese attacked the Manchus here and the deaths which followed have been estimated at 20,000; probably more than in all of the fighting in the important battles of Hankow and Nanking. The Manchus were practically exterminated. The northeast part of the city, where they lived, was left it is said without one brick on top of another.

The neighborhood of the city abounds in tombs, monuments and other relics of great antiquity. Many of the early "Yellow" Emperors are buried here, though the marks of their tombs have long since been effaced and few of them can be identified with any degree of certainty. It was here that one of the rulers of China was buried with such a wealth of gold and silver that his sons feared the temptation it would offer to robbers and constructed many other grave mounds so that no one could tell which contained the treasure. The large number of tumuli in the vicinity give credence to the legend. Shih Hwang-ti (240-209 B.C.) is buried at the city of Lint'unghsien, 15 miles east of Sianfu. It was this Emperor who sought to begin the history of

China anew by burning all the books of the country and to keep out the Mongols and the Tartars by building the Great Wall. His tomb, which was an exact duplicate of his Sianfu palace, was so magnificent that it passed into a proverb and formed the basis for some *Arabian Nights* tales. It was fifty feet high and a mile and a half in circumference. Near the city is buried We Tse-tien, the only Empress who ever ruled over China in her own name. In the former Manchu quarter stands a stone on which is imprinted the figure of a human hand, somewhat larger than life size. According to legend, this mark was left by the Empress though it is also said that it is the imprint of the hand of Yang Kuei Fei, a famous concubine who played an important part in the history of China. Sianfu or a neighboring city is reputed to have been the birthplace of the legendary Fu Hsi.

South of the Tartar City is the famous Pei Lin, or " Forest of Stones," a collection of more than 1,400 monuments on which the history of the place for 2,000 years has been inscribed, some of the records being pictorial. The best known of these monuments is the Nestorian Tablet, which bears the date of A.D. 781 and gives in 2,000 Chinese characters a record of the establishment in China " of the illustrious religion of Syria." This, the only known record of that early effort to Christianize China, was found in 1625 west of the city at what was most probably the site of the old Nestorian temple and was placed in the Pei Lin.

In the Lama temple at the northwest corner of the city there is a massive carved bowl of yellow marble, some four feet in diameter. Tradition puts this down as the baptismal font of the old Nestorian temple.

Ten miles from Pinchou, northwest of Sianfu, there is a famous image of Buddha, carved out of the living rock. The image is forty feet high, and a pendant image is larger than life size. The work is said to belong to the T'ang dynasty (A.D. 618-906).

Of the many rich shops in the city, probably the most

notable are the furriers. Curio shops abound, where the articles offered for sale are usually of much greater antiquity than those found in the shops nearer the coast. As the place has been untouched by tourist travel, prices are comparatively low. The museum in Sianfu has a few wonderful examples of Chinese art. The most famous things are the huge stone horses cut in bas-relief and the great bronze bell, which was used as the model for the famous bells of Kyoto. The city of Kyoto was laid out after the plan of Sianfu.

Sianfu has a large Moslem population and is headquarters for the Mohammedanism of the north. The Mohammedan mosque, dating from the second century, is worthy of note. During the great Mohammedan rebellion of 1861-1876, Sianfu held out while every other city and village for miles around was razed. Extensive bituminous coal fields exist near Sianfu, awaiting the arrival of a railway to make their development possible.

Shensi Province.

The province of Shensi has an area of 75,290 square miles and a population of 9,465,558. The northern two-thirds of the province is cut off from the southern third by the Tsingling range, which is a labyrinth of hills and high mountains, some of the peaks rising to heights of 12,000 feet. The general altitude is 8,500 feet. Some of the streams in this broad range fall 600 feet in 30 miles. The northern slopes are steep and cold and the southern slopes are gentle and lie in a temperate climate. The range is crossed by two important trade routes. The valley of the Yellow River is mostly a dry and barren area, while the valley of the Wei is important agriculturally. On the whole the soil of the province produces fine crops, provided the rains are abundant, but in time of drouth famines ensue. One of the worst famines in the recent history of China was that in Shensi which followed soon after the Boxer uprising. In some of the districts the death rate was 70% and despite the expenditure of almost

20

£1,000,000 in relief, the deaths were about 2½ million. The province suffered severely during the Mohammedan rebellion of 1874, which is estimated to have swept away about half the population. Immigration has since been encouraged by the government, with the result that "the population is practically representative of the greater half of China, for there are immigrants from Shansi, Shantung, Honan, Hupeh, Szechuan, and Yunnan." Salt, nickel, gold and iron are found in the province. The best known industries are "iron work at Tungkwan, straw plaiting at Hwayinmiao, incense sticks and bamboo furniture at Chihshui, and coal at Weinan Hsien."

THE LOESS PLAIN.

On any road to Sianfu one passes through a part of the great loess district of western and central China, which stretches through the provinces of Shensi and Kansu. The area covered by the loess was estimated by Baron Richthofen to be 375,000 square miles. North of Sianfu the deposit attains a maximum depth of 1,000 feet. Through this loess deposit small streams have made canyons sometimes several hundred feet deep. The roads through the plain are especially atrocious, being quagmires in the rainy season and deep with dust in the dry.

According to Richthofen and other authorities, loess is the dust of northern Asia produced through many centuries and blown over north China by the prevailing winds. This fine powdery material mixed with sand covers what was the original surface of the land with a varying depth which is usually several hundred feet. Rivers in the loess country sweep through this loose material and find their beds on the original soil beneath, with the result that all flow between steep, precipitous banks. The soil is so rich that no fertilization is needed, as in other parts of China, and with suitable rainfall abundant crops are produced, but crop failures from drouth are not uncommon. According to local belief, there is small famine every three years and a large one every ten.

A striking feature of the loess country is the vertical cleavage of the soil. From a height, the plain appears to stretch away for miles unbroken by any depression, but on closer examination, it is found to be full of ravines, many of them several hundred feet deep and only a few yards wide. Crops here are not the same as in the south; millet, wheat, oats, corn and sweet potatoes taking the place of rice as staples.

LANCHOWFU.

West of Shensi in the province of Kansu (population 5,927,997), is the far western capital of Lanchowfu, with a population of 500,000. Being so near to the high Mongolian plateau, Kansu suffers great extremes of heat and cold. Two roads connect Lanchowfu and Sianfu, the most important being the northern. It was formerly a beautiful thoroughfare, bordered by trees. It is now being rebuilt for motor traffic. Lanchowfu is situated on the Yellow River which is crossed by a bridge of boats in the summer and by ice in winter.

PAOTINGFU.

This city, 91 miles from Peking on the Peking-Hankow Railway, was formerly the official capital of Chihli (Hopei), but with the growing importance of Tientsin, the latter city has usurped practically all the functions of the provincial capital. The city is enclosed by a wall four miles in circuit built in 1402, and has a population of 80,000. It is the location of a modern university, founded in 1901, and is an important center for missionary work. During the Boxer trouble twenty-five foreigners, mostly American missionaries, were massacred here. The sacred mountain of Wu-tai-shan, about 115 miles distant, can be reached in five stages. It is visited more conveniently from Ting-chow.

TAIYUANFU.

This city, the capital of Shansi, is the terminus of the Cheng Tai Railway, running from Shai Kai Chwang, where connection is made with the through trains of the

Peiping-Hankow line. Shai Kai Chwang is 172 miles from Peiping, and Taiyuanfu is 323 miles from Peiping by rail. The Cheng Tai line passes through a mountainous section of the country, of great scenic beauty. Population of Taiyuanfu, 100,000. There are two hotels of semi-foreign style.

The city is surrounded by a wall eight miles in circuit, being laid out like the Tartar city of Peiping. Two broad streets run north and south and two east and west, connecting the eight gates and dividing the city into rectangles. Some of the fine streets are bordered with very old trees. The place is of interest to foreigners because of the fact that it was the scene of one of the most bloody massacres of the Boxer uprising. Forty-five missionaries of Shansi were induced to come to the capital and place themselves under the protection of the governor. But as soon as all were there, they were treacherously massacred by the officials. Altogether with those who came later, more than seventy missionaries, Catholic and Protestant, were killed. The Empress Dowager on her flight from Peiping stopped here and listened eagerly to the stories of the tortures. The mission boards, invited by the Chinese government to settle on an indemnity for the massacre, suggested a fine of half a million taels, not as an indemnity for the lives of the missionaries, but to establish a modern university to remove the cause of hostility. Since that time the railway has been built, many foreigners have taken up residence here, a modern university has been established and the whole aspect of the place changed so far as the interests of foreigners are concerned. In 1907 a permanent exposition was opened here for the display of the products of the province, which include camels' hair rugs, furs, cotton goods, pottery, jewelry, carved furniture, ores, etc. The province is well known for its suppression of the growing and use of opium, its schools, anti-foot binding movement and other reforms. Its fruit, especially grapes, are very famous. Cotton mills, iron works and other industries have been developed.

"One of the mountain peaks of the plain is pointed out as the ' Ararat ' of China, and is commonly called Jen-tsu-shan (Mountain of the Ancestors of Man), and the story is told that when the whole race were destroyed by a great flood, two persons saved their lives by jumping on the backs of two mighty lions, and were carried by them to the top-most ledge of this mountain, and thus saved from the general destruction. These two afterwards became the parents of the whole human race. On the top of this mountain is a very old temple."

Eighty miles north of Taiyuanfu is the sacred mountain of Wu-tai-shan, visited the whole year round by a steady stream of pilgrims from all parts of the country, some coming from Mongolia and Thibet.

Fifteen miles south of the city is located the famous temple of Chin Sz, of the Tang Dynasty, with very old trees and a great spring located in the temple grounds. Nearby are primitive paper and chemical industries. Motor roads built by the government and the American Red Cross extend from Tatung in the extreme northern end of the province, connecting with the Peking-Suiyuan Railway, to the southern end of the province, touching important cities like Taichow, Linchow, Taiku, Pingyao, Fenchow, Pinting and Liaochow. Ricshas, motor buses and motor cars are used for long distance travel on these roads.

The elevated plain to the south of Taiyuanfu is covered with villages. Many coal mines in the vicinity have been worked by primitive methods for centuries. It has been estimated that the anthracite resources of Shansi and adjacent territory are equal to those of Pennsylvania and with the development of mining this will be one of the richest sections of China.

PEIPING-MOUKDEN RAILWAY.

This line of the Chinese government railway system maintains a regular daily service between Peiping and Moukden, with an additional through train which, in conjunction with the South Manchuria and the Chinese

Eastern railways, connects with the Trans-Siberian through-service to Europe. In addition to the regular fare on this "train de luxe," seat tickets and sleeping berth fees must be added.

Principal points on the Peiping-Moukden Line are:

Miles from Peiping		Miles from Moukden
0	Peiping	523
84	Tientsin Central	439
87	Tientsin East	436
114	Tangku	409
168	Tangshan	455
241	Peitaiho	282
251	Chinwangtao	272
262	Shanhaikwan	261
396	Chinchoufu	127
416	Koupangtzŭ, change for Newchwang	107
486	Hsinminfu	37
522	Fengtien (Moukden) (S. M. R. Station)	1
523	Moukden (Fengtien) (C. G. S. Station)	0

HOPEI (CHIHLI) PROVINCE.

Hopei Province has an area of 115,830 square miles, and a population of 34,186,711. About half of the area lies outside the Great Wall and is now a part of the disputed territory known as Manchukuo. The greater part of the province is a dead level plain, the northern part of that great plain which stretches along the east coast of the country for 700 miles to the south through Honan to the Yangtsze. The plain is well watered, though the streams are unfit for navigation and the uncertain rainfall makes occasional famines inevitable. In the northeast are many rugged hills and mountains and one peak which reaches an elevation of nearly 10,000 feet. The climate is invigorating, the summers being intensely hot and the winters intensely cold. Indeed, there are few places where such extremes of temperature are met, the summer temperature often rising as high as at Hongkong, while in the winter zero weather is common. The principal cities are: Peiping, Tientsin, Tungchow, Chengtingfu, and Shanhaikwan.

GRAND CANAL.

Like the Great Wall of China, the Grand Canal remains as evidence of the advanced state of civilization in China twenty centuries ago. This great engineering work extends from Hangchow in Chekiang Province to Tientsin on the Gulf of Chihli, a distance of 650 miles. The section between the Yangtsze and the Yellow River was begun about 485 B.C., that is 24 years after the Republic of Rome was established and during the most glorious time of Athens. It was not until more than a thousand years later that the section south of the Yangtsze was built, while the work was completed on the Northern section in the thirteenth century. Kublai Khan is often credited with the construction of the Grand Canal, but parts of it were in use long before his time.

It is variously known by the the the Chinese as the Yuho (Imperial River), Yun-ho (Transport River), or Yun-liang-ho (Tribute-Bearing River). Until recent years a large amount of rice was sent through the Grand Canal from the Yangtsze Valley provinces to Peiping, but with the partial silting up of the canal, the coast steamship lines have usurped that function. With the completion of the Tientsin-Pukow Railway, Tientsin and Hangchow are now connected by rail and the usefulness of the Grand Canal is less than ever before.

PEITAIHO BEACH.

This summer resort, which is very popular with foreign residents of North China and draws many visitors from the Yangtsze Valley, is 150 miles north-east of Tientsin, 240 miles from Peiping and 282 miles from Moukden on the Peking-Moukden line. Hotels—Peitaiho, Strand, Oriental, open only during the season. Minimum rates $9 daily or about $210 monthly. The resort is on the sea coast, nine miles from the port of Chinwangtao. Peitaiho Beach is reached by a branch of the Peiping-

Moukden line from Peitaiho station, 13 miles. The branch operates only from May 1 to October 5 as Peitaiho Beach is purely a summer resort and during the winter is inhabited by only a few villagers. The climate is dry and bracing and is especially fine during the summer months when the temperature is about ten degrees lower than in Peiping. The excellent sea bathing which is enjoyed along the extensive beach during about six months of the year and the magnificent scenery add to the popularity of the place as a summer resort. The vicinity of Peitaiho abounds in delightful walks and game is plentiful in the neighborhood. The principal diversions are sea bathing, tennis and fishing. Some very fine sea bass have been caught.

This attractive settlement has been developed since 1895, when the first cottages were built. The fine, long stretch of sandy beach was known for some years before that date by neighboring missionaries, but it was not until the building of the Peiping-Moukden Railway that development was made possible. Quite a number of cottages were built only to be destroyed by the Boxers in 1900. Following the suppression of the Boxers, the Germans sent a detachment of soldiers to the resort and built a light railway from the main line to the beach.

With the withdrawal of the German troops, the light railway was removed and for many years the place was reached only by suffering the hardships of travel over unimproved roads. The settlement grew in spite of these difficulties of travel and transport, and in 1917 it finally was connected with the main line of the Peking-Moukden Railway. When foreigners first began to develop Peitaiho, they were not permitted to own land in their own names, but later the settlement was included within the area of the treaty port of Chinwangtao. This arrangement permits the purchase of land by foreigners and the registration of title deeds in foreign consulates.

The Peitaiho Beach railway station is located at that part of the resort known as Rocky Point, a few hundred yards from the beach and approximately in the center of a group of settlements. Cottages extend to the west of the mouth of Tai Ho, the small river from which the resort derives its name, and to the east an equal distance to the Lighthouse Promontory. All of this territory is connected by well-built macadam roads and donkey paths. The principal means of transportion are donkeys and ricshas.

Cottages at Peitaiho are in great demand and those who wish to obtain accommodations should communicate with agents in Tientsin early in the year. Rentals for the season range from Tls. 300 upward. Cottages usually are fully furnished except for linen and silver. Local shops supply all necessary provisions. Cooks, house-boys and amahs should be taken to Peitaiho, but coolies may be employed locally.

CHINWANGTAO.

Equally famous as a summer resort and as a port for the shipment of coal is Chinwangtao, a station on the Peiping-Moukden railway, and port on the Gulf of Pechili, the port and the railway station being connected by a short railway line operated by the Kailan Mining Administration. The port is connected with Shanghai by a regular steamer service.

Chinwangtao was opened to foreign trade in 1898, but owing to the Boxer troubles a customs house was not set up until three years later. A breakwater, constructed by the admirals of the allied fleet in 1901, was purchased by the Kailan Mining Administration. This is the only port of the Gulf of Pechili except Hulatao which is not ice-bound at any time of the year.

MOUKDEN (FENGTIEN).*

Moukden, formerly the capital of Manchuria, has a population (official) of 334,050 Chinese, 25,219 Koreans,

---

* Moukden, the name most frequently used by foreigners, is an adaptation of the old Manchu name. Fengtien is the Chinese name of the city although it is also known by the Chinese as Shenyang or or Liaoning and as Hoten by the Japanese.

23,330 Japanese and 1,990 foreigners. Moukden was nominally opened as a treaty port by treaty between China and the United States in 1903 but as the Russo-Japanese War broke out soon after that, it was not actually opened until three years later. Three railways meet here. It is on the main line of the South Manchuria Railway, which extends from Dalny and Port Arthur in the south and at Changchun in the north connects with the Chinese Eastern Railway and with the Trans-Siberian route. The branch of the South Manchuria Railway from Antung on the Korean border connects here with the main line. At Antung, it connects with the Korean railways and thence by means of the ferry from Fusan to Shimonoseki with the railways system of Japan. Moukden is also the terminus of the Peiping-Moukden line of the Chinese government railways and of the Moukden-Hailung-Kirin Railway (Feng-Hai). In addition there are two small branch lines, one of the South Manchuria Railway to the Fushun mines and of the Peiping-Moukden Railway to the Pei Ling (Northern Tombs). There are two railway stations, the Fengtien station of the South Manchuria line and the modern Moukden City station of the Peiping-Moukden line. Important trains of the latter line proceed to the Fengtien station, which is the more conveniently located of the two. The new Yamato Hotel, conducted by the South Manchuria Railway is about five minutes from the station by motor car. Other hotels are Oriental (Russian), Lengmueller (German) and Keining (German). An electric tram line connects the station with the city, distant about three miles, or Russian carriages may be secured. The usual fare is $1 an hour or $6 for an entire day. A motor bus line also operates between this station and both gates of the west suburb, fare 15 sen. Mule carts are useful in carrying baggage and ricshas may be had at the station or in any part of the city. The consulates, French, British, Japanese, Soviet and American, are situated outside the west wall of the city in or near the so-called "Foreign Settlement" which is not a foreign settlement and has always been administered by the Chinese authorities. On the South Manchuria railway only Japanese money is accepted, or Chinese money at a discount.

This ancient birthplace of the Manchu dynasty, which ruled China for so long, is the largest and most important city in Manchuria, and is of great historical interest and political importance. It was here that Nurhachu, the Manchu chieftain, established himself in 1625, after effecting a confederation of the tribes of the neighborhood and from here he conducted his successful campaign against China which resulted in the establishment of the Manchu dynasty. Before that time the capital of the Manchus had been at Hsingching, about 100 miles east of Moukden. When Peking surrendered in 1644, the government was transferred to that city, but Moukden has always retained an official importance greater than that of other provincial capitals.

On arrival at either of the Moukden stations nothing is seen of the old city as the nearest point is nearly three miles away to the east. The station is surrounded by the Japanese settlement, with many fine new buildings, among which the most conspicuous are the hospital and medical school belonging to the South Manchuria Railway. The southern of the two good roads leading to the city passes a large monument erected to the memory of the Japanese soldiers who fell in the battle of Moukden, which was fought from February 19 to March 14, 1905. Near the northern road is a monument to the Russian soldiers. Between the two roads are situated most of the consulates and other foreign buildings.

Entering the walled city of Moukden by either of these two western roads, one passes through a gateway, which has taken the place of the old gate through the outer wall. The other gates are closed at night, and a military guard is stationed at all gates. This outer wall is built of mud and is about 11 miles in circumference, but it is now broken down in many places so that pedestrians may cross.

A mile or more inside this rampart stands the inner city, a little more than a mile square and surrounded by a massive battlemented brick and stone wall, 40 feet high and 30 feet wide at the summit. Until recent years there was a high tower over each gate, but only one of these now stands. Interesting views of the city may be had from several points on the wall, but there is no walk around the top of it. The space between the inner and outer walls is called the suburbs and is the residential part of Moukden.

Broad main streets run through the city connecting the eight gates, their most noteworthy feature being the large artistic shop signs which extend high above the fronts of the shops and are ornamented with brilliantly colored peacocks, dragons, birds and other designs. Two towers are conspicuous, breaking the line of the more northern street from east to west, the Drum Tower and the Bell Tower. The former contains the old drum beaten to summon the guard to the defense of the city; the latter contains a large bell sounded slowly for curfew and more rapidly when there is a serious fire. The more easterly of the two, the Bell Tower (Chung Low or Joong Low) can be ascended and affords a good view. The street between these towers is the principal one in the city.

In the center of the city stands the old imperial palace of Nurhachu (Chin-lan-tien or Jin-lan-dyen), well worth a visit although the unique collection of old porcelain and Manchu antiquities for which the place was formerly famous has been removed to Peiping. The buildings which are just as when used by the Manchu conquerors, are from time to time used as barracks for soldiers and might be kept in better repair. The throne room and the summer pavilion with its high roofs and balconies are especially interesting. A pass to visit the palace must be obtained through one's consul. No charge is made but a tip is usually given to the custodian. One entire side of the street, immediately south of the palace is occupied by handsome government buildings, all erected since 1905, the central entrance being that of the governor's yamen.

Most of the prominent buildings inside the city belonged to the government, such as the law school, Bank of China, (near the west wall), a large girls' school near the east wall, etc.

At the southeast corner of the city wall is a curious old relic of nature worship, a temple to the fox. There is a deep hole or cave in which the animal or its spirit is supposed to dwell. Thirty years ago crowds went to this temple for healing, and there are many tablets erected by grateful patients, but of late years it has been neglected and has fallen into ruins. A short distance from this temple the Boxers had their headquarters where many Chinese Christians were killed.

Less than a mile east of the inner wall is a stretch of water called the Small River. In summer the river bank becomes the favorite pleasure resort of Moukden and is worth visiting in the afternoons to see the crowds in the booths, the pleasure boats moving slowly about, and the lotus blooms growing in profusion on the surface of the water. Farther north, near the outer wall, is an interesting Buddhist temple, the " Tien Hsi Miao." The Buddhist hells may be seen here at any time, and the huge images of Buddha and his satellites, also the covered walk by which he goes from one image to another. Worshippers frequent the temple only on the 1st and 15th of each moon, usually early in the day.

Outside the city, the most interesting sight is the tomb of Nurhachu's son, the Emperor Ta-tsung the second of the Manchu line, who was buried here in 1644. It is called the North Tomb (or Pei Ling). The tomb is on a wooded eminence four miles to the northwest of the city and may be reached by carriage or motor. The main approach to the tomb from the south is well worth walking along, though forbidden to vehicles. In front of the triple south gate which is kept closed is a fine archway of, fretted white marble. Visitors alight at the guard-house before the western gate of the enclosure. Inside the wall are beautiful avenues of old pines, curious stone animals, an artificial hill with fine glimpses of the surrounding country from its top, and a second wall with battlements and towers. The gates of this inner enclosure will be opened by the custodian who shows the party round and who should receive a tip. Entrance is not allowed to the innermost enclosure surrounding the tomb itself, a circular mound. In front of its gate is an interesting erection where sacrifices are offered to the spirit of the dead. Outside the outer wall lie extensive woods, in which, to the northwest, one may find a smaller tomb, that of the wife of the Emperor. The best time to visit this North Tomb is in May or June on a cloudless day, but it is beautiful in sunshine at any time, and an ideal spot for a picnic. The Manchu custodians who live in a little house at the gate are very obliging and will provide boiling water for tea.

About ten miles to the northeast of the city is the tomb of Nurhachu who was buried here in 1629, called the East Tomb (or Tung Ling). It is finer and has more extensive and more picturesque woods than the North Tomb, but is not so accessible and for that reason it is seldom visited.

Close to the outer wall of the city is a Christian Arts College, carried on unitedly by the three Protestant missions at work in Manchuria, the United Free Church of Scotland, the Irish Presbyterian Church, and the Danish Lutheran Church. There is also a Union Theological Hall. Near these and inside the wall are a Chinese Christian church and the buildings of the Irish Presbyterian Mission. Outside the brick wall in the south suburb stands the Roman Catholic Cathedral, a conspicuous building with graceful twin spires. All the buildings connected with the mission are gathered round it—schools, orphanage, priests seminary, convent, etc. This mission was established by French priests in 1832 and now numbers about 50,000 converts in Manchuria. Immediately outside the east gates is the largest Protestant Church in Manchuria, attended by from 500 to 700 Chinese Christians every Sunday. The congregation is governed and financed entirely by the

Chinese. It is a part of the Presbyterian church of Manchuria and was established by the United Presbyterian, now the United Free Church of Scotland, which began work in Manchuria in 1872. On the banks of the Small River are the premises of the United Free Mission (Scottish) which includes the largest hospital in North China (140 beds for men and boys) a woman's hospital (70 beds), Girls' Normal College and school, and a number of dwelling houses. Besides the hospital there is the Moukden Medical College, a large handsome collection of buildings opened in 1912. The three missions unite in this institution.

The country surrounding Moukden is very rich agriculturally and the city is next only to Yingkou in its importance as a centre for the manufacture of bean oil and bean cake. The annual production of oil is about 13 million pounds and of bean cake about 100 million pounds. A large part of the oil is used in Manchuria or shipped to China, while Japan takes practically all of the bean cake for use as fertilizer.

Thirty miles to the northeast of Moukden is the Fushun colliery, under Japanese ownership, connected with Moukden by a branch railway. Coins and household implements dug out of the mines indicate that they were worked as long ago as the 12th century, mostly by Korean immigrants who developed the mines in order to secure coal for their pottery works. With the rise of the Manchus to power the mines were closed by imperial edict as it was feared that their operation would have an adverse influence of *feng shui* on the imperial tombs which are near by. It was not until 1901 that permission was secured to work them. Two companies at that time began operations one purely Chinese and the other a Russo-Chinese company. The property came into the hands of Japanese at the time the Portsmouth treaty was signed at the close of the Russo-Japanese War. The coal field covers an area of about 25 square miles with one coal seam ranging from 75 to 400 feet in thickness. The total content is estimated at more than a billion tons, or a supply that cannot be exhausted in less than a century. These mines now have a daily output of about 10,000 tons, and as the South Manchuria Railway is connected directly with the mines, this large output easily finds its way into the avenues of commerce.

MANCHURIA (MANCHUKUO).

This division of China known to the Chinese as Kwantung, has an area of about 370,000 square miles and an estimated population of 20 millions. For more than 2,000 years the territory now known as Manchuria or Manchukuo was peopled by a number of Tartar tribes, known to the Chinese as barbarians, and parts of it were at various times under the control of China or Korea, and ruled separately. In the seventeenth century the Manchu tribe, previously of but small importance, began its rise to prominence. Their chief, Nurhachu, effected a combination of tribes and before his death was able to set up an independent and powerful government in Manchuria. His successors fulfilled the dream of their chief in 1644 when Nurhachu's grandsons began their rule over the whole of China. The population of Manchuria was then drawn upon heavily to supply Tartar garrisons in the principal cities of China, and the result was that whole sections of the country were entirely cleared of their inhabitants. Some of these sections have remained without population for more than two centuries and Manchuria is to-day a rich field for immigration from the crowded sections of both China and Japan. It is divided into three provinces: Shengking (or Fengtien), Kirin and Heilungkiang, with populations, respectively, of 13 million, 5 million and 2 million. Shengking has an area of 70,000 square miles, Kirin 110,000, and Heilungkiang 190,000. In Shengking the ranges of the Sungari mountains are covered with great forests of elm and pine, which are being rapidly thinned, the logs being floated in rafts down the Yalu to Antung. The plains of the province supply large quantities of soya beans for export. The Chinese population is largely made up of immigrants from Shantung. Colonists from China proper are also replacing the native Manchu population of Kirin province. The products are practically the same as in Shengking, large quantities of beans being grown for export, and, in addition, much wheat supplied to the mills at Harbin. Chinese have colonized an important part of Heilungkiang, but the greater part of the province remains peopled by pure Manchus, nomad Mongols, and the Tungusic tribes, who live by fishing and hunting.

In 1898 the Russians leased Port Arthur and the adjoining peninsula from China and proceeded to connect their leased territory with the Siberian Railway by the construction of the Chinese Eastern Railway, and to establish the ice-free port of Dalny (Dairen).

In 1900 the Boxer outbreak devastated the country. Every foreign building was burned, which in Moukden alone meant two hospitals, two Protestant churches, six mission houses, the Roman Catholic cathedral and other buildings. The Catholic bishop, two French priests, two French sisters and a large number of Chinese converts were killed. The Russian punitive expedition swept the country of Boxers and Chinese troops alike. In Moukden the Chinese soldiers fired the principal streets before fleeing. The Russians were from that time on the preponderant foreign influence in the government of Manchuria.

In the Russo-Japanese war of 1904-5, which came as a result of Russian aggression in Manchuria, thousands of Chinese noncombatants were killed and wounded and tens of thousands had their homes destroyed. After the close of the war the Japanese took the place of the Russians as the influential foreign power in South Manchuria, the Russian influence continuing in North Manchuria with Changchun as a meeting place. The whole country remained, however, a part of China, under Chinese government, the two foreign powers exercising sovereignty only on their respective railways, settlements and mines. In 1932 under Japanese leadership the independent government of Manchukuo was set up.

21

During 1910-11, Manchuria was visited by a remarkably deadly epidemic of pneumonic plague, 44,000 deaths taking place without a single recovery. The Chinese authorities in Moukden, with the help of British missionary doctors and others, worked hard and with gratifying success to prevent the spread of the infection. A young doctor, Arthur Jackson, died of plague and is buried about a mile outside Moukden on ground given by the Chinese government. In April, 1911, an international conference was held in Moukden to investigate the nature of the disease and to devise methods for the prevention of a future epidemic.

SHAN-HAI-KWAN.

Shan-hai-kwan, marking the boundary between China and Manchuria, is 260 miles from Peiping. The city, which is unimportant commercially, has always been a place of strategic importance as it is located at the eastern end of the Great Wall where that structure joins the sea. The line of the wall can be seen from here for many miles crossing valleys and climbing precipitous mountain sides, sometimes to a height of 1,000 feet. A visit to a celebrated Taoist temple on the top of one of the near-by hills is well worth the trouble, because of the magnificent view that is to be obtained at its elevation of 1,500 feet. The city is one of some historical interest, for it was from here that Wu Sen-Kwei, who was in command of the local garrison, appealed to the near-by Manchus to come to the aid of the Ming dynasty and regain Peking from the rebels. The Manchu troops occupied the city in May, 1644, and shortly thereafter made their victorious entry into Peking. In fact most of the history of the city has to do with the military affairs of China and Manchuria.

Shan-hai-kwan was a scene of great activity during the Boxer siege, for it was here that the foreign forces were landed for their march on Peking and the city was then occupied by foreign troops. The Station Hotel, which was built then, affords accommodation for travelers.

There is a fine beach which many foreigners visit during the summer.

HARBIN.

Harbin is an important railway center where passengers from Europe, Vladivostock, China or Japan change trains to continue their journey. Here the southern section of the Chinese Eastern Railway which connects with the South Manchuria at Changchun, forms a junction with the main line, the eastern continuation of the Siberian trunk line. Though there are four stations in Harbin, all trains converge at the commodious Central Station, where there are large waiting rooms and a restaurant. Harbin is 495 miles from Vladivostock, 874 miles from Peiping, and 5,100 miles from Leningrad. Hotels: Moderne, Grand, Metropole and Orient, all under Russian management. Runners of the principal hotels meet all trains and look after tickets and baggage.

Harbin is a comparatively new town, owing its existence to the construction of the Chinese Eastern Railway, and was not of much importance until the Russo-Japanese war, after which its growth became phenomenal. It now has a population of about 200,000, half Chinese and half Russian, thus having the largest European population of any city in Asia. The city is built on the leased ground of the Chinese Eastern Railway, a tract of 29,000 acres, and consists of three parts, Old Harbin, New Town and Wharf District. The station is located in New Town, Old Harbin being about two miles distant. The latter was formerly the business center of the place, during the construction of the railway, but with the establishment of the station, the interests of the city followed. Old town is the refuge of Russian emigrants who disagreed with the Soviet regime and here is one place where the color and life of old Russia may still be seen. The old section is now important only as the location of the barracks, residences of the railway officials, etc. With the rise of Soviet power in Russia, New Town has all of the appearance of a European city, with wide regular streets, which radiate from the cathedral. The hotels, railway agencies, post office, banks, etc., are all located in this section, near the station. The wharf section on the river northwest of the station is an important business center. Harbin is especially interesting as the meeting place of Russia and China where the life of each country can be observed and compared. The business hours are peculiar as most offices open at 8 o'clock and close at 3. The long afternoons and evenings are gay with dinners and parties and the night life rivals that of Shanghai.

The principal industry of Harbin is flour milling, the capital invested in the local mills amounting to more than five million dollars. All of the wheat comes from the farms of North Manchuria.

CHANGCHUN (HSIN KING).

Three railways converge at Changchun, it being the northern terminus of the South Manchuria Railway, the southern terminus of the Chinese Eastern Railway and the western terminus of the Changchun-Kirin line. Passengers traveling by any of these lines for a destination beyond Changchun must change cars here. With the establishment of the new State of Manchukuo the name of the place was changed to Hsin King and it is the capital of the new country, eclipsing Moukden in political importance. The Yamato Hotel is near the South Manchuria Railway station. Changchun, like Harbin, owes its importance to the railway and contains nothing of any historical interest. It is an important center for the bean trade and is also famous for its horse fair which is held daily in a suburb of the city outside the South Gate. The horses are of Mongolian breed, mostly fit only for draught purposes, but a few good riding horses are offered for sale. The city has a population of about 150,000. A few cabarets near the railway station are reminiscent of the dance halls of the Wild West.

The Changchun-Kirin Railway connects with Kirin, 80 miles distant. Kirin is an important trading town with a population of about 200,000, located on the navigable portion of the Sungari River.

DAIREN (DALNY).

This is the Southern terminus of the South Manchuria Railway, 246 miles south of Moukden, and the principal seaport of Manchuria. Yamato Hotel. Dairen is a Japanese leased territory and the only free port in the Orient. Japanese money is in circulation and notes issued by the Bank of Chosen are mostly used. Dairen and its vicinity are included in what the Japanese military authorities designate as "prohibited areas" and photographing and sketching are unlawful. The population is about 300,000, including 100,000 Japanese and 200,000 Chinese. All others number less than 500.

The territory now occupied by Dalny was included in the lease of Port Arthur obtained by Russia from China in 1898. Though a place of great natural advantages as a port, it had never been developed by the Chinese, and was then merely a collection of fishermen's huts. Russia immediately began an extended scheme of improvement and in six years accomplished wonders, laying out beautiful streets planted with trees and lined with fine residences. The city is built close to the shore at an elevation of a little more than fifty feet, giving an excellent drainage system. The principal streets radiate from circles where spacious public gardens are located.

In six years the Russians spent about 20 million roubles on Dalny and then it fell into the possession of the Japanese as one of the richest prizes of the Russo-Japanese war. The Russian plans have been carried out and amplified by the Japanese and Dalny is now one of the most rapidly growing and most modern cities in the Far East. A new breakwater and lighthouse have recently been completed and the city has replaced Newchwang in importance as a Manchurian port. It has a system of tramways, macadamized roads, electric lights, telephones, and an equipment of wharves and other public works of which any city might be proud. Steamers sail twice weekly for Shanghai, and there is also steamer connection with the principal ports of Japan, and several lines are now running direct from Dairen to ports on the Pacific Coast.

Hoshigaura (Star Beach) is about five miles from the city, connected by an electric tram line and good motor road. A cliff garden has been laid out and a hotel built there, with several bungalows in European and Japanese style, which are let to visitors. Ro-ko-san is a pretty spot near Dalny reached by a good motor road. It is on the seacoast where divers, for a small fee, will give exhibitions of their skill in the clear sea water. Port Arthur, made famous during the Russo-Japanese War, is connected with Dairen by motor road.

South Manchuria Railway.

The main line of the South Manchuria Railway through Manchuria from Changchun to Dairen, and its branch lines and all the rights, privileges, and properties, including coal mines formerly owned by the Chinese Eastern Railway, were acquired by the Japanese Government on September 5, 1905, by virtue of the treaty of peace between Japan and Russia. The operating company, the South Manchuria Railway Company, was established by Imperial Ordinance on June 7, 1906. The original authorized capital was 200,000,000 yen, since increased to 440,000,000 yen.

The length of the main line between Changchun and Dairen is 435 miles. There are daily express trains between Changchun and Dairen, and between Moukden and Fusan. On the branch lines, there are seven trains daily each way between Dairen and Port Arthur (Ryojun); seven trains daily each way between Tashihchiao and Yingkou (Newchwang); and six trains daily each way between Moukden and Fushun. No first class cars are attached to the trains on the last two lines. "Yamato" hotels are operated by the railway company at Dairen, Port Arthur, Moukden, Changchun and Hoshigaura.

Principal points along the line (express train stops) are:

Miles from Dairen		Miles from Changchun
0	Dairen	435
5	Chou-shui-tzu	430

Branch line to Port Arthur connects here with main line.

20	Chinchou	415

The walled town, population about 10,000, lies about one mile northwest of the station. Nanshan, a plateau beginning southwest of the station, was the scene of one of the most fiercely contested battles of the Russo-Japanese War.

28	Er-shih-li-tai	407
65	Wa-fang-tien	360
90	Wan-chia-ling	345
110	Hsiung-yo-cheng	325
148	Ta-shih-chiao	287

Branch line to Yingkou or Newchwang connects with main line.

168	Hai-cheng	276
206	Liaoyang	229

One of the oldest towns in Manchuria, its history going back to 1400 B.C. Formerly a place of some commercial importance, but of recent years its trade has dwindled. Contains several interesting old temples. Population 40,000.

236	Su-chia-tun	199

Branch line to the Fushun colliery.

Miles from Dairen		Miles from Changchun
246	Moukden or Fengtien	188
290	Tiehling	145
	The most important city between Moukden and Changchun and a great center for the bean trade.	
311	Kai-yuan	124
324	Ma-chung-ho	111
	A prolongation of the Great Wall may be seen here.	
330	Chang-tu	105
	The town, population 14,000, is five miles northwest of the station.	
364	Szu Ping Chieh	171
	This unimportant town is noted as the meeting place of the Japanese and Russian commissioners after the war.	
397	Kung-chu-ling	38
435	Changchun	0

PORT ARTHUR.

This world-famous place is 39 miles from Dairen with which it is connected by railway and steamship lines and the best motor road in Asia completed in 1924 at a cost of Y.1,350,000. The road traverses a beautiful country with fine landscapes and occasional glimpses of the sea. Hotel, Yamato. The place is known as Ryojon by Japanese and as Lushun by Chinese. As this is a Japanese fortified area sketching and photographing are prohibited.

Port Arthur, once the pride of the system of coast defenses which China was developing, was taken by the Japanese in 1894, a victory which assured the success of Japan in the war with China. Russia, Germany and France, acting as friends of China, prevented Japan from taking possession of the place, but four years later brought pressure to bear which forced China to lease the position to Russia. Under the Russians the original fortifications were improved upon until it became known as the "Gibraltar of the Far East."

In the Russo-Japanese war, Admiral Togo attacked the place, February 8, 1904, blockading the harbor. The presence of mines in the channel made it impracticable to continue the sea attack, but the blockade was maintained. The land forces began a siege of the place in May, the siege being marked by many battles until the surrender of the position on January 1, 1905. The Japanese, in the surrender, took as prisoners 878 officers and 23,491 men. The booty included 59 permanent forts, four battleships and more than fifty smaller ships.

The principal points of interest in Port Arthur are, of course, connected with the great battle which brought it into fame. Good carriage roads lead to the vicinity of nearly all the forts and the Chinese drivers know the names and locations of all of them. The principal batteries are on Tiger's Tail Promontory and Golden Hill. The Japanese are very jealous of this stronghold and visitors who carry cameras should be careful not to arouse the suspicions of the authorities, who are always ready to suspect espionage.

The first object of interest is Monument Hill which is directly back of the station. This is a mole, something over 400 feet high, which divides the old town from the new. On this hill is the national mausoleum containing the remains of 22,000 soldiers who died in the siege of Port Arthur. A monument 218 feet high is erected on the summit in honor of their memory. A stairway leads to a platform at the top of the monument, where an excellent view of the bay may be obtained.

From Monument Hill a visit can be made to Memorial Museum. This is most interesting as it contains an excellent collection of various kinds of war material, military stores, ammunition and uniforms. The approach is lined by models of trenches, wire entanglements, etc., the whole making a very interesting and impressive exhibit of the machinery of war. The museum is open from 8 a.m. to 5 p.m., Mondays excepted.

It will be found worth while to continue on from the Museum to the main line of fortifications which includes East Cockscomb Hill (Tungchi-kuan-shan or Higashi-eikwan-zan), Eagle's Nest Hill (Bo-dai), Two Dragon Hill (Er-lung-shan or Niryu-zan). At each one of these old forts the shattered trenches and battered fortifications give mute, grim evidence of the terrific struggle for their capture and of their brave defense.

Lunch may be had at the Yamato Hotel in the city, and in the afternoon a trip should be made to 203 Meter Hill. There will be ample time to climb to the summit of this historical mound and return in time to board the 4 o'clock train for Dairen. Not until one has visited this rocky stronghold will he realize the stupendous task which confronted the Japanese attackers. It is one of the highest hills surrounding the city and was considered a strategic point of great importance. The Japanese attack on the hill began on November 27 and ended on December 6, 1904, when the stronghold fell after nine days and nights of desperate struggle. With the possession of the eminence, the Japanese had a great advantage and in less than one month the fortress fell. The effort made to reach this point will be amply repaid by the view of the magnificent panorama. A pair of field glasses will add greatly to the pleasure of this excursion.

NEWCHWANG (YINGKOU).

For more than forty years Newchwang was the only treaty port in Manchuria, and it was formerly of great commercial importance. The name of the place now known as Newchwang to foreigners is really Yingkou, the real Newchwang being 30 miles up the river. When the place was opened for foreign residence, the foreigners found Yingkou to be more suitable than Newchwang and arbitrarily settled there, changing the name of the place to suit the requirements of the treaty. The country is flat and uninteresting and the town has nothing of interest to offer the visitor.

MOUKDEN TO ANTUNG (AMPO LINE).

During the Russo-Japanese war the Japanese built a narrow-gauge line of railway from Moukden to Antung, a distance of 189 miles, for military uses. This was later turned over to the South Manchuria Railway Co., and made a standard-gauge railway on which there is now an express-train service traversing the distance in 6 hrs. 40 m. The railway passes through some very interesting scenery and presents numerous examples of engineering skill. On the line are 24 tunnels and 212 bridges. At Antung connection is made with the Korean (Chosen) railways and through them, by way of Fusan, with the railway system of Japan.

There are no towns along the line of any importance, and Antung does not merit a visit except as the gateway to Korea.

CHEFOO.

The principal port of call for Shanghai-Tientsin steamers is Chefoo, two days' journey from Shanghai, located on the west of Chefoo Bay. The steamer track distance between Shanghai and Chefoo is 498 or 514 nautical miles, depending on whether the North or South channel is used. The air line distance is 390 miles. Hotels: Broadway, Astor House, Beach, Imperial, Sea View. Consulates: Great Britain, Belgium, France, Japan, Sweden, United States and Soviet Russia. Opened to foreign trade in March, 1863. The Chinese population is about 150,000. There are about 1,100 foreign residents and many others spend the summer here. It is the summer station for the entire United States Asiatic fleet which is stationed during the winter in the Philippines. The presence during the summer months of the officers and men of the fleet adds a great deal to the life and prosperity of the port. The dry salubrious climate and the beautiful shore makes Chefoo popular as a summer residence for foreigners, though it has few places of interest. The trade amounts to about 40 million taels annually. The real name of the place is Yentai, but foreigners have arbitrarily given it the name of Chefoo, which properly belongs to a large village on the opposite side of the bay. The principal exports are eggs, bean cake, silk, peanuts, lace, fruit, salt fish and straw braid. It is an important distributing point for kerosene.

Chefoo is a well-known center for silk and lace manufacture, and both articles can be purchased here at lower prices than elsewhere. Near Chefoo grow the dwarf oaks from the leaves of which pongee, or "Shantung," silk is produced. The best known gold mine in China is at Chouyuoen, about 40 miles southwest of Chefoo, and has produced several million dollars' worth of the metal.

A daily motor bus service over a good road connects Chefoo with Weihsien, an important station distant 187 miles on the Tsingtao-Tsinanfu Railway. There are a number of other roads into the interior. Among them being a road to Muping, 20 miles long.

Missions: China Inland, Church of England, American Presbyterian, American Baptist, Roman Catholic. The large school of the China Inland Mission for the children of missionaries is a conspicuous object on the beach to the east of the town. It is attended by about 350 children from all parts of China.

WEIHAIWEI.

The former British leased territory of Weihaiwei is on the south side of the Gulf of Pechili, near the extremity of the Shantung promontory, about 115 miles from Port Arthur and an equal distance from Tsingtau, two days by steamer from Shanghai. Weihaiwei, formerly a Chinese naval station, was captured by the Japanese in 1895 and held by them pending payment of the indemnity agreed upon at the close of the war. The battle of Weihaiwei, one of the principal encounters in the war between China and Japan, was distinguished by the gallant conduct of Admiral Ting, commander of the Chinese squadron. He had retreated here after a defeat on the Yalu, but despite the battered condition of his vessels prepared to resist the Japanese attack which began on January 30th. The modern forts of the Chinese fell in quick succession. However, despite the continued success of the Japanese, Admiral Ting held out bravely until February 12th, when he sent up the white flag of surrender and then committed suicide, several of his officers following his example. Japan remained in possession of the place three years. Great Britain then aided China in securing funds for the payment of the indemnity, and in return was given the lease of Weihaiwei. The lease provided for the occupation of the place by Great Britain " for so long a period as Port Arthur shall remain in the occupation of Russia." The territory was surrendered to China in 1930 as the result of negotiations between China and Great Britain.

The territory is covered by mountains, the highest range being Mount MacDonald (1,589 feet) whose summit is crowned with the remains of old temples and altars, erected at a time when this was one of the sacred mountains of China. From the summit the whole of the city and bay may be seen. Other high points include Mount Lansdowne (1,367 feet), Mount Goschen (1,343 feet) and Temple Peak (1,240 feet). "The formation of the rocks can only be described as extraordinary, conformity being conspicuous by its absence. For absolute confusion of rocks the tourist is recommended to explore the coast to the east of Water Witch Bay. An interesting example of brecciated structure may be seen near Three Peaks Point, in a cliff some 150 feet in height. A magnificent monolith of white quartz twelve feet high adorns the crest

of Mount MacDonald. Gold has been found both in
alluvial deposits and in reefs and has been worked by the
Chinese."

The leased territory included the island of Liukung,
all the islands in the bay and a belt of land for ten miles
along the coast, the whole territory amounting to 285
square miles. It included more than 300 villages, with a
total estimated population of 150,000. Since the British
occupation the place has been greatly improved, many
roads having been built and a large hotel erected. With
Tsingtau, Chefoo and other northern coast points, it shares
in the summer-resort patronage from the more southern
places. The climate is fine the whole year and sea bathing is possible from May to October. One of the summer
diversions which is growing in popularity is fishing for
sea bass; specimens of more than 15 lbs. have been caught.

The bay offers excellent anchorage, the harbor being
guarded by the island of Liukung, two miles long. Weihaiwei is a port of call for coast steamers, having direct
connection with Shanghai, Chefoo, Tsingtau and Tientsin.

TSINGTAU.

Three hundred miles north of Shanghai (430 miles by
steamer track), at the entrance to Kiaochow Bay is the
city and port of Tsingtau, a favorite summer resort and
important commercial city. It is the eastern terminus of
the Shantung Railway which connects with the Tientsin-
Pukow Railway at Tsinan. There are both day and night
trains between the two cities. There is frequent boat
service to ports in Japan as well as to Shanghai and other
ports on the China Coast, while several European lines
make Tsingtau a port of call. Population, about 168,000
including 14,500 Japanese and 700 Europeans. Hotels:
Grand, Strand, while numerous pensions provide satisfactory accommodations.

Tsingtau was formerly a small and unimportant
fishing village before it came within the range of German
ambitions. Germany desired a suitable military and naval

base in Far Eastern waters and discovering that Tsingtau met this need, steps were taken as early as 1895 to negotiate with China for a lease of the territory. An attack on three German priests at Yenchowfu in 1897 led to a section of the German Asiatic fleet being despatched to Tsingtau. The forces were landed without opposition and the port fell into German hands on November 14, 1897. The following year the territory was leased to Germany for a period of 99 years.

On August 16, 1914, at the outbreak of the Great War, Japan demanded that Germany surrender the leased zone and on Germany's refusal to comply with the demand, the place was attacked by Japanese forces. It was surrendered to Japan on November 7, 1914, and held by them until December, 1922, when it was returned to China under agreements reached at the Washington Conference.

The town has been built since the German occupation and credit for its development is shared principally by Germans and Japanese but the Chinese administrations have in many ways continued the good work started by their foreign predecessors. It is well laid out, has many handsome foreign residences and the streets are well lighted. In the period the place was held by Germany and Japan many factories were erected and the railway built to Tsinanfu and it is now one of the leading industrial centers of China, in addition to which it is also the second port of China from the point of view of tonnage. The area of the leased territory was 193 square miles, in addition to which a sphere of influence 30 miles from all points of the leased territory was recognized. This brought the total area up to about 2,750 square miles.

Kweichow Bay is nineteen miles long by fifteen miles wide and is almost surrounded by mountains, affords good shelter and has been greatly improved. The entrance is half a mile across, marked by a lighthouse. A long pier and a large dock are among the many improvements which the Germans added to the harbor and these have since been considerably augmented. Among the notable conservation schemes carried out is the planting of trees on the barren hillsides. Many good motor roads have been built, connecting with villages in the interior.

It was while under the administration of Japan that the port saw its greatest commercial development. As the gateway to one of China's greatest provinces it is a commercial center of constantly increasing importance. The local industries include cotton spinning mills, a cigarette factory, refrigerating plants, silk filature, peanut oil mills, brewery, tanneries and match factories. It is said to be the largest peanut shipping port in the world. Other important items of export are tobacco, beef and coal.

The places of interest in Tsingtau are the great harbor, enclosed by breakwaters, free from ice and open the year round; Chungshan Road, the most popular business street, running through the heart of the city, lined on both sides by rows of shops, and presenting a scene of active life day and night, the Tien-hou Temple, dedicated to the Goddess of the Sea, the oldest and the most interesting historically of any structure in the city, the bathing beach, shelved very gradually and free from stones and rocks; the First Park, covering an extensive area at the foot of Iltis Hill, and containing a recreation ground, golf links, several nurseries for trees and flowers and attractive avenues lined with cherry trees; the forts, relics of the world war and the aquarium.

Various interesting excursions may be taken from Tsingtau, the principal one being to the Laoshan Mountains and Telakuan. Of the shorter journeys the most popular ones are to the Iltis Mountain, the lighthouse, Prinz Heinrich Mountain, Syfeng, "Jagdschlosschen" (Hunters' Inn), Tsangkou, Litsun, Schatskou at the foot of the beautiful Laoshan, and the Bay of Schatskou. Short sea trips may be taken to various islands, Cape Jaeschke, Pearl Mountains (Sleeping Temples) and the romantic mountains and monasteries of Tai-tsching-kung and Hua-ye-nan.

The Laoshan Mountains with their wooded tops, waterfalls and delightful scenery form one of the most attractive regions along the China coast. The mountains may be reached in about one hour by motor car from Tsingtau. Two of the most popular excursions in the mountains are through Rocky Valley to the Laoting, 3,600 feet elevation; and to the temple Wei-erl-pu, 1,800 feet elevation.

The region known as Iltis Huk, beyond the Strand Bathing Beach, has now developed into an important and popular resort for foreigners with more than a hundred foreign residences and three miles of beautiful sandy bathing beaches. One of the beauty spots of Tsingtau is the picturesque little harbor known as " the old harbor " or " fisherman's cove "; it would excite a thrill from any artist.

Excellent sea fishing is to be had all the year round and fishing boats completely equipped with tackle and bait can be hired for the day at $5 to $25, according to the distance to be covered, motors being fitted to the boats which are engaged for the longer distances. The bathing beaches are the best in the Orient and are quite safe at all times. The average summer temperature is 70 to 75 degrees, the high range rarely reaching 90 degrees.

TIENTSIN-PUKOW RAILWAY.

The Tientsin-Pukow Railway line was opened for traffic in 1912, and affords the quickest service between North China and the eastern part of the Yangtsze Valley. The trip from Pukow to Tientsin, a distance of 631 miles, occupies about twenty-seven hours, making it possible to go from Shanghai to Peiping in thirty-six hours. At Tientsin the road connects with the government railways of North China, and at Pukow it connects by ferry with the Nanking terminus of the Nanking-Shanghai Railway.

The negotiations for the construction of this line resulted in dividing the work between Germany and Great Britain. The northern portion, from Tientsin to the

22

Grand Canal, was built by German capital and engineers, while the southern portion, from the Grand Canal to Pukow, was built by British capital and engineers. Both sections are under purely Chinese control. Passengers will notice a striking contrast between the German and British portions of the line. On the former all the stations have been equipped with pretentious buildings of brick, stone and tile, each one being of a different style of architecture, but all containing Chinese ideas as interpreted by the German architects. In the British section the stations are severely plain. Construction on the British section cost £10,600 per mile and on the German section about £14,000 per mile. The greater part of the road runs through level plains with a few miles of mountainous country in Shantung. Between Tientsin and the Yellow River the country is very flat, and the soil contains a large proportion of loess.

Important points on the line are:

Miles from Tientsin		Miles from Pukow
0	Tientsin	631
78	Tsangchow	553
148	Techow	483
220	Tsinanfu	411
	Connection is made here with the Shantung Railway for Tsingtau. A few miles north of Tsinanfu the Yellow River is crossed.	
265	Taianfu	366
308	Chufou	323
318	Yenchowfu	313
377	Lincheng	254
392	Hanchuang. The railway crosses the Grand Canal near this station. To the west is a lake which serves as a storehouse for the overflow of water from the canal.	239

Miles from Tientsin		Miles from Pukow
420	Hsuchowfu. At this point the ırunk line from Kaifengfu to the coast joins the Tientsin-Pukow line. The station stands on the old bed of the Yellow River.	271
523	Pengpu	108
631	Pukow. A ferry across the Yangtsze connects with Nanking.	0

TIENTSIN.

Located at the junction of the Haiho and Peiho rivers and the Grand Canal, about 80 miles from Peiping and 35 miles by river from the coast. Northern terminus of the Tientsin-Pukow Railway, about 630 miles. There are three railway stations, Tientsin Central, Tientsin West and Tientsin East. Travelers who stop at Tientsin should leave the train at the East Station as it is the nearest to the hotels. Passengers to and from Peiping change cars at Tientsin Central. Tram-cars, ricshas, and motor cars take one to any part of the city. Population, about 1,500,000 which includes about 10,000 foreigners. Hotels: Imperial, Astor House, Court.

As the river port for the old capital and the entrepôt for the northern provinces, Tientsin has for centuries played a most important part in the commerce of China. It has been equally important from a military standpoint, for it is the key to the capital and has figured prominently in all of the many attacks on Peking. Since 1910 it has been the capital of the province of Chihli (now known as Hopei). Because of the windings of the river, Tientsin was formerly 56 miles, by water, from the sea. Through an elaborate conservancy scheme, this distance has been reduced to 35 miles and the city is now an ice-free port owing to the introduction of modern ice breakers. The Chinese population is made up almost entirely of traders, merchants, and persons connected with the various large manufacturing plants. Of late years the city has become an educational center. Li Hung Chang made this his residence from 1871 to 1898 and, under the favor of Peiping, ruled over Tientsin and the surrounding country like a feudal lord. Under his leadership, Tientsin became known as a center of reform. It was here that he tried his experiments in education and army reforms—policies which were later ably carried out by the famous old viceroy's *protégé*, Yuan Shih K'ai.

Formerly there were eight foreign concessions in Tientsin—those of Great Britain (three areas), France, Japan, Italy, Belgium, Russia, Germany, and Austria, each under its own consular jurisdiction. The last two, however, were taken over in 1917 when China declared war, and since have been administered by the Chinese police. In 1920 the local Chinese authorities, acting under a presidential mandate, assumed charge of the Russian consular functions and the policing of the Russian concession, leaving the municipal council to continue to function in minor municipal affairs and the undeveloped Belgian concession was voluntarily returned in 1930.

The oldest foreign concessions in Tientsin are the British and French, which were established in 1860. The plans for the settlement were drawn by General "Chinese" Gordon, whose name has been given to the principal administration hall. The Japanese, after the war of 1895, received a concession and since 1900 the other concessions were granted and additions made to older concessions.

Amalgamation of the three British concessions—known as the British Concession, British Extension, and Extramural Extension—took place in February, 1918. New land regulations came into force, and one council consisting of British and Chinese members now operates in the three areas. The Crown leases of the old concession expire in 1960, while those of the extensions have leases for 999 years.

Walls were built around Tientsin in 1403, and remained until 1901, the year following the Boxer outbreak

when they were pulled down by order of the foreign
provisional government. The ground they occupied was
utilized for the building of a fine thoroughfare, while the
material contained in the walls was used for railway
ballast. During the Boxer outbreak, the Chinese government sent troops against the foreign concessions of Tientsin, which were besieged for 27 days until the city was
taken by the Allied troops. The city was governed by an
international commission from 1900 to 1902, and during
this time many important public works were completed.

The railway to Peiping was built in 1897 and proved
such a financial success that the track was doubled the
following year. The building of this railway, the tearing
down of the city walls, and the good example set by the
fine foreign concessions have led to great improvements in
the Chinese City. Broad streets have been laid out and
kept in a good state of repair, and a tramway system built
reaching to almost every part of the town. Many of the
old temples have been turned into modern schools, devoted
to Western learning.

The largest and most imposing temple in the city was
built as a memorial to Li Hung Chang. It is surrounded
by extensive grounds laid out in the miniature landscape
effect of which the Chinese are so fond. It is located to
the north of the Viceroy's yamen. An excellent view of
the city may be obtained from the Drum Tower in the
center of the Chinese City.

An interesting history attaches to the immense bronze
bell in the Hai Kuang Sze Temple, which for twenty years
was a conspicuous feature of Victoria Gardens. The bell
was removed from the public park to make room for
the War Memorial which was unveiled on the anniversary
of Armistice Day, 1921. An inscription in English and
Chinese tells the story of the bell and records the fact
that the seven artisans who engraved the Buddhist *sutras*
on the bell all died within 100 days after they had
completed the engravings.

Aside from the few places of interest mentioned above,

Tientsin holds little attraction for the Occidental sightseer, and comparatively few tourists stop in Tientsin on the journey between Shanghai and Peiping. Its foreign settlements are modern with well-paved streets, handsome buildings and efficient administrations, but in these features there is nothing that cannot be seen elsewhere. The business man and student of industrial development, however, will find much of interest.

Next to Shanghai, Tientsin is the most important industrial center of China. Flour milling is the leading industry, as might be expected, since Tientsin is favorably situated to draw on the vast grain supplies of the northern plains and the provinces to the west. There are twelve large flour mills; the cotton mill industry comes second, with mills employing many thousand operatives. Because of its proximity to the great grazing districts of North China, Tientsin is the chief wool-exporting center of China also the principal fur exporting center.

On the way to Tientsin from the coast, Taku will be passed at the mouth of the Haiho, on the southern bank of the river. It is memorable as being the former location of the Taku forts, four times the point of attack by foreign forces. Under the protocol following the Boxer troubles, the forts were demolished, China agreeing not to fortify or to maintain troops on the route between the capital and the sea. A large number of foreign troops are usually quartered in Tientsin. The city formerly enjoyed some prominence and prosperity through the fact that it was the shipping point for the tribute rice coming to Peiping from the southern provinces. This was shipped to Tientsin as the northern terminus of the Grand Canal and thence transported to the capital, but with the development of railways and steamship lines the Grand Canal is no longer used save for local traffic.

TSINANFU.

This city is the capital and commercial center of Shantung Province, lying in the center of a rich territory.

To the north and south runs the Tientsin-Pukow Railway; in the east it is connected with Tsingtau and the peninsular region of Shantung by the Shantung Railway, built by the Germans and recently returned to the Chinese by the Japanese who had held it since the capture of Tsingtau in the first months of the World War. From the west the junks of the Yellow River bring agricultural products and return up the river with the manufactured products turned out in Tsinanfu and imported goods distributed here. The city has a population of about 400,000 and does a trade of approximately $40,000,000 annually. It is 260 miles west of Tsingtau and an equal distance south of Tientsin. Foreign hotels: Hotel Stein, Chao Tai Railway Hotel, Tientsin-Pukow Railway Hotel. Runners meet the trains.

The city owes its location to the natural springs, for which it is famous throughout a great part of China. The flow of the springs has never ceased or diminished and has made the region around Tsinan free from the devastations of drouth which have been visited on other parts of North China. On a part of the plain watered by the overflow from the springs the only rice cultivated in North China is grown. According to local history a city was established on the present site of Tsinanfu during the lifetime of the great Yu, or about 4,000 years ago. At any rate a city bearing the name Tsinanfu was located 25 miles to the east of the present city. About A.D. 300 for some unknown reason this city was moved bodily to the present site of Tsinanfu, the name being transferred as well. According to the legend lines of men were formed shoulder to shoulder between the two cities and the bricks forming the wall were passed from hand to hand, all being moved in one night. There was so much breakage that although the walls before being moved were 20 li in circumference, the bricks served to build only 12 li here.

As evidence of the great antiquity of the place and of the associations it had with famous characters of ancient history, residents point out inside the south gate of the city a well said to have been dug by Emperor Shun. The well is still in daily use. The present city walls were built in 1371. The stone suburban wall, outside the city wall proper, is of recent construction, having been erected as a means of protection against the Taiping rebels.

The Yellow River, five miles to the north, runs in flood time high above the level of the city, which is protected by thick embankments. The city is on the edge of the great plain which extends from Tsinanfu to Peiping broken only by a few small hills, while to the south it is on the edge of the Taishan *massif*. The city is built at the foot of a range of these limestone hills and receives an excellent supply of water from the famous " 72 springs " which are doubtless fed from the hills. The north wall runs through a spring-fed lake and within the city walls a large area, about one-fourth of the total, is unfit for building purposes because under water. This lake " is divided into lots which belong to various owners, who raise thereon reeds, lotus roots, and beautiful water lillies, besides frogs—a table delicacy here—and fish. Separating the lots are lanes of clear water, lined during the summer season on both sides with tall reeds, through which run boats that are in great demand during the hot weather, carrying pleasure-seekers to the various tea-houses and temples located in various parts of the lake. In addition to the " 72 springs " which are conspicuous in all parts of the city there are many other smaller springs. The water flows through the city in open channels and most of it finds its way into the Hsiao Hsing Ho, a canalized stream which in the past carried most of the commerce of the city.

Among the points of interest in Tsinanfu may be mentioned the Confucian (or Public) Library, with its picturesque gardens located on the edge of the lake and accessible from the mainland. Some of the notable inscriptions found in Shantung province have been preserved here. A short distance from the library is the Provincial Assembly Hall.

Shoppers will find the most attractive articles on the wide and well paved main street which runs from east to west. To foreigners the most interesting articles are imitations of precious stones, manufactured locally.

Up to the time of the Boxer trouble Tsinanfu was one of the most conservative cities in China, having little to do with foreigners or foreign institutions. Since that time, however, it has become very progressive and is now the location of many government schools, hospitals, etc., conducted on western lines. It has also become a center for missionary work. In the south suburb is located the very interesting museum known as the Tsinan Institute, a department of Shantung Christian University. This museum has attracted so much attention among the Chinese that the average daily attendance is about one thousand. Adjoining the site of the institute is the Union Medical College of the Shantung Christian University. Its fine building was erected in 1910. Just outside the suburban wall are the other buildings of the university. Here have been erected buildings to the value of about $1,000,000. The university is a union work of the several missions of Shantung and North China. The hospitals and other enterprises of the American Presbyterian Mission are located in the east suburb.

Tsinanfu was voluntarily opened for foreign settlement by the Chinese government in 1906, being the first city in China in which such action was taken. Many foreign firms and several foreign hotels are now located here as well as a fine foreign settlement covering a little more than one square mile. Since the opening of the Tientsin-Pukow railway the settlement has been growing rapidly until the wide well-kept streets and foreign style buildings give it quite a western appearance.

The beautiful "Hill of the Thousand Buddhas" is near the city and may be easily reached from the south gate by chair or ricsha. "The view from the temple on this hill over the city lying at its feet, out over the plain and across the Yellow River, four miles from the city to the north, is very extensive, and when the fields are covered with growing crops, a very beautiful one, but it is surpassed in the extent and variety of the scenery by that from Pagoda Hill, from the top of which can be seen not only the plain to the north with the Yellow River winding through it, but also the rugged mountainous country extending as far as the eye can reach to the south. From the top of this Pagoda Hill may be seen, on clear days, the form of Taishan, the sacred mountain of Shantung, lying fifty miles to the south and surrounded on all sides by billowy hills. There is a legend which represents Tsinan as being fastened to the pagoda on the summit of Pagoda Mountain by an invisible rope, which if ever severed through any evil influence will allow the city to float out into the swamp lying north of the town."

The Temple of the Dragon's Cave, eight miles from the city, is one of the most picturesque in China. The temple lies at the bottom of a deep gorge and there are several caves in the surrounding limestone cliffs.

SHANTUNG PROVINCE.

The area of Shantung is 55,984 square miles, and it has a population of 30,803,245. The hilly and mountainous portions of the south and east occupy almost half the area of the province, the remainder being a plain. The mountains of the eastern portion follow the shore line closely, rising sheer from the sea and making landing difficult. Only towards the extremity of the promontory are there any natural harbors. There are now no forests in the province, though near the home of Confucius at Chufu the noble groves indicate the former beauty of the country. There are many fine orchard tracts including pears, apples, apricots, peaches, nectarines, plums, cherries, walnuts and persimmons and some important vineyards. In the hills are the wild mulberry and oak plantations from which pongee silk is made. The soil of Shantung has been tilled continuously for many centuries and is consequently greatly impoverished, but continues to produce a minimum of three crops every two years. Wheat, millet, maize, sorghum, sweet potatoes, peanuts, hemp, indigo, tobacco and a variety of bean and pea crops are regularly grown. Because the Shantung farmer raises so many crops such as tobacco and peanuts which are sold for cash he has more money to spend and is generally looked on as being more prosperous than the farmers of other provinces. The Shantung men are very much larger than the southern Chinese, being of about the same average stature as Europeans. Men six feet tall are not infrequently seen. They are "stalwart, well-built men, steadfast, blunt, outspoken, persevering, not so easily roused as the men of the southern provinces, nor so easily pacified, but yet sharing other common characteristics of the race." Most of the watchmen and policemen employed in Shanghai are Shantung men.

A large part of the present province of Shantung was once the feudal state of Lu, which was granted by the founder of the Chow dynasty to his brother Tan, "who there carved out for himself a realm and reigned, loved by his subjects and revered in all later ages, as the sainted patriarch Chou Kung, a sort of Alfred among the lords of old." Of all the feudal States abolished by Emperor Shih Hwang-ti, that of Lu was probably the most persistent in its attempts to regain independence. There were princes of Lu under the Han dynasty and as late as the Mings— sixteen centuries after the consolidation of the Empire of China—attempts were made to re-establish the State.

YELLOW RIVER (HWANG HU).

Five miles north of Tsinanfu the Yellow River is crossed by the Tientsin-Pukow Railway on the famous Yellow River bridge, the most important bridge in China and one of the longest in the world, its length being 4,180 feet. Work on this structure was begun in 1906 and extended over a period of more than three years, the total cost being about $5,000,000. Owing to the swiftness of the current, the shifting habits of the stream and the lack of solid foundations, the construction of the bridge was beset with a great many difficulties, but is now believed to be proof against any changes of the very treacherous river. The foundations are sunk about 60 feet below the low water level, the bridge being built on reinforced concrete piles of that length. So many piles have been driven that it is believed the bridge would be secure even if the earth should be washed away from the concrete foundations of the piers.

This great stream, about 2,500 miles in length, drains an area of 475,000 square miles. Scarcely a decade in the last century has passed without some devastating outbreak of this river. Enormous sums of money have been spent in the construction of powerful dykes and the natural sand banks of the stream have in places been faced by stone embankments. In 1848 the embankment broke at Laoyang Hsien; in 1868 at a point near Chengchow; in 1869 another break occurred at the same place and a large area was flooded. When the water receded it was found that the land had been covered by sand and rendered unfit for cultivation.

Between the noted bridge and the sea, there was completed in the spring of 1923 an important conservancy work on a contract calling for a payment of $1,500,000. This consisted in cutting a new 6,000-foot channel across a bend in the river and building a dam just below the intake. The river was successfully turned into its new channel. The completion of this work was expected to mark the beginning of a new phase in the age-long and hitherto losing battle of the Chinese people with this great river which, because of its frequent floods and change of course, and consequent loss of life and property, has justly earned the name of " China's Sorrow."

The river has been following this course only since 1852. During 146 years, from 1048 to 1194, the river poured its waters into the sea at Tientsin through the mouth of the Peiho. Then the course was changed and it emptied into the Yellow Sea 400 miles to the southward until 1852 when the present course was adopted in a time of flood. It is unique among the great rivers of the world in that it is of practically no value for navigation owing to its shifting currents.

" What must be said of the mental status of a people who for forty centuries have measured their strength against such a Titan racing past their homes above the level of their fields, confined only between walls of their own construction? While they have not always succeeded in controlling the river, they have never failed to try again. In 1877 this river broke its banks, inundating a vast area, bringing death to a million people. Again as late as 1898, 1,500 villages to the northeast of Tsinanfu and a much larger area to the southwest of the same city were devastated by it." *

TAI SHAN.

The great sacred mountain of Tai Shan (elevation 5,068 feet) is north of the city of Taianfu, a station on the Tientsin-Pukow railway and in plain view to the east of the railway. Taianfu is 45 miles south of Tsinanfu. This is one of the principal points of religious pilgrimages in north China and a not inconsiderable part of the revenue of the city comes from catering to the needs of pilgrims. Tai Shan is probably the most venerable sacred mountain in the world, pilgrims having made their periodical visits to the place for several thousand years. According to tradition Emperor Shun sacrificed there in the 23rd century B.C. The mountain is covered with temples and is the location of many spots of great fame.

For many centuries Tai Shan has held a high place in the religion and mythology of the Chinese. It was a sacred spot when the Chinese were nature worshippers and has never lost its prestige. Confucianists, Buddhists and Taoists alike make pilgrimages to it. Many of the early Emperors visited the place and left mementos in

---

* " Farmers of Forty Centuries," by Professor F. H. King.

the form of temples, obelisks and monuments, though many of these objects now pointed out by the guide are of later date than he would have you believe.

The annual pilgrimage to the mountain takes place from February to May, when as many as ten thousand people make the ascent daily. Members of a guild of chair-bearers carry one up and down the mountain, making the round trip in one day but most of the devout prefer to proceed on foot while some ascend on their knees. It is curious to note that members of the guild which has a monopoly of chair carrying are Mohammedans who have no sympathy with the religious significance of the mountain. The chair with its basket-like seat of ropes is a contrivance peculiar to Tai Shan and found in no other part of China. It is a very uncomfortable conveyance unless softened by pillows or blankets. The ascent to the top, about 15 miles, takes six hours and the descent half that time. On the descent the chair bearers race at incredible speed down the steep slopes. An old local law inflicts severe penalties on coolies who slip or allow a chair to drop in making the trip, but they are as sure-footed as goats and it is said that these penalties are not enforced once in a decade. The usual charge for a chair is $4.00 to $5.00 for the round trip. During the winter months the mountain is closed to travelers as the ice on the road makes the trip too dangerous.

The remarkable road which leads to the summit of the mountain, starting outside the north gate of Taianfu, is paved its entire length, and in the numerous steep elevations there are said to be 6,300 stone steps. This road at places is twelve to fifteen feet wide and is a splendid testimonial to the engineering skill of the ancient Chinese. For the first half of the way the road leads though fine groves of cyprus and follows a mountain stream whose cascades and waterfalls add much to the beauty of the scenery. Above the 3,000 foot level the cyprus are replaced by pines. About halfway up the hill one of the principal temples is reached, marked by a gateway which is known as

"The Middle Gate of Heaven." Passing this gate, the road is fairly level for a mile, and then comes to the foot of the grand stairway "one of the great sights of the world. The stairway consists of over 2,000 steps . . . running straight up to the summit. . . . The steps themselves appear to be an endless flight. . . . Heavy chains, riveted into the rock, line either side of the stairway to assist the exhausted climber up the last few hundred steps." At the summit there is another conspicuous gateway called "The Third Gate of Heaven," really the end of the climb. From here the summit is reached by an easy grade and one reaches the small plateau on which all the temples of Tai Shan are located. Here there are a number of pretentious temples, the highest one being dedicated to the Taoist " Emperor of the Sky." The chief temple is dedicated to the "jade lady," a goddess of Chinese mythology who is supposed to relieve her devotees of the dread curses of barrenness and blindness. A slightly smaller temple honors the memory of Confucius and contains a copy of the famous image of the sage, the original of which is found in the temple at Chufou. Parts of the temples at the top are very old but being kept in good repair the older parts are often unnoticed by the casual sightseer. The cast-iron tiles on the temple to " The Old Lady of the Mountain " have been in use since the 15th century. Near by are cliffs over which devotees formerly threw themselves to the rocks below. So great was the loss of life that the authorities have guarded the place with a high wall, yet in spite of this, some lives are sacrificed each year.

The view from the top of Tai Shan is one of the finest in China. To the south one can see almost the whole valley of the Wen Ho, while to the north, though Tsinanfu is hidden, a part of the course of the Yellow River may be followed. Confucius claimed he saw the sea on the east, and Nanking on the south, a feat which is impossible to the modern traveler, but the horizon is 85 miles distant and if the great sage did not view the sea itself, he at least

saw a spot located very near to the seashore. The view
from the top embraces what might be called the "Holy Land
of China" where her greatest sages, Confucius and Mencius,
lived, taught and are buried. " In all the cities and villages of Shantung, stones from Tai Shan are much in
request as talismans. It is believed to be unlucky for a
house to be so built as to face a turning or a cross road.
To ward off the ill luck, stones are inserted in the wall of
the house so situated, with the inscription ' The stone from
Tai Shan accepts the responsibility.' " Such stones have
been found in use in every province in China.

Among the many places in and about the city of
Taianfu three temples are of especial interest. The
" Buddhist Hell," not far from the railway station depicts
in life-sized clay figures all the horrors of future punishment. In 1899 the Boxers gathered and practised their
manual of arms in this place, going out from here to kill
the first of the missionary martyrs. Only a three minutes'
walk from this place is the Brass Temple, also devoted to
" The Old Lady of the Mountain," but usually quite deserted. Here is the famous Golden Palace or brass tower
which formerly stood on top of the mountain but was
brought down here for some unknown reason about 1770.
Twelve huge figures may be seen in the temple halls,
remarkable not only for their good casting but also for
their fine carving. The largest and most popular temple
of the city is the Tai Miao, dedicated to the Emperor Shun,
in the northeastern part of the city. An Emperor of the
Han dynasty is generally credited with planting the gnarled old cypress trees which to-day fill the temple courtyard.
Large trees growing out of crevasses in the walls attest to
the great age of the place, and there seems to be fairly
good evidence that some of the trees still standing date
from the Han dynasty. There is a well preserved locust
of the Tang period, A.D. 600 to 900. Some of the large
metal incense burners were made during the Sung dynasty,
960 to 1280. In one of the outer courts of the temple
visitors are sometimes shown an extraordinarily large slab

of jade presented by Emperor Chien Lung in 1736, held in great repute by reason of the local belief that one end is always warm and the other end always cold. During the pilgrim season one is likely to overlook the very interesting objects about the temple because of the greater interest of the mass of humanity which passes before one. Pilgrims from many provinces, but especially from Shantung, then throng the temple by thousands. A brisk trade in souvenir toys carried on at this time furnishes a livelihood for the citizens for the remaining eight months of the year.

The Tientsin-Pukow Railway maintains a good hotel at Taianfu. The hotel can make all arrangements for seeing the mountain.

CHUFOU.

Ninety miles south of Tsinanfu on the Tientsin-Pukow Railway is Chufou, famous as the place where Confucius lived and the location of his tomb. When the railway was under construction the late Duke of Kung, a lineal descendant of Confucius, objected to the defilement of the sacred place by such a barbarous thing as a foreign railway and so was able to keep it out of Chufou. It is therefore necessary for the visitor to ride five miles in a Chinese cart or wheel-barrow from the railway station in order to reach the tomb.

The principal point of interest at Chufou is the great cemetery, covering about 600 acres and containing the bones of the Kung clan in all its branches for 2500 years. It lies outside the north gate of the city and is reached by a road about a mile long leading between rows of magnificent old cedars. From the outer enclosure of this park-like cemetery an avenue of trees leads to an inner enclosure at the south end of the great cemetery containing many monuments commemorating imperial visits to the tomb, some of them dating back to the Sung dynasty. Near the center of the enclosure are knolls which cover the remains of Confucius, his only son, and a grandson, the latter being the author of " The Doctrine of the Mean."

23

The tablet marking the resting place of the great sage bears the simple inscription, "Ancient, Most Holy Teacher." Near the tomb is a monument marking the spot where a disciple lived in a hut for six years mourning the death of his master. All the other disciples mourned for only three years.

The great Confucian temple, one of the finest in China, occupies, with its grounds and outlying buildings, one whole side of the town, about one-third of the total area. The lofty green tiled roofs are visible for a long distance. The carved stone pillars, a mass of interlaced dragons and tracery, that support the great shrine, the Ta Ch'eng Tien, ' Hall of Perfection,' wherein the statue of Confucius reposes, are marvels of Chinese sculpture. " The sacrificial vessels are of priceless porcelain and bronze. The inscriptions are countless, many of the tablets having papers pasted to them intimating that rubbings are not to be taken without due authority. Under the eaves are masses of gay colored wood carving, enclosed in wire netting as a protection against birds and bats, yet the buildings are by no means as clean as they might be. On the veranda of the Ta Ch'eng Tien may be seen the famous sounding stones, the caps of two small pillars that, for some reason of which the secret is lost or well kept, ring with a musical note when struck. The marble stairs and ramps leading to the shrines are masterpieces. Everything, in fact, that devotion and money can supply has been done to make the temple buildings the grandest specimen of Chinese architecture, and, as usual, they stand in a park of splendid trees. The roots of one very ancient cypress are carefully enclosed in a marble parapet. From this ancient stump, which is said to have been planted by Confucius himself, a tall and vigorous stem, itself some centuries old, projects straight aloft to proclaim that the old root has sap and life in it yet. An extremely interesting and complete collection of ancient musical instruments is kept in the temple. Estates reckoned at 48,000 *mow*, say 8,000 acres, are devoted to the support of the temple and the supply of the enormous number of pigs, sheep and cattle required for the sacrifices, for symbolism has not taken root here and instead of burning cheap paper images the worshippers of Confucius perform the full sacrificial rites laid down in the books of old. In a word the Prophet is by no means without honor in his own country." Many things intimately connected with the life of Confucius are to be seen. The well from which he drank and the room in which he taught are carefully preserved.

Though this place derives its greatest fame from the fact that it is the burial place of Confucius it also has renown as the burial place of Shauhau, son of the famous third Emperor of China, Hwang-ti. Shauhau reigned from 2594 to 2511 B.C., a period of 83 years, of which the Chinese legends give little information beyond the fact that the custom of embroidering representations of birds on the uniforms of civil officials and of beasts of prey on those of military officials originated during this period.

TSOWHSIEN.

Seventeen miles south of Chufou on the Tientsin-Pukow railway is Tsowhsien, the birthplace of Mencius, the sage who stands next to Confucius in the estimation of the Chinese and whom many foreigners place first. About midway between Chufou and Tsowhsien are two cemetery plots, five miles apart, the larger and more accessible one containing the grave of Mencius' mother, a woman very famous in Chinese legend. The sage is buried in a more isolated place, too far away for the casual visitor. However, both places may be visited by one willing to make the journey in a wheelbarrow or cart. The grave of Mencius may also be reached from Chufou by traveling about eight miles.

The chief point of interest in the town is the temple to Mencius, outside the south gate, with memorials of imperial visits second only in importance to those in the Confucian temple at Chufou. On the way to the temple one sees a memorial arch bearing the inscription. " Ancient Site of the Third Change of Residence." This refers to a famous story told of the mother of Mencius. She first lived near a cemetery but found that her son amused himself by mimicking the mourners; she then moved near a market place, where the young Mencius imitated the bickerings of the tradesmen. The third removal, commemorated by the arch, was to a site near a school, where the mind of Mencius developed rapidly under the good examples so constantly before him.

Tsowhsien like Chufou has its local duke, a descendant of Mencius. About 1000 families in the town claim to be descendants of the sage, though a large part of the clan migrated to Soochow.

HSUCHOWFU.

The most important city on the Tientsin-Pukow Railway south of Tsinanfu, is Hsuchowfu, 417 miles from Tientsin. The Yellow River formerly ran near here and the old bed of the river can be seen to the north of the city. It is recognizable because it lies higher than the surrounding country though it is now built over with houses and is under cultivation. It is one of many cities which in the past has been threatened with destruction by this scourge of rivers. According to local legend the river once threatened to engulf and destroy the city and a human sacrifice was called for to appease the wrath of the river god. The young daughter of the mayor responded by throwing herself from the city wall into the flood which promptly subsided. A monument erected in her honor has disappeared but on a part of the city wall which still remains there is a crumbling bronze figure of a cow with wide open mouth, to swallow the river if its flood waters should ever again reach the city wall. The river has long since changed its course and flows several hundred miles to the north and most of the city wall has been torn down but the cow and the legend remain.

Hsuchowfu is of growing commercial importance as the junction of the Tientsin-Pukow and the Lunghai railways. The eastern terminus of the latter road is at Haichow, a new port in an important salt producing district. To the west the road connects Hsuchowfu with Kaifeng and the Peiping-Hankow Railway and will eventually reach Sianfu. It was the country traversed by this line which provided the background for the romantic historical novels of China, notably the "History of the Three Kingdoms."

PUKOW.

This southern terminus of the Tientsin-Pukow railway is on the northern bank of the Yangtsze, 628 miles from Tientsin. Passengers arriving here are transported across the river to Nanking by railway ferry. Those proceeding to Shanghai are landed near the station of the Shanghai-Nanking railway. Plans are under way to make this place the industrial center of China.

HONGKONG AND SOUTH CHINA

 ONGKONG is a crown colony of Great Britain, ceded by treaty with China, January 25, 1841. The principal city is Victoria, on the north shore. Distance from London 10,000 miles, from San Francisco 6,000 miles, from Shanghai 850 miles. Time, 7 hours 35 minutes in advance of Greenwich. Population: Chinese, nearly 500,000; foreign, 13,000.

Arrival.—Steamers usually dock on the Kowloon side of the harbor and passengers disembarking must walk a short distance to the Star Ferry Pier from where a regular ferry service is operated every ten minutes to Victoria. Porters from leading hotels meet all steamers and take care of baggage for which a small charge is made. There are practically no customs formalities as Hongkong is nominally a free port.

Hotels.—Hongkong, Peninsular, Gloucester. The Repulse Bay Hotel is located a few miles out of town. If a prolonged stay is intended, arrangements can be made for reduced weekly and monthly rates.

Money.—Hongkong has its own currency, the value of which fluctuates daily with the price of silver. The Hongkong dollar is usually worth about 10% more than the Chinese dollar. Chinese coins do not pass as legal tender and the tourist should refuse to accept them.

Newspapers.—Daily: Hongkong Daily Press, South China Morning Post, Hongkong Telegraph, China Mail.

Posts and Telegraphs.—The General Post Office is a handsome building on the water front and extending back to Des Voeux Road. Offices of the Eastern Extension Australasia and China Telegraph Co., the Great Northern Telegraph Co., the Chinese Government Radio Administration and the Chinese Telegraph Administration are located near the water front.

Consulates.—Belgium, Brazil, Chili, Denmark, France, Italy, Japan, Mexico, Netherlands, Norway, Nicaragua, Panama, Peru, Portugal, Siam, Spain, Sweden, United States.

Local Sightseeing Trips.—As the steamship connections at Hongkong allow travelers only a short stay in the colony, the traveler is advised to take advantage of one of the many local sightseeing trips arranged by the travel agencies. These include trips to the Peak, motor excursions to Repulse Bay, one of the finest drives in the world, a visit to the mainland at Kowloon, etc. Visits to Canton and Macao can also be arranged at Hongkong.

The occasional piratical attacks still made in the waters about the entrance of the West River come as reminders of the almost forgotten fact that Hongkong is one of the Ladrones, or "Thieves" Islands, a name which early Portuguese traders appropriately gave them. But Hongkong itself has long ago outgrown its old name, and as a British crown colony has been transformed from a pirate-fisherman village with a population of a few thousand to one of the most important business centers in the Far East, with a port which in the amount of tonnage entering and leaving its waters is one of the most important in the world. In the troubles which preceded the war with China, the British traders who were driven from Canton by the hostility of the Chinese found refuge in the Portuguese colony of Macao, but as this directed Chinese hostility toward Macao, the British soon left and settled on the island of Hongkong, feeling that they ought not to compromise the safety of the Portuguese settlement by remaining there. For a time the little community lived on board the ships until residences could be established, and there was some moving back and forth between Macao and the island. In 1840 the British expeditionary force arrived and made Hongkong its headquarters. The island has been under the British flag ever since that time. However, in the early days the colony was found to be so unhealthful that the project of abandoning it was seriously discussed. In 1844 the colonial treasurer drew up a report in which he set forth the large number of deaths and gave it as his opinion that "it was a delusion to hope that Hongkong could ever become a commercial emporium like Singapore." These pessimistic views, though they found some adherents, did not prevail, and such was the progress made that about forty years later Sir William des Voeux was able to write: "It may be doubted whether the evidences of material and moral achievement, presented as it were in a focus, make anywhere a more forcible appeal to eye and imagination, and whether any other spot on the earth is thus more likely to excite, or much more fully justifies, pride in the name of Englishman."

Hongkong is to-day without doubt the most beautiful city in the Far East and one of the foremost commercial centers. It is an important point for the trans-shipment of goods destined for other points in the Orient. The harbor, with an area of 15 square miles, is well sheltered, being enclosed on two sides by lofty hills, which rise on the mainland to a height of 3,000 feet. However, it is in the typhoon area, and on several occasions great damage has been done to shipping in port. Many thousands of lives were lost in the typhoon of 1874. Warnings of these disturbances are now sent out by wireless, greatly decreasing the danger, as shipping is able to take shelter. The manufacturing interests of the city are yearly growing more important and now include several large sugar refineries, rope and glass factories and cement works. Several large dry docks and ship-building works are located here.

Except for a tradition that after the fall of the Mings some of the courtiers fled to Hongkong and there found safety from the Manchus, the place cannot be said to have had a place in history before it became a British colony. A similar tradition is connected with Kowloon on the mainland. It is said that in the year 1287 the last Emperor of the Sung dynasty, flying from Kublai Khan, took refuge there in a cave. The incident is commemorated by an inscription on a large granite boulder on a hill near Kowloon City; the three characters which are said to form the original inscription mean "Sung Emperor's Pavilion." When the territory was ceded to Great Britain the Chinese petitioned the Hongkong Government that the rock might not be injured, on account of the tradition connecting it with the imperial personage. In 1898 a resolution was passed by the Hongkong Legislative Council preserving in perpetuity the land on which the rock stands for the benefit of the public.

The island of Hongkong is known to the Chinese as Heung-kong (Fragrant Stream or Good Harbor), but

Anglo-Saxons have ever found the nuances of Chinese pronunciation difficult and the blunter official name has come into common usage. The island is 11 miles long, from 2 to 5 miles wide with a circumference of 25 miles and an area of 30 square miles. The channel which separates the island from the mainland is one mile wide between Victoria and Kowloon, narrowing to ¼ mile at Lyemun Pass. The island is covered with rugged hills and small valleys through which flow a few rocky streams. A fine motor road winds around the greater part of the island, following close on the beach or climbing the sides of the steep hills which fringe the shore. A motor trip over this road, stopping at Repulse Bay, is one of the features of nearly every visit to Hongkong. Many other winding roads which would do credit to any city in the world have been built reaching the top of the Peak. Most of them are beautifully shaded and afford excellent opportunities for fine walks. A form of exercise very popular in Hongkong is to ride to the top of the hill on chairs or in the tram and walk back to the city. The return trip can be made in from one hour to an hour and a half by a good walker. The cable tramway leading to the top is a very interesting piece of engineering and no visit to Hongkong is complete without a trip over the line. Picnic excursions on launches to the many small harbors and beaches about the island are popular. With the building of roads in the New Territories interesting motor car trips are made possible.

The colony, Britain's first outpost on the China coast, was established in 1842 when the island of Hongkong was ceded by the treaty of Nanking, this treaty confirming a cession which had been made one year earlier. In 1844 it was made a crown colony and has since enjoyed steady growth and almost uninterrupted prosperity. The colony was increased in 1860 by the acquisition of the Kowloon peninsula, just across the harbor from Hongkong, and an additional piece of territory was acquired by lease in 1898, the whole territory now amounting to 400 square miles.

The colony is administered by a Governor, who is

aided by an Executive Council of seven members. The Legislative Council is composed of the Colonial Secretary, the Commander of the Troops, the Treasurer, the Attorney-General, Director of Public Works, Captain-Superintendent of Police, Secretary for Chinese Affairs, four British and two Chinese unofficial members. The port remained free until 1909, except for opium, but since that time duties on spirits and wines have been added. Traveler's personal baggage is rarely examined.

The winter months of November to February offer the best season in which to visit Hongkong, when the climate will be found very pleasant and cool. March, April and May are usually very damp and rainy and during the summer very hot weather prevails, with practically no cool days to relieve the monotonous heat.

Officially, there is no city of Hongkong, that being the name of the colony, while Victoria is the name of the principal city; but outside of official documents the name Victoria is rarely used, the city being commonly given the name of the island. The city is built in a graceful curve five miles long around the shores of the bay on the north of the island. The business houses of the foreground and the residences in the rear stretch back in a succession of tiers which reach several hundred feet up the side of the peak. The background of this impressive picture, as viewed from the harbor, is the Peak, 1823 feet high. In the effort to escape the enervating damp heat of the summer, many houses have been built on the Peak, most of them being perched on narrow ledges quarried out of the sides of the hill and reached by precipitous flights of steps. Part of the water-front street is known officially as Connaught Road, but the name Praya is usually given to the entire stretch of street. Parallel with this road runs Des Voeux Road and above that Queen's Road. The latter was formerly just above high-water mark and the ground now between it and the shore has been reclaimed. The principal business houses and shops are found on these three streets. Close to the business streets are located the Chinese residences. They are not packed together on narrow streets as in the cities of China proper, for the streets of Hongkong are fairly wide. Instead, the residences are high tenement-like structures, containing many small rooms and a population almost as dense as in the crowded cities of the mainland. These rather squalid buildings afford an interesting contrast to the fine residences of the foreigners on the Peak.

"There are grander sights to be seen in the world, but few more picturesque and graceful than that of Hongkong, the entrance to the harbor and the panoramic view from the mountain. Coming from east or west, you pass by islands, or rather rocks, which are grey and naked, and glitter in the sunshine. It is a desolate region; not a vestige of vegetation, not a trace of human life. Gliding between them, the vessel approaches to a point from which Hongkong is seen, at no great distance; a greyish mass standing out in relief, though the neighboring land can yet scarcely be distinguished. Little by little objects can be discerned; masses of verdure here and there on the peaks; a pane of glass glittering on the summit of a pavilion amongst the trees. Suddenly the vessel makes a curve, and the narrow channel discloses a fleet of ships, junks and sampans; the extended curve of quays; the regular line of buildings, and above them, rising on a succession of hill slopes, the villas in tiers along the zigzags of the mountain roads."

Every visitor to Hongkong takes a trip to the Peak to see the fine panorama which stretches out on all sides. At one's feet lies the city outlined against the busy harbor, where large steamers look like sampans. Eighty miles to the north, if the day is clear, may be seen a grey speck, which is Canton. Nearer at hand on the island are Pok-folum reservoir, the village of Aberdeen to the south, and Mountain Lodge, the summer residence of the governor of the colony.

The interesting Botanical Gardens occupy a tract of eight acres and are worth a visit. They can be reached by chair in ten minutes from the principal hotels. Some of the finest scenery on the island can be seen on a trip to the Tytam reservoir, about five miles distant from the city. An interesting ricsha ride may be taken over Jubilee Road to the fishing village of Aberdeen. It is at this point that the Dragon boat races of Hongkong are held annually. At Pokfolum is the important publishing plant of the French mission. It comprises a complete type-casting plant, where types of all the Oriental languages are cast, said to be the most complete collection of types of this kind in existence. The first dictionary of the Thibetan language was published here. This is also the location of the mission's sanatorium, which stands on a large well-wooded tract. In the vicinity are a number of pretentious Chinese graves belonging to wealthy native families.

The principal educational institution of the colony is Hongkong University, established largely through the liberality of British, Chinese and Parsee gentlemen living in Hongkong. The foundation stone was laid on March 16, 1910. The handsome building, occupying a site about halfway up the side of the Peak, is a prominent landmark from the harbor.

As the principal tourist point on the China coast, Hongkong abounds in curio shops stocked with Chinese, Indian and Japanese goods. Most of the Chinese articles come from Canton and Swatow, the distinctive local products being Canton furniture and Swatow lace. The large porcelain shops, while offering nothing extraordinary, are well stocked. Several of them have their goods marked in plain prices, with labels giving descriptions of the pieces, a practice which is not common in any other part of China.

Mission work began in Hongkong practically from the establishment of the colony, for mission institutions which had previously found in Macao refuge from Chinese opposition moved over to Hongkong with the British occupation. St. John's Cathedral (Anglican) was erected in 1842. Its architectural pretensions are not great but the interior wood work shows fine Chinese carving. Other local reli-

gious buildings are St. Peter's (for sailors); St. Stephen's
(for Chinese), Union Church, Wesleyan Chapel, Roman
Catholic Cathedral, St. Joseph's Church, St. Francis'
Church and Church of the Sacred Heart. There are a
Jewish synagogue, two Mohammedan mosques and one
Sikh temple. A number of Protestant mission chapels are
maintained in various parts of the city. St. Joseph's
College is a school for boys managed by the Christian
Brothers (Roman Catholic). The Italian Convent educates
girls and maintains an orphanage. The Asile de la Sainte
Enfance, conducted by French sisters, takes care of many
Chinese foundlings. Roman Catholic, Protestant, Jewish,
Parsee and Mohammedan Cemeteries occupy sites in
Wongnai Chung Valley.

Ferries which leave every ten minutes convey passengers for Hongkong across the harbor to Kowloon. Kowloon is a walled city of small importance, but will give the
hurried visitor a good idea of the character of purely
Chinese cities, if he has not time to visit Canton or other
larger and more interesting places.

The Canton-Kowloon Railway affords the quickest
route between Hongkong and Canton, though travelers
usually arrange to travel one way by steamer and the
other by rail, as both routes are beautiful and interesting.
The express train makes the trip in three hours. The
Kowloon terminus of the railway is close to the ferry landing, but the Canton station is 2½ miles from the foreign
settlement of Shameen. However, it is connected by a
good macadam road, with ricshas always available. The
British section of this road, 22 miles, extending from
Kowloon to Lowu, on the Chinese frontier, is one of the
most expensive pieces of road in the world, costing about
£10,000 per mile. The most difficult engineering feat was
the tunneling of Beacon Hill for a distance of 7,200 feet,
The Chinese section, which connects with the British, is
89 miles long, giving the whole road a length of 111 miles.
The road will ultimately be the southern terminus of the

Canton-Hankow Railway, which will place Canton and
Hongkong in direct rail communication with Paris.

CANTON.

Eighty miles from Hongkong, at the apex of the delta
of the Pearl river, is Canton, the commercial metropolis of
South China, the Chinese city with which foreign traders
and missionaries first came in contact and the city which
for many years has played a very important part in the
political affairs of the country. Population, 1,042,360.
There are several Chinese hotels of semi-foreign style but
most foreign travelers stop at the Victoria on Shameen
Island. Tourists should not undertake visits to Canton
without a guide or interpreter.

Old as Canton is in comparison with the most ancient
cities of Europe, it belongs to a much later date in Chinese
history than that of the older cities of the north. It was
a few centuries before the Christian era when the immigrants from the basin of the Yellow River in the north
reached the present site of Canton as the most southern
frontier of the rapidly expanding Chinese people. According to local tradition, at about the same time five fairy
men arrived from the north on the backs of goats, each
bearing a stalk of grain and a message bidding the people
in Canton to live in peace and prosperity—advice which
they have only half followed, for during the centuries of
its existence the city has usually been prosperous but it
has seldom been peaceful. The fairies disappeared. The
goats turned to stone and can still be seen by the skeptical
in the Temple of Five Genii. From this circumstance
Canton is known as "The City of Rams."

It is from Canton that practically all the Chinese in
America come, and they with their neighbors of Fukien
settled in Hawaii, the Philippines, and overran Java, Siam,
Singapore and the other places of the Far East. Many
of these emigrants return to their loved birthplace after
amassing fortunes abroad, bringing with them advanced
ideas of government. Those who do not return keep in

touch with relatives at home through letters and cash remittances, giving all Cantonese a broader view of the world than that possessed by their more secluded country-men as well as adding a great deal to the local wealth.

The Chinese have a saying, "Everything new origin-ates in Canton," and this is especially true of things political. It was in this southern city that the plots which resulted in the overthrow of the Manchu monarchy were hatched, and during the brief but dramatic struggle of the Republican Revolution the principal parts were played by Cantonese. For many years before this, the quick-witted Cantonese had taken high honors at the official examinations, much to the displeasure of the ruling Manchus, who saw in every one of them a potential enemy to the monarchy.

Halfway from Hongkong to Canton, the comfortable passenger steamers which make the trip daily pass through Bocca Tigris (Tiger's Mouth), the name given by early Portuguese traders to the narrow point in the estuary. A little farther on is Whampoa, where the famous British and American clipper tea ships of the middle part of the 19th century dropped anchor while loading to start on their race with the first tea of the season to the American and English markets.

For many centuries the older part of Canton was surrounded by a wall and moat about six miles in circumference and the streets were world-famous for their narrowness. The wall has been torn down, the moat filled up and the city possesses many miles of well paved streets 80 to 150 feet wide and the motor car has long since ceased to be a novelty. The streets in the city itself have been widened and in many ways Canton is, as it has been for more than a century, the most modern city in China. Motor roads have also been built to many points outside the city. Motor buses afford a popular means of transportation inside the city as well as to many distant points in the East River and North River districts.

Banked for miles along the river are thousands of Chinese water craft on which live a population of perhaps a hundred thousand. Tens of thousands are born, live and die on these boats, forming a community complete in itself, containing beggars, priests, workmen and thousands of families whose ancestors were also members of the boating population of Canton. The occasional typhoons create havoc on the river and cause great loss of life among this boating population.

The Portuguese first came to Canton in 1511, but the foreign trade of the city far antedates their visit. The tall minaret known as the Plain Pagoda, is in reality a Moslem mosque built by Arabian voyagers and traders more than a thousand years ago that they might have a place of worship on their visits to Canton. The Arabian trade with China ended many centuries ago, but the Mohammedan religion remains as it does in almost all parts of China.

Early British traders came to Canton about 100 years after the Portuguese and for many years carried on trade with the Chinese, all of the dealings being through the famous Chinese merchant's guild known as the Co-hong of Canton. In the latter part of the 18th century sailing vessels came from Liverpool, Salem, Boston and New York and returned laden with silks and tea. The American vessels left the Atlantic coast with cargoes of cotton prints and other cheap goods. They sailed through the Straits of Magellan and on the west coast of Canada traded their cargo to Indians for furs or in Hawaii bartered with the natives for sandalwood. These articles, highly prized by the Chinese, were exchanged at Canton for tea and silk. The sailing vessel might return home in two years and if the voyage met no ill luck, the owner would make a fortune from one trip. Until the Treaty of Nanking was signed (1842) all the foreign trade of China was confined to Canton and both the Chinese and the foreign merchants who engaged in it made enormous profits. With the opening of other ports, Canton has lost its old dominant position, but still remains a very important center of Chinese trade.

When the foreign residents of Canton returned from their exile after the war with Great Britain, in 1841, they found their residences and factories in ruins and the small island of Shameen was granted to them as a place of residence. It was then only a sandy mud flat, but has since been converted into a handsome residence section, one of the many examples of the way in which Europeans have made spots of beauty out of areas which the Chinese considered as waste land. It is here that the foreigners live and the traveler will find accommodations at the Victoria Hotel. One-third of the island is French and two-thirds British. It has been planted with trees and is one of the pleasantest places of residence in tropical China. Zest rather than danger is added to residence there by reason of the occasional disturbances in Canton.

Several hundred temples in addition to pavilions, ancestral halls and other show places are located in Canton. The most famous of Canton temples no longer exists for its hundreds of priests have been driven out and it is now the home of the Non Wo Middle School Among the places well worth visiting are: the Flowery Pagoda or Fah-tap, a nine storied, octagonal pagoda, 270 feet high (it was formerly believed to be so sacred that no vermin could be found in it). The Five Storey Pagoda (now a museum), Temple of Five Genii and the Calamity Bell, which never sounds except to herald calamity to the city, Smooth Pagoda, Mohammedan Mosque, Temple of the Three Great Buddhas, Temple of Horrors, Temple of Honan, Chan's Temple, Provincial Mint, Kwangtung Arsenal at Shektseng, the Provincial Assembly Building, the flower gardens in Fati, the old viceroys' yamen are among the famous sights.

Among the show places of modern Canton are two structures erected in memory of Dr. Sun Yat-sen, the father of modern China, who was a Cantonese by birth. There are the Sun Yat Sen Memorial Hall and Memorial

24

Tower. The Memorial Hall is said to be one of the
finest pieces of modern architecture in Asia. The tower
surmounts a hill and from its topmost floor there is a
wonderful view of the entire city of Canton.

Canton is the home of many Chinese industries, and
the Cantonese workmen are famous for their skill. The
finest blackwood furniture in China is made here while
their tortoise shell, lacquer, stoneware, fans and pottery
enjoy a world-wide reputation. No trip to Canton is
complete without a visit to the street where the workmen
inlay kingfisher's feathers and silver, and to the ginger
works, where candied ginger was put up for our grand-
fathers.

Among the unique industries of Canton are silk
weaving in its intricate forms, crystal eye-glass making,
glazing cloth with half ton stones without heat, tobacco
pressing and cutting, ivory carving, bone cutting and
carving, blackwood or ebony work, grass matting weaving,
lacquer work, mother-of-pearl work, inlaid ware, peanut
oïl presses, primitive dye works, manufacture of pewter
ware, incense sticks, and glass blowing.

Among the most important missionary enterprises in
the city is Lingnan University, supported by the American
Union Missions. The Roman Catholic cathedral is located
in Canton and the chapel in Shameen. The American
Presbyterian and Baptist churches maintain many
missionary enterprises in Canton, including theological
seminaries, girls' and boys' schools, etc. The Baptist
Publication Society's printing office is located in Tung-
shan, east of the city.

KWANGTUNG PROVINCE.

The area of Kwangtung Province is 100,000 square
miles and its population is 37,167,701. It lies almost wholly
in the tropics and the area, well divided between mountain
and plain, is watered by four large rivers. The principal
products are silk, sugar, indigo, rice, tea, tobacco, salt,
oil, fish and live stock. The graceful banyan tree is found

in all parts of the province except the coast. There are banana plantations along the East River, while olives, lichees, pumeloes, oranges and other fruits are also grown and find their way to the Yangtsze Valley markets. Camphor trees are abundant at Sunning and there are dense palm groves in the Sunwi district. The palms are cultivated for fans, of which millions are exported annually. Though the province is densely populated, tigers and leopards are still numerous and have been seen within twenty miles of Canton. The coast line of the province is nearly 800 miles long, and the deforested hills which mark a great part of it are barren and desolate. The view from the sea gives no hint of the existence of the rich agricultural districts of the interior.

Because of its excellent harbors and its nearness to old trade routes, it became the center for an extensive foreign trade in ancient times, being in touch with the Arabs and the Roman Empire for many centuries before the development of modern foreign trade began. More recently it was the scene of the pioneer work of foreign merchants and missionaries, holding first place as a mercantile and missionary center until superseded by the development of foreign activity in the Yangtsze Valley. From this province come the ablest and most enterprising of merchants to be found in all the ports of China. The "Canton Guilds" and the "Swatow Guilds" are powerful in the trading communities of the country, being found in force in Shanghai, Tientsin, Hankow and other large commercial centers. The province contains a large population of Hakkas, whom the Cantonese insist on regarding as aliens. For the most part the Hakkas occupy scattered villages and hamlets in the mountains. They are a vigorous people, mainly agricultural, and are probably better educated than those who live in the crowded plains. Kwangtung province has furnished most of the emigrants to Singapore and other parts of the Straits Settlements, America, Australia and South Africa. Remittances of millions of dollars annually from these emigrants help to relieve the poverty of this overcrowded province. Some of the wealthiest men in the province are returned emigrants who amassed fortunes abroad. Piracy has always prevailed near Canton, where the delta of the West River with its numerous estuaries and coves affords ideal hiding places for the pirates.

One little-known part of the province is the island of Hainan. The central and southern portions of this island are covered with densely wooded hills inhabited by aborigines. There are many valuable and undeveloped forests of hardwood including rosewood and mahogany. The natives cut nothing but aromatic woods which are sold in all parts of China for use as beads, etc. There are great opportunities for development here, but efforts in that direction have been retarded by the climate of the place, its lack of communications, etc. Tropical plants from Singapore have been grown here with success and it is believed that rubber and camphor would thrive.

MACAO.

Distant 35 miles from Hongkong is Macao, a Portuguese colony equally interesting for its history, for the natural beauty of its location and for the quaint mixture of the Orient and mediæval Europe, as seen in its buildings. The steamer trip is made in four hours from Hongkong and should not be omitted from any tour to southern China. It is also possible to visit Macao from Canton by the comfortable boats which sail nightly.

Macao is the oldest outpost of Europe in its intercourse with China. The Portuguese established themselves here in 1557, and by a fortunate circumstance gained the good will of the Chinese authorities. The coast was menaced by a strong band of pirates, whom the Chinese officials were unable to overcome, and the Portuguese colonists were asked to help. They responded with such success that the pirates were driven away, and out of gratitude the Chinese asked the colonists to settle on the narrow end of the peninsula, which has since been

the home of their descendants and successors. The land
was held at a nominal rental from the Emperor of China
of 500 taels a year, but in 1848 the Governor took
advantage of other difficulties which engaged the attention
of China to refuse further payments and drove out the
Chinese customs house, together with every vestige of
Chinese authority. It was probably because of this that
he was treacherously murdered the following year and
his head taken to Canton. The complete sovereignty of
Portugal over the place was not fully recognized by China
until 1887, when a new treaty was signed.

For several centuries Macao was the principal trading
point between China and the west, especially in the first
half of the eighteenth century. The cession of Hongkong
to Great Britain created a dangerous competitor and
after that Macao steadily declined as a commercial center.
Hongkong was made a free port and when the authorities
of Macao attempted by reducing the customs dues to
regain the trade they had lost, it was found the change
had come too late. Its harbor silted up and the colony
lost its important trade. Many of the Macanese have
removed to Hongkong, and Macao is now chiefly a pleasure
resort for South China. Some fine old European furniture
remains in many of the older houses of the city and one
is occasionally able to pick up a good piece in the second-
hand shops. It is known as "the Monte Carlo of the Far
East" and the whole purpose of the government of the
place might appear to be to derive revenue from gambling,
opium and lotteries, which have been driven out of Chinese
cities. The revenue goes to the support of the home
government of Portugal. The *fan tan* houses of Macao
are famous along the whole China coast and one of the
principal sources of income of the place is from the sale
of lottery tickets. But despite its vice, Macao is as
quiet and has an appearance as puritanical as that of a
New England village and there is not a dance hall or
dance orchestra in the colony.

The area of the colony of Macao is eleven square

miles, and it has a population of about 78,000. Of the original thousand Portuguese families which settled in the place, little remains but the Portuguese names, for long intermarriage with the Chinese has resulted in the domination of Chinese blood. Of the present population, the Portuguese of pure blood are confined almost exclusively to the government officials, police and soldiers, a total of probably less than 100. The troopers from the Portuguese colony of Goa, in their Indian costumes, add color to the street scenes of the place.

The blue, pink, yellow and brown buildings of Macao rise on a hillside overlooking a beautiful crescent-shaped bay, the appearance of the city being quite unlike that of any other in the Orient. The buildings are neither Chinese nor foreign, but a strange combination of the two, clearly showing the survival of mediæval Portuguese influence. Standing out high against the sky line is the fine facade of the San Paulo (St. Paul) cathedral, built in 1594 by the Jesuits, and destroyed by fire in 1835. Japanese Catholics who fled from their homes to escape official persecution helped to build the cathedral. The Praia Grande, one of the famous streets of the Orient, fronts the sea for a mile and a half, the entire length being faced by a stone embankment. The harbor is picturesque and for many years that was all that could be said in its praise, for it had silted up until it was too shallow for small Chinese junks. In recent years a great deal of money has been spent on its improvement and it is now one of the best harbors in South China. The small steamers from Hongkong and Canton use the inner harbor, lying between the peninsula and the island of Lappa. An excellent view of the entire city and the surrounding territory can be had from the residence of the bishop, the building at the top of the hill, near the Boa Vista Hotel. The parapets around the residence and the little chapel are always open to visitors. Another fine view is obtained from the parapet of the old forts.

The incorporated name of the city is "City of the

Name of God, Most Loyal of the Colonies," a name accorded it in 1642. Though there might be some differance of opinion regarding the first part of the name, it has always lived up to the latter part and its history contains many passages telling how the brave Macanese held the place against attacks of Dutch and Chinese.

Camoens (1524-1580), the prince of Portuguese poets, lived in Macao as a political exile and wrote his greatest poem here. Camoens took part in the military occupation of Macao in 1558, for he was then in compulsory military service, as a result of his attacks on the authorities. He remained in Macao many months after the termination of his service. The grotto in which he worked is always open to visitors. It is situated in the Casa garden, one of the prettiest spots in the Orient. The grotto, near the center of the garden, is formed by several huge boulders, and the bust of the poet now stands on the spot where he sat when writing the latter part of his epic poem "The Lusiad."

Near the entrance to the garden is the English Church and in the old Protestant Cemetery at the back lie buried many who were prominent in the early history of foreign intercourse with China. Among the graves are those of Rev. Robert Morrison, the pioneer missionary who made the first translation of the Bible into Chinese; George Chinnery, the painter; Sir Philip le Fleming Senhouse, the British Admiral; and Lord Henry Churchill, captain of "The Druid." Many of the gravestones bear the names of American seamen from Salem and Boston, mementos of the time when Massachusetts skippers and representatives of the East India Company were keen rivals for the tea trade of South China. In spite of the fact that it is no longer a city of any commercial importance, Macao retains a few factories and carries on a small trade in tea, silk, tobacco, and firecrackers.

WEST RIVER.

Until so recent a date as 1897, West River, the

principal waterway of South China, was closed to all navigation by foreigners, and the rich territory through which it flows was sealed to the outside world. But in that year the river was opened to foreign trade and since then it has formed one of the most interesting parts of the itineraries of many travelers.

The river rises in the mountains of Yunnan and flows into the sea a short distance from Macao, the length of the stream being about 1,000 miles. A trip on one of the sternwheel steamers which ply from Hongkong will take the traveler into the heart of China, where he will have an opportunity to see Chinese life as it exists untouched by foreign influence.

The river at the point where it flows into the sea is divided into a delta of countless streams and a trip of sixty miles or more through narrow creeks surrounded on all sides by cultivated rice fields is necessary before the West River proper is reached. The principal towns passed on the trip to Wuchow-fu are Kum-chuck, Tak-hing and Samshui. Arrangements for a West River trip should be made through travel agencies in Hongkong.

SWATOW.

Swatow is a city with a fine harbor 180 miles from Hongkong at the mouth of the Han River. Population 60,000. As a seaport connected with the important towns of Chao Chow-fu and San-ha-up, Swatow was opened to foreign trade by the treaty of 1858. But the early traders, who began carrying emigrant coolies from the place soon turned their attention to kidnapping; and so many Chinese were carried away to be sold into what was practical slavery, that there developed intense hatred of the foreigners. No foreigner entered the city gates for several years after the promulgation of the treaty, and it was not until recently that they were able to travel in the vicinity without annoyance and insult. However, all that is changed now and Swatow has a number of foreign residences and a foreign hotel, the Astor House. Emigration from Swatow has been revived along legitimate lines and now amounts to about 100,000 yearly, the returning emigrants numbering about 80,000. Water works and an electric light plant are among the modern improvements. Swatow and surrounding country are not especially interesting except for the local manufactures and curios. The city is famous for grass cloth, pewter ware, drawn work and fans. Although these articles are all on sale in Hongkong, they can be secured at cheaper prices in Swatow. Formerly Swatow owed the reason for existence to the fact that it was the port for Chao Chow-fu but it is now the business center of this part of the country. A projected and partially completed motor road will connect the place with Canton.

CHAO CHOW-FU.

A line of railway 27 miles long connects Swatow with Chao Chow-fu, population 400,000, the scene of the exploits of Han Yu, China's prototype of St. Patrick, who is patron saint of the Chao Chow plain and a national hero honored in all parts of China. In A.D. 814 the Emperor made elaborate arrangements to receive a bone of Buddha at the court and Confucianists of the day saw in this a great danger to Chinese civilization. The statesman Han Yu, who was noted for his outspokenness, wrote a memorial against the proposed action, its effect being later described as follows: "Truth began to be obscured and literature to fade; supernatural religions sprang up on all sides, and many eminent scholars failed to oppose their advance until Han Yu, the cotton-clothed, arose and blasted them with his derisive sneer." For this rash action Han Yu was banished to Chao Chow, then peopled by tribes but little removed from a state of barbarism. In less than a year he had established schools here and had given such a stimulus to education that the residents of the place were noted for their learning centuries afterwards. According to local tradition the rivers of Chao Chow were then infested by crocodiles which devoured the domestic animals and kept the people in a state of terror. Han Yu was implored to rid the country of these reptiles which he proceeded to do according to the classic Chinese custom. He wrote an ultimatum to the crocodiles, which was thrown into the water with a pig and a goat, and the reptiles thereupon disappeared, never to be seen again. Shrines in the neighborhood commemorate this exploit and the ultimatum remains to this day a model of literary style. It may also be added that there are no crocodiles in the neighborhood.

AMOY.

Three hundred miles north of Hongkong at the mouth of the Pei Chi, or Dragon river, is the island of Haimon, on which the city of Amoy is located. Nearby is the smaller island of Kolongsu, where the foreign colony live. The city was opened to foreign trade in 1842. Hotel: Insular on Kolongsu. As hotel accommodations are very limited it is advisable to make reservations in advance.

"Perhaps no place along this entire coast has had a more interesting and exciting story to tell than this same small island, scarcely eight miles across. Many are the stirring events which have taken place here and in the neighborhood. For hundreds of years it was the rendezvous of bold buccaneers and unscrupulous adventurers, who, ravishing and plundering its inhabitants without mercy, made off with the spoils only to return another day to renew their wild depredations more violently than before. It has been the theater of many a fierce struggle, and the strong strategical position, or gateway to all the vast territory beyond (even Formosa itself), coveted alike by the Manchus, the Long-haired Rebels, the Dutch and the Japanese."

The Portuguese settled here in 1544, about the time they were driven from Ningpo by the Chinese government, but as in Ningpo, trouble arose between the foreigners and the Chinese government and the foreigners were expelled and their vessels burned. A hundred years later the famous Koxinga, the staunch defender of the Ming dynasty, held the place against the Manchus and even changed its name to Subengsu, which means "the island that remembers the Mings." "He collected a band of followers several thousand strong, and set up his standards (1647) on the island of Kolongsu, an island just opposite Amoy. He had, it is said, a fleet of 8,000 war junks, 240,000 fighting men, 8,000 ironsides; and with all the pirates that infested the coast of southern China under his command he claimed to have a combined force of 800,000 men. In training his men, we are told, he used a stone lion weighing over 600 pounds to test the strength of his soldiers. Those who were strong enough to lift this stone and walk off with it were selected for his own body-guard named the 'Tiger Guards.' They wore iron masks and iron aprons; they carried bows and arrows painted in red and green stripes, matching with long-handled swords used for killing horses; and they were stationed in the van that they might maim the horses' legs. They were his most reliable troops and were called 'Ironsides.'"

At length, in 1680, after the death of Koxinga, the Manchus succeeded in establishing their authority in Amoy, long after they had subdued the remainder of the country.

The city was built probably during the Ming dynasty and now has a population of about 120,000, with 100,000 additional living in the other villages of the island. The city is separated from the rest of the island by a high rocky ridge. The bay with its numerous islands, a few crowned by pagodas, presents a beautiful scene. The foreign settlement is on Kolongsu, a small island between Amoy city and the mainland, and is one of the prettiest in all China. During the autumn and winter (October to February) the climate here is delightful. Several good bathing beaches on the island make sea bathing a popular recreation during the warm months from May to October. Amoy lies in the typhoon area, but the island of Formosa acts as a protecting barrier against their worst fury.

One of the famous sights of China is a stone bridge 20

miles up the river from Amoy, now a part of a motor road. The bridge, 1100 feet long, is constructed of giant spans of granite, some of them being 70 feet long, 6 feet wide and 5 feet thick, weighing 200 tons. Local history affords no clue as to how these giant slabs were put into place, nor does any one know where they were quarried. A huge rocking stone near the Chinese city has been locally famous for centuries.

Long before Amoy attained any importance, another city called Zayton flourished in this neighborhood. Opinion differs as to whether it was Chuan Chow-fu, or Haiting of the present day, but there is no doubt about its being one of the greatest commercial centers of the world, carrying on a huge trade with India. It was from this ancient city that the word *satin* originated. The tea trade also flourished here from early days and our English word *tea* is probably derived through the Dutch from the Amoy word *te*. It was from Amoy that the tea-laden ship sailed, whose arrival in Boston harbor resulted in the historical "Boston Tea Party," the starting point of the American Revolution.

In addition to the Roman Catholics, three Protestant organizations, the Presbyterian Church of England, the London Missionary Society and Reformed Church in America, maintain chapels, a hospital and schools in Amoy.

FOOCHOW.

Foochow, the capital of Fukien province, is located on the north side of the Min river, 33 miles from the sea and 455 miles from Hongkong, about the same disttance from Shanghai. Vessels drawing more than eleven feet can come to Pagoda Anchorage, ten miles distant from the city. The population of the city is 700,000 and including that of the suburbs, is estimated at 1,000,000. There is no foreign hotel.

In the district around Foochow there are about 200 miles of road on which operate motor busses and motor cars. The city is lighted by a modern electric light plant erected and operated by progressive Chinese. Good ricshas and fairly good carriages can be hired. The city is clean and has an air of prosperity.

The walled city is about two and one-half miles from the river bank, but a crowded suburb fills up the space between with a numerous population. The wall, with a circuit of six and one-fourth miles, is built around three hills (Wushishan, Yushan, and Pingshan), which give the city a picturesque appearance. Foochow is known as "the Banyan City," and this magnificent shade tree is found at its best in Fukien province.

The scenery approaching Foochow from the sea and about the city is magnificent. Vessels from the sea leave the wide shallow stream for the narrower Kimpai Pass, a half mile wide and enclosed by bold rock walls. The pass of Mingan is even narrower, enclosed by towering terraced cliffs which have been compared to those of the Rhine. "All around were monuments of the past. At the entrance stood a tower on the crest behind Sharp Peak; it was erected by a wife to welcome back her husband from a voyage, but when he saw the strange mark he concluded he had mistaken the estuary, and sailed away never to return. Here was a post to commemorate a wreck, here an old beacon superseded by electric telegraphy; yonder were forts to guard the passes. Here was one of a pair of mandarin's feet in the live rock. Sacrilegious quarrymen were not debarred from carving away its fellow by the blood which followed the strokes of the chisel, but detached it and took it up to build a bridge, where it assumed the offensive and kicked the masons into the river; so the hint was taken and the foot was allowed to follow them; this one remains here to prove the story."

Owing to the shallowness of the river, ocean going vessels for years have anchored at Pagoda Anchorage, 10 miles from the city. In the war with France in 1884, the French fleet steamed into the river as far as the Anchorage and destroyed the arsenal. As a means of preventing another attack of that kind farther up the river, junks loaded with stones were sunk off Kushan Point, adding more difficulties to the navigation of the stream. In recent years the Min River Conservancy Bureau has been making important improvements.

South of the city and connecting it with Chungchau Island is the "Bridge of 10,000 Ages" or the "Long Bridge." It is about one-fourth of a mile long, and 13 to 14 feet wide. It has 28 piers and was completed in 1323. Connecting Chungchau (Middle Island) with the south bank of the river is the "Bridge in Front of the Granaries," built after the same design, but only about one-fourth as long as the "Bridge of 10,000 Ages."

Foochow came into prominence in 1853 as a market for black teas, including the famous Bohea tea, grown in the Bohea Hills in the extreme north of the province. In the early '60's the harbor at Pagoda Anchorage was usually crowded with British and American "clippers," fast sailing vessels which carried the tea to various parts of the world. The once-important tea trade has declined greatly in recent years because of competition with teas from Ceylon and elsewhere.

Foochow excels in the production of lacquer-ware, the finest being made by the noted She Shao-an family which has followed the trade for many generations. In the exhibits of lacquer-ware at the St. Louis Exposition, the first prize went to Foochow. The manufacture of silver jewelry in which kingfishers' feathers are inlaid is interesting to visitors. Silk and woolen stuffs are produced; also goats' hair rugs are manufactured, and furniture is made by a branch of the Fukien Industrial Mission. Camphor, paper, poles, lumber, green tea, oranges and other fruits are exported.

Foochow poles used in Shanghai and North China for building purposes are exported in the famous junks which add so much to the picturesqueness of Shanghai and other harbors. Large quantities of Fukien pine logs are turned into lumber here and exported. The export of green tea is important and the Chinese tea growers appear to be turning their attention more to the production of green tea, which is popular among the Chinese, than to the black tea formerly shipped abroad.

Two well-preserved pagodas are among the interesting local sights. The Black Pagoda with seven stories and 156 feet high was built in A.D. 785 to commemorate the birthday of an emperor. The White Pagoda, also of seven stories and 261 feet high, was erected in A.D. 903 as an act of filial piety. The Foochow Hot Springs, outside the Water Gate and the East Gate of the city, are famous among the Chinese and are credited with great curative powers. Numerous bath houses have been built where the springs abound and are well patronized.

The name Foochow first appears in Chinese history during the T'ang dynasty. When that dynasty fell it became an independent State under the rule of the King of Min, but a century later was reunited under the Sung dynasty. If the visitor is fortunate he may be able to see some of the dog-worshipping aborigines who live in the hills near by. Their race is unmixed with Chinese and they worship a dog as their great ancestor.

The Min River is navigable for almost 300 miles from Foochow and the scenery along its course is splendid, probably the finest in all of China. The Yungfu Monastery, Hai Shan Monastery, Moon Temple and Kushan Monastery, near Foochow, all have beautiful sites and are fine specimens of Chinese architecture.

Missionary work is important in Foochow. It was established in 1847 and has continued without interruption since that date. Among the prominent enterprises is the Union College for men, supported by a number of missionary societies. The American Board, American Methodist Episcopal Board and the Church Missionary Society maintain schools, colleges, hospitals, orphanages, etc. The Roman Catholic foundling asylum is situated a short distance ouside the South Gate of the city, and is under the direction of the Spanish Dominicans.

Kuliang is a popular mountain resort situated five miles east of Foochow at an elevation of 1,800 to 2,000 feet. During the summer months it is frequented by the foreign residents of Foochow, and also by foreign visitors from Hongkong, Swatow, Amoy, Shanghai, and other places in Central and North China, making a total summer population of several hundred. It may be reached from Foochow by a chair ride of four hours.

FUKIEN PROVINCE.

The province of Fukien is one of the smallest, containing an area of 46,332 square miles and a population of 13,157,791. The province is an almost unrelieved stretch of hills and mountains, the only plains being small and near the coast. In addition to tea growing, the chief industries are paper making and cloth weaving. The timber supply of the province has been greatly diminished. The export of timber in 1846 was estimated at £2,000,000 but in recent years the entire trade was but little more than one-tenth of that amount. The chief timber supplies at present come from the head-waters of the Min. The mountainous character of the country makes transportation difficult and the roads consist chiefly of rough blocks of granite which follow the easiest routes through a country where a dead level is unknown. The need for transportation is inadequately supplied by streams, all crowded with boats. The southern half of Fukien is undeveloped and is little known to foreigners. It is broken and mountainous, sparsely populated and densely wooded. The province was one of the first to gain by the development of foreign trade, owing to the large demand for Fukien tea, but with the development of Ceylon and India teas, this trade has fallen off. The partial failure of this industry and the natural difficulties encountered in gaining a livelihood in such a picturesque and mountainous country has caused a large emigration from the province, second only to that of Kwangtung. All of the Chinese in the Philippine Islands come from Fukien, and are known by the Filipinos as *"Amoy-istas"* because the earliest immigrants came from Amoy. In ancient times Fukien, like other parts of South China, was inhabited by a number of semi-barbarous tribes, each under a separate ruler. As a result the province exhibits great linguistic difficulties, almost every community having its separate dialect, often unknown thirty miles away.

YUNNAN PROVINCE.

The province of Yunnan lies in the extreme southwest of China. Area 146,714 square miles, population 9,839,180. It is of a mountainous character with large open plateaus of considerable altitude. Till the opening of the Tonkin-Yunnan railway by French enterprise the province was isolated, communication being difficult, slow and costly. Now, however, the journey from the sea at Haiphong to Yunnanfu the provincial capital, may be made by rail.

The province is of considerable interest, bordering as it does on Tonkin to the south and Burmah to the west. The people are of a quiet, friendly disposition and the traveler is happily free from the prying curiosity which is so exacting and persistent in some other provinces.

The valleys are occupied by Chinese who speak the usual mandarin language of the interior, while in the mountains one may find an almost endless variety of aboriginal tribes such as Lolos, Miaotze, and numerous others, affording a fine scope for study along ethnological lines. There are many Mohammedans in all parts of the province; hence certain forms of provisions are available that are not usually found in a purely Chinese community. Beef, mutton, fowls and many kinds of fruit and vegetables are plentiful.

The climate is very much like that of Northern California, but the summers are much more moderate. The thermometer ranges from 30° to 85° with a sunny, rainless winter—the rainfall being confined to the months from May to October. Winter is thus the time to travel and nothing can be finer or more enjoyable than a cross-country journey over the mountains of Yunnan in its brilliant winter weather. Coolies for transport of goods, and ponies for riding are to be had always at reasonable rates. Cot beds, blankets and the usual impedimenta of the careful traveler are necessary.

Many parts of the province are practically unknown to travelers. In the time of the Ming dynasty banishment to the "frontiers of Yunnan" was a much dreaded punishment. But as the province becomes better known and more closely investigated it reveals attractions that are bound to make it a favorite region with the tourist and explorer. While Yunnanfu is at present the best known portion of the province, the roads that connect with the southwest, northwest and southeast parts of Yunnan offer to the traveler attractions that will be hard to resist.

In the southeast corner of the province, eighteen days from Yunnanfu, lies the little custom outpost of Ssu-mao, a place opened to the foreign trade which it was hoped might be developed across the Shan States from British Burmah. Here, in this remote spot, one or two foreigners in the employ of the Chinese customs pass their time in the midst of a highly interesting population. While the Chinese are the ruling race, there is a medley of folks interesting in its variety and attractive because of its problems—Shans in the valleys, Wahs in the hills and many other kinds wedged between. A market day in Ssu-mao is a moving picture of intensest interest. Beyond Ssu-mao in the triangular patch between China, Burmah and Tonkin is a kind of no man's land, where adventure and discovery invite those whose temperament leads along that path.

To the northwest, where China impinges on Thibet and the debatable land of the Thibetan border, there is much country of a character that appeals to the ardent traveler —high mountain ranges with deep sheltered valleys where shy unknown peoples live and the sportsman may still find prey worthy of his mettle—bears, deer, leopards and many

kinds of game birds such as *Lopho horus Thibetanum;*
tragapans and various kinds of pheasant, golden, Reeves,
Amherst and the common China sort. To enjoy this kind
of travel leisure and temperament are needed: having
which the opportunities for enjoyment are practically
unlimited.

The rate of travel along the main roads averages
from 20 to 25 miles per day, going by the regular stages
which are fixed by "old custom" and so form the most
useful unit in calculating the journey. The best inns and
other accommodations and provisions for the road are to
be found at the regular stages, so the seasoned traveler
tries to make his halting places coincide with these. On
the smaller roads one has to trust his luck and rely upon
his foresight and backbone.

From Yunnanfu to Suifu in the Yangtsze valley is a
journey of twenty-six stages—traveling leisurely. The
road passes through two large cities and the usual collection of market villages and hamlets. Foreign residents,
missionaries, may be found at Tungchuan and Chaotung,
at which points pleasant breaks may be made in the
journey.

To the west the road runs to Talifu, a journey of
thirteen days, where a halt should be made to look over the
very interesting country connected with the abortive rising
of the Mohammedans in the middle of the last century.
English and French missionaries reside at Talifu and are
available for local information.

At Tali the road divides—the traveler for Burmah and
the west goes by the official road that leads to Bhamo and
the valley of the Irrawady. The road crosses the valleys
of the Mekong, Salwen and Shiveli rivers and affords a
comprehensive insight into the character of this little
known, much debatable frontier country. The time needed
from Tali to Bhamo is about twenty-five days. The chief
towns on the way are Yungchang and Tengyueh. At the
latter are a consulate, customs house, and mission station.
The road is impossible during the rainy season.

From Tali to the northwest a road runs up to Batang.
in the Thibetan marches of China. The time required between the two cities is approximately the same as to Bhamo.
The character of the country and people are quite different,
however, both country and people being of a wilder and
less conventional type. The people are of a very
heterogeneous character but are quiet and friendly
towards foreigners. The Roman Catholic missions have
some very strong and well-developed stations on the way,
where travelers are made welcome and afforded such
assistance as may be required.

YUNNANFU.

Yunnanfu is the capital of Yunnan, and is the largest
city in the province. It lies in a well-watered extensive
plain on the east of a charming lake 23 miles long by 12
wide that lends much charm to the landscape. The elevation
of the plain, 6,500 feet, ensures a comfortable climate and
is a most refreshing change from the depressing heat of
Tonkin and other shoreward places. The city contains
about 100,000 people, is surrounded by a good wall, and
is famous for its jade-cutting and metal works such as
bronze idols, incense burners, etc.

The Confucian temple in the center of the city is
worthy of notice. The buildings of the main temple are
of imposing size and well preserved, though dirty and
neglected. A small grove of cypress trees gives a touch
of rusticity and solitude, while the bridges and tanks
maintain the classic touch with the past. Across the big
lake, the transit of which takes about three hours, there
is a lofty ridge with a very precipitous face towards the
east. Here the ingenuity of the people has combined with
their religious zeal to build a series of temples, galleries
and grottoes in the face of the cliff, with ornamental
balustrades excavated in the original rock at a point
whence there is a sheer drop to the water far below. A
magnificent view opens across the lake to the picturesque

city of Yunnanfu and its amphitheater of mountains to the
north and east. At one point is a lunch room with a
round table and seats cut from the solid rock.

Ten miles northeast of the city is Hei Lung Tan
(Black Dragon Spring), where there is a fine temple in a
grove guarding a beautiful spring of pure water which
gushes from the limestone and goes meandering across the
plain, carrying fertility in its course.

About ten miles directly east from the city is a bronze
temple of equal fame and beauty, Chin Tien, locally
known as "The Copper Temple." This gem lies in a
miniature forest and is approached from the main road by
a series of paved terraces across which gateways are built
and named "The First Gate of Heaven," "The Second Gate
of Heaven" and so on. The approach to the main temple
is impressive though dilapidated. The temple is built
wholly of bronze, even the banner and flagstaff being of
that metal. A wall encloses the temple, built to imitate
a city wall; and indeed the resemblance to a miniature
city is very striking. The temple was built during the
Ming dynasty and is said to be one of two similar
structures in China.

A short distance from the south gate of the city
is an interesting ruin, worthy of notice by the amateur
archaeologist. An adobe building in a disreputable
condition of forlorn despair is an object of pride to the
local Mohammedans as being the tomb of Seyyid ed jel,
a Mongol prince who was governor of Yunnan from 1274
to 1279, the date of his death.

In the vicinity of Yunnan are many ruins, the result
of the Mohammedan rebellions which devastated the
province from 1855 to 1873 and came very near success;
being thwarted only by the defection of the principal rebel
general, after which a ferocious massacre took place and
the country was pacified in the time-honored method of
killing off all the rebels who could be found.

While the city itself is smaller than most provincial
capitals, there are few places that offer more attractions

in such agreeable surroundings than Yunnan. There is a growing foreign community in which the French naturally predominate, but no traveler need long remain a stranger in this hospitable city.

The French government supports a hospital and schools for both boys and girls where the French language and literature is taught gratuitously. Electric light, telephones, telegraphs, a mint and arsenal, are evidences that Yunnan is swinging into the modern current in common with the rest of China. The people of the capital are quiet and reticent, generally friendly, and phlegmatic enough to pay little attention to a casual stranger. There is a large student population in the schools, some thousands being here from all parts of the province.

The approach to the province is from Haiphong, the principal port of the French colony of Tonkin. Haiphong is reached by frequent steamers from Hongkong. The French customs regulations in Tonkin are stringent in regard to merchandise, but passengers' baggage is subjected only to the ordinary scrutiny and rarely is there any objection raised. The exception is in the case of firearms, for which a special permit is necessary before they can be brought across the frontier at Ho Kou. The customs officials at that point will arrange this matter for the traveler.

INDEX.

In the following index Chinese names of places and geographical names are marked with * while personal names are marked †.